Criminal Justice *In Transition*

Editorial contributors

Bryan Gibson

Clerk to the North-west Hampshire Justices and a former co-editor of Justice of the Peace. Co-author of Bail: The Law, Best Practice and the Debate (Waterside Press, 1993)

Paul Cavadino

Clerk to the Parliamentary All-Party Penal Affairs Group and Principal Officer, NACRO. Co-author of Bail: The Law, Best Practice and the Debate (Waterside Press, 1993)

Andrew Rutherford

Director of the Institute of Criminal Justice, University of Southampton. Chairman of the Howard League. Author of Prisons and the Process of Justice (Heinemann, 1984), Growing Out of Crime: The New Era (Waterside Press, 1992) and Criminal Justice and the Pursuit of Decency (Oxford, 1993)

Andrew Ashworth

Professor of Criminal Law and Criminal Justice, King's College, University of London. Editor of the Criminal Law Review. Author of Sentencing and Criminal Justice (Weidenfeld and Nicolson, 1992)

John Harding

Chief Probation Officer for Inner London and chair of the Association of Chief Officers of Probation Young Offenders Committee

Contents

Criminal Justice *In Transition*

A survey of sentencing law and practice including the effects of
the Criminal Justice Act 1991, Criminal Justice Act 1993, the
rulings
ound to

Criminal Justice *In Transition*

Bryan Gibson
Paul Cavadino
Andrew Rutherford
Andrew Ashworth
John Harding

WATERSIDE PRESS
WINCHESTER

Criminal Justice *In Transition*

Published 1994 by
WATERSIDE PRESS
Domum Road
Winchester SO23 9NN
Telephone or Fax 0962 855567

ISBN Paperback 1 872870 20 1

First edition, *Introduction to the Criminal Justice Act 1991*
published 1992.

Printing & binding Antony Rowe Ltd, Chippenham SN14 6QA

Part III: Appendices

Criminal Justice *In Transition*

Abbreviations used in this work

CYPA 33 Children and Young Persons Act 1933

CJA 67 Criminal Justice Act 1967

CYPA 69 Children and Young Persons Act 1969

PCCA 73 Powers of Criminal Courts Act 1973

MCA 80 Magistrates' Courts Act 1980

CJA 82 Criminal Justice Act 1982

MHA 1983 Mental Health Act 1983

CJA 1988 Criminal Justice Act 1988

CJA 91 Criminal Justice Act 1991

CJA 93 Criminal Justice Act 1993

CJ and PO Bill of 1994
Criminal Justice and Public Order Bill of 1994

Foreword

In the foreword to the first edition of this work, *Introduction to the Criminal Justice Act 1991,* we commented that:

> The Criminal Justice Act 1991 calls for a reappraisal of existing ideas and approaches to sentencing. Understood and applied as intended, the Act may be seen, with hindsight, as the single most important criminal justice measure this century.

With the benefit of that hindsight, the original version of the CJA 91 can now be seen as a bold reforming measure—but one for which neither the courts nor the public seemed to be ready. Yet it is impossible to erase the ideas which underpinned the original version of the Act, many of which have found their way into judicial thinking despite subsequent reversals of policy beginning with the Criminal Justice Act 1993.

Politics and Criminal Justice

Increasingly, criminal justice has been at the forefront of the political agenda. Since the U-turn of 1993 the pace has not slackened. What began as a *volte face* over unit fines and previous convictions has turned into 'freefall' with the Opposition as keen as the government to raise the stakes. Since July 1993 'law and order' has come to mean a constant menu of new pronouncements. Key developments of the past twelve months have included:

• The Criminal Justice Act 1993 which *inter alia* eliminated the 'two offence rule' in relation to the seriousness of offences, replaced unit fines and increased the relevance of previous convictions and responses to previous sentences in sentencing decisions. That Act also made the fact that an offence has been committed whilst on bail a compulsory aggravating factor.

• The Bail (Amendment) Act 1993 which conferred a right of appeal against a grant of bail on the prosecutor in certain instances.

• The Criminal Justice and Public Order Bill of 1994 which contains further sentencing changes—'escalatory' in nature and running counter to the philosophy behind the 1991 legislation as promulgated in the government's White Paper *Crime, Justice and Protecting the Public* (1990, Cm 965) and the Home Office *General Guide to the Criminal Justice Act 1991* (HMSO, 1990).

One feature has been the handing back of wider discretion to the courts. In the charged atmosphere created by tags such as 'prison works', 'young thugs' and 'bail bandits' many courts could view this as a licence to 'get tough', even if the facts about crime fall short of the media hype.

To take an example, a politically convenient target has been the 'persistent young offender'—yet a report by the Policy Studies Institute, commissioned by the Home Office and published in 1994, questions the assumptions behind this main plank of current strategy by showing that even if all such offenders were locked up this would have only a marginal effect on the crime rate.

In the background to the changes there has been *inter alia*:

• A 'tough' law and order atmosphere reinforced by high profile if untypical cases involving young offenders.

• Extensive work to review (and in Ministers' rhetoric 'toughen') National Standards for probation work, the enforcement of community sentences, parole and early release from prison.

• A Home Office Circular on 'The Cautioning of Offenders' (HOC 18/94: reproduced in *Appendix III, post*) the import of which was summed up by the Home Secretary as 'Your first chance is your last'.

• Speeches and public statements by Home Office Ministers advocating a greater use of imprisonment. Senior judges have expressed concern at the implied criticism by the executive of judicial practice. This shifting view of the separation of powers has caused concern on several occasions during the government's present term of office.

• Tough new Sentencing Guidelines from the Magistrates' Association precipitated by the 1993 Act (see *Appendix II, post*).

Forward looking and considered policies—made following wide consultation and leading to the Criminal Justice Act 1991—have been eroded without proper scrutiny. Every government has the right to legislate, but criminal justice issues are too important to be rushed through Parliament in the way that they are being at present, propelled by power politics. Not only has criminal justice become heavily politicised—but there has been a denial of true democracy, a diminution of open government, with experts forced to respond by fax or telephone to what has become a truncated, sometimes 24 hour, consultation process. As an editorial in *The Magistrate* (Vol 50, No 4, May 1994) commented:

'Most organisations representing those involved in the administration of criminal justice have expressed their reservations in robust terms . . . What is at issue is the reactive "knee jerk" nature of the way in which these policies have been formulated and hastily scrambled through the legislative process without there being a coherent, or any, overall strategy which addresses the fair and orderly administration of criminal justice.'

The Criminal Justice and Public Order Bill—like the 1993 Act a 'rushed' measure—when published in December 1993 contained other significant reversals of policy, including proposals for secure training centres for 12 to 14 year olds and the doubling of maximum sentences of detention in young offender institutions for 15 to 17 year olds, as well as some fundamental changes to the Bail Act 1976 and the right to silence. A large number of changes have been added to the Bill during its passage, often at a few days' notice. These have not been minor adustments, but items which are central to the work of the criminal courts—tagged on to an existing Bill to suit the political moment. This 'legislation by amendment' includes:

• Powers to bind over parents to ensure compliance with a community sentence by their child, even though present parental binding over powers are unpopular with youth court magistrates—being divisive as between parent and child.

• Abolition of the mandatory requirement for pre-sentence reports before custody or certain community sentences are used—thereby placing at risk the information base for proper decision making

• The extension of secure remand powers to 12 to 14 year olds

• A statutory arrangement for discounts to be given for guilty pleas (seemingly not discussed with the courts at all albeit that the principle is well established at common law)

• Wide new powers to stop and search suspects

• The replacement of committal proceedings (ie committal for trial) by a system of transfer to the Crown Court, including 'paper' submissions to challenge the evidence—to relieve witnesses from giving evidence twice (a laudable notion) but also to speed cases through the courts (a move which becomes equivocal within the 'tough' new context).

The CJA 1991 set out a comprehensive sentencing framework and was accompanied by a philosophy, well documented in the Home Office publications *supra*. It is open to question whether there is now any clear strategy—other than that the post-1991 Act shifts point in an opposite direction. There is now tension between what is left of the original CJA 91 and the subsequent changes, and a degree of confusion, which runs the risk of undermining what is left of that 1991 Act.

No-one has clearly articulated the change of thinking, which would appear to be driven by the determination of Ministers. Criminal justice practitioners—faced with courts exercising their new found discretion in the light of daily political pronouncements—may find themselves somewhat perplexed. Reactive, or 'knee-jerk', changes are no substitute for mature policies. Something more considered is called for.

There should be a presumption against criminal justice legislation being used to meet short term ends—a removal of these fundamentally important issues from frontline party politics, something which before the 1980s was close to reality.

In retrospect

The CJA 91 contained the most wide-ranging changes to sentencing law for over 40 years. The Act, implemented in October 1992, was—despite opposition from some judges, JPs and sections of the media—hailed by many as a long overdue reforming measure and it was widely predicted that it would make a fundamental impact on sentencing law and practice in England and Wales.

Behind the Act lay the idea of 'just deserts' or 'commensurate sentences', ie sentences which are proportionate to the seriousness of the current offence of which an offender stands convicted. Within a comprehensive sentencing framework, individual sentencing choices—custody, a new and extended range of community sentences and unit fines—shared recognizable features. The purpose was to encourage more consistent, visible and accountable decisions. The philosophy of the CJA 91 and its main aims are summarised in *Chapter 1* of this work,

In the event, the expectations of the framers of the legislation were short lived. Just just twelve months after Royal Assent, in a remarkable turnaround the government reversed some of the key provisions of the Act already mentioned *supra*—whilst inside 18 months a tougher law and order climate emerged and this coincided with growing hostility (fuelled by the media) to aspects of the 1991 Act. There was also a feeling among some of the judiciary that the Act placed undue restraints on their discretion (arguably unfounded). Largely as a result of the tougher climate, further proposals for change featured in the Criminal Justice and Public Order Bill of 1994. All these changes have been in a more punitive direction with an emphasis on the need to increase the use of custody (the prison population saw a 12 per cent increase in the 12 months to February 1994).

The extent of the shifts in the political climate can be seen from some of the more significant post-CJA 91 developments—by way of amendment to that Act and in relation to criminal justice generally:

• The 'two offence rule' has been replaced by one that allows the offence and one or more offences associated with it (ie any number of offences) to be taken into account when assessing seriousness (s1 and s6 CJA 91 as amended by the CJA 93).

• The rule against previous convictions and responses to earlier sentences being taken into account when assessing seriousness has been reversed, *supra* (s29(1) CJA 91 as substituted by the CJA 93).

• A new statutory rule has been created whereby if an offence is comitted on bail this fact must be treated as an aggravating factor (s29(2) CJA 91 as substituted by the CJA 93).

• The statutory unit fines scheme has been replaced by new arrangements under which fines must reflect the seriousness of the offence whilst taking account of the financial circumstances of the offender, *supra* (s18 CJA 91 as substituted by the CJA 93).

• Maximum sentences have been increased for certain offences (CJA 93 and CJ and PO Bill).

• The Court of Appeal has revived deterrent sentencing—albeit in a limited form (see *Chapter 1(c)*).

• The Magistrates' Association has published revised sentencing guidelines containing 'entry points' for offences—in some instances custody or a community sentence—which look more punitive generally (see *Appendix III, post*).

• Proposals for secure training centres for offenders aged 12 to 14, *supra* (CJ and PO Bill).

• A proposal to increase from one year to two years the maximum sentence of detention in a young offender institution for 15 to 17 year olds, *supra* (CJ and PO Bill).

• A proposal to extend the ambit of s53 CYPA 1933 in relation to younger offenders and to a wider range of offences (CJ and PO Bill with CJA 93).

• The prosecution has been given a right of appeal against a refusal of bail in a wide range of cases (Bail (Amendment) Act 1993).

• Proposals for automatic custodial remands in certain situations and an added ground for refusing bail, ie that an alleged indictable or either way offence was committed whilst the offender was on bail (CJ and PO Bill).

• A proposal that courts be given discretion to dispense with a pre-sentence report if the court deems a report unnecessary—tempered in the case of those below 18 years of age with a requirement that an earlier report must be available (CJ and PO Bill).

• A proposal to allow courts to bind over parents to ensure compliance by their child with a community sentence (CJ and PO Bill).

• A proposal to extend powers to remand juveniles in secure facilities (CJ and PO Bill).

• Proposals concerning discounts for timely pleas of guilty (CJ and PO Bill).

• Proposals to abolish the right to silence, reduce corroboration requirements under the law of evidence and to give the police additional powers in relation to 'stop and search' and 'body samples' (CJ and PO Bill).

• A proposal for the replacement of committal proceeding (ie committal for trial in the Crown Court) with a system of transfer to the Crown Court with a view *inter alia* to bringing offenders to trial more speedily (CJ and PO Bill).

• A new Home Office circular on 'The Cautioning of Offenders' tightening the circumstances in which an offender may be cautioned rather than prosecuted (HOC 18/94).

Whither the philosophy of the 1991 Act?

The original version of the CJA 91 relied on a preparedness to rethink old ideas and a degree of commitment by criminal justice practitioners—including sentencers—to making the Act work. In changing direction, the government has not only reversed major aspects of its sentencing policy but has handed to the courts broad fields of discretion. The U-turns also raise questions about the extent to which the philosophy and underlying principles of the Act have survived—something we have tried to answer in *Chapter 3, Sentencing Principles.*

There is judicial authority to the effect that the main principles of the Act remain intact (see *Chapter 1(b)*)—but equally there is a risk that, with the original framework fundamentally altered, courts will see this as an excuse to pay only lip-service to those principles. Each day seems to bring some new inroad into the philosophy behind the Act and the government has probably not completed its agenda for change with the 1994 Bill. Predictably, recent statements suggest that the one relatively unscathed area of sentencing, community sentences, is also likely to come in for scrutiny with all that this entails for a fundamental aspect of the Act's sentencing framework.

Criminal Justice in Transition

In this work we have attempted to deal with all the changes which have occurred between 1991 and 1994—together with further historical data where appropriate. The Criminal Justice and Public Order Bill is dealt with as it stood at the end of April 1994 as when it had completed its passage through the House of Commons and was about to begin its committee stage in the House of Lords.

The scheme of the book is as follows: *Chapter 1* deals with *Key Developments* since implementation. *Section (a)* of that chapter deals with the *Origins of the CJA 91, (b)* with *Changes Made by the CJA 93 et al, (c)* with *Judicial Guidance* and *(d)* with *Sentencing Trends After the CJA 91.*

The *Dynamics of Change—1987 to 1994* are discussed in *Chapter 2* which attempts to set the developments in the context of modern penal policy.

Current sentencing law and practice are dealt with in detail in *Chapters 3* to *13*—taking full account of the Criminal Justice Act 1993 and the proposals contained in the Criminal Justice and Public Order Bill of 1994 so far as practicable.

Relevant *Statutory Provisions*—including the CJA 91 as amended and updated extracts from other statutes—are reproduced, in chronological order, with annotations and notes on the Criminal Justice and Public Order Bill proposals in *Appendix I;* the full text of the *Magistrates' Association Sentencing Guidelines* (1993) in *Appendix II;* the revised *Home Office Circular on Cautioning* (HOC 18/94) in *Appendix III;* the *National Mode of Trial Guidelines* in *Appendix IV;* and the joint paper *Seriousness, Suitability and Restriction of Liberty,* produced by the Magistrates' Association, the Association of Chief Officers of Probation and the Justices' Clerks' Society in *Appendix V.*

Acknowledgements

The work did not begin and end with the contributors. Thanks are also due to Nikki Kenny for typing the manuscripts, to Jonathan Black for allowing his chart *Sentencing and Other Powers* to be reproduced in an updated form, to the Magistrates' Association for their kind permission to reproduce the *Sentencing Guidelines* and to many other people who have assisted in a somewhat less formal way by providing material, information and opinions.

Bryan Gibson Co-ordinating editor, May 1994

The Waterside Press series

This work continues a series which comprises:

Introduction to the CRIMINAL JUSTICE ACT 1991

A basic guide to the CJA 91 for general readers and containing an outline of the legislation as originally enacted—including chapters on General Principles, Custodial Sentences, Community Sentences, Unit Fines and Anti-discrimination. The book also contains a summary of the law affecting the Youth Court and of the law on Parole and Early Release of Prisoners—as well as much useful background information.

The Youth Court

A specialist work designed to meet the needs of people involved in the youth court (introduced by the CJA 91). Items covered include: jurisdiction, powers and procedures, remands, practice developments affecting juveniles and young offenders, summaries of relevant judicial guidance and annotated *Statutory Provisions* affecting the youth court.

Criminal Justice Act 1991 LEGAL POINTS Commentary & Annotated Guide for Practitioners

This work contains a technical legal commentary on all the main aspects of the CJA 91 together with annotated *Statutory Provisions* and summaries of judicial guidance in relation to the analogous provisions of the Criminal Justice Act 1982.

MATERIALS on the Criminal Justice Act 1991

This work contains virtually all the source materials which appeared between Royal Assent and implementation of the Act in October 1992.

Criminal Justice In Transition and The Youth Court One Year Onwards

which are intended as second editions of the first two works mentioned above, save that the statutory provisions which formerly appeared in book three, *Legal Points,* are now annexed to *Criminal Justice in Transition*. Both books bring events up to date as at April 1994.

A full list of Waterside Press publications on criminal justice topics appears at the end of this work together with ISBN numbers.

SENTENCING AND OTHER POWERS

Based on an original chart compiled by Jonathan Black 1994

SENTENCE	AUTHORITY	AVAILABILITY	NOTES
1 ABSOLUTE DISCHARGE An order discharging the offender without any further obligation, usually where there has been a purely technical offence.	S7 PCCA 1973	Every case	Used when the court considers that 'it is inexpedient to inflict punishment and that a probation order is not appropriate'. Logically, therefore, no other penalty can be used for the same offence.
2 CONDITIONAL DISCHARGE An order releasing the offender from court without any immediate penalty, but subject to the condition that he or she commits no further offence during a period of up to three years fixed by the court.	S7 PCCA 1973	Every case	As for 'Absolute discharge' *supra*
3 BIND OVER An order whereby an offender enters into a recognizance (or pledge) to be of good behaviour (or to keep the peace or both) for a period fixed by the court in a sum of money fixed by the court.	Common law (and referred to in Justices of the Peace Act 1361).	Every case Note: The Law Commission has recommended the abolition of this power.	In magistrates' courts this is an ancillary power, ie it cannot be imposed as the sole sentence. Not to be confused with the quasi-civil remedy where on a private complaint a person can be required to enter into a recognizance or to find sureties for his of her good behaviour in the future.
4 FINE A monetary penalty the value of which is determined by the seriousness of the offence taking into account the financial circumstances of the offender. Note: Some statutes, eg Revenue Acts, set a fixed penalty (although magistrates have power to mitigate such penalties).	The statute which creates the offence sets the maximum amount of the fine. The CJA 91 determines the way in which individual fines are calculated.	Every case	In magistrates' courts the originating statute lays down maximum fines, usually £5,000 or less. A 'standard scale' prescribes five levels of maximum penalty. This simplifies the process of amendment. Fines are often linked to an alternative or additional power of imprisonment. Sentencing guides—local or national—provide starting points for sentencing. In the Crown Court fines are usually unlimited, and in the discretion of the judge.

SENTENCE	AUTHORITY	AVAILABILITY SENTENCES	NOTES
5 PROBATION ORDER An order requiring an offender aged 16 or over to be under the supervision of a probation officer for a period of between 6 months and 3 years. Extra requirements may be added to the order under which the offender must: • attend at a probation centre for up to 60 days • attend at a specified place and take part in activities for up to 60 days • refrain from doing something during a period of time • undergo treatment for a mental condition (and see **22** *post*) • live at a particular place such as an approved hostel • undergo treatment designed to reduce or eliminate dependence on alcohol or drugs	COMMUNITY S2 PCCA 1973 (as amended by CJA 1991)	Every case where the offender is aged 16 or over	The court must be of opinion that the supervision of the offender by a probation officer is desirable in the interests of: • Securing the rehabilitation of the offender, or • Protecting the public from harm from him or her, or • Preventing the commission by him or her of further offences. • The offender must express a willingness to comply with the requirements which must be explained to him or her in ordinary language. • Requirements can be inserted if the court has consulted a probation officer about the offender's circumstances and is satisfied that it is feasible to secure compliance. • The restriction of liberty under the order must be commensurate with the seriousness of the offence. • A pre-sentence report is *mandatory* where requirements are to be added and *desirable* where an ordinary probation order is contemplated. (But note the implications of the CJ and PO Bill of 1994: see *Chapter 12*).
6 COMMUNITY SERVICE ORDER An order that the offender undertake between 40 and 240 hours of unpaid work for the benefit of the community under the auspices of the probation service. The work must be completed within a year.	S14 PCCA 1973 (as amended by the CJA 1991)	The offence must be 'punishable by imprisonment', ie the court must have *power* to imprison in the case of an adult.	A community service scheme must exist in the area where the defendant resides (now everywhere in England and Wales). The effect of the order must be explained in ordinary language and the offender must consent to it. • The court must obtain a pre-sentence report (but consider the CJ and PO Bill of 1994: see *Chapter 12*) and be satisfied as to the suitability of the offender for community service. • National standards for the operation of orders exist to ensure that demands are made on offenders. • A community service order can be combined with a fine as a sentence (but not with a probation order except by way of a combination order *post*).

SENTENCE	AUTHORITY	AVAILABILITY	NOTES
7 COMBINATION ORDER An order under which an offender aged 16 or over is supervised by a probation officer for a period of between 12 months and 3 years and must also perform between 40 and 100 hours community service.	S11 CJA 1991	The offence must be 'punishable by imprisonment', ie the court must have *power* to imprison in the case of an adult.	As with a probation order, the court must be satisfied that a combination order is desirable in the interests of securing the rehabilitation of the offender or protecting the public from harm from him or her or preventing the commission of offences by him or her. The offender must also be suitable for community service. • A pre-sentence report is mandatory (but consider the CJ and PO Bill of 1994, *Chapter 12*). • The offender must consent to the community service part of the order and to any requirements in the probation part of the order. • A combination order can be used in conjunction with a financial penalty or with other community orders (other than probation and community service which can only be combined within a combination order).
8 CURFEW ORDER An order requiring an offender to remain at a specified place for specified periods of between 2 and 12 hours a day for a period of up to 6 months. The order can be enforced by electronic monitoring ('tagging').	S12 CJA 1991 S13 CJA 1991	Every case where the offender is 16 or over.	A pre-sentence report is *not* mandatory. • Different lengths of time can be specified for different days and different places. • The order must avoid conflict with religious beliefs or school attendance. • The offender must consent to the order. • The order must make a person responsible for monitoring the whereabouts of the offender during the curfew period.

SENTENCE	AUTHORITY	AVAILABILITY	NOTES
9 SUPERVISION ORDER An order requiring an offender under 18 years of age to be supervised by a local authority social worker or a probation officer. Requirements may be included whereby the offender: • lives at a particular place • attends a specified place at a specified time • takes part in various (highly intensive) forms of supervised activity • refrains from specified activities • remains at home for specified periods of not more than 10 hours between 6pm and 6am for not more than 30 days during the first 3 months of the order • receives psychiatric treatment • attends school regularly • does not reside with a specified person • lives in accommodation provided by the local authority for a specified period not exceeding 6 months.	S12 CYPA 1969 (as amended)	Every case where the offender is under 18.	There is no minimum period. The maximum period is 3 years. • Requirements 'to attend' and 'to participate' may be inserted for up to 90 days. • The offender's consent is required where extra requirements are added. • A pre-sentence report is mandatory if requirements are to be added and desirable where a straightforward supervision order is contemplated (but consider the CJ and PO Bill of 1994: see *Chapter 12*).

SENTENCE	AUTHORITY	AVAILABILITY	NOTES
10 ATTENDANCE CENTRE ORDER An order to attend at a centre, usually under police, probation or education service management for between 12 and 36 hours. Attendees take part in physical training, social skills exercises and similar disciplines	S19 CJA 1948 (as amended)	The offence must be 'punishable by imprisonment', ie the court must have *power* to imprison in the case of an adult. The offender must be under 21.	Available only where there is an attendance centre to which the offender will have reasonable access. The maximum hours of attendance are 24 for offenders under 16 years of age and 36 hours for those aged 16-21. The offender's consent is *not* required.
		CUSTODIAL MEASURES	
11 IMPRISONMENT A custodial sentence of between 5 days and 6 months in the magistrates' court. Beyond this, for an either way offence, the offender may be committed to the Crown Court for a longer sentence where this is indicated by the seriousness of the offence or the need to protect the public from serious harm from the offender. Consecutive sentences amounting to 12 months in aggregate can be imposed by a magistrates' court when sentencing for two or more either way offences. Notes: (1) Imprisonment is for adults only, ie those aged 21 years and over. For offenders under 21 years of age see *Detention in a Young Offender Institution*, *post*. (2) A former power to imprison for less than five days, ie for one day in the court or at a police station, in s134 MCA 1980 was repealed by s49 CJA 1988.	The maximum sentence is fixed by the statute which creates the offence, and the correct approach by ss1 and 2 CJA 91 as amended.		The offender must be given the opportunity of legal representation before sentence unless he or she has already served imprisonment. The 'threshold criteria' for custody are that: • the offence, or the combination of the offence and one or more offences associated with it, is so serious that only custody can be justified; or • the offence is a violent or sexual offence and only such a sentence would be adequate to protect the public from serious harm from the offender; or • the offender has refused to consent to a community sentence that requires such consent. Other requirements: • A pre-sentence report is mandatory except in the Crown Court when the offence is triable only on indictment (but see the CJ and PO Bill of 1994: *Chapter 12*). • The *length* of the sentence must be commensurate with the seriousness of the offence or the offence and one or more offences associated with it or with the need to protect the public from serious harm from the offender. • Reasons must be given in open court for the sentence. • These must be explained in ordinary language

SENTENCE	AUTHORITY	AVAILABILITY	NOTES
12 SUSPENDED SENTENCE OF IMPRISONMENT Not strictly another form of sentence but a variant of 11 *supra*, ie an option to withhold imprisonment for between 1 and 2 years (fixed by the court) subject to the condition that the offender commits no other offence punishable by imprisonment during this, the 'operational period'.	S22 PCCA 1973 (as amended by the CJA 1991). Otherwise as for imprisonment, *supra*.		The same rules apply as for sentences of immediate imprisonment, *supra*. NB that the sentence must be explained to the defendant in ordinary language. The power to suspend can only be exercised in 'exceptional circumstances': see *Chapter 7*.
13 DETENTION IN A YOUNG OFFENDER INSTITUTION Boys aged 15-17 = 2 to 6 months* Girls aged 18-20 = 2 to 6 months* * Maximum 12 months where there are two or more 'either way' offences.	S123 and sched 8 CJA 1988 as amended by the CJA 1991. Otherwise as for imprisonment *supra*.	Available for any offence punishable with imprisonment' or for failure to comply with the terms of supervision after release from a young offender institution (maximum 30 days).	The offender must be given the opportunity to be legally represented. He or she must satisfy the same 'threshold criteria' as for imprisonment *supra*. The court must give reasons for the sentence in open court and explain them in ordinary language. See also now *Secure training centres: Chapter 10*
14 COMMITTAL TO THE CROWN COURT FOR SENTENCE (EITHER WAY OFFENCES) An order by a magistrates' court sending an offender to the Crown Court for greater sentence than magistrates have power to impose, ie more than 6 months or 12 months where there are two or more either way offences.	S38 MCA 1980 and S56 CJA 1967 (as amended by CJA 1991 and CJA 1993)	Either way offences only. Purely summary offences can be committed to the Crown Court to be dealt with at the same time as an either way offence if 'punishable by imprisonment' or disqualification from driving.	The magistrates' court must be of opinion either: • that the offence or the combination of the offence and one or more offences associated with it was so serious that greater punishment should be inflicted for it than the magistrates' court has power to impose (ie 6 months or 12 for two or more either way offences); or • in the case of a violent or sexual offence committed by a person aged 21 years or over (but see the CJ and PO Bill of 1994: *Chapter 12*) imprisonment for longer than the magistrates' court has power to impose is necessary to protect the public from serious harm from the offender.
15 COMMITTAL FOR TRIAL OF SUMMARY OFFENCES	S41 CJA 1988	Can only be committed for trial along with either way offences.	Before they can be committed for trial, summary offences must either be:- • punishable with imprisonment, ie the court must have *power* to imprison in the case of an adult; or • by disqualification *and* arise out of or be connected with the either way offence which is being committed for trial.

SENTENCE	AUTHORITY	AVAILABILITY	NOTES
16 COMPENSATION An order for payment of money to compensate the victim for any loss, damage or injury arising from the offence (or any other offence taken into consideration). The maximum compensation in the magistrates' court is £5,000 per offence of which the offender stands convicted.	S35 PCCA 1973 and s40 MCA 1980 (as amended by the CJA 1991)	Every case. Compensation can be a *sentence in its own right* or is capable of being an order ancillary to some other sentence. Preference must be given to compensation over a fine out of an offender's financial resources: see *Chapter 9*	The victim does not need to apply to the court, which can make an award of its own motion. No order can be made for loss resulting from the death of the victim. The court must take into account the means of the offender. An order should not be made by magistrates where there are difficulties in assessing the amount of the loss or where complex questions of civil law arise. A magistrates' court must give reasons for not ordering compensation in a case where it has power to make such an award. Compensation can be awarded in traffic cases: • in respect of damage following an offence under the Theft Act • in relation to injury, loss or damage for which the offender is not insured • where the loss extends to circumstances where damage is caused to other property when a vehicle is taken without consent.
ANCILLARY ORDERS			
17 RESTITUTION An order to restore to a victim the actual goods stolen or the direct proceeds of the sale of such goods.	S28 Theft Act 1968	Every case under the Theft Act 1968 or the Theft Act 1972.	The victim does not need to apply to the court. Of limited use by its very nature. May be used with a *Deferred sentence, post.*
18 DEPRIVATION OF PROPERTY ORDER An order to forfeit items used in the course of an offence or intended for such use. Note: Some statutes give courts specific powers of forfeiture eg Firearms Act 1968, Misuse of Drugs Act 1971 and Obscene Publications Act 1959.	S69 CJA 1988	Every offence.	There are provisions for third parties claiming ownership of property to apply to the court for its return. Applicants must satisfy the court that they did not realise the property would be put to unlawful use. Applies to any property used to commit or facilitate commission of the offence (including offences taken into consideration) or intended for that purpose. No other penalty need be used. The court must take account of the value of the property, the seriousness of the offence and the overall effect of the sentence.

SENTENCE	AUTHORITY	AVAILABILITY	NOTES
19 COSTS The basic rule has always been that the losing party pays. In criminal cases the costs of the prosecution are borne by the state or local authority etc, but the offender may be ordered to reimburse these.	S18 Prosecution of Offences Act 1985, *et al* (which also deals with 'costs thrown away', ie costs ordered to mark the fact that time or money has been wasted)	Every criminal case (including breach of an order)	The court has a discretion how much to order but *must* have regard to the means of the party concerned. The court cannot award costs at the end of a case if it imposes a penalty of £5 or less.
20 NO SEPARATE PENALTY (NSP)	Inherent powers	Every case where a penalty has already been imposed for another offence.	This is a non-statutory device to record a conviction or finding of guilt, where sentences have already been imposed for other (often more serious) offences and further punishment is not appropriate.
SPECIAL		**CATEGORIES**	
21. JUVENILES APPEARING IN MAGISTRATES' COURTS	S7 Children and Young Persons Act 1969.	Every case, summary or either way.	A juvenile appearing before an adult court after conviction must be remitted to the youth court for sentence unless the court proposes to deal with him or her by way of: • absolute discharge or conditional discharge • fine, or • a parental bind over (ie an order binding over parents for the good behaviour of their child) in all cases together with any ancillary orders. Sentences for juveniles which are exclusive to the youth court, ie not available to adult magistrates' courts in respect of offenders below the age of 18, include: supervision order, attendance centre order, community service order (16 or over) and detention in a young offender institution. These are set out in full in the companion to this work *The Youth Court One Year Onwards*

SENTENCE	AUTHORITY	AVAILABILITY	NOTES
22 MENTALLY ILL PEOPLE			
HOSPITAL ORDER An order whereby a defendant is detained in hospital for medical treatment until he or she is discharged by the hospital authorities or Mental Health Review Tribunal.	Mental Health Act 1983	Every case where the offence is punishable by imprisonment.	The court must obtain medical reports from two doctors qualified within the terms of the 1983 Act and in which there is agreement on the diagnosed medical or psychiatric condition (again as defined in the Act) and an offer of a hospital place or guardianship provision.
GUARDIANSHIP ORDER Similar to a hospital order but placing the offender under the guardianship of either a local authority social services department or some other approved person (a relative).	Mental Health Act 1983	Every case where the offence is punishable by imprisonment.	A defendant can be remanded in custody for preparation of reports. The court need not have convicted the individual concerned because of problems over his or her mental state, but must be satisfied that the acts or omissions alleged have been committed. A guardian can require the patient to live at a specified place, undergo medical treatment, receive training or education.
RESTRICTION ORDER In severe cases magistrates can commit an offender to the Crown Court which may impose a restriction on the release of the offender.	Mental Health Act 1983	Every case where the offence is punishable by imprisonment and the order is made by the Crown Court.	Under ordinary hospital orders the date of release becomes a matter for the hospital authorities not the court (or in guardianship cases the local social services department). Hence the need for restriction orders in severe cases.
CONDITION OF MEDICAL TREATMENT ATTACHED TO A PROBATION ORDER A requirement attached to a probation order (see 5 supra) that the probationer undergo in-patient or out-patient treatment at a named hospital, or under the supervision of a named doctor	S3 PCCA 1973 (as amended by CJA 1991)	Every case where a probation order is appropriate.	The requirement can be imposed on the recommendation of a qualified doctor (within the meaning of the Mental Health Act 1983) and a probation officer. Because the order is within the framework of a probation order the offender must consent.

SENTENCE	AUTHORITY	AVAILABILITY	NOTES
23 DEFERMENT OF SENTENCE An order postponing the decision about sentence to a later date, not more than six months away.	S1 PCCA 1973	Every case	The purpose of deferment is to allow the court to assess the behaviour and attitude of the offender during an extended period of adjournment after conviction. • Reasons for deferment must be given and explained to the offender to enable him or her to respond accordingly. • The offender must consent. • The use of this power (strictly not a sentence) has been restricted by case law and statute. If the offender has complied with the court's expectations, it should not impose a custodial sentence—but, if not, it can use custody if appropriate. • The offender may be brought back to court and dealt with before the end of the period of deferment if he or she commits a further offence within that period.
24 RECOMMENDATION FOR DEPORTATION	S3 Immigration Act 1971	The offence must be punishable by imprisonment, ie the court must have *power* to imprison in the case of an adult.	Applies to all 'non-patrials' as defined in the 1971 Act. • The offender must be given at least 7 clear days notice of the intention to recommend deportation before the decision to so recommend is made. • The final decision rests with the Home Secretary. • Unless the court otherwise directs, the offender is kept in custody until the Home Secretary makes his decision. • A recommendation for deportation is *not* an alternative to sentence. Some form of sentence should be passed for the offence.

Part I

Criminal Justice In Transition

1 Key Developments

a) Origins of the CJA 91

b) Changes Made by the CJA 93 *et al*

c) Judicial Guidance

d) Sentencing Trends After the CJA 91

2 The Dynamics of Change— 1987 to 1994

1 Key Developments

This chapter charts developments in sentencing law and practice since 1991 as follows:

- (a) *Origins and Content of the Criminal Justice Act 91*
- (b) *Changes Made by the Criminal Justice Act 1993 et al*
- (c) *Judicial Guidance*
- (d) *Sentencing Trends After the CJA 91.*

a) Origins of the CJA 91

The immediate origins of the CJA 91 are to be found in the White Paper *Crime, Justice and Protecting the Public* (1990, Cm 965) and the Green Paper *Punishment, Custody and the Community* (1988, Cm 424). These documents were the outcome of a decade or more of research and deliberation during which the government opted for a de-escalatory approach to criminal justice. The background to these events is set out in *Chapter 2*.

Critically, the White Paper made the point that reduction of crime is the ultimate objective of criminal justice, but that the role of court sentences in this should not be over-stated. Crime prevention strategies and new initiatives in policing were the main ways of achieving a reduction in crime whereas the primary task of the courts was to impose *proportionate* and *consistent* sentences. The White Paper used the term 'just deserts' to describe this approach which was expanded on in the Home Office *General Guide to the Criminal Justice Act 1991* (1991) published following Royal Assent.

A new sentencing structure

The CJA 91 created, for the first time, a comprehensive sentencing framework. The Act introduced criteria for the use of fines, community sentences and custody which were complementary to and consistent with each other—together with a new system of unit fines in magistrates' courts. Significantly, the Act also created new enforcement powers and a revised system of parole and early release from custody. The overall effect on the powers of the courts can be summarised as follows:

- *Absolute* and *conditional discharges*
Discharges were not affected by the CJA 91 but the relevant provisions were consolidated and re-enacted: see s1A to s1C PCCA 1973, *Appendix I post.*

- *Unit fines*
Under the statutory unit fines scheme contained principally in s18 CJA 91—and which was based on the experiences of four pilot projects—magistrates' courts (but not Crown Courts) were required to determine the seriousness of an offence

28

in units on a scale from one to 50 and then to multiply these units by the offender's own disposable weekly income as assessed by the court under regulations contained in the Magistrates' Courts (Unit Fines) Rules 1992 SI 1852. Compensation to victims of crime continued to take priority over fines out of an offender's available financial resources pursuant to s35 PCCA 1973. To assist the enforcement of any financial penalties a new scheme for deducting monies from income support was introduced by s24 CJA 91. Unit fines were abolished by the CJA 93: see *Chapter 1(b) post.*

• *Community sentences*
In future community sentences were to be used where the current offence (or that offence and one offence associated with it: but see *Changes Made by the CJA 93, post*) was **'serious enough'** to justify this: s6 CJA 91. After the CJA 91 these sentences comprised six possible types of court order as follows:

(a) **probation orders** with or without extra requirements (the purpose of probation being set out in the 1991 Act as rehabilitation, protection of the public from harm from the offender, or preventing further offences by him or her)
(b) **community service orders**, ie unpaid work in the community
(c) **combination orders**, introduced by the CJA 91 and containing elements of community service and probation.
(d) **curfew orders**, introduced by the CJA 91 (not brought into force).
(e) **attendance centre orders** for people aged 10 to 20 years inclusive.
(f) **supervision orders**, ie supervision a local authority social worker or probation officer for people aged 10 to 17 years inclusive.

• *Custodial sentences*
Following the CJA 91 the criteria for the use of custody applied equally to all offenders regardless of age. Under s1 CJA 91, custody was only to be used only

—where the current offence (or that offence and one offence associated with it: but see *Changes Made by the CJA 93, post*) was so serious that only a custodial sentence was justified; or
—to protect the public from serious harm from the offender (this criteria applying in relation to violent or sexual offences only); or
—on refusal (or on breach) of certain community orders.

• *Associated offences*
The CJA 91 introduced the notion of associated offences (defined in s31 CJA 91: see *Chapter 3* and *Statutory Provisions* in *Appendix III* to this work). In relation to the seriousness threshold justifying either custody or a community sentence a rule was invoked that only the current offence and *one other* offence associated with it could be considered when assessing whether the threshold had been reached—but **not** other offences beyond these two, and specifically **not** previous convictions as such (the effect of the then s1, s6 and s29(1) CJA 91). The so called 'two offence rule' did not apply: (a) to unit fines; (b) when fixing

the *length* of a custodial sentence or the *extent* of the restrictions on liberty contained in a particular community sentence; or (c) when assessing the *suitability* of a community order for the offender.

Other key points

The original version of the CJA 91 also contained a variety of important ancillary provisions. The Act rested on certain underlying premises (not contained in the legislation but publicised in government documents such as the white paper *Crime, Justice and Protecting the Public* and Home Office *General Guide* to the Act, *supra*—and enjoying varying degrees of support from the judiciary). The main points can be summarised:

• *Just deserts*
The sentence imposed for an offence should equate with the **seriousness** of the offence. The Act uses the term 'commensurate' with the seriousness of the offence: see in particular s2 (length of custody), s6 (community sentences) and s18 (unit fines). The word 'commensurate' has survived subsequent changes except in relation to fines where it has been replaced by the word 'reflect', ie fines must now reflect the seriousness of the current offence or offences: see *Chapter 9*.

• *Present offence*
The sentence must be for the **present offence**. The Act provided that the seriousness of an offence should not be aggravated on account of other convictions or responses to sentences—and see the 'two offence rule' mentioned under the heading *Associated offences, supra* and *Circumstances of other offences, post*. The rule against taking account of previous convictions and responses was reversed by the CJA 93: see *Chapter 4*.

• *Circumstances of other offences*
The **circumstances** of other offences (but **not** just the bare fact of conviction) could be taken into account if these shed light on the seriousness of the present offence: s29(2) CJA 91. This implied that information about the facts of previous convictions would be forthcoming on the basis of which courts might make appropriate decisions; but in most instances this information failed to materialise except, generally speaking, in the Crown Court—something that might have been foreseen. There is as yet no convenient recording system for this purpose within any of the criminal justice agencies. The content of the original s29(2) has become redundant: see generally *Chapter 4* of this work.

• *Seriousness and seriousness thresholds*
More generally, the seriousness of an offence would be assessed on the basis of all relevant information (including that contained in a *Pre-sentence report*, post) and taking account of **aggravating** and **mitigating** factors: see in particular s3 CJA 91. Two specific 'seriousness thresholds' were introduced (and still remain):

—following the CJA 91 a **community order** could only be used where the offence was **'serious enough to warrant such a sentence'**; and —a **custodial sentence** could only be passed if the offence was considered to be **'so serious that only a custodial sentence can be justified'**.

• *Information and reasons for decisions*
The sentencing provisions contained in Part I of the CJA 91 were accompanied by procedural and other requirements requiring certain information to be taken into account before sentence.

Thus, *inter alia*, courts were placed under a duty to obtain a pre-sentence report before either a custodial sentence (in most cases) or most types of community order were used. The CJA 91 required courts to give reasons *inter alia* for any decision that only custody could be justified and to explain that decision to the offender in ordinary language: see generally *Chapter 5* of this work. A proposal to allow courts to dispense with PSRs where they consider them unnecessary is contained in the CJ and PO Bill of 1994.

• *Restriction of liberty*
All forms of sentence were to be viewed as a form of 'restriction of liberty'— albeit in differing degrees. Under the CJA 91 itself the selection of an appropriate community order fell to be tested by considering whether the restrictions contained in the particular order or orders were commensurate with the seriousness of the offence—as well as whether the order was the most suitable one for the offender: see s6 CJA 91. This aspect remains unaffected by subsequent changes.

• *Suitability*
In addition to any considerations concerning 'restriction of liberty', a community order must be the one most suitable for the offender: s6 CJA 91—again unaffected.

• *Pre-sentence reports*
Following the CJA 91, PSRs were to form an integral part of the information gathering and sentencing process—providing information relevant to both seriousness and suitability. PSRs would also contain background information and where appropriate a proposal for a community sentence, and would be prepared in accordance with *National standards, post*. PSRs became mandatory before most custodial or community sentences could be passed: see *Chapter 12*. Proposals to alter this—and to allow courts to dispense with PSRs—are contained in the CJ and PO Bill of 1994.

• *Mitigation*
Notwithstanding the focus on commensurate sentences and sentencing thresholds, courts were empowered take into account any mitigating factors unconnected with the offence itself ('offender mitigation') and reduce the sentence from that which the level of seriousness of the offence might otherwise require: see s28 CJA 91 discussed under the heading *Mitigation of sentence, post*. This

aspect remains unaffected.

• *Parole and early release from custody*
Under Part II CJA 91 offenders would serve definite, in many instances longer, periods in custody of at least half the sentence imposed. Prisoners sentenced to less than four years would be released automatically after half the sentence; would be supervised on licence (if the sentence was 12 months or more) to the three-quarters point of the sentence; and, if reconvicted before the end of the sentence, would be liable to serve the remaining part of the original sentence in addition to the penalty for the new offence. Prisoners serving four years or more would be eligible for discretionary conditional release between the half-way point and the two-thirds point of the sentence, and would also be supervised on licence to the three-quarters point of the sentence; and if reconvicted of an offence committed before the end of the sentence would be liable to serve the remainder of the original sentence in addition to that for the later offence. This placed offenders 'at risk' throughout the full period of the sentence: *Chapter 13, post.*

• *Enforcement*
New, more stringent, enforcement powers were introduced to allow eg for re-sentencing on breach of a community order (and if viewed by the court as a 'refusal' this could also justify a custodial sentence); and criminal courts were handed new powers to send an offender back to prison if in breach of his or her licence: see *Parole and early release from custody, supra.* It was urged that these powers gave certainty to sentences, ie in the mind of the offender—and the public would know what a sentence meant and that it would be carried through according to clear statutory criteria and *National standards, post.* This was also a reason why, post-CJA 91, community sentences could be regarded as a more significant sentence than previously—the original intention being to encourage courts to use them at higher levels of seriousness than before.

• *National Standards* for relevant aspects of probation practice, social work and post-custody supervision were introduced in support of the Act. The purpose was to enhance the quality of reports and to reinforce the enforcement provisions of the Act. The standards are in the process of revision as this work goes to press: see *Chapter 12.*

Implementation of the 1991 Act

The CJA 91 represented a shift in sentencing culture. The Act rested on the philosophy of proportionality in sentencing and certain assumptions needed to be understood if the otherwise bare sentencing framework was to work: see *Chapter 3, Principles of Sentencing.* A great deal of time and effort was invested in training for the judiciary (particularly the magistracy) and in the provision of supporting information. At a Home Office Special Conference held in November 1991, John Halliday of the Criminal Department at the Home Office said '. . . experience shows that legislation only "works" . . . in relation to policy objectives if there is widespread understanding of its purposes, and concerted efforts are made by practitioners to plan and organise for implementation.' He went on to make a number of pertinent comments, saying first that there was:

'. . . a large amount of change; some of it quite radical. The Act can be seen as a first attempt to construct a truly comprehensive piece of legislation governing sentencing. It covers the whole process: virtually the whole range of disposals available; the reasoning to be applied when reaching decisions; the methods by which sentences can be calculated and implemented; and, in the case of custody, the whole process from reception, right through to the expiry of the term imposed. The sheer scale of the attempt, taken as a whole, is probably unprecedented. Previous reforms have tended to be more piecemeal.'

He also pointed out that:

'The Act breaks new ground in another way. This Act—as distinct perhaps from any others on the subject—seeks to incorporate a clearly stated set of principles about sentencing—a sentencing philosophy, if you like . . . Governments habitually explain their policies in White Papers—in this case, the White Paper "Crime, Justice and Protecting the Public". In this case, the Act seeks to incorporate the policies in statutory form.'

And further that:

'The key underlying principle of the sentencing provisions is that: "The court should try to arrive at a sentence which is commensurate with the seriousness of the offence, taking account of aggravating and mitigating circumstances". The so-called theory of "proportionality"—the punishment fitting the crime—or "just deserts".'

'Proportionality' must now be understood in the light of the subsequent changes. Following Royal Assent in July 1991 there was much debate about the extent to which it actually altered or replaced traditional sentencing bases. The White Paper *supra* had stated eg: 'It is unrealistic to construct sentencing arrangements on the assumption that most offenders will weigh up the possibilities in advance and base their conduct on rational calculation' (p 6). Shortly after the CJA 91 was implemented the Court of Appeal sought to reconcile the new legislation with deterrent sentencing by holding that a commensurate sentence means one that is 'commensurate with the punishment and deterrence which the seriousness of the offence requires': see *Cunningham* (1993) 14 Cr App R (S) 444, discussed in *Section (c)* of this chapter, *Judicial Guidance*.

Rehabilitation *does* have a statutorily acknowledged part to play in sentencing under the Act, notably in relation to probation orders and combination orders: *Chapter 8*. But the primary test of whether a community sentence is appropriate at all remains the seriousness of the offence. Indeed, whilst preserving former sentencing considerations the Court of Appeal has also confirmed that the pursuit of secondary aims and objectives must be consistent with the use of sentences which are commensurate with the seriousness of the offence or imposed to protect the public.

John Halliday of the Home Office had originally observed:

'The very existence of criminal law, law enforcement agencies, the courts, sentences, etc., can safely be assumed to have some deterrent effect. Complete withdrawal of the police in the early part of this century during the police strike in 1919 was seen to lead to increased offending. "Crime as opportunity" was identified as a significant factor by researchers during the 1970s. Many people seem to be deflected from crime after initial exposure to the sanctions which exist: one in three adult males will have at least one serious criminal conviction by the age of 30; but 6% of any population seems to be responsible for about 60-70% of the crime committed by that population. Large numbers are deterred (no doubt for a variety of reasons, but including fear of detection, and the due process of law, including sentencing). A relatively small number of very persistent offenders are clearly not.

Reconviction rates on release from custody, or from community sentences, give no obvious message in relation to deterrence. Such evidence as there is suggests that those given community sentences have no worse and, if anything, rather better reconviction rates; and that longer custodial sentences do not result in lower reconviction rates than shorter ones. It follows that, at the point of sentencing the individual offender, the use of custody cannot be given validity by the presumed deterrent effects and the Act reflects this, in requiring that custody be used only where justified by the seriousness of the offence.'

Such views had become fairly widespread as at implementation in October 1992. Whatever occured subsequently, the shifts engineered by the CJA 91 were not merely 'fashionable', but based on mature consideration and research.

The Home Office had been quick to promote the underlying philosophy of the Act, albeit that there had been relatively little in the way of an authoritative judicial opinion concerning the legitimacy of the approach prior to implementation. However, in an address to the Justices' Clerks' Society in Cambridge, on 28 September 1992, Lord Mackay of Clashfern PC, Lord Chancellor, remarked:

'It would be appropriate to say something about the Criminal Justice Act in view of the fact that it will come into force very shortly. The implementation next week of the main provisions of the Act marks an important step forward in the way we respond to offenders in court . . . For the first time a piece of legislation lays out a sentencing philosophy, the philosophy of proportionality, that the sentence should primarily match the seriousness of the offence. This approach builds on principles derived from the Court of Appeal judgments and from legislative provisions affecting young offenders since 1982 . . . The Act should lead to a more coherent approach to sentencing and more consistent outcomes.'

Notwithstanding such exhortations it took less than a year for important aspects of the original CJA 91 to be altered by government, a phenomenon discussed in *Chapter 2, The Dynamics of Change 1987 to 1994.* The Court of Appeal judgments which interpreted the statutory sentencing framework introduced by the CJA 91 are discussed in *Chapter 1(c), post.* The extent to which the philosophy of the CJA 91 remains intact following the CJA 93 is discussed in *Chapter 3, Sentencing Principles.*

Other reforms

The original CJA 91 brought about several other important reforms.

Abolition of certain sentences

The CJA 91 abolished extended sentences of imprisonment and the partly suspended sentence. However, ordinary suspended sentences of imprisonment were retained, ie the power to suspend a complete prison term for a fixed period of up to two years. A new test restricted suspended sentences to cases where there were 'exceptional circumstances': see *Chapter 7*. There is *no power* to suspend custodial sentences on offenders below the age of 21. Both these items are unaffected by subsequent changes.

The youth court

An important change was the replacement of the juvenile court by a new youth court—the intention being to capitalise on the ethos of the juvenile court which had been at the forefront of developments in the 1980s.

The youth court was established to deal with young people below the age of 18 (as opposed to 'under 17' as was the case in the former juvenile court) using more flexible powers. The significance lay as much in the fact of the creation of the new court—and that the new 10 to 17 year age range (and within this the new, older element, ie 16 and 17 year olds, referred to in the White Paper as 'near adults') would undoubtedly attract special attention from criminal justice practitioners along the lines of that which occured in the former juvenile court—as it did in any changes made by the CJA 91 to magistrates' sentencing powers in relation to this age group.

Under the 1991 Act people below the age of 18 became subject to the same sentencing framework as adult offenders but subject to the 'welfare principle' contained in s44 Children and Young Persons Act 1933.

The youth court provisions were reinforced by a fresh onus on parental responsibility in relation to younger offenders within the youth court age band, interlinking with the idea that offenders should be dealt with on the basis of their individual maturity. The intention was that '... the way in which young people are dealt with in the criminal justice system should more closely reflect their age and development, as should the extent to which their parents should be expected to take responsibility for their actions': Home Office *General Guide*. The new jurisdiction and the sentencing changes are outlined in *Chapter 10*. A comprehensive treatment is contained in the companion volume to this work *The Youth Court One Year Onwards*.

The Criminal Justice and Public Order Bill of 1994 contains proposals for secure training centres for those aged twelve but under 15 years, new remand powers for 12 to 14 year olds and provisions empowering courts to bind over parents to ensure compliance with community sentences.

Remand of juveniles

The Act introduced a new system of remand for juveniles awaiting trial or sentence. Under these changes the remand of juveniles to prison under what were previously called 'unruly certificates' were to be phased out over a period of four years in favour of remands to local authority accommodation with a new power to make a 'security requirement' for defendants aged 15 and 16. There is a transitory stage until the arrangements are finalised: see *Chapter 10* and the companion volume to this work *The Youth Court One Year Onwards*.

In March 1994, Michael Howard, the Home Secretary amended the Criminal Justice and Public Order Bill so as to extend court powers to make security requirements to include 12 to 14 year olds.

Children's evidence
Quite separately from the youth court provisions, the CJA 91 made important changes in relation to evidence given by children. The law was revised to allow this to be given unsworn, and for video evidence to be received by courts in certain instances. These evidence provisions, not being matters affecting sentencing, have been omitted from this edition. They can be found reproduced in *The Youth Court* (Waterside Press, 1992).

Cash limits and other miscellaneous items
The Act incorporated several miscellaneous items. It provided for the cash limiting of magistrates' courts and of the probation service; for the appointment of court security officers in magistrates' courts; and for the private management of prisoner escorts and the contracting out of prisons. These items—whilst of considerable importance for the administration of justice as a whole—do not directly affect sentencing or court procedures and are not dealt with in this work.

b) Changes Made by the CJA 93 *et al*

There have been two tranches of statutory changes since the Criminal Justice Act 1991—those contained in the Criminal Justice Act 1993 and the proposals contained in the Criminal Justice and Public Order Bill of 1994 which is still on its way through Parliament as at the time of going to press. The main sentencing changes and proposals can be summarised:

CJA 1993:

- abrogation of the 'two offence rule'
- reversal of the rule against taking previous convictions or responses into account re the seriousness of the current offence
- abolition of unit fines
- offending on bail becomes a mandatory seriousness factor
- increase in certain penalties

CJ and PO Bill 1994

- secure training centres for offenders aged 12 to 14
- a doubling of maximum sentences of detention in a young offender institution from one year to two years
- extension of the ambit of s53 Children and Young persons Act 1933 (long sentences of detention for 'grave crimes' committed by juveniles)
- youth courts to be given power to bind over parents to ensure compliance with community sentences on their children
- the extension of secure remand powers to 12 to 14 year olds
- courts given a discretion to dispense with pre-sentence reports
- courts to consider giving a discount for a guilty plea

In addition, the Bill makes a number of changes to the law relating to bail. These are briefly summarised at the end of this part of *Chapter 1*.

Changes contained in the Criminal Justice Act 1993

The Criminal Justice Act 1993 received Royal Assent in July of that year and the relevant sentencing provisions came into force between August and November. These changes were as follows:

Sentencing criteria—abolition of the 'two offence rule'
The statutory criteria in the CJA 91 for the imposition of custodial sentences and community sentences each contained a reference to the 'two offence rule'. This rule never applied to fines.

Abolition of the 'two offence rule'—Custody
The first criterion for passing a custodial sentence, contained in section 1(2)(a)

CJA 91 was 'that the offence, or the combination of the offence and *one other* offence associated with it, was so serious that only such a sentence can be justified for the offence' (italics supplied). Section 66(1) CJA 93 changed the wording of section 1(2)(a) to:

'. . . the offence, or the combination of the offence and one or more offences associated with it, was so serious that only such a sentence can be justified for the offence'.

Whereas previously the court could consider the combined seriousness of no more than two offences when deciding if only custody was justified, it can now look at the combined seriousness of any number of offences. Some commentators expressed anxiety about this change suggesting that it might lead to the unnecessary imprisonment of minor offenders. They suggested that the change might give the impression that courts could now eg—by adding up the value of a number of minor offences—thereby sentence a petty offender as though he or she were a more serious criminal.

The Magistrates' Association's *Sentencing Guidelines*, issued in September 1993 (see *Appendix II, post*), emphasised that

'. . . when there are several offences, the overall sentence should be kept in proportion to the totality of the offending behaviour with which the court is dealing'.

If someone is convicted of a number of unconnected petty thefts, none of which individually involve a large amount of money but which add up to a much larger total, the CJA 93 amendments do not mean that a court must treat such an offender as if he or she were a much bigger thief who was before the court for a single big 'job' which involved stealing the aggregate amount of all the small thefts put together—and this would seem to be a wrong approach. As always, the court must have regard to the totality—ie the overall seriousness—of the offending behaviour. This principle was expressly preserved in section 28(2) of the CJA 91, which states:

'... nothing . . . shall prevent a court ... in the case of an offender who is convicted of one or more other offences, from mitigating his sentence by applying any rule of law as to the totality of sentences.'

Abolition of the 'two offence rule'—Community sentences
Section 6 CJA 91 lays down criteria for imposing community sentences. The original s6(1) stipulated that a court should not pass a community sentence unless it was of the opinion 'that the offence, or the combination of the offence and *one other* offence associated with it, was serious enough to warrant such a sentence'. Section 6(2) stated that any community sentence must be in the court's opinion 'the most suitable for the offender' and that the restrictions on liberty imposed by the sentence must be 'commensurate with the seriousness of the offence, or the combination of the offence and *other* [ie without limit] offences associated with it' (italics supplied).

Section 66(4) CJA 93 amended s6(1) so that it now refers to 'the offence, or the combination of the offence and *one or more* offences associated with it' (italics supplied). Whereas previously the court could look at the combined seriousness of the offence and one associated offence when deciding whether the offending was serious enough to warrant a community sentence, it can now look at the combined seriousness of any number of offences.

The same considerations apply as are mentioned in relation to custody, *supra*, ie a court need not aggravate an offence merely because there are now more than two offences. Each case will depend on its own merits.

Criteria for length or extent of sentences brought into line

Section 2 CJA 91 laid down criteria for the length of custodial sentences. In most cases this is governed by s2(2)(a), which in its original form provided that the length of a sentence should be 'commensurate with the seriousness of the offence, or the combination of the offence and other offences associated with it'. Section 66(2) CJA 93 made a change in this wording, which now reads:

'commensurate with the seriousness of the offence, or the combination of the offence and one or more offences associated with it'.

Before and after this change, the court could look at the seriousness of any number of offences when fixing the length of a custodial sentence. The change of wording made the formulation identical to that in the amended section 1(2)(a) and thus made it clear that 'a court would be free to consider one offence with just one other if it considered that to be an appropriate mix' (David Maclean, Home Office Minister, House of Commons, 17 June 1993).

In relation to community sentences, s66(4) amended s6(2) CJA 91, substituting 'one or more offences' for the words 'other offences'. Before and after this change, the court could look at the seriousness of any number of offences when deciding on the degree of restriction on liberty to be contained in a community sentence. The change of wording made the formulation consistent with s6(1) *supra*—and indicates that a court would be free to consider one offence with just one other if it considered that to be an appropriate mix.

Reversal of the rule about previous convictions and responses

One of the most controversial provisions in the original version of the 1991 Act was s29(1) which stipulated that an offence should not be regarded as more serious by reason of any previous convictions or failures to respond to previous sentences; but that the court could take into account aggravating factors of the current offence disclosed by the circumstances of other offences.

Section 66(6) CJA 93 substitutes a new s29(1) which states:

'In considering the seriousness of any offence, the court may take into account any previous convictions of the offender or any failure of his to respond to previous sentences.'

The Magistrates' Association *Sentencing Guidelines, Appendix II post*, recommend that courts should '. . . identify which convictions or failures are

39

relevant for this purpose and then consider what the effect of such previous convictions or failures is in relation to seriousness.'

A new s29(3) and new s29(4) CJA 91 provide that probation orders and conditional discharges made before 1 October 1992 (which would otherwise not count as a 'sentence') shall be treated as sentences for the purposes of s29; and that convictions before 1 October 1992 in respect of which a probation order or conditional discharge was made (which would otherwise not count as a 'conviction') shall be treated as convictions for these purposes.

The CJ and PO Bill of 1994 amends s29(4) to provide that a conviction in respect of which an *absolute* discharge was made before 1 October 1992 shall also be treated as a conviction for these purposes. The Bill adds a new s29(5) providing that a *conditional* discharge made after 30 September 1992 (which would not otherwise count as a 'sentence') is to be treated as a sentence for the purposes of s29; and a new s29(6) providing that a conviction in respect of which an absolute or conditional discharge was made after 30 September 1992 (which would not otherwise count as a conviction) shall be treated as a conviction for these purposes.

Effect of the changes to s29

Some commentators have argued that these amendments run the risk of making it easier to send minor offenders to prison unnecessarily, pointing out that they contain no direct or explicit reference to the limiting principle of proportionality. However, comments made by the Lord Chief Justice, Lord Taylor of Gosforth, in an address to the Annual General Meeting of NACRO on 11 November 1993, suggest that the common law rules laid down by the Court of Appeal before the CJA 91 should still be regarded as valid. These were to the effect that, while previous convictions reduce or eliminate the mitigation which could otherwise have reduced the proper sentence for the offence, a criminal record cannot justify increasing the sentence to a level disproportionate to the seriousness of the current offence. The Court of Appeal had said previously that an offender should not be '. . . sentenced for the offences which he has committed in the past and for which he has already been punished': *Queen* (1981) 3 Cr App R (S) 241. In his address to NACRO, Lord Taylor said:

'I believe that the philosophy of the Criminal Justice Act 1991 as it was originally envisaged still holds good. I believe, though, that the amendments have improved it and have made it more realistic...

'That is not to say that the rule which the courts have evolved long before the Criminal Justice Act should be ignored—namely that a person should not be sentenced a second time for offences which have already been punished in the past. That is a basic principle of judicial precedent and I see no conflict between that and having regard to previous record and to previous sentences which have been imposed on the offender. Now, it seems to me, the balance is right. The court will approach the question of seriousness, of course, by looking primarily at the instant offences which have to be dealt with, but looking at them not in a vacuum or in blinkers but against a previous history...'

Lord Taylor also said:

'I know that there are certain worries that the modification of the 1991 Act might persuade judges that they can tot up a number of very trivial offences and make the whole offending sufficiently grave to justify a prison sentence. I hope that the criteria which will be applied, and have been applied, by the Court of Appeal will show that that is not a legitimate approach.

'Can I just give one example? Last week in the Court of Appeal (Criminal Division) we had the case of a woman who had committed many offences of very minor shoplifting, not as a member of a gang doing it commercially—that puts the matter into a different league—but simply on her own behalf. She had been given a suspended sentence of 12 months suspended for two years for not just shoplifting but also burglary and taking part in a robbery. During the period of the suspended sentence she went into a supermarket with her boyfriend, put a number of goods into the basket, intended to pay for most of them but could not resist taking £3.27 worth of bacon and slipping it into her pocket . . . She was convicted of that offence and the Crown Court, I am sorry to say, sentenced her to three months' imprisonment for the bacon and activated the suspended sentence. Now that is precisely what ought not to happen, because the triviality of the type of offence—notwithstanding the background of previous offending, notwithstanding that it was committed during the period of suspension—simply did not justify taking that course. In a case of that kind it is not justifiable to impose a prison sentence for the offence.'

Amendments to the wording of related provisions

Section 66 CJA 93 made corresponding changes to the wording of other provisions, which are consequential on the changes in wording in s1, s6 and s29 CJA 91 *supra*. The amended provisions are s7(1) CJA 91, which lays down procedural requirements for courts passing community sentences; s12D(1) Children and Young Persons Act 1969, which obliges courts imposing specified activities requirements instead of custodial sentences on juvenile offenders to state their reasoning in open court (see *Chapter 5, post* and for a more detailed treatment *The Youth Court One Year Onwards*); and s38(2)(a) of the Magistrates' Courts Act 1980, which contains the criteria for committals to the Crown Court for sentence.

Offending on bail a 'seriousness factor'

In view of the changes to the law affecting the admissibility of previous convictions or responses, the original s29(2) CJA 91 (which dealt with the relevance of 'aggravating circumstances': see *Section (a)* of this chapter) became redundant.

A new section 29(2) CJA 91, substituted by s66(6) CJA 93, deals with an entirely different matter as follows:

'In considering the seriousness of any offence committed while the offender was on bail, the court shall treat the fact that it was committed in those circumstances as an aggravating factor.'

When this provision was debated in the House of Lords on 26 July 1993, Earl Ferrers, Minister of State at the Home Office, made it clear that—despite the mandatory wording—an increased sentence need not follow in every case where an offence was committed while on bail. He said:

> 'The Government do not intend that an offence committed on bail will always lead to a longer sentence. That would be absurd where the two offences are totally unconnected, or the second offence is a trivial one. The measure is aimed at the career burglar who regards bail with indifference, and is caught and convicted again. If, in the court's opinion, the fact of offending on bail does not make the offence so serious that it deserves a jump to the next level of sentence, there is nothing in the provisions of the Criminal Justice Act 1991 to prevent such a conclusion being reached.'

For an extended treatment of this aspect and an updated treatment of the law of bail in general see *Bail: The Law, Best Practice and the Debate* by Paul Cavadino and Bryan Gibson (Waterside Press, 1993).

Abolition of unit fines and substitution of means related fines

Section 18 CJA 1991 introduced a new statutory system of unit fines in magistrates' courts. Section 19 provided that in other cases courts fixing the amount of a fine 'shall take into account among other things the means of the offender so far as they appear or are known to the court', and stipulated that this should apply whether it had the effect of increasing or reducing the fine.

In the wake of adverse (if sometimes misinformed) publicity and disquiet among some of the magistracy, s65 CJA 93 (to be read with sched 3 CJA 93) replaced s18 CJA 91 with new provisions which apply to all courts and repealed section 19 CJA 91. The new s18(1) CJA 91 requires a court to inquire into the financial circumstances of the offender before fixing the amount of a fine. Section 18(2) *ibid* provides that:

> 'The amount of any fine fixed by a court shall be such as, in the opinion of the court, reflects the seriousness of the offence.'

A new s18(3) provides that, in fixing the amount of any fine, a court shall take into account the circumstances of the case 'including, among other things, the financial circumstances of the offender so far as they are known, or appear, to the court.' Section 18(5) stipulates that s18(3) applies whether taking into account the financial circumstances of the offender has the effect of increasing or reducing the fine.

Section 18(4) empowers courts to make such determination of the offender's financial circumstances as they see fit where he or she has been convicted in his or her absence, or where the offender (or the parent or guardian of a young offender) has failed to comply with an order to give a statement of financial circumstances or has in any other way failed to comply with the court's inquiry into his or her financial circumstances.

Schedule 3 to the 1993 Act, paragraph 2, replaces s20(1) CJA 91 (which empowered courts to order offenders to provide a statement of means). The new s20(1) gives courts the power to order an offender to provide a statement of financial circumstances *following* conviction and before he or she is sentenced, and a new s20(1B) extends the power so that it applies to parents or guardians of young offenders. A new s20(1A) extends the power to make a financial circumstances order so that it applies *before* conviction where the court has been notified of the offender's intention to plead guilty in absence in accordance with the provisions of s12 Magistrates' Courts Act 1980.

Paragraph 3 of the Schedule operates to replace s21 CJA 91 (which provided for the remission of fines fixed under the unit fines scheme). The new s21 provides that where a court has determined the offender's financial circumstances under s18(4) in the absence of sufficient information it may, on subsequently inquiring into financial circumstances, remit the whole or part of the fine if it is of the opinion that the imposition of a fine was inappropriate or the original fine was too high.

Paragraph 4 of the Schedule repeals s22 CJA 91, which fixed terms of imprisonment for default in paying fines under the unit fine scheme. The effect of repealing this section is that periods of imprisonment for fine default will now be set in accordance with s23 CJA 91 which specifies maximum periods for given amounts. (Section 22 continues to apply to offenders who were fined under the unit fine scheme if those fines remain unpaid).

Paragraph 5 of the Schedule operates to replace s57(3) and s57(4) CJA 91 (which relate to the responsibilities of parents or guardians for financial penalties). The new s57(3) requires the court, when setting the amount of a fine or compensation order, to take into account the financial circumstances of a parent or guardian who is ordered to pay the fine of a young offender. Section 57(4) stipulates that the means of local authorities are not to be taken into account in fixing the level of a fine or compensation order when the authority is ordered to pay.

Increased penalties for certain offences

Section 67(1) CJA 93 amends sched 2 to the Road Traffic Offences Act 1988 in order to increase the maximum penalty for causing death by dangerous driving, or by careless driving while under the influence of drink or drugs, from five to 10 years.

Section 67(2) amends s53(2) Children and Young Persons Act 1933 to include these offences in those eligible for sentences of detention under section 53(2) ('grave crimes').

Andrew Ashworth and Bryan Gibson have commented (*Altering the Sentencing Framework,* [1994] Crim. L.R. 109):

'... there is now a need for reconsideration of sentencing policy for these offences, in particular the relevance of unforeseen harm. The difference in maxima between dangerous driving (two years) and causing death by dangerous driving (10 years) is now huge, and yet it is well known that a given piece of bad driving may lead to no collision, a collision with injuries, a collision with one death or a collision with several deaths. There is a danger that, for sentencing purposes, true culpability may be replaced by mere causation.'

Changes proposed in the Criminal Justice and Public Order Bill of 1994 (Summarised)

The Criminal Justice and Public Order Bill completed its passage through the House of Commons on 13 April 1994. It had its second reading in the House of Lords on April 25 and began its committee stage in that House in May. As it then stood, the Bill makes the following changes to the law on sentencing, bail and young offenders.

Secure training orders
Clauses 1 to 15 of the Bill provide for the introduction of a new 'secure training order' for 12 to 14 year old offenders. Those eligible for the order will be young offenders who have been convicted of three or more imprisonable offences. The order is a 'custodial sentence' for the purposes of s1 to s4 CJA 91 (restrictions etc as to custodial sentences). Juveniles sentenced to a secure training order will be detained in a new system of secure training centres. There will be five centres, each with 40 places. The maximum sentence will be two years—and sentences will be determinate, with half spent in custody and half in the community under supervision. The criteria for secure training orders and the relevant provisions of the Bill are contained in the companion volume to this work *The Youth Court One Year Onwards*.

The centres will be built on Prison Service land subject to statutory rules to be made by the Home Secretary under the Prisons Act 1952. The Bill's financial memorandum states that the overall costs of the order including supervision in the community 'are expected to be in excess of £30 million a year'.

Long term detention
Clause 16 extends the powers of courts to order young people aged 10 to 13 to be detained for long periods. At present children of this age who commit murder are sentenced to detention at Her Majesty's Pleasure (the juvenile equivalent of a life sentence) under section 53(1) Children and Young Persons Act 1933; and those who commit manslaughter can be sentenced either to detention at Her Majesty's pleasure or to detention for a fixed number of years under section 53(2) of the same Act. Clause 16 would permit courts to impose such sentences for any offence carrying a maximum sentence of 14 years' imprisonment in the case of an adult. This would bring the position of 10 to 13 year olds into line with that for 14 to 17 year olds.

The clause also provides for s53 sentences to be available for 10 to 17 year olds for the offence of indecent assault on a woman; and confirms the existing position whereby they are available for 14 to 17 year olds for the offences of causing death by dangerous driving and causing death by careless driving while under the influence of drink or drugs.

Maximum length of detention in a young offender institution
Clause 17 increases the maximum length of detention in a young offender institution for 15 to 17 year olds from 12 months to two years.

Demonopolisation of local authority secure accommodation
Clauses 19 and 22 enable local authorities to make arrangements for secure accommodation to be provided by voluntary organisations or the private sector instead of being run by local authorities direct.

Secure remands
Clause 20 extends the age range of children on whom courts are empowered to impose a 'security requirement' when remanding them to local authority accommodation. The CJA 91 empowered courts to do this when remanding 15 and 16 year olds (though this provision has not yet been implemented): the Bill empowers courts also to impose security requirements on children aged 12 to 14 and provides for this to be brought into force progressively for children aged 14, 13 and 12. Clause 21 provides for the costs incurred by local authorities in complying with remands by courts to be defrayed by central government.

Police detention
Clause 23 alters the rules governing the detention of arrested juveniles after charge before they are brought to court. At present the law provides that juveniles cannot be held overnight in police detention unless a custody officer certifies (a) that it is 'impracticable' to transfer the juvenile to local authority accommodation, or (b) where the juvenile is aged 15 or over, that no secure accommodation is available and that keeping him in other local authority accommodation would not be adequate to protect the public from serious harm from him or her. The Bill changes the minimum age in criterion (b) from 15 to 12.

Binding over parents
Schedule 9, paragraph 44, empowers courts, when binding over a parent or guardian to take care of and exercise control over a young offender, to include in the bind-over a requirement that the parent or guardian should ensure that the child complies with the requirements of a community sentence.

Bail
Part II of the Bill contains a series of measures which change the laws on granting bail. Clause 24 provides that someone with a previous conviction for actual or attempted murder, manslaughter or rape who is now accused of another such offence should automatically be refused bail and remanded in custody. Clause 25 removes the statutory presumption in favour of bail when a defendant is accused of an either way offence allegedly committed while on bail.

Clause 26 gives the police power to impose conditions when granting police bail. Clause 27 brings the criteria for refusing police bail more closely into line with the Bail Act criteria for refusing court bail. Clause 28 gives the police a power of arrest for failure to answer police bail.

Clause 29 enables the CPS to apply to a court if new information has come to light since bail was granted and to ask for bail to be withdrawn or for additional bail conditions to be imposed.

Transfer proceedings

Clause 40 and sched 4 provide a new procedure for transferring cases from the magistrates' court to the Crown Court for trial. This will replace committal proceedings.

Guilty pleas

Clause 44 requires courts, when determining sentence on an offender who is pleading guilty, to take into account the stage at which the offender indicated his or her intention to plead guilty and the circumstances in which the indication was given; and, if the court passes a reduced sentence because of a guilty plea, to state that it has done so. In so far as written pleas of guilty are concerned, sched 5 to the CJ and PO Bill introduces a new s12 MCA 1980 under which *inter alia* magistrates' courts will be able to deal with such a plea at any time within 14 days of the summons return date without the need to give notice of adjournment.

Fines

Clause 142 and Schedule 8 increase the maximum fines for certain offences. This includes five-fold increases in the maxima for a range of offences associated with cannabis and other Class C drugs. There are also minor modifications to s24 CJA 91 (attachment of income support) so that *inter alia* attachment can be requested of the DSS following transfer of a fine from one court to another.

Pre-sentence reports

Schedule 9, paragraph 34, removes the mandatory requirement for courts to obtain a pre-sentence report before passing a custodial sentence or certain community sentences. It provides instead that, before passing such a sentence, the court must obtain a pre-sentence report unless 'the court is of the opinion that it is unnecessary to obtain a pre-sentence report'. Where the offender is under 18, the court cannot decide that it is unnecessary to obtain a report unless the offence is triable only on indictment or the court has a previous pre-sentence report on the offender.

Electronic monitoring

Schedule 9, paragraph 35 of the Bill provides for the area by area introduction of curfew orders with electronic monitoring (sometimes referred to as 'tagging'). According to the Bill's financial memorandum, it is planned to conduct pilot trials of curfew orders with electronic monitoring at a total cost of nearly £1.4 million.

c) Judicial Guidance

There has been a large number of rulings of the Court of Appeal since the CJA 91 came into force. In this part of this chapter extracts are printed from the more significant of these together with summaries of the effect of a range of other cases. The first part provides a *General Overview* followed by an analysis of *Particular Offences*.

General Overview

A wide range of matters relating to the CJA 91 have fallen to be decided by the higher courts. However even before this began to occur, on 1 October 1992, the same date on which the sentencing and early release provisions of the CJA 91 came into force, the Lord Chief Justice, Lord Taylor of Gosforth PC, issued a *Practice Statement* concerning the relevance to sentencing decisions of the new rules governing early release contained in Part II of the Act. Lord Taylor's statement urged sentencers to take account of the fact that most offenders would serve longer in custody under the new provisions (see *Parole and Early Release, Chapter 13, post*) and is reproduced in *Chapter 7* of this work, *Custodial Sentences* under the heading *Length of sentence*.

'So serious' that only custody can be justified

Court of Appeal rulings after 1 October 1992 began to indicate types of offence which were regarded by the Court as 'so serious' that only custody can be justified. In *Cox* (1993) 14 Cr App R (S) 479 and later cases the Court adopted the formulation of Lord Justice Lawton in the case of *Bradbourn* (1985) 7 Cr App R (S) 180—'the kind of offence which when committed by a young person would make right-thinking members of the public, knowing all the facts, think that justice had not been done by the passing of any sentence other than a custodial one'.

Later in this chapter the details of offences which were, and which were not, held to be 'so serious' that only custody could be justified in a range of cases between October 1992 and June 1993 are summarised. Also listed are instances in which the Court of Appeal held that the combined seriousness of two offences (the 'two offence rule' being in operation until the passing of the CJA 93: see *Section (b)* of this chapter) justified a custodial sentence under the original wording of section 1(2)(a) of the Criminal Justice Act 1991, ie 'that the offence, or the combination of the offence and one other offence associated with it, was so serious that only such a sentence can be justified for the offence'.

The cases establish that—even where the offence itself is 'so serious' that only custody can be justified—the sentencing court may nevertheless pass a community sentence because s28 CJA 91 allows it to mitigate sentence by reason of mitigating factors relating to the offender: see for example, *Oliver and Little (1993)* 14 Cr App R (S) 457, *Cox, supra, Baverstock* (1993) 14 Cr App R (S) 471, *Hill* (1993) 14 Cr App R (S) 556, *Reynolds* (1993) 14 Cr App R (S) 694, *Duncan* (unreported, 4 March 1993), and *Newman* (unreported, 25 March 1993). In *Cox* the Lord Chief Justice, Lord Taylor, said:

'. . . We have reached the conclusion that only a custodial sentence could be justified for this offence . . . That, however, is not the end of the matter. Section 1(2) enjoins the court not to pass a custodial sentence unless it is of the opinion that the criteria of seriousness are met. The court is not *required* to pass such a sentence even when they are. Although an offender may qualify for a custodial sentence by virtue of section 1(2), the court is still required to consider whether such a sentence is appropriate having regard to the mitigating factors available and relevant to the offender (as opposed to such factors as are relevant to the offence)'.

A commentary on *Reynolds* at [1993] Crim LR, p467 commented:

'The question for the court is, in effect, *"assuming that there is no mitigation at all available to the offender,* is the offence so serious that only a custodial sentence could be justified?" If the court decides that the offence does reach this level of seriousness, it then pauses to consider whether under section 28 there is any personal mitigation available to the offender which allows the court to pass a sentence other than custody.'

Nature of section 28 mitigation

The cases indicate that the factors relevant under section 28 of the 1991 Act continue to include many familiar considerations which have traditionally been regarded as mitigating factors. Examples mentioned in the reported judgments include:

• made admissions, pleaded guilty: *Sanderson* (1993) 14 Cr App R (S) 361, *Godden and Boosey* (1993) 14 Cr App R (S) 386, *Baverstock, supra, Corkhill* (1993) 14 Cr App R (S) 543, *Nixon* (unreported, 18 January 1993), *Husbands* (1993) 14 Cr App R (S) 709, *Jones* (unreported, 2 March 1993), *Hayton* (1994) 15 Cr App R (S) 71.

• co-operation with the police: *Cunningham* (1993) 14 Cr App R (S) 444, *Corkhill, supra, Prunty* (unreported, 18 January 1993).

• gave evidence at trial against co-accused: *Godden and Boosey, supra.*

• the offender's youth: *Godden and Boosey, supra, Small* (1993) 14 Cr App R (S) 404, *Okinian* (1993) 14 Cr App R (S) 453, *Cunningham, supra, Cox, supra, Winterton* (1993) 14 Cr App R (S) 529, *Hill, supra, Husbands, supra, Duncan, supra.*

• being seven years younger than co-defendant: *Dorries and Dorries* (1993) 14 Cr App R (S) 608.

• previous good character: *Sanderson, supra, Godden and Boosey, supra, Flynn and Flynn* (1993) 14 Cr App R (S) 422, *Okinian, supra, Cunningham, supra, Cox, supra, Winterton, supra, Corkhill, supra, Hill, supra, Nixon, supra, Prunty, supra, Dorries and Dorries, supra, Husbands,supra, Duncan, supra, Huntley* (1993) 14 Cr App R (S) 795, *Audit* (1994) 15 Cr App R (S) 36.

• no previous involvement in offences of same type: *Morgan and Morgan* (1993) 14 Cr App R (S) 619, *Reynolds, supra*.

• no offences for last nine years: *Newman, supra*.

• genuine remorse, expressed regret: *Sanderson, supra, Godden and Boosey, supra, Oliver and Little, supra, Winterton, supra, Corkhill, supra, Prunty, supra, Morgan and Morgan, supra, Godfrey* (1993) 14 Cr App R (S) 804.

• serious and continuing efforts since offence to tackle the causes of offending: *Cameron* (1993) 14 Cr App R (S) 801.

• offender had repaid stolen money: *Godfrey, supra*.

• immature personality: *Baverstock, supra*.

• having a disturbed family background involving drunkenness and violence aimed at him: *Audit, supra*.

• a long period of suspense before trial: *Winterton, supra;* or while on bail pending appeal: *Hill, supra*.

• being ostracised and having to give up a job: *Corkhill, supra*.

• loss of a child born since the offence: *Godfrey, supra*.

• offender's parents both invalids and depend on him for assistance: *Cawley* (1994) 15 Cr App R (S) 209.

• father suffers from most unfortunate illness: *Morgan and Morgan, supra*.

• good work record: *Sanderson, supra, Smith* (1993) 14 Cr App R (S) 617, *Godfrey, supra, Audit, supra*.

• having successfully brought up a large family, none of whom had been in trouble with the law: *Flynn and Flynn, supra*.

• some positive response to suspended sentence supervision/satisfactory completion of most of probation order: *Neville* (1993) 14 Cr App R (S) 768, *Decino* (unreported, 21 April 1993).

• bankruptcy as a result of offence: *Robinson* (1993) 14 Cr App R (S) 559.

• injuries to offender as a result of offence: *Hayton, supra*.

• prison would significantly worsen the offender's depression and set back the progress of current treatment for this: *French* (1994) 15 Cr App R (S) 194.

• repetition of the offence (by a youth receiving treatment for psychotic mood swings) would be less likely if he received counselling and help at a probation centre than if he served a short term in custody: *Duncan, supra*.

Previous convictions and other current offences

A number of judgments contained guidance on the construction of the *original* version of s29 CJA 91, which concerned the relevance of previous convictions and other current offences in sentencing. The most important of these cases was *Bexley, Summers and Harrison* (1993) 14 Cr App R (S) 462; and other relevant judgments included *Godden and Boosey, supra, Baverstock, supra, Moriarty* (1993) 14 Cr App R (S) 575, *Kyle* (1993) 14 Cr App R (S) 613, *Jones, supra, Utip* (1993) 14 Cr App R (S) 746, *Evans* (1993) 14 Cr App R (S) 751, *Price* (unreported, 30 March 1993), *Allright* (1993) 14 Cr App R (S) 797, *Hayton, supra, Breeze* (1994) 15 Cr App R (S) 94, *Clarke* (1994) 15 Cr App R (S) 102, and *Bennett* (1994) 15 Cr App R (S) 213.

The judgments emphasised that, under the then s29, the instant offence could not be regarded as more serious because of 'the mere existence of previous convictions'. However, under s29(2) as it then stood, the circumstances of other offences could shed light on the instant offence so as to disclose aggravating factors. These would usually bear on the offender's guilty mind—for example they might show an aggravating element of planning, deliberation and selection or they might disclose some added gravity of purpose in the instant offence. It might be that these cases will not be unhelpful in coming to terms with the post-CJA 93 law in that, under s29(1), a degree of relevance ought to be present before previous convictions or responses are taken into account in order to increase the seriousness of the current offence, *semble*. Examples were:

• the circumstances of previous burglaries of elderly widows' houses disclosing the deliberate targeting of elderly widows: *Bexley, Summers and Harrison, supra*.

• the circumstances of other offences in which a stolen credit card was used to buy a large amount of luxury goods, or to defraud many people on a large scale, disclosing this as the motive for stealing a credit card: *Bexley, supra*.

• the circumstances of previous shoplifting offences showing that the offender was working as one of a gang or otherwise operating as a professional commercial shoplifter: *Summers, supra*.

• the circumstances of previous violent offences suggesting that on this occasion the offender had deliberately barged a stranger in the street in order to start a fight in which he could use his knife: *Utip, supra*.

• the circumstances of previous offences disclosing that the offender was effectively in the business of dismantling stolen vehicles in order to reconstruct them and add them to the parts of others, to sell them on: *Evans, supra*.

• the circumstances of previous offences showing a determination to continue driving with excess alcohol despite past experience: *Hayton, supra*.

• the circumstances of previous burglaries committed against the elderly occupants of sheltered accommodation showing the offender's indifference to the effect he might have on householders and elderly people: *Cawley, supra*.

Following these judgments, s66 CJA 93 substituted for the previous section 29(1) the new version which provides that, in considering the seriousness of any offence, the court may take into account any previous convictions of the offender or any failure to respond to previous sentences. The full implications of this change are considered in *Chapter 4*.

Seriousness and breach of previous sentences

It was held in *Bexley, Summers and Harrison, supra, Bee* (1993) 14 Cr App R (S) 703, *Evans, supra* and *Cawley* (1994) 15 Cr App R (S) 25, that, under the original version of s29, the fact that the current offence put the offender in breach of a suspended sentence could not be taken into account as affecting the seriousness of the offence. In *Summers, supra* the Court of Appeal held that the fact that the offences were committed while subject to a probation order and a conditional discharge was excluded from consideration in relation to seriousness. In *Godfrey, supra* the Court of Appeal held that s29 prevented a court from taking into account the fact that the current offences were committed in breach of a conditional discharge. The same reasoning would have applied to an offence committed while subject to a community service order or a combination order.

However, from 16 August 1993, this position was superseded by the new version of s29(1) substituted by s66 CJA 93, which states:

'In considering the seriousness of any offence, the court may take into account any previous convictions of the offender *or any failure of his to respond to previous sentences*' (emphasis added).

The implications of this change are considered in *Chapter 4*. It was made clear in *Neville, supra* and *Decino, supra* that courts should give credit for a partial response to, or a partially successful completion of, a community sentence.

Deterrence, prevalence and offending on bail

Appeal rulings have clarified the relevance to the assessment of seriousness of a number of considerations, including deterrence, the prevalence of similar offences and the fact that an offence was committed on bail.

In *Cunningham, supra* the Court held that the sentencer may take into account the need for deterrence when assessing seriousness. Lord Taylor CJ said:

'The purposes of a custodial sentence must primarily be to punish and deter. Accordingly, the phrase "commensurate with the seriousness of the offence" must mean commensurate with the punishment and deterrence which the seriousness of the offence requires.'

However, the degree of deterrence which is appropriate in sentencing must be related to the seriousness of the offence. Lord Taylor continued:

'What section 2(2)(a) does prohibit is adding any extra length to the sentence which by those criteria is commensurate with the seriousness of the offence, simply to make a special example of the defendant.'

This rules out the so-called exemplary sentence, where a sentence beyond the level customarily considered to be justified by the seriousness of the offence is imposed in order to make a special example of the individual.

In the same case, and in *Baverstock, supra* and *Newman, supra*, the Court of Appeal held that the prevalence of the offence is a legitimate factor to be considered by a sentencer in assessing seriousness. In *Cunningham* Lord Taylor said:

'The seriousness of an offence is clearly affected by how many people it harms and to what extent. For example, a violent sexual attack on a woman in a public place gravely harms her. But if such attacks are prevalent in a neighbourhood, each offence affects not only the immediate victim but women generally in that area, putting them in fear and limiting their freedom of movement. Accordingly, in such circumstances, the sentence commensurate with the seriousness of the offence may need to be higher there than elsewhere. Again, and for similar reasons, a bomb hoax may at one time not have been so serious as it is when a campaign of actual bombings mixed with hoaxes is in progress.'

In an article in *Justice of the Peace* on 27 March 1993, the editor of that journal argued that this 'begs the question of how prevalence is to be defined and how it is to be established and assessed.' He wrote:

'The point must be that the offence is on the increase, nationally or locally—or that it is "getting out of hand" or causing particular alarm. An increase in the recorded incidence of a particular offence can be established by reference to national or local criminal statistics, but it is not clear how such evidence would be put before a court or tested to see whether the figures reflected a "true" increase or simply an increase in the reporting and recording of crime. To establish that an offence is getting out of hand or causing particular alarm will often be harder still. What will clearly not suffice is for the sentencer to rely solely on his or her recollections of previous cases heard in his or her court, on reports in local newspapers, or on public statements by the police, by interest groups, or by local or national politicians: the court will need to be satisfied about prevalence and this implies that evidence of some sort will be needed to be considered and tested before the court has any sound basis for aggravating seriousness. Arguably, the cases in which "prevalence" can be reliably established as a relevant factor will be few in number, perhaps arising from local outbreaks of offences such as racial harassment, or the stealing and racing of motor vehicles. Further guidance may be needed in due course.'

The judgments in *Baverstock, supra, Bexley, Summers and Harrison, supra, Price, supra,* and *Allright, supra* reinforced the Court's guidance in the earlier case of *Attorney General's Reference Nos 3, 4 and 5 of 1992* (1993) 14 Cr App R (S) 191 that the fact that an offender is on bail at the time of the offence amounts to an aggravating factor. This has now been placed in statutory form by the new s29(2) as substituted by s66 CJA 93, which states:

'In considering the seriousness of any offence committed while the offender was on bail, the court shall treat the fact that it was committed in those circumstances as an aggravating factor.'

When this provision was debated in the House of Lords on 26 July 1993, Earl Ferrers, Minister of State at the Home Office, made it clear that a lengthening of sentence need not follow in every case where an offence was committed while on bail: see *Section (b)* of this chapter under the heading *Offending on bail*.

Meaning of 'associated offence'

Two cases concerned the meaning of an 'associated' offence—ie one which can be considered in combination with the instant offence in assessing seriousness. In *Crawford* (1993) 14 Cr App R (S) 782 the Court held that an earlier offence for which the offender had received a suspended sentence, which was now being activated, was not an associated offence. Although the definition of an associated offence in s31(2)CJA 91 includes an offence of which the offender has previously been convicted but for which he is now being sentenced, as a matter of law activating a suspended sentence is not passing a sentence.

In *Godfrey, supra* the Court of Appeal held that a previous offence for which the offender was conditionally discharged was not an associated offence if the court did not now impose a penalty for it, but would become an associated offence if the offender were now sentenced for it. This decision presumably also applies when a court revokes a probation order or community service order and resentences for the original offence.

Protecting the public from serious harm from violent and sexual offences

The case of *Robinson* (1993) 14 Cr App R (S) 448 established that attempted rape falls within the definition of a 'sexual offence' contained in s31(1) CJA 91. Like other attempts, attempted rape is charged as an offence contrary to the Criminal Attempts Act 1981, and this statute was omitted from the list of statutory provisions included in the definition in s31(1) CJA 91. However, Lord Taylor CJ said:

'Section 37 of the Sexual Offences Act 1956 provides for the prosecution and punishment of rape and attempted rape as well as other sexual offences. In Schedule 2, Part I, rape and attempted rape are listed together in the column marked "Offence". Attempt to commit rape is treated in exactly the same way as the full of offence of rape, in effect, for these purposes, as identical. In other words, attempted rape is an offence under the 1956 Act for the purpose of specifying the court's statutory powers of sentence. Although this offence is *indicted* under the Criminal Attempts Act 1981, it is in our judgment properly regarded as an offence "under" the Sexual Offences Act 1956. In these circumstances we have concluded that attempted rape comes within the definition of a "sexual offence" for the purposes of the Criminal Justice Act 1991.'

In the particular case the offence also fell within the definition of 'violent offence' because the victim did in fact suffer physical injury as a direct result of the offence. The judgment pointed out that the definition of 'violent offence' did not include psychological harm, or require that the physical injury should be serious.

An article by Dr David Thomas in *Sentencing News*, Issue 1, January 26, 1993 commented:

'While this decision resolves the problem of the status of attempted rape, it has limitations—the reasoning of the Court is clearly applicable only to those attempts which are mentioned specifically in Schedule 2 to the Sexual Offences Act 1956 ... Schedule 2 specifically mentions attempted rape, attempted unlawful intercourse, attempting to procure a woman to have sexual intercourse by threats, attempted intercourse with a defective, attempted incest, attempting to cause prostitution and attempted procuration, but in relation to attempted buggery, only attempted buggery of a boy under 16, a woman or an animal is mentioned. It seems to follow that attempted buggery of a male over 16 is not a "sexual offence" for the purposes of CJA 1991, s31.'

The CJ and PO Bill of 1994 amends the statutory definition of a 'sexual offence'. For details see *Sexual or violent offences*, in *Chapter 7, post*.

In *Utip, supra* it was held that s2(2)(b) CJA 91 applied, permitting a longer sentence than would otherwise be justified, to a violent offender whose previous record showed a ready resort to violence and to weapons with or without provocation; who on this occasion had barged a stranger in the street in order to start a fight in which he could use his knife; and who when at large was a danger to the public.

In the case of *Clarke, supra* the Court upheld a sentence of six years' imprisonment for an unprovoked attack involving striking three blows with a hammer to the victim's head, saying that this was commensurate with the seriousness of the offence. However, the Court also said that, if it had not taken this view, it would alternatively have upheld the sentence under s2(2)(b) to protect the public as the appellant's personality disorder rendered him prone to anti-social and aggressive behaviour. The information before the Court which led it to the latter conclusion was drawn from the circumstances of the offence, the existence of previous violent offences and information about the appellant's attitude and mental state contained in a pre-sentence report and a medical report.

In *Bowler* (1994) 15 Cr App R (S) 78 a sentence of six years' imprisonment was upheld as a longer than normal sentence on an appellant who had pleaded guilty to indecent assault on a girl aged six by putting his hand up her skirt and touching her private parts through her knickers, then pulling the girl on to his knee, before letting go when another adult intervened. He had eight previous convictions for indecent assaults on adult women, usually by touching or grabbing at the private parts; was of limited intelligence and probably suffering from brain damage, with no insight into his behaviour; had been treated with drugs to suppress his libido but was not willing to undergo further such treatment; and was described as having a sexual preference for the specific behaviour of touching women's knickers. The Court of Appeal said that it was not necessary for there to be evidence that serious harm had actually been caused in the past for a judge reasonably to form the opinion that there was a danger that serious harm might occur in the future. Mrs Justice Smith said:

'There are worrying indications that the appellant has recently turned his attention towards young girls. In the view of this Court an indecent assault on a

54

young girl might well lead to serious psychological harm. In addition to that, as has been pointed out in the course of argument, there are some adult women who might be seriously disturbed by conduct such as this. Many women might shrug off this kind of unwelcome attention which this man gives to women indiscriminately, but some will not. It seems to us that the purpose of this section should include the protection of those women, less robust than average, who may be vulnerable to the kind of conduct that this man is likely to perpetrate and who might, in those circumstances, suffer serious psychological harm.'

In the contrasting case of *Creasey* [1994] Crim LR 308 the Court of Appeal overturned a sentence of five years' imprisonment passed as a longer than normal sentence under s2(2)(b) CJA 91 on an offender who had pleaded guilty to three counts of indecent assault on a boy aged 13. On three occasions the appellant had followed the boy on his way home from school, placed a hand on the boy's genitalia through his trousers and attempted to masturbate him. He had previous convictions in 1961 for two counts of unlawful sexual intercourse with a girl aged under 13, and in 1975 for two counts of indecent assault on a boy aged eight similar on their facts to the previous offence. The Crown Court had had reports indicating that the appellant was of a paedophiliac orientation, unlikely to respond to a treatment programme, likely to offend in a manner similar to his previous offences, and unable to recognise or accept responsibility for his behaviour. The Court concluded that the case did not fall within the criteria required under s2(2)(b) as the reports did not show that there was likely to be serious harm to the public from the defendant. The offences were unpleasant and distressing but did not amount to such offfences as would necessitate protecting the public from serious harm. The sentence was reduced to 21 months' imprisonment.

In a commentary on this case at [1994] Crim LR 308, Dr David Thomas commented:

'In the present case, the Court appears to have concluded that the harm done to potential victims of similar offences likely to be committed by the appellant in the future—indecent assaults on young boys through their clothing—was not 'serious harm' for the purposes of the section; in *Bowler*, where the requirements of the section were held to be satisfied, the likely future offences were relatively similar (touching girls through their underclothes) except in respect of the sex of the potential victims ... These decisions, and others, seem to indicate that there is considerable uncertainty in the proper use of section 2(2)(b), and further considered guidance is desirable. As the cases show, the use of the section may mean a very substantial difference in the sentence imposed.'

Bowler was cited, but *Creasey* apparently was not, in *Mansell, The Times,* 22 February 1994, in which the Court of Appeal upheld a sentence of five years' imprisonment passed as a longer than normal sentence on an offender convicted of three counts of sexual offences against young men aged between 18 and 22 years by rubbing himself against them while each was fully dressed. The Lord Chief Justice, Lord Taylor, said that the victims had been put in extreme distress and added:

'The judge had to perform a balancing act. In theory someone who was addicted to conduct which could cause serious harm to members of the public might need to be prevented from doing that for a long time. Where harm was likely to be serious and looked likely to continue for a very long time, an indeterminate sentence might be appropriate. However, the judge in each individual case had to try to balance the need to protect the public with the need to look at the totality of the sentence and to see that it was not out of all proportion to the nature of the offender.'

The use of suspended sentences

The cases of *Sanderson, supra, Okinian, supra, Lowery* (1993) 14 Cr App R (S) 485, *Robinson, supra, Baldassari* (unreported, 15 March 1993), *Garcia* (unreported, 15 March 1993), *Huntley, supra, Cameron, supra, French, supra, Hartland* (1994) 15 Cr App R (S) 201 and *Khan* (1994) 15 Cr App R (S) 320 considered what circumstances do and do not amount to 'exceptional circumstances' justifying a suspended sentence.

In *Okinian, supra* Lord Taylor CJ declined to lay down a definition of 'exceptional circumstances', saying that this would depend on the facts of each individual case. However, he added:

'. . . taken on their own, or in combination, good character, youth and an early plea are not exceptional circumstances justifying a suspended sentence. They are common features of many cases. They may amount to mitigation sufficient to persuade the court that a custodial sentence should not be passed or to reduce its length.'

In *Robinson, supra* (involving breach of trust by a woman who managed a sub-post office with her husband) the Court observed that the instances in which a suspended sentence would be appropriate following the CJA 91 would be 'few and far between'. It held that the bankruptcy and serious debts of the appellant and her husband, the loss of the husband's job and his hospitalisation did not amount to 'exceptional circumstances'. In *Sanderson, supra* the Court held that the reliance of the appellant's wife and mother upon him, his previous good character and the provocation provided by the victim did not justify suspending the sentence.

In *Lowery, supra* where a police officer with a severely disabled wife had committed a serious breach of trust, it held that the 'catastrophic' effects of arrest and conviction—he had lost his employment and his house, made two suicide attempts, been hospitalised, developed a reactive depressive illness and needed continuing psychiatric care—did not amount to 'exceptional circumstances'.

These cases suggested, therefore, that personal mitigation is more likely to lead to a court's passing a community sentence rather than a custodial one, or shortening a custodial sentence, than to the use of a suspended sentence.

The commentary by Dr. David Thomas on the cases of *Sanderson* and *Lowery* at [1993] Criminal Law Review 226 stated:

'The combined effect ... appears to be that previous good character, youth, a long period of public service, provocation, a plea of guilty, the commission of the offence as a result of significant domestic difficulties, extra-legal consequences in the form of loss of career, home, and substantial diminution of pension rights, cannot constitute "exceptional circumstances" for this purpose, either alone or in combination with each other. It seems clear that in future suspended sentences will be permissible only in extremely unusual cases, where the mitigating factors are both rare and compelling.'

A different view was taken in the article 'The Use of Suspended Sentences' by David Foot, in *Justice of the Peace*, 4 September 1993, which argued:

'The cases of *Sanderson, Lowery* and *Robinson* were cases which fell to be determined on their own facts. One can only say that, when the particular constellation of circumstances in each fell to be determined by the Court of Appeal, it found these constellations not to be exceptional. But if some features of each had come together in a different combination, one cannot say that the outcome would have been the same...

'Consider the features which the Lord Chief Justice, in *Okinian,* said could not either singly or in combination constitute exceptional circumstances (ie good character, youth, early plea). They are all what might be called basic judicial discriminations which apply to almost all defendants, or do not, as the case may be. But the same cannot be said of the more complex concepts which Dr. Thomas includes in his list of features which cannot justify suspension of a sentence. Take, for example, provocation. While provocation *per se* may well be a common feature of most violent offences, the level of provocation varies on a continuum, both in intensity and duration ... At some point on the continuum, it must logically become the case that the level of provocation is exceptional. And, indeed, in the case of *R v Huntley* such a level was found.'

In *Huntley, supra* an offender of previous good character had assaulted with a bottle a woman who had had an affair with the offender's cohabitee, resulting in a child. The victim had taunted the offender about the affair over time and immediately before the offence. The Court of Appeal overturned a sentence of 18 months' immediate imprisonment and substituted a suspended sentence of 12 months' imprisonment. David Foot argued:

'One cannot tell from reading this judgment whether or not the judges took into account the good character of the appellant when forming the view that the circumstances were exceptional. If they did so, I would argue that this is permissible. Whilst, standing alone, good character cannot be exceptional, if someone had reached mature years without showing any disposition to violence, then, when there is evidence of exceptional provocation, the court is surely entitled to see the good character of the defendant as supportive of the claim that the provocation was, indeed, exceptional.'

In five other cases the Court held that there were exceptional circumstances justifying suspension. The most striking of these is the case of *Baldassari, supra*. The appellant, who pleaded guilty to handling stolen goods, had been left porcelain (worth £27,000 in 1986), which she knew to be stolen, in the will of a friend who had bought it in good faith. The Court of Appeal referred to the fact that she was a widow with children, one of whom was at a fee-paying school, was running her own industrial cleaning business employing a substantial workforce and was buying her own property; that the impact in these circumstances of an immediate custodial sentence was very severe; and that she had some years previously been instrumental in tracing the person responsible for a very serious crime who was subsequently brought to trial.

In *Garcia, supra* the appellant was involved in the importation of cannabis; but the prosecution accepted that he had not known the nature of the contents when asked to bring a parcel of cannabis into the country and that, having discovered this, he refused to hand it over on arrival to two people who came and asked him for it. In *Cameron, supra* where a father of previous good character had been imprisoned for assaulting his young son, he had co-operated with intensive treatment by the NSPCC who had decided with the local authority that his children's best interests would be served by reuniting them with their father. The Court suspended the sentence on the grounds that the sooner the offender was released to begin the process of reuniting the family, the more likely it was to be successful. In *French, supra* the appellant had given her car to two men who had been ringing motor vehicles, reported it stolen and claimed from her insurance company. She had a significant psychiatric history and had been receiving psychiatric treatment for depression, which had worsened during a very long period awaiting trial. A psychiatric report said that it was highly likely that, if imprisoned, she would become significantly depressed and that this would jeopardise progress which was being made in current treatment.

In *Khan, supra* the Court of Appeal suspended a sentence of 12 months imprisonment imposed on a solicitor who had been concerned in a series of mortgage frauds by a client which resulted in losses to building societies of between £145,000 and £150,000. Medical reports obtained for the purpose of the appeal indicated that the appellant was suffering from a paranoid psychosis which would have significantly jeopardized his concentration and judgment and for which medical treatment was available. The court held that the appellant's serious health problems were capable of being 'exceptional circumstances'.

In *Attorney General's Reference No 5 of 1993 (Hartland), supra* the Court of Appeal substituted a sentence of two years' immediate imprisonment for a suspended sentence of twelve months' imprisonment passed with a £1,250 compensation order on an offender who had been convicted of arson, being reckless whether life would be endangered. Following a dispute with a group of men in the course of which his girlfriend had been knocked to the ground and momentarily knocked out, the offender had gone in the early hours of the morning to the house where the men lived and had thrown a brick through the window followed by a petrol bomb, causing minor damage to the house. The Court said that considerations such as good character, a plea of guilty and the return of money in cases involving property were not to be regarded as 'exceptional circumstances'. The court took account of the offender's good character and accepted that the offence was out of character and committed while brooding over his girlfriend's experience and when affected by drink; but in view of the gravity of what had been done, it held that a suspended sentence was unduly lenient.

In *Bradley* [1994] Crim LR 381 the appellant had been sentenced to nine months' immediate imprisonment after pleading guilty to forgery, obtaining by deception and theft. She was a college teacher and manager of a school within the college, and had diverted about £7,000 from the income of the school for her personal benefit. She had no previous convictions; had been in hospital for serious reactive depression, and continued to suffer from depressive conditions; she had a history of mental health problems since childhood including post-traumatic stress, and the prognosis was poor while she was under a custodial sentence. The Court of Appeal considered that the facts of the case were not so exceptional as to justify suspension of the sentence but, in view of the medical evidence, it reduced the sentence to four months' imprisonment.

In a commentary on *Bradley* at [1994] Crim LR 382, Dr David Thomas commented that the Court of Appeal decisions on the application of the 'exceptional circumstances' requirement in s5(1) CJA 91 are difficult to reconcile with each other. It is submitted that a comparison of the way a depressive condition was regarded in this case and in *French, supra* lends considerable force to Dr Thomas' contention.

'Serious enough' for a community sentence

In the cases of *Small, Cox, Summers, Harrison, Hill, Bee, Duncan, Newman* (all *supra*), *Tetteh* (1994) 15 Cr App R (S) 46 and *Breeze, supra* the Court explicitly or implicitly indicated that the offences were serious enough to warrant the making of a community sentence. Details of these cases are listed later in this chapter.

The nature of a pre-sentence report

The Court of Appeal in *Okinian, supra* considered whether a social inquiry report prepared some time earlier could amount to a pre-sentence report for the purposes of satisfying s3 CJA 91. It held that it was for the trial judge to decide whether the report available to the court was adequate for sentencing purposes and constituted proper compliance with the statute. The report must, however, be in writing, be made or submitted by a probation officer or social worker, and give appropriate information about the offences before the court. The Court of Appeal said:

'Provided the report is in writing and is made or submitted by a probation officer or social worker and gives appropriate information about the offender in relation to the offences which bring him before the court, the judge is not obliged to ensure that every detail of information put before him by counsel is checked and confirmed in a further pre-sentence report or by way of addendum. If he considers that a further written report is required to confirm further information, he may of course adjourn the case, but he is not obliged to do so.'

Although this case concerned a social inquiry report, the principles enunciated in it are not restricted to situations where a social inquiry report was prepared before 1 October 1992. They help to define what a judge can decide constitutes a pre-sentence report for the purposes of satisfying section 3 of the Criminal Justice Act 1991.

The editor of *Justice of the Peace,* in an article published in that journal on 30 January 1993, 157 JPN 67, commented:

'Assuming for one moment that the report was deficient in a material particular, eg his suitability for community service, the court could either: (i) adjourn the case so that the report could address this issue; or, better still (ii) stand the case down so that a short written addendum could be added to the report detailing the offender's suitability for community service.'

In *Butterfield* (unreported, 30 March 1993) the Court emphasised that the requirement to obtain a pre-sentence report before passing a custodial sentence or certain community sentences in summary and triable-either-way cases was mandatory '. . . even if all concerned in the trial took the view that no purpose would be served by the preparation of a report.'

Breach of community sentences by reoffending

The judgments in *Oliver and Little, supra* and *Ipswich Justices ex p Best* (1993) 14 Cr App R (S) 685 case considered whether the Crown Court and magistrates' court respectively have retained the power to sentence offenders for the original offences when they have reoffended during the currency of a probation order imposed before October 1992.

Oliver and Little, supra decided that Schedule 2 to the CJA 91 (which provides a single procedure for dealing with breaches of probation orders, community service orders and combination orders, and for offences during the currency of such orders) applies to orders made before as well as after 1 October 1992. This means that the Crown Court has a power to sentence offenders for the original offences, whether the order was imposed before or after 1 October 1992, provided that the order is still in effect when sentencing takes place.

However, the *Ipswich Justices* case established that magistrates' courts do not possess such a power. The difference turns on the ability of the Crown Court to proceed of its own volition to deal with a breach of probation by reoffending, whereas (under Part II of Schedule 2 to the CJA 91) magistrates are dependent in such circumstances on the matter coming before them at the instance of the offender or of a probation officer.

Another change made by the CJA 91 is that a court can only revoke an order if it is still in force when the court sentences for the new offence. Thus in *Bennett, supra* a sentence passed by the Crown Court for the original offences was held to be unlawful when the offender had reoffended during the currency of a probation order but the order had expired when sentence was passed.

These rules also apply to reoffending during the currency of a community service order or a combination order.

The general rule is therefore as follows:

• Where an offender is convicted of a further offence before the Crown Court, the Crown Court may revoke an existing community order (or revoke and re-sentence) if the order is still in effect and it appears to the court to be in the interests of justice to do so.

• Where an offender is convicted of a further offence by a magistrates' court, the magistrates' court may revoke an existing community order or commit to the Crown Court with a view to revocation *only* if an application is made by the

60

offender or the probation officer. The magistrates' court has no power to act of its own volition.

Probation officers may consider that, when an offender has been sentenced to custody, it would be appropriate to apply to a magistrates' court for a revocation of the order. Probation services may wish to examine arrangements with their local courts to ensure the speedy hearing of such applications.

Other cases of relevance are:

Moffatt (unreported, 26 May 1993) where a magistrates' court had committed an offender to the Crown Court to be dealt with for a breach of probation and the Crown Court had resentenced the offender for the original offences. The Divisional Court held that the magistrates' court had had no power to commit for the breach of probation because no application had been made by the offender or the probation officer.

Cawley, supra where a probation order had been revoked and the offender resentenced when he was convicted of an offence committed before the probation order was made. The Court held that it would seldom if ever be in the interests of justice to resentence an offender for offences for which he had been placed on probation after the current offence was committed.

Neville, supra where it was made clear that, when a probation order is revoked and the offender is also sentenced for the original offence, credit must be given for any time spent in custody on remand before the order was made; and that an allowance should be made for partial completion of the order.

The principles laid down in these cases will also apply to breach of other community sentences. On giving an allowance for partial completion of an order, see also *Decino, supra* where a suspended sentence was activated and the Court took account of the fact that there had been some response to a suspended sentence supervision order.

Particular offences

In this section are listed examples of offences which the Court of Appeal held to be so serious that only custody could be justified. In the cases of *Cox, Hill* and *Duncan, post* the Court *nevertheless substituted a community sentence* because s28 CJA 91 allowed it to mitigate sentence by reason of mitigating factors relating to the offender. In 'How serious is "so serious"?' (*Sentencing News*, Issue 3, July 27, 1993) Dr. David Thomas commented:

'... the fact that an offence satisfies the requirement of seriousness does not necessarily mean that a custodial sentence will follow. Even though the offence is so serious that only a custodial sentence could be justified, the sentencer must consider under section 28 of the Act whether mitigating factors personal to the offender allow a less severe sentence to be imposed ... In considering the significance of these decisions, it is also necessary to bear in mind that many are decisions of two-judge courts, and that frequently counsel for the appellant concedes that the offence passed the seriousness threshold but asks for a reduction in length—possibly the most practical strategy when the appellant is in custody and has served a few months of the sentence.'

Violent offences

Unlawful wounding: Following an argument between a taxi driver and his passenger over a fare, in the course of which the passenger damaged the taxi, the passenger called his wife to get a crowbar from their house; upon which the driver returned to his taxi to get a chisel, struck the victim two blows to the top of the head, knocking him to the ground and then struck him further blows to the face. The wounds required 17 stitches, there was a suspected fracture of the orbit of the left eye, bruising and a deformed nose: *Sanderson, supra.*

Unlawful wounding: The offender shot at a schoolboy at a distance with an air rifle, hitting him in the thigh with a pellet. The offender said that he had intended to scare rather than hit the boy after previously hearing an air pellet pass close to him: *Corkhill, supra.*

Unlawful wounding: Following a fight between one of the offenders and the victim earlier in the day, the two offenders went to the victim's house at 9.55 pm armed with a truncheon and a spanner. When he answered the door, they entered his house and fought him, causing general bodily bruising, a facial cut, a bruised shoulder and pain in the knee: *Morgan and Morgan, supra.*

Unlawful wounding: The offender went towards the victim with a knife and waved it in front of his face, leaving him with a wound which required 14 stitches: *Duncan, supra.*

Assault occasioning actual bodily harm: The offender, left in charge of his cohabitee's 10 month old daughter, slapped her across the cheek with his hand after she had been crying at night, so that she bore the red marks of the slap the following day: *Barnes* (1993) 14 Cr App R (S) 547.

Assault occasioning actual bodily harm: When a policewoman was standing in front of his car, the offender pressed the accelerator. She jumped out of the way to avoid being hit and, as the car accelerated away, the bonnet clipped her arm: *Actie* (1993) 14 Cr App R (S) 598.

Assault occasioning actual bodily harm: The offender knocked on the victim's door after the latter had complained about his children's behaviour, punched the victim about the face, then followed the retreating victim into his flat and punched him again: *Bryan* (unreported, 16 March 1993).

Assault occasioning actual bodily harm: After drinking, the offender for no clear reason punched the victim on the back of the head, continued to punch him in the face and, when he fell to the ground, again punched him: *Audit, supra*.

Robbery: While on bail the offender with an accomplice entered a corner shop brandishing a knife and demanded money from the shopkeeper who had a small child in his arms. During a struggle, he seized the till containing about £2,700: *Cunningham, supra*.

Non-violent offences

Burglary: Two offenders broke into a house by forcing a rear window and stole a television set and some sound equipment valued at £700, of which £300 worth was recovered; and committed a second burglary offence in which the offender stole a video recorder, cigarette lighter, watch, pocket knife and £100 in cash, to a total value of £740, none of which was recovered: *Oliver and Little, supra*.

Burglary: The offender with three others entered a bungalow while the owners were on holiday, ransacked the bedroom and another room and, when arrested, had a credit card, jewellery and other items stolen in the burglary: *Reynolds, supra*.

Burglary and handling stolen property: The offender and a co-accused were observed making a forced entry to the house of a recently deceased woman whose death had been announced in the newspapers, loaded property worth over £5,000 in a car and drove off. Keys, an iron bar, gloves and other addresses of recently deceased people were found in the car, and at the offender's home over £5,000 worth of property from eight previous similar burglaries was found: *Lewis* (1993) 14 Cr App R (S) 744.

Burglary and taking a vehicle: The offender with others had stolen a car with the purpose of using it to commit burglary, broke into a newsagent's shop in the early hours and stole the till containing cash, cigarettes and other items to a total value of about £2,900, effecting entry by breaking a window that cost £323 to repair: *Price, supra*.

Theft: The offenders, who were selling furniture door to door, had browbeaten an elderly couple, removing their old settee and two armchairs and replacing it with new furniture, for which they later returned to collect payment: *Flynn and Flynn, supra*.

Theft: The offender and two accomplices staged a fake robbery in the course of which an accomplice was tied up in a shop of which he was deputy manager in order to conceal the theft of stock worth about £1,500: *Cunningham, supra.*

False accounting: On 11 occasions a police officer failed to pay into the court office fine payments which he had collected from police stations and diverted it to his own purposes. The total sum involved was £1,506 and the prosecution accepted that he intended to repay the money when he was in a position to do so: *Lowery, supra.*

Theft: The offender, who was a key holder to supermarket premises where he worked, stole £1,100 from the safe at night, stole £3,000 on a second similar occasion, and on a third occasion was recorded on video machine opening the safe to see if there was any cash in it: *Robbins* (unreported, 22 December 1992).

Theft and obtaining property by deception: The offender stole goods valued at nearly £1,500 from the store where he worked, sold some to acquaintances, and took others with forged till receipts to neighbouring branches of the same firm and obtained refunds for them: *Hill, supra.*

Theft and false accounting: The offender, who managed a post office and shop with her husband, falsified accounts for the post office to the extent of about £2,500 over two years, initially to cover innocent shortfalls in the accounts which she sought to cover up by increasingly dishonest behaviour: *Robinson, supra.*

Theft: While on bail the offender had made off with cash and goods worth £839 from a service station which he was in charge of on a night shift: *Price, supra.*

Theft: The offender with two others had set out in the late evening or early hours in a car, with a rechargeable drill and tools intended to enable them to break open telephone boxes. When they were apprehended, their car contained a BT coin box and coins. Although the amount stolen was only £40.20, the planned nature of the expedition and the fact that this offence could deprive members of the public of use of the telephone were cited as factors affecting seriousness: *Decino, supra.*

Driving offences

Causing death by reckless driving: The offenders raced each other over a considerable distance at excessive speeds on a road where there were a number of other vehicles, overtaking other cars on the inside. When they were alongside each other and B's car in the nearside lane was rapidly gaining ground on a slower moving car ahead, he pulled out sharply into the outside lane, caught the front of G's car, lost control, hit the central barrier, flew over at least one car, overturned and somersaulted, fatally injuring his passenger: *Godden and Boosey, supra.*

Reckless driving: The offender, riding a motorcycle with no lights at night in wet weather, was pursued by the police. He drove along a pavement at 25 to 30 mph, turned into a walkway, went on to another road, overtook a car by going on to the pavement, ignored a give way sign, went on to a narrow pathway, lost control of the motorcycle and fell off: *Cox, supra.*

Causing death by reckless driving: The offender, driving at 70 mph in a 60 mph limit, crossed double white lines and went on to the wrong side of the road to overtake two cars at a point where there was no visibility as to what might be coming in the other direction; had to swerve back acutely to the inside to avoid an oncoming car; lost control of the vehicle which struck the nearside verge, went completely out of control and struck a car coming in the opposite direction causing the death of the driver: *Winterton, supra.*

Reckless driving: The offender after drinking was seen by police officers driving at high speed, braked violently and swerved into a kerb; continued to travel through built up areas at speeds of up to 90 mph, went the wrong way round a roundabout and then swerved and demolished a pair of bollards; then mounted a pavement and stopped: *Moriarty, supra.*

Reckless driving: The offender attempted to overtake a van by entering part of the carriageway reserved for traffic turning right when coming from the opposite direction; found himself in difficulty because his car was not proceeding fast enough to overtake the van before reaching an approaching traffic island; made his way on to the opposite carriageway and struck a pedestrian who was crossing the road: *Smith, supra.*

Cases where two offences in combination were held to be 'so serious', ie under the original s1 CJA 91

Driving with excess alcohol and while disqualified: Driving at 5.10 am while 30% over the legal limit of alcohol in the blood, making no reply to police officers and then giving a false name; *plus* while on bail for that offence, driving while disqualified, again giving a false name when apprehended: *Cawley, supra.*

Acting as a look-out when a stolen car was dismantled *plus* while on bail, being involved in the theft of a radio cassette player and a rear passenger shelf, worth a total of £430, from a parked car: *Baverstock, supra.*

Handling a stolen cheque book and card with an intention to use them extensively as a plan of campaign to defraud many people on a large scale *plus* later using them to pay for goods and obtain cash (both offences committed while on bail): *Bexley, supra.*

Acting as a look-out while two others burgled a house during the day, smashing the front door in and stealing property worth £1,900 including a television set, stereo system, video recorder, watch, wallet and credit cards *plus* committing a similar offence with another person who acted as look-out in the early evening but in which nothing was taken: *Husbands, supra.*

Offences held not to be 'so serious'

These included the following:

Assault occasioning actual bodily harm: The appellant, aged 19, angered because the victim aged 16 had lent his shirt to a friend without his permission, chased him upstairs together with a co-accused, cornered him, punched and headbutted him. Later he and the co-accused punched the victim about the head and body and then kicked him while he was on the floor. The victim had four swellings around his forehead area and a further swelling behind his right ear: *Nixon, supra.*

Supplying a Class B drug and possession of a Class A drug: The offender bought an LSD tablet for £5 for his own consumption. On two occasions he supplied about £10 to £15 worth of cannabis to two friends, making no money out of this: *Prunty, supra.*

Burglary: The offender with an accomplice had entered a private club, gone into the cellar and forced open the spirits store. He was seen emerging from the cellar by the steward. On investigation, nothing had been taken but the drayman's entrance cover had been moved to allow access to the street: *Tetteh, supra.*

Burglary: The offender broke into a house at 10 pm, knowing the householder had gone on holiday and, when a neighbour went to investigate, made good his escape by breaking the glass of a back door. Nothing was taken and a relatively modest amount of damage was caused: *Bennett, supra.*

Theft: The offender, aged 19 at the time of the offence, was made a shift manager at a busy shop supplying pizzas and on three occasions stole a total of £1,080 from the takings which he should have paid into the bank: *Small, supra.*

Theft: The offender shoplifted several pairs of jeans valued at £75, and committed a second offence of shoplifting two video cassettes worth £28: *Summers, supra.*

Handling and obtaining property by deception: The offender used a stolen credit card to buy petrol and cigarettes worth £23.36, with five offences of obtaining property valued at a total of £119 from filling stations with another credit card during one week taken into consideration: *Harrison, supra.*

Theft: The appellant issued cheques on bank accounts which he held in his own name at Barclays Bank and Lloyds Bank, knowing that there were no funds to cover them. Three cheques were issued on the Barclays account totalling £455 and one on the Lloyds account for £400: *Awoyemi* (unreported, 5 February 1993).

Obtaining by deception: The offender made false statements in order to obtain two cheques for £63.86 from the DSS for unemployment benefit. He had had three days' employment in which he had earned £74 which he had not declared and was overpaid by £59: *Bee, supra.*

Theft and criminal damage: The offender drove into a car park with two associates and broke into and stole a Ford Fiesta, forcing the ignition barrel off and starting the car with a screwdriver. When police officers blocked him from driving out of the car park, he reversed the car at high speed, collided with his own car, manoeuvred the car to try to get away, then jumped out but was caught and arrested: *Jones, supra.*

Theft: The offender had stolen a motorcycle worth about £1,000 and had dismantled it with a view to using it for spare parts: *Evans, supra.*

Theft: The appellant, who was in a chemist's shop with a pushchair, selected a bottle of eau de toilette, placed it in the hood of the pushchair, covered it with cloth and left the store: *Brown* (unreported, 16 Match 1993).

Theft: The offender took a box of wine valued at £11.50 from a shelf in a store and left the store without paying for it: *Church, supra.*

Theft: The offender had taken a supermarket trolley with something over £200 worth of goods: *Crawford, supra.*

Theft and going equipped for theft: The appellant stole a car stereo worth between £40 and £50 and two speakers worth between £20 and £30 new; went equipped for theft with a screwdriver, knife, blade and torch; stole 12 cans of lager; and stole a quantity of petrol from a motor car: *Cook* (unreported, 23 March 1993).

Theft: The appellant went to the offices of a company and asked if he could use the toilet: on the way out he stole a lady's handbag which was hanging over the chair by her unattended desk. While on bail, he stole a stereo and some cassette tapes from a car: *Allright, supra.*

Attempted theft: The offender had put his hand into the handbag of a lady standing on a bus, using a raincoat draped over his arm to try to conceal what was happening: *Newman, supra.*

Obtaining property by deception: The offender had fraudulently encashed social security pension allowance book vouchers over a one week period to a total value of £264.70. This was part of a sophisticated fraud in which others were the main conspirators and the offender received £15 for each encashment: *Breeze, supra.*

Offences held to be 'serious enough' for a community sentence

Assault occasioning actual bodily harm: The appellant, aged 19, angered because the victim aged 16 had lent his shirt to a friend without his permission, chased him upstairs together with a co-accused, cornered him, punched and headbutted him. Later he and the co-accused punched the victim about the head and body and then kicked him while he was on the floor. The victim had four swellings around his forehead area and a further swelling behind his right ear: *Nixon, supra.*

Unlawful wounding: The offender went towards the victim with a knife and waved it in front of his face, leaving him with a wound which required 14 stitches: *Duncan, supra.*

Burglary: The offender with an accomplice had entered a private club, gone into the cellar and forced open the spirits store. He was seen emerging from the cellar by the steward. On investigation, nothing had been taken but the drayman's entrance cover had been moved to allow access to the street: *Tetteh, supra.*

Reckless driving: The offender, riding a motorcycle with no lights at night in wet weather, was pursued by the police. He drove along a pavement at 25 to 30 mph, turned into a walkway, went on to another road, overtook a car by going on to the pavement, ignored a give way sign, went on to a narrow pathway, lost control of the motorcycle and fell off: *Cox, supra.*

Theft: The offender, aged 19 at the time of the offence, was made a shift manager at a busy shop selling pizzas and on three occasions stole a total of £1,080 from the takings which he should have paid into the bank: *Small, supra.*

Theft: The offender shoplifted several pairs of jeans valued at £75, and committed a second offence of shoplifting two video cassettes worth £28: *Summers, supra.*

Handling and obtaining by deception: The offender used a stolen credit card to buy petrol and cigarettes worth £23.36, with five offences of obtaining property valued at a total of £119 from filling stations with another credit card during one week taken into consideration: *Harrison, supra.*

Theft and obtaining property by deception: The offender stole goods valued at nearly £1,500 from the store where he worked, sold some to acquaintances, and took others with forged till receipts to neighbouring branches of the same firm and obtained refunds for them: *Hill, supra.*

Theft: The appellant issued cheques on bank accounts which he held in his own name at Barclays Bank and Lloyds Bank, knowing that there were no funds to cover them. Three cheques were issued on the Barclays account totalling £455 and one on the Lloyds account for £400: *Awoyemi, supra.*

Obtaining by deception: The offender made false statements in order to obtain two cheques for £63.86 from the DSS for unemployment benefit. He had had three days' employment in which he had earned £74 which he had not declared and was overpaid by £59: *Bee, supra.*

Theft and criminal damage: The offender drove into a car park with two associates and broke into and stole a Ford Fiesta, forcing the ignition barrel off and starting the car with a screwdriver. When police officers blocked him from driving out of the car park, he reversed the car at high speed, collided with his own car, manoeuvred the car to try to get away, then jumped out but was caught and arrested: *Jones, supra.*

Theft and going equipped for theft: The appellant stole a car stereo worth between £40 and £50 and two speakers worth between £20 and £30 new; went equipped for theft with a screwdriver, knife, blade and torch; stole 12 cans of lager; and stole a quantity of petrol from a motor car: *Cook, supra.*

Theft: The appellant went to the offices of a company and asked if he could use the toilet: on the way out he stole a lady's handbag which was hanging over the chair by her unattended desk. While on bail, he stole a stereo and some cassette tapes from a car: *Allright, supra.*

Attempted theft: The offender had put his hand into the handbag of a lady standing on the bus, using a raincoat draped over his arm to try to conceal what was happening: *Newman, supra.*

d) Sentencing Trends After the CJA 91

The following is a summary of available research findings and statistical data:

Phase I (October 1992 to January 1993)

Following implementation of the Criminal Justice Act 1991 on 1 October 1992, sentencing trends fell into two phases - a four month phase in which the use of custody fell, followed by a sharp reversal of this downward trend in the second phase from February 1993 onwards.

In interpreting the prison population figures, we have to be careful to allow for the usual seasonal variations in the prison population. In the two months immediately before implementation, from the end of July to the end of September 1992, there was a fall in the prison population of 800. Such a fall is not unusual at that time of year (the prison population usually falls in summer because of reduced activity by Crown Courts).

However, in the two months after the Act there was a fall in the prison population of nearly 3,000 from 45,835 at the end of September to 43,064 at the end of November: this was a very striking fall, as the prison population is usually rising at that time of year to a peak at the end of November.

The population continued to fall to 40,606 at the end of December 1992 (but it always falls in December because of reduced activity by the courts over Christmas). At the end of January it had risen to 41,561 - but, here again, it always rises in January from the artificially low end of December figure. Overall, however, the number of prisoners four months after implementation was more than 4,000 lower than before implementation, representing a real and substantial fall in the use of custody by the courts.

There had been a fall in the number of offenders coming before the courts; but this was a longer term trend and could not account for the very sharp drop in the use of custody immediately after the Criminal Justice Act 1991. The evidence indicates that the Act produced a real reduction in the courts' use of custody.

Home Office Statistical Bulletin 24/93, 'Cautions, Court Proceedings and Sentencing, England and Wales, 1992' (September 1993) showed that between 1991 and 1992 there was a fall of 6% in the number of offenders sentenced to immediate custody, following a rise of 10% between 1990 and 1991.

The proportionate use of immediate custody for persons of all ages sentenced for indictable offences had increased from 15.1% in 1991 to 15.7% in the first three-quarters of 1992; but, following the implementation of the Criminal Justice Act 1991, it fell to 11.6% in the last quarter of 1992. The figures broke down as follows:

• At magistrates' courts, the proportionate use of immediate custody for indictable offences was nearly 5.5% in the first three-quarters of 1992 and fell to 3% in the last quarter. For adult males the fall was from 6% in the first three quarters to 3% in the last quarter. The largest falls occurred for burglary (from 15% to 9%) and theft and handling (from 6 to 2%).

• At the Crown Court, the proportionate use of custody for indictable offences was 45.5% in the first three quarters of 1992, but fell to 40% in the last quarter. For adult males there was a fall for all offence groups, with substantial falls occurring for burglary (56 to 50%), theft and handling (36 to 26%) and fraud and forgery (41 to 34%).

As a result of the reduction in the use of custody after the Act, the number of prisoners held in police cells was rapidly reduced (and this practice was ended in February 1993); few prisoners in penal establishments were any longer held three to a cell (the number fell from 1,272 in March 1992 to 108 in March 1993, and the number two to a cell from 9,160 to 6,872); and prison population projections for the end of the century were scaled down by several thousand. Although comparative European figures for early 1993 will not be available for some time, it is likely that during this period we lost our usual position as the West European country with the highest proportion of its population in prison.

Community sentences in Phase I
What happened to the use of community sentences during this phase? The earliest clues began to emerge from surveys by probation service organisations. The National Association of Probation Officers (NAPO) collected information in February and March 1993 from 28 court areas. In 27 of the 28 areas the number of community service orders had increased since the Act by amounts ranging from 10% to 60%. However, the number of probation orders had fallen in all but three areas, by amounts ranging from 5 to 30%.

The fall in probation orders did not necessarily represent a straight shift from probation towards community service. The Act's criteria required courts to be satisfied that an offence is 'serious enough' to warrant a community sentence before making one; and there was some evidence from local surveys of a fall in the number of minor offenders receiving probation orders. For example, Howard Thomas, Chief Probation Officer for North Wales, wrote as follows of the first three months of the Act:

'The first quarter's figures in this area indicate that there has been a dramatic fall in first offenders coming on to our books by way of a probation order, a mere 4 per cent now of all cases against the last national average figure of 12 per cent and our own previous full year total of 11 per cent. The Act therefore being quite influential in this regard.' ('Green Shoots or Otherwise', *Justice of the Peace*, 5 June 1993).

However, another reason for the decline in probation orders was identified by HM Inspectorate of Probation in its report 'The Criminal Justice Act 1991 Inspection' (May 1993), which said:

'Sentencers were finding it difficult to see the probation order without additional requirements as a community sentence that sufficiently restricted liberty ... where probation officers mentioned a number of different possible community orders in the PSR, sentencers were more likely to use those where the restriction of liberty was most apparent. This was putting the "straight" probation order at a disadvantage.' (para. 6.6).

The Association of Chief Officers of Probation (ACOP) carried out an early survey of the use of combination orders, which looked at all such orders carried out in eight areas, representing about 25% of the service's national caseload, from 1 October to 15 December 1992.

There were wide variations in their use, but it was estimated that at that rate there would be 4,000 to 4,600 combination orders made nationally in a year. 76% were made by magistrates' courts (including youth courts) and only 24% by Crown Courts—although, as it is the most intensive community sentence, it had been expected that it would be used normally by Crown Courts.

In many cases combination orders were passed when probation was proposed in a pre-sentence report, but the report also mentioned that community service was available. In the NAPO survey combination orders accounted for around 5% of all orders with 80% coming from the magistrates' courts.

In its inspection on the Criminal Justice Act 1991, HM Inspectorate of Probation examined all combination orders made up to the date of the inspection (February 1993) in six probation areas—Devon, Essex, South Glamorgan, Merseyside, West Sussex and Warwickshire—a total of 160 orders. 62% of combination orders were made in magistrates' courts, 8% in youth courts and only 30% in Crown Courts. Very few combination orders had been proposed in pre-sentence reports and most (three-quarters or more) had been made without such a proposal having been put forward. Such orders were often made when there was a strong proposal for probation with an observation that community service was available:

'One consequence was that some people sentenced to a combination order had lifestyles or personal characteristics which made it questionable whether they would be able or willing to comply with the requirements of the sentence or National Standards. People who misused drugs, including alcohol, seemed to be the largest classifiable group in this category, but there were others who, for example, had no fixed accommodation or had an ingrained antipathy to authority.' (para. 7.8)

About half the combination orders seemed to be pitched around the middle of the community sentences 'band', about a quarter lay towards the top and the rest were in the lower third. There was a minority which were, by probation service criteria, made on offences which were not so serious as to warrant such a sentence. The Inspectorate concluded:

' ... it was fairly clear that combination orders were being used by courts for offences of a wide range of seriousness.' (para. 7.11)

Home Office Statistical Bulletin 17/93, 'Summary Probation Statistics, England and Wales, 1992' (July 1993) confirmed these trends. The statistics showed that:

• In 1992 community service order commencements reached their highest level ever at 43,000, a 4% rise over 1991. Early indications for the first few months of 1993 suggested that the number of community service orders was continuing to rise. Provisional court sentencing information for 1992 indicated that between 1991 and 1992 community service orders rose as a proportion of all sentences for indictable offences at both the Crown Court and magistrates' courts.

• In 1992, 41,000 people began a probation order, 9% fewer than in 1991 and the lowest number since 1986. The Bulletin observed:

'The reduction was concentrated in the October-December period after the CJA was implemented and the reasons for it include a fall in the total numbers sentenced for indictable offences and in the proportion of those sentenced at the magistrates' courts who were put on probation, changes in the availability of sentences and a reduction in the numbers put on probation for summary offences. Early indications for the first few months of 1993 suggest that the number of probation orders have remained lower than in recent years.'

The proportion of probation orders which had additional requirements increased from 25% in 1991 to 29% in the last quarter of 1992.

• 1400 people started combination orders in the three months following their introduction on 1 October 1992. A third of these orders had the maximum community service element of 100 hours specified. 'The lengths of the probation part of the order seem similar to those for standard probation order,' said the Bulletin. Early indications for the first few months of 1993 suggested that the number of combination orders was continuing to rise.

Further details were given in Home Office Statistical Bulletin 24/93, *Cautions, Court Proceedings and Sentencing, England and Wales, 1992* (September 1993). The figures in this bulletin were compiled from information provided to the Home Office by the police: the Bulletin said that, because the returns for summary offences were incomplete, the figures 'have been estimated and are subject to revision'. They showed that:

• the number of probation orders made by courts in 1992 fell by 3,700 to 43,800; supervision orders fell by 400 to 5,900; and attendance centre orders fell by 1,000 to 7,200. The number of community service orders increased by 1,600 to 44,100. The combination order had been given to 1,300 offenders in the last quarter of 1992.

• the proportionate use of the probation order for indictable offences fell by one percentage point to 9% in magistrates' courts and rose by one percentage point to 13% at the Crown Court. The proportionate use of community service orders rose by one percentage point at both magistrates' courts and the Crown Court to 8 and 14% respectively. The proportionate use of attendance centre and supervision orders remained the same at both types of court.

• the proportionate use of community sentences as a whole at the Crown Court rose from 26% in the first three quarters of 1992 to 37% in the fourth quarter. At magistrates' courts the proportionate use of community sentences for indictable offences fell from 21% to 20% between these two periods.

73

Home Office data monitoring exercise
Home Office Statistical Bulletin 25/93, 'Monitoring of the Criminal Justice Act 1991—Data From A Special Collection Exercise', contained figures from a special data collection exercise for offenders sentenced for indictable offences in nine magistrates' courts and 10 Crown Court centres in the summer of 1992 and early 1993. The changes in the proportionate use of particular types of sentence in the nine magistrates' courts between summer 1992 and early 1993 were as follows:

	Pre-CJA	Post-CJA
Immediate custody	6%	5%
Suspended sentences	4%	1%
Community sentences	19%	21%
Fines	37%	42%
Discharges	31%	29%
Other	3%	2%

The figures for the ten Crown Courts were:

	Pre-CJA	Post-CJA
Immediate custody	44%	42%
Suspended sentences	18%	5%
Community sentences	24%	37%
Fines	7%	6%
Discharges	6%	7%
Other	1%	3%

It is particularly striking that the large fall in the number of suspended sentences passed in Crown Courts, following the 1991 Act's restriction of such sentences to cases with 'exceptional circumstances', did not lead to an increase in immediate custody. This suggests that suspended sentences were in general replaced by non-custodial penalties.

The fall in the proportionate use of custody was most apparent among offenders with a substantial number of previous convictions. For example, at the nine magistrates' courts the proportionate use of custody for offenders with between six and 20 previous convictions fell from 9 to 6%, and for those with 21 or more previous convictions it fell from 19 to 13%.

The average sentence length of those sent into custody remained the same at magistrates' courts for adult male offenders. At Crown Courts it rose by an average of three months for violent offences and fell by an average of two months for property offences, the fall being more apparent among those with 21 or more previous convictions.

The 1991 Act's provisions for mandatory pre-sentence reports before courts can impose certain sentences made little overall differences in the magistrates' courts, where the proportion of offenders sentenced with a social inquiry report before the Act was identical to the proportion sentenced with a PSR after the Act: 30% in both cases. However, the provisions made a marked impact at the Crown Courts where the percentage increased from 57% to 73%, with a particularly large increase (from 37 to 61%) for those pleading not guilty.

Fines

Following the introduction of the unit fine system on 1 October 1992, the overall use of the fine for indictable offences at magistrates' courts rose to 45% in the final quarter of the year compared with 42% in the first three quarters, indicating that the new system was achieving some success in increasing the credibility of the fine.

Home Office *Statistical Bulletin* 25/93 compared sentencing data for indictable offences (collected from nine magistrates' courts) for the summer of 1992 with data from January and February 1993. In the sample courts the proportionate use of the fine increased from 37 to 42% between the two periods. There was a particularly marked increase in the use of the fine for unemployed offenders, from 31 to 48%. Although the average fine at the participating magistrates' courts remained almost unchanged at about £110, the average amount increased for those employed from roughly £140 to £230, while the average amount for those unemployed fell from nearly £90 to under £70.

Phase I (Early February 1993 onwards)

The second phase began at the height of an intensive media campaign about crime. There is little doubt that this affected the climate in which sentencing and remand decisions were made, and there was a sharp increase in the prison population, shown in the following table. The rise continued throughout the year as strong media pressure for harsher policies towards offenders continued; the new Home Secretary, Michael Howard, made a series of strident speeches and public statements advocating a greater use of imprisonment; and the statutory restrictions on using prison sentences contained in the 1991 Act were weakened by the Criminal Justice Act 1993.

Date	Total prison population	Remand prisoners	Young offenders in custody (under 21)
1992			
30 September	45,835	9,455	7835
31 October	43,905	9,163	7455
30 November	43,064	9,200	7263
31 December	40,606	8,272	6783
1993			
31 January	41,561	9,281	7,060
28 February	42,882	9,933	7,488
31 March	43,195	9,996	7,659
30 April	43,391	9,997	7,682
31 May	43,585	10,181	7,784
30 June	44,246	10,632	7,876
31 July	44,830	10,572	7,892
31 August	45,633	11,407	8,016
30 September	46,211	11,445	8,256
31 October	46,886	11,829	8,393
30 November	47,153	11,885	8,288
31 December	45,214	10,763	7,780
1994			
31 January	46,902	12,100	8,078
28 February	47,906	11,923	8,217

It can be seen from the above that, in the 12 months to February 1994, the overall prison population increased by 5,024 (12%), an average increase of 419 a month; the number of remand prisoners rose by 1,990 (20%); and the number of young prisoners aged under 21 rose by 729 (10%). This rate of increase over such a short period is unprecedented in recent years.

Home Office *Statistical Bulletin* 25/93 contained details of the early upswing in the use of custody between January and February 1993. It said:

'Data from the Lord Chancellor's Department for January and February of 1993 show an increase of custody from 42 to 46% for all (Crown Court) centres in England and Wales.'

In a sample of nine magistrates' courts from which figures were collected for the *Bulletin*, there was a one percentage point increase in the proportionate use of immediate custody for indictable offences from 4% to 5% between January and February.

As well as an increase in custody, there was also a move between January and February upwards from fines and discharges towards community sentences in magistrates' courts. At the same nine magistrates' courts the proportionate use of fines fell from 44% to 40%; discharges fell from 29% to 27%; probation orders increased from 7 to 9%; community service orders rose from 7 to 9%; and supervision orders rose from 2 to 3%.

A Parliamentary answer to Joan Ruddock MP on 18 October 1993 (col. 136) contained figures for the proportionate use of immediate custody for defendants sentenced at the Crown Court following committal for trial. In September 1992, immediately before implementation of the CJA 91, the proportion was 48%; in January 1993 it was 42%; in February 1993 it rose to 46%; and a steady rise followed until in August 1993 the proportion was 54%.

It could be argued that the harsher climate might have produced a considerably higher prison population were it not for the restraint on sentencers which the framework of the Criminal Justice Act 1993 continued to exert. However, on 13 May 1993, the then Home Secretary, Kenneth Clarke, announced that the restrictions on the use of custodial sentences contained in the CJA 91 were to be amended and that the unit fine system would be abolished. These changes were subsequently included in the Criminal Justice Act 1993 and implemented in August and September 1993.

Community sentences

Monitoring by the Association of Chief Officers of Probation during 1993 indicated that commencements of probation orders had risen during the year and that the number in the third quarter of 1993 was comparable to the third quarter of 1992, before the implementation of the CJA 91. Commencements of community service orders remained higher than before the CJA 91, with a trend towards longer orders. Commencements of combination orders had continued to rise. (*Finance and Resource Newsbrief*, ACOP, March 1994).

Youth courts

The National Association for the Care and Resettlement of Offenders (NACRO) monitored sentencing in youth courts after the Act by analysing returns submitted by 15 social services departments (covering 10% of youth courts).

The first six months of the monitoring exercise were from 1 October 1992 to 31 March 1993, during which time 3,005 cases were processed by the courts in the sample. 38.3% resulted in conditional or absolute discharges; 2.2% in bind-overs; 15.3% in fines imposed on young offenders; 1.9% in fines imposed on parents; 2.6% in compensation orders; 12.8% in attendance centre orders; 13.3% in supervision orders (including 1.0% in supervision plus IT and 0.8% in supervision plus specified activities); 2.2% in probation orders; 5.8% in community service orders; 4.5% in detention in a young offender institution; and 0.3% in section 53 orders. Points worth noting include:

• There was little use of the combination order. Such orders were used in only 20 cases (0.7%), 9 of which were on 16 year olds and 11 on 17 year olds.

• There was relatively little use of the probation order. 63 such orders were made (2.2%), of which only 6 were made on 16 year olds and the remaining 57 were on 17 or 18 year olds. (18 year olds would be sentenced as 17 year olds, having reached this age during the proceedings). In comparison, there were 386 supervision orders, of which 110 were made on 16 year olds and 113 on 17 year olds. 17 year olds were receiving supervision orders in the same proportion as 16 year olds.

• 5.8% of disposals (169) were community service orders, of which the majority (125) were on 17 and 18 year olds. The national figure for 14 to 16 year olds in 1991 was 5%. 30 orders (1.0%) exceeded 120 hours, seven of which were on 16 year olds and 23 on 17 and 18 year olds.

• Relatively little use was made of the power to order parents to pay fines: 15.3% of sentences were fines on young people and only 1.9% were fines on parents.

For the 15-17 year old age group (ie those eligible for custody), detention in a young offender institution made up 5.2% of all sentences. This compares with a national figure of 8% for 14-16 year olds in 1991.

However, incomplete figures received by NACRO for 1st April to 30 September 1993 indicated that some toughening of sentencing had occurred since the first six months. 5.9% of cases received sentences of detention in a young offender institution, compared with 4.5% in the first six months of the Act, and 6.5% received community service orders, compared with 5.8% in the earlier period. In other respects the figures were similar to the first six months of the Act.

Section 53 CYPA 1933
A separate survey by NACRO of the use of sentences under section 53 of the Children and Young Persons Act 1993 using information supplied by the Home Office showed that, in the first six months' operation of the Criminal Justice Act 1991, 72 young people received a sentence under section 53(2).

Thirty-five of these were young people aged 17 to 18, who became eligible for section 53 sentences by the provisions of the 1991 Act. Therefore, 37 young people under 17 were sentenced under section 53 over the six months, an annual rate of 74: this compares with 102 in 1991.

Overall, therefore, there was no dramatic increase in the use of section 53 following the 1991 Act.

However, the long delays which can occur before cases reach the Crown Court may mean that 17 year olds will feature more prominently in future statistics. 23.6% of cases sentenced under section 53 were burglary offences (18.1% if aggravated burglary is excluded) compared with 12% in 1991.

Juvenile remands

In June 1993 the Association of Chief Officers of Probation (ACOP) and the National Association for the Care and Resettlement of Offenders (NACRO) published a report entitled 'Awaiting Trial', which contained the findings of a survey of juveniles remanded to prison service custody in England and Wales between April 1992 and March 1993. This period covered the six months before implementation of the Criminal Justice Act 1991 on 1st October 1992, and the six month period immediately following its implementation. The report showed that the daily number of juveniles held on remand in custody had nearly doubled from 47 in April 1992 to 95 in March 1993. The average daily number in the six months after implementation of the Criminal Justice Act 1991 (October 1992 to March 1993) was 83, compared with an average of 57 in the six months before the Act - an increase of 46%. This rise reversed a previous downward trend, from an average of 94 in 1989 to an average of 56 in the first nine months of 1992.

The above figures are for the number of juveniles held on remand at one time. Over the six months from October 1992 to March 1993 a total of 566 juveniles were remanded in custody, a 29% increase on the 440 such remands in the previous six months. Much of this increase was due to a sharp increase in admissions in the final three months of the survey, between January and March 1993.

The report discussed how far, if at all, these trends had been affected by the Criminal Justice Act 1991. From 1st October 1992 this had stipulated that courts should remand juveniles to prisons and remand centres only when this was necessary `to protect the public from serious harm'. However, the Act also allowed courts to make custodial remands on their own initiative: previously the court had to consider a report from the local authority before making a 'certificate of unruliness'. The report said:

'Where there have been significant increases these were largely recorded in January and, particularly, February and March 1993. These months coincide with sustained media interest in juvenile crime and a major public and political debate about "persistent offenders". In consequence it is difficult to judge the extent to which the legislation itself has made an impact, or whether the increase has been due more to other pressures.'

The report observed that those working with young offenders and defendants considered that the media debate in the early months of 1993 had 'presented a misleading picture to the public, as a result of which attitudes hardened.'

2 The Dynamics of Change 1987 to 1994

When the Criminal Justice Act 1991 received Royal Assent it was reasonably assumed by many observers that the criminal justice mould of the post-war years had been broken. The significance of the 1991 Act was widely acknowledged, building as it did a new approach which emerged after the Conservative government was returned to office in June 1987. A brief review of key events during the late 1980s is an essential pre-requisite to understanding how the Act and its reforming intentions came to be so quickly reversed.

Criminal justice policy

In general, criminal justice policy-making tends to be an equivocal process. Objectives often lack consistency and, not infrequently, appear to be contradictory. Furthermore, the relationship between policy and practice is uncertain, not least because the agenda of practitioners only rarely dovetails with that of policy-makers. Occasionally, however there are interludes where the main patterns of criminal policy are somewhat easier to discern.

Douglas Hurd was Home Secretary from September 1985 to October 1989 and the latter 28 months of his relatively lengthy stewardship of the Home Office was one such period of relative clarity of vision in criminal policy. The 'Hurd vision', of course, represented a composite of ideas and intentions not only of the Secretary of State but also of other Home Office ministers, most notably John Patten, and of senior civil servants such as Sir Brian Cubbon and David Faulkner—respectively, at that time permanent under-secretary and deputy-under-secretary (with responsibility for criminal policy) at the Home Office.

Three themes

The themes that flowed from the Hurd vision were never neatly articulated within some hierarchy of policy purposes, but are more appropriately viewed as a set of priorities that gathered (and in some instances, lost) pace over the period under review. The overriding theme was that community penalties make much more sense in crime control terms with respect to many offenders than resort to an over-burdened prison system. While this had been a policy preoccupation at the Home Office over at least two decades, the distinctive feature of Hurd's approach was the concerted determination urgently to achieve results. At an unusual gathering of the full team of Home Office ministers, held at Leeds Castle on 28 September 1987, an explicit expansionist versus reductionist choice regarding the size of the prison population was presented by senior civil servants. (No account by any of the participants at the Leeds Castle Seminar has yet been published, but for a useful assessment of this and other meetings initiated by the Home Office, based on interviews with some of those present, see Lord Windlesham, *Responses to Crime Vol. 2*, Oxford University Press, 1993, pp 215 *et al*).

Ministers opted for the latter course and the chain of events from the Green Paper of June 1988 to the White Paper of February 1990 and leading to the Criminal Justice Act 1991 was set in place. In challenging the legitimacy of the use of prison for repeat property offenders, this scepticism about imprisonment was certainly not extended to serious violent and sexual offenders, and in due course the 1991 Act enabled sentencers to exceed the 'just deserts' ceiling in sending such persons to prison. The primary resolve was to reverse the inexorable climb in prison numbers that had dogged criminal policy throughout the post-war years.

A second and related theme was the special focus upon young persons. In particular, ways were sought to reduce the number of young adults (persons aged 17-21) held within prisons. In early 1988 Douglas Hurd, in a speech to magistrates, stated that the figure of 21 per cent of young adults sentenced to custody for indictable offences was too high (speech to the South East London Branch of the Magistrates' Association, 15 January 1988).

A few months later the Green Paper drew attention to the substantial fall in the number of juveniles receiving custodial sentences since 1981, adding that it was 'reasonable to look to a significant drop in the number of young adults sentenced to custody' (*Punishment, Custody and the Community*, Cm 424, 1988, p7).

Subsequently, considerable thought was given to how the probation service and other agencies might most urgently respond to this challenge via local 'Action Plans', but broader notions of taking action for disadvantaged youth depended upon a degree of inter-agency collaboration across central government which was to remain elusive.

The third theme was the articulation of a principled jurisprudence of sentencing. Although this issue was still handled with considerable sensitivity, there was, compared with a decade earlier, a more confident sense among ministers that progress could be made without unduly stepping on sensitive judicial toes. Far-reaching proposals, such as a sentencing commission, had been dismissed in favour of building upon the experience of the criteria for custodial sentences pioneered in relation to young offenders by the Criminal Justice Act 1982. It was decided that statutory criteria should apply regardless of age, and that sentencing decisions be shaped so as to ensure proportionality between seriousness of the instant offence and severity of the penalty. But this search for an explicit guiding principle ran counter to the pragmatic and eclectic British sentencing tradition and, almost certainly, contributed to the opposition by some judges to aspects of the 1991 Act.

It is necessary to add, in concluding this preliminary review of the political background to the CJA 91 that these policy initiatives by the Home Office were accompanied by extensive consultations, training exercises and 'special conferences' across the criminal justice process. Unprecedented efforts were made closely to consult senior members of the judiciary, although officials later appeared to regret that more could not be done during the actual drafting stage.

Other influences

Congruent to the Hurd vision was the far-reaching report of Lord Justice Woolf (as he then was) on the riots at Strangeways and other prisons which had occurred in April 1990, stressing the need for inter-agency consultative arrangements that actively recognised the interdependence of the criminal justice process (*Prison Disturbances April 1990*, Report of an Inquiry by Lord Justice Woolf and Judge Stephen Tumim, Cm 1456, 1991, pp260-264).

Further support, with particular reference to mentally disordered offenders, also came from the series of reports issued by the inter-departmental review chaired by Dr John Reed.

There were also some promising indicators of change at the level of practice. For example between March and September 1992 the prison population fell by almost 2,000 and then by a further 2,000 during October, the first month of the implementation of the CJA 91. It was a reasonable assumption that prison numbers would continue to decline as the use of community penalties expanded. During this period the Home Office also promoted other de-escalatory measures such as formal cautioning by the police and the provision of better information for the courts in making remand decisions.

However, when the main provisions of the Act came into force, the sky was by no means one of cloudless blue. It was with Kenneth Baker's arrival at the Home Office in November 1990 (succeeding David Waddington, who had stood by the Hurd vision) that signs of slippage were first apparent. Mr Baker offered an eager ear to the campaign mounted by some senior police officers for a more restrictive approach to the granting of bail, and his speeches gave a wide currency to the term 'bail bandit'. In response to media concentration on 'joy riding' episodes, he also rushed through the Aggravated Vehicle-Taking Act 1991. But it was the arrival of Kenneth Clarke at the Home Office in April 1992 that posed the first substantial threat to the reductionist agenda.

Kenneth Clarke pursued his predecessor's observation that additional institutional places were required for persistent juvenile offenders, and within a few months was promising that this was a gap which would be filled by additional sentencing powers. Initially, it appeared that he intended to reinvent the discarded and discredited approved schools, but any such notion soon gave way to proposals for a new form of centrally provided secure accomodation. In the midst of widespread public anxiety aroused by the murder of two year old James Bulger and the subsequent charges brought against two ten year old boys, Clarke scrapped a projected White Paper on young offenders and proceeded forthwith with legislative proposals for secure training orders (Statement on juvenile offending, House of Commons, 2 March 1993. The Bulger case was, of course, strictly speaking irrelevant to the issue of giving the courts additional custodial powers, as juveniles aged 10 or over found guilty of homicide could already be sentenced to detention at Her Majesty's pleasure).

This announcement carried a double-edged warning to adherents of the CJA 91 by focusing on young people and on the issue of persistent, as opposed to serious, offending. But Clarke had done nothing to disguise his lack of enthusiasm for the 1991 Act, and he had made a point of avoiding any personal association with its implementation. While Michael Jack, who had succeeded John Patten as Minister of State, was left to express any remaining ministerial support, Clarke's political office worked overtime to present the Home Secretary as the saviour of criminal policy from an ill-advised liberal course chartered by his predecessors.

The pace of events

Events now moved at an extraordinary pace. Speaking in Scotland the Lord Chief Justice, Lord Taylor, gave expression to the misgivings of many judges by deploring the 'ill-fitting straitjacket' which the Act had imposed upon sentencers, with s29 singled out for his deepest wrath (speech to the Law Society of Scotland, Gleneagles, 21 March 1993).

Kenneth Clarke responded by promising urgently to review the working of the Act. In the meantime the Magistrates' Association joined the fray with misgivings not only about s29 (admissibility of previous convictions and responses) but regarding the operation of the new system of unit fines (introduced into magistrates' courts but not Crown Courts and which had attracted a concerted and damaging media campaign and the well-publicised resignation of a few JPs). Clarke acted with extraordinary haste and announced on 13 May that he would amend the CJA 91 by introducing additional clauses to the Criminal Justice Bill of 1993 (which having started its life in the House of Lords was about to reach the Commons).

Under the Criminal Justice Act 1993, s29 was replaced so as to reinstate the importance of previous convictions or responses in relation to sentencing decisions (see *Chapter 4*) and unit fines were summarily dispatched to a footnote of British penal history. These provisions of the CJA 93 took effect on 16 August and 20 September 1993 respectively.

With the resignation of the Chancellor of the Exchequer, and his replacement by Kenneth Clarke, the Home Office found itself with its fourth Secretary of State since Douglas Hurd. But any hopes that Michael Howard might seek to restore the Hurd vision were quickly dashed. At the Conservative Party Conference in October 1993, Howard left no doubt that a complete policy U-turn was in the making. He told delegates: 'Let us be clear. Prison works. It ensures that we are protected from murderers, muggers and rapists—and it will make many who are tempted to commit crimes think twice' (speech to the Conservative Party Conference, Blackpool 6 October 1993). The Home Secretary's strong public advocacy of an increased use of imprisonment produced a strong contrary reaction from the judiciary exemplified in an *Observer* newspaper article citing the views of six senior judges.

This clarion call for expanding the prison system exemplified the stark and shrill note being struck by Home Office Ministers in relation to every stage of the criminal justice process from restricting cautioning decisions by the police, to tougher bail decision-making and to greater 'austerity' within prisons. Not surprisingly, the decline in prison numbers halted in January 1993 and, numbers grew by 5,024 (or 12 per cent) between February 1993 and February 1994.

Two policy turns
This chapter has considered two turns of criminal justice policy in England and Wales during the period 1987 to 1994. The first turn, described as Hurd's vision, sought a considered and rational way forward that placed greater emphasis upon a range of community penalties, thereby reducing resort to imprisonment for certain categories of offenders. As important as the details of the CJA 91 and other policy initiatives was the calming influence which government was able to bring to the mood and temper of the times—borrowing Winston Churchill's words from his famous speech on penal reform, House of Commons, 20 July 1910.

The CJA 93 enacted in July of that year replaced these and other aspects of the CJA 91 with provisions giving wide discretion to courts: see *Chapter 1(b)*, *ante*. The second turn, initiated by Kenneth Clarke and vigorously pursued by Michael Howard, sought to reverse much of the progress made.

As David Faulkner observed: 'The Government's change of direction in its policies on crime and criminal justice is probably the most sudden and the most radical which has ever taken place in this area of public policy' (*The Guardian* 11 November 1993).

Whilst it is premature fully to piece together the dynamics underlying this latest turn or to be certain where it will lead, a few preliminary observations are in order.

'Swarming circumstances'
There appear to be three significant 'swarming circumstances' (David Garland *Punishment and Modern Society* Oxford University Press, 1990, p285) associated with the new change of direction set for criminal policy in the early 1990s. Firstly, considerations of party politics played a crucial role. Within the Conservative Party there was growing unease that the Government had strayed too far from its traditional posture on crime and punishment. Certainly Mr Clarke and Mr Howard did nothing to quell such concerns. Public anxieties about crime were also seized upon by the Labour Party, adding to perceptions that the law and order issue was being stolen from the Tories. Certainly the ambiguities of Labour's position on the Government's legislative steps since 1993 served to put additional pressure upon Michael Howard to sound tough.

A second consideration arises from 'new managerialism' with its expectations of instrumental results for 'cost effective' (if not always 'market tested') criminal justice activities. It seems likely that the emerging ethos of pragmatic expediency works against principled endeavours such as the course set by Douglas Hurd and others in the late 1980s. Yet, ironically, the excessive use of custody is far from being cost effective and it can be argued that the Hurd approach, in addition to being more principled, was also more likely from a pragmatic standpoint to achieve beneficial results.

Finally, there are the individual and collective activities of practitioners, but here the terrain remains especially difficult to describe with precision. The two most influential groups, the police and the judiciary, might at first glance appear to have contributed to the new tough tone of criminal policy. However some senior judges, notably Lord Woolf and five others interviewed by the *Observer* newspaper, have publicly raised profound anxieties about contemporary developments. Furthermore, the police leadership is taking a cautious and considered approach, not least—at the time of writing—because of profound opposition to key elements of the Police and Magistrates' Courts Bill. Other practitioner groups, notably within the probation service, have actively lobbied to retain what is left of the Hurd vision.

The future in the hands of practitioners

As this volume goes to press, the transition of criminal justice during the early 1990s is not complete and its eventual outcome remains uncertain. Although for the immediate future the policy compass appears to be set, ultimately this may be largely rejected at the level of day-to-day practice. Perhaps, as never before, the shape and direction of criminal justice is very much in the hands of its practitioners.

Part II

Law and Practice

3 Sentencing Principles

As outlined in *Chapter 1*, the choice of penalty under the Criminal Justice Act 1991 is dictated primarily by the seriousness of the offence or—in the case violent or sexual offences only and in relation to custody only—by either the seriousness of the offence or the need to protect the public from serious harm from the offender.

Original purposes of the CJA 91

A key term used throughout the original version of the 1991 Act—and still used following the CJA 93 in relation to custody and community sentences—is 'commensurate'. Sentences should be commensurate with the seriousness of the current offence (or offences, *post*) of which the offender stands convicted. This focus on the current offence was reinforced under the original version of the CJA 91 by a rule that a court could only take into account a maximum of two associated offences when assessing whether the threshold for custody or a community sentence had been reached and the further rule that it could not take direct account of previous convictions—for which the offender would *ex hypothesi* already have suffered an appropriate penalty or remain subject thereto. Neither could responses to earlier sentences be taken into account, each sentence being seen, in effect, as a self-contained punishment. Failure to respond to a community sentence eg would be dealt with at the time of the failure by enforcement of that order—not by loading some future sentence.

Notwithstanding the abolition of the 'two offence rule' and the reversal of the rule concerning previous convictions and responses by the CJA 93 (as to which see *Chapter 1(c)*, *ante* and *Chapter 4, Section 29 CJA 91*), the seriousness of the current offence (or offences) remains the central and overriding focus for sentencing decisions. The principle is generally referred to as 'proportionality' in sentencing. The original Home Office *General Guide to the Criminal Justice Act 1991* (HMSO, 1990) stated:

> 'The severity of the sentence . . . should reflect primarily the seriousness of the offence which has been committed. Whilst factors such as preventing crime or the rehabilitation of the offender remain important functions of the criminal justice process as a whole, they should not lead to a heavier penalty in an individual case than that which is justified by the seriousness of the offence or the need to protect the public from serious harm.'

A significant tranche of early rulings of the Court of Appeal on key aspects of the CJA 91 served to cast doubt on whether the CJA 91 had resulted in any diminution in the importance of older common law sentencing considerations such as 'deterrence', 'retribution' and 'rehabilitation'. In particular, in *Cunningham* (1993) 14 Cr App R (S) 444, Lord Taylor LCJ, stated that a commensurate sentence means a sentence which is commensurate with the punishment and deterrence which the offence requires: see *Chapter 1(c), Judicial Guidance.*

The effect of the 1993 changes and the judicial rulings can be said to have altered the government's initial notions of proportionality to the extent that

• the interplay of a greater number of associated offences

• the possibility of relevant previous convictions or adverse responses, and

• a wider range of secondary sentencing considerations

affect the seriousness of the current offence in a given case. But it remains the case that it is wrong for a court to go above the seriousness ceiling of the current offence or offences, *semble,* or to sentence out af all proportion to the matter before the court—so that the principle of proportionality remains intact to this extent (*post* and see *Chapter 4*).

Protection of the public
The words in the foregoing extract from the Home Office *General Guide to the Criminal Justice Act 1991* '. . . a need to protect the public from serious harm' refer to a limited exception to the general rule of proportionality applicable only in the case of violent or sexual offences—and only to custodial sentences.

In such cases, the need to protect the public from serious harm from the offender overrides the basic rule that sentences should equate directly to seriousness. This aspect is unaffected by subsequent changes.

The White Paper, *Crime, Justice and Protecting the Public* drew a sharp distinction between offences against property and offences against the person for which special rules were considered to be in order. A court may thus pass a custodial sentence even where the seriousness of the offence might not, in itself, justify this, or pass a longer custodial sentence than is commensurate with the seriousness of the current offence where public safety so dictates. There are no statutory rules relating to associated offences or to previous convictions and responses when this sentencing limb is relied on. A court has complete discretion to take account of whatever relevant information is before the court in order to assess whether the test in s1(2)(b) CJA 91 is satisfied: see *Chapter 7.*

Protection of the public and non-custodial sentences
At first sight it might be considered that community sentences and financial penalties have no part to play in relation to offenders who represent a risk to the public. In relation to the dangerous offender, it is hard to imagine that any court would consciously allow an offender who represents such a risk to go unrestrained. However, in some circumstances the offender's willingness to co-operate with an appropriate community sentence can be seen as reducing the risk of serious harm: see *Powell* (1992) 13 Cr App R (S) 202, an indecent assault case, where the Crown Court made a probation order with a requirement that the

offender reside at a hostel which specialised in providing treatment for young men convicted of sexual assault; but considered that, when the offender had failed to co-operate with and had absconded from the hostel, custody was justified on resentencing for the original offence to protect the public from serious harm.

It should be noted that one of the statutory bases for using probation orders and combination orders is, *inter alia*, that such orders are desirable in the interests of '... protecting the public from harm from [the offender] or preventing the commission by [the offender] of further offences': s2(1)(b) PCCA 73 (as substituted by s8 CJA 91); and s11(2)(b) CJA 91. Clearly, what is intended here is protection from a lower level of risk than that already envisaged *supra* (the word 'harm' is used, not the words 'serious harm').

With community sentences, the aim is to achieve protection of the public over the longer term, through supervision, as opposed to immediate incarceration. The full criteria for probation orders and combination orders are contained in *Chapter 8*.

Philosophy behind the CJA 91

The first edition of this work commented that the philosophy behind the CJA 91 was a key to understanding the 1991 changes. That philosophy was not contained in the legislation—although it was discernible from it. As a result of widescale training and the apparent acceptance by practitioners of the emergent thinking, preparations seemed to be well advanced as at implementation of the Act in October 1992.

Quite apart from the the arguments contained in the White Paper, the Home Office *General Guide to the Criminal Justice Act 1991, supra*, distilled matters by stating that the Act '... is founded on the following basic principles' (comments in square brackets added):

(i) the severity of the sentence in an individual case should reflect primarily the seriousness of the offence which has been committed. Whilst factors such as preventing crime or the rehabilitation of the offender remain important functions of the criminal justice system as a whole, they should not lead to a heavier penalty in an individual case than that which is justified by the seriousness of the offence or the need to protect the public from serious harm from the offender ;

(ii) a sharper distinction than hitherto should be drawn between property offences and offences against the person—that is crimes of a sexual or violent nature. The Act recognises that additional restrictions may need to be placed on the liberty of a sexual or violent offender in order to protect the public from serious harm from the offender. [The corollary being that property crimes can be dealt with by lesser sentences than custody, either community sentences or fines. The 1991 Act reduced the maximum sentence for theft from 10 years to 7 years; that for 'non-domestic' burglary from 14 years to 10 years];

(iii) the procedures for administering sentences once they have been imposed should be rigorous and fair so as to ensure that the sentencer's intentions are properly reflected in the way in which the sentence is served;

(iv) community penalties should play a full part in their own right in the structure of penalties. They should not be viewed as 'alternatives to custody';

(v) the way in which young people are dealt with in the criminal justice system should more closely reflect their age and development, as should the extent to which their parents should be expected to take reponsibility for their actions [see *Chapter 10, The Youth Court In Outline*];

(vi) criminal justice services should be administered as efficiently as possible, and without discrimination on improper grounds, particularly those of race or sex [see *Chapter 6*].

Traces of the proportionate approach could be found before the CJA 91 in Court of Appeal rulings on sentencing, notably in relation to young offenders where seriousness was one of three statutory criteria for custody since 1982. The main effect of the CJA 91 was (subject to the protection of the public criteria, *supra*) to make sentences exclusively referable to the seriousness of the offence—or predominantly in the case of community sentences. However, the Court of Appeal has long recognized the relevance of other, secondary sentencing considerations and some of these have been renewed in rulings subsequent to that Act. In *The Structure of a Decision* (Judicial Studies Board, 1986) the Board advised courts that in looking to the object of a sentence they should consider the need to:

- Punish the offender
- Deter the offender
- Deter others
- Rehabilitate the offender
- Compensate the victim
- Protect the public
- Reflect public concern

Objects of sentencing examined

Judicial comment concerning the purpose of particular sentences is noted in *Chapter 1(c), Judicial Guidance, ante.* Certain general points can be made:

Punishment
The need for punishment was a feature of the White Paper, *Crime, Justice and Protecting the Public, supra,* with its 'just deserts' approach to sentencing. Commensurate sentences connote punishment geared to seriousness—but where the CJA 91 broke fresh ground was in firming up a hitherto somewhat loosely acknowledged principle that punishment should relate to the current offence, so that eg punishment should not be increased on account of previous offences. This can be described as punishment as a charge or levy for misbehaviour, or punishment pure and simple, over and done with once a sentence is completed. The punishment effect might be short lived in some instances, but geared closely to the offence.

This punitive effect could also be seen eg in changes under which probation orders became 'sentences of the court' (as opposed to 'welfare' based orders), in the idea that community orders involve 'restrictions on liberty', and under the fining provisions under which—for the first time—fines could be increased for the better off. This was highly visible under the unit fines provisions and continues, in muted form, following the CJA 93 amendments.

The above punishment approach remains valid and, indeed, has been expressly endorsed by the Court of Appeal in cases dealing with the nature of commensurate sentences: see *Chapter 1(c) Judicial Guidance, ante*. The White Paper spoke of the need for 'tougher' sentences in certain instances, principally in relation to offences against the person and this exists via the special protection of the public criteria.

Compensation

Compensation remains a central object of sentencing—enhanced by statutory provision and a climate in which the position of victims of crime has been high on the political agenda: see eg Home Office Circular 'Compensation in the Criminal Courts' (HOC 53/93) reproduced in *Chapter 9, post*. Compensation continues to take priority over a fine out of available income: s35 PCCA 1973 (although a specific reminder which existed in the unit fines provisions has been removed—presumably as being superflous to conventional 'cash' fines).

Deterrence

Deterrence and the prevalence of offences has been given a fresh lease of life by the Court of Appeal, both these items going to the seriousness of the offence: see *Chapter 1(c), Judicial Guidance*. In the White Paper, *Crime, Justice and Protecting the Public* it had been argued that the claims made for certain secondary sentencing aims were often not substantiated, or even discredited eg the available evidence suggested that deterrence of the individual offender or deterrence of others was only likely to work in certain unusual situations. Notwithstanding the Court of Appeal rulings on deterrence, it remains a fact that imposing a disproportionate sentence on someone in the hope of achieving deterrence may often fail to achieve its purpose, because many offenders do not 'weigh up the possibilities in advance so as to base their conduct on rational calculation' (White Paper, para 2.8).

Rehabilitation

Rehabilitation remains an object of sentencing—but this object presents analogous problems in terms of certainty of outcome. If rehabilitation can be achieved within a proportionate sentence, so much the better, but the effects of a sentence on an individual are often unpredictable. It is not legitimate within the framework of the CJA 91 to impose a custodial sentence, or a longer custodial sentence than would otherwise be appropriate, on the basis that this would rehabilitate the offender. However, in relation to community sentences, rehabilitation has a statutory role. It is one of the pre-requisites to the making of a probation order that supervision by a probation officer is 'desirable in the interests of— (a) securing the rehabilitation of the offender ...' (section 8(2)(a) Powers of Criminal Courts Act 1973, as amended by the CJA 91). The same is true of combination orders (section 11(2), *ibid*).

Protection of the public

Whilst this is an an object of sentencing, over two decades prior to the CJA 91 the Court of Appeal repeatedly emphasised the general rule that the danger posed by the offender to the community did not justify passing a sentence disproportionate to the offence for which it was imposed—although there were occasional decisions which are difficult to reconcile with this principle, for example *Kirk* (1989) 11 Cr App R (S) 453. The overwhelming majority of decisions reaffirmed the principle succinctly summarised by Lord Bridge in *Tolley* (1978) 68 Cr App R 323: 'The principle ... is clear, that punishment should fit the crime and the fact that an offender's mental condition makes it likely that he may, if at liberty, be a danger to himself and others does not justify the use of the penal system as a kind of long stop to make good the shortcomings of social services and the mental health system.' The same principle was stated as follows by Evans J in *Richardson* (1990) 12 Cr App R (S) 311: 'We were therefore addressed on the option of whether the appropriate sentence in the present case should be increased beyond what would otherwise be proper by reason of the need to provide for the future protection of the public. We are satisfied that the underlying principle is ... that the punishment shall fit the crime; that it is not proper to increase custodial sentences for reasons unconnected with the crime and which would be directed solely towards increasing the period of detention.' The only statutory exceptions to the principle that a disproportionate sentence of imprisonment could be imposed on grounds of dangerousness before the CJA 91 were where it was appropriate to use an extended sentence (abolished by s5(2)(a) CJA 91) or a life sentence.

Assuming that the former Court of Appeal rulings hold good, it follows that the 'protection of the public' ground for custody introduced by s1(2)(b) CJA 91—and the corresponding power to increase the length of a sentence on this ground: see s2(2) CJA 91—represent the only proper basis for departing from a commensurate sentence.

A definite meaning to sentences

Another aspect of the philosophy was that, under the CJA 91, sentences commensurate with seriousness, or imposed to protect the public, would be readily understood by both offenders and the public. The framework created the potential for sentences to become less disparate judged one against another. To ensure that the administration and carrying out of sentences is rigorous and fair, including proper enforcement, the 1991 Act introduced new powers under which, eg those failing to carry out community orders would, in most instances, be at risk of custody through resentencing (see, eg sched 2 CJA 91).

Custody was given more definite meaning via a new system of *Parole and Early Release, Chapter 13, post,* introduced by Part II of the Act. These provisions restructured the parole scheme, abolished remission on custodial sentences and introduced more definite rules for early release on licence of prisoners sentenced to below 12 months and to 12 months but below four years in prison. Many prisoners will serve longer in custody. They will also be liable to recall—ie they are 'at risk'—during the whole of the remainder of their sentence. Magistrates' courts were given power to fine released prisoners for breach of the conditions of their licence: s38(1) CJA 91; and to suspend the prisoner's licence and to order his or her recall to prison: s38(2). The Carlisle Report (*The Parole System in England and Wales: Report of the Review Committee*, 1988, Cm 532) on which the new provisions are based said its proposed scheme '... should provide the springboard for a thorough re-assessment of present sentencing levels. We therefore recommend that the implementation of our proposals should be accompanied by a determined attempt on the part of the government and the judiciary to secure a corresponding reduction in sentencing at all levels ... [We] are quite clear that it would be an unbalanced approach and add undesirably to the overall quantum of punishment to enhance the meaning of sentences in the way we propose without at the same time working for a reduction in present tariffs, which have evolved within a quite different framework': pp 72-73. Lord Taylor has responded with a corresponding Practice Statement: see *Chapter 13*.

Other steps towards giving sentences more definite meaning can be found in the National Standards for sentences supervised by the probation service introduced by the Home Office, the Department of Health and the Welsh Office. These operate alongside National Standards for 'pre-sentence reports', which *inter alia* require reports to include information relevant to seriousness and the protection of the public as well as the suitability of the offender for particular sentences: see *Chapter 12*.

Impact of the CJA 93 on the philosophy of the CJA 91
The CJA 91 adopted as its guiding principle the idea of proportionality in sentencing, 'just deserts' or deserved punishment. Proportionate sentences should be seen as fair by all concerned: they do not rely on some of the more doubtful claims about whether an offender might be reformed or whether other people in the community might be deterred.

Subsequent changes raise questions about the extent to which the philosophy behind the Act still holds good. The abolition of the 'two offence rule', the reversal of the rule against previous conviction and responses, the abolition of unit fines and the proposed diminution in the requirements affecting pre-sentence reports contained in the CJ and PO Bill of 1994 all have the capacity to impact on the proportionate approach. Properly understood and correctly applied, the changes do not undermine this—although much now rests on the a proper use of discretion, on good sentencing practice rather than legal prescription. Previous convictions eg will, as a result of the revised s29 CJA 91, need to be relevant to seriousness before they can be allowed any effect; it will similarly be wrong eg to make a community service order unless the restriction of liberty that this connotes is 'commensurate' with seriousness—and unwise to do so unless there is sound information before the court indicating that the order is suitable for the offender, *post*.

Certain extra-judicial comments of Lord Taylor LCJ, to the effect that the philosophy of the CJA 91 holds good are reproduced in *Chapter 1(c), ante* under the heading *Effect of the changes to s29*.

The Sentencing Framework

The CJA 91 introduced, for the first time, a comprehensive sentencing framework within which the criteria for different types of sentence bore similar characteristics. This framework continues, but is affected at several key points by the CJA 93.

Only discharges stand outside the framework as such. The CJA 91 made no substantive changes to the statutory provisions concerning absolute or conditional discharges—but sched 1 to the 1991 Act inserted new provisions in the PCCA 1973 to bring the relevant law in line with that in the remainder of the 1991 Act: see s1A to 1C PCCA 1973 reproduced in *Appendix I* to this work.

Fines

Under the original s18(2) CJA 91, the amount of a fine was the product of '... the number of units which is determined by the court to be commensurate with the seriousness of the offence or other offences associated with it' and the individual offender's own disposable weekly income. Proportionality in sentencing was highly visible and this was reinforced throughout the unit method: for a comprehensive treatment see *Introduction to the Criminal Justice Act 1991* (Waterside Press, 1992); and for the asssessment regulations see *Materials on the Criminal Justice Act 1991* (Waterside Press, 1993).

Unit fines were abolished and a new scheme of means related fines introduced by the CJA 93 (principally by way of a new s18 CJA 91). The 1993 provisions give increased scope for the use of discretion by courts—the statutory requirements in relation to the assessment of seriousness and the extent to which the offender's financial circumstances are taken into account being more flexible.

Under the present s18 fines must 'reflect' the seriousness of the current offence (or that offence plus 'one or more' offences associated with it). 'Reflect' seems to have less rigid connotations than 'commensurate'—but proportionality is substantially preserved. There was never a limit to the number of associated offences which could be taken into account when setting a fine.

The court must take into account the circumstances of the case including the 'financial circumstances' of the offender so far as known: s18(3) *ibid*. There is a duty to inquire into an offender's financial circumstances before setting the amount of the fine: s18(1) *ibid*. The terminology is now 'financial circumstances' as oppposed to 'means': see generally *Chapter 9, Fines and Compensation, post*.

A correct and full use of fines—being by far the most common disposal in magistrates' courts—is critical to the sentencing process as a whole. Work was undertaken by the Magistrates' Association in conjunction with representatives from the stipendiary bench and the Justices' Clerks' Society in producing, in the summer of 1993 and within a matter of weeks of the CJA 93 receiving Royal Assent, a revised version of the Association's *Sentencing Guidelines*. These contain guideline fines for many criminal offences and road traffic offences and 'entry points' of custody or community sentence for some more serious offences.

The guidelines are reproduced in *Appendix II, post*.

There is nothing to prevent a court operating a non-statutory unit fines system or a flexible 'unit approach' as an aid to decision making under the post-CJA 93 law. Such schemes continue to be commonplace.

Community sentences—the 'serious enough' test

The CJA 91 introduced 'community *sentences*'. These comprise one or more of a range of six 'community *orders*' (note the terminology indicated in italics). These orders can be used individually, or in combination (with one exception in relation to combination orders, *post*), and in conjunction with financial penalties. The main provisions are s6 to s13 CJA 91. The range of community orders, depending on age, is as follows:

> *Age 16 years upwards*: **probation**: s2, 3 PCCA 73, as substituted by s8, 9 CJA 91; **community service**: s14, 15 PCCA 73, as amended by s10 CJA 91; **combination order**: s11 CJA 91* ; **curfew order**: s12 CJA 91* (not yet in force). *Age 10 to 17 years inclusive*: **supervision order**: s7(7), s12 CYPA 1969 (largely unaffected by the CJA 91 except for new enforcement procedures and the fact that this new age range was introduced by s68 and sched 8 CJA 91). *Age 14 to 20 years inclusive*: **attendance centre order**: s17, 18 CJA 82, as amended by s67 CJA 91.

Orders introduced in 1991 are marked with an asterisk. A 'combination order' combines probation and community service (in consequence of which probation orders and community service orders cannot, themselves, be combined with one another: s6(3) CJA 91). According to the Home Office *General Guide to the Criminal Justice Act 1991, supra,* the combination order '... is aimed particularly at persistent property offenders, who might now be given custody'.

The other new order, the 'curfew', can be supplemented by a condition of electronic monitoring: s13 CJA 91. Community sentences are intended as restrictions on liberty, *post*. Whilst such sentences feature between financial penalties and custody in terms of their general severity, the individual community orders, or mix of orders, do not form any tariff or hierarchy. It can be argued that they overlap with fines and custody at the two ends of the seriousness scale. This is because where an offence is 'serious enough' to warrant a community sentence, this does not oblige the court to pass such a sentence if a fine reflecting the seriousness of the offence would be more appropriate; and when an offence is 'so serious' that only custody can be justified, a court could nevertheless decide to pass a community sentence because of mitigating factors relating to the offender under s28 CJA 91, *post*.

Under the original CJA 91 a community sentence could only be passed by a court where '. . . the offence or the offence and *one other* offence associated with it was serious enough to warrant such a sentence' (emphasis supplied), ie the so called 'two offence rule', *supra:* s6(1) CJA 91.

The only specific changes in relation to community sentences made by the CJA 93 are to s6(1) CJA 91 which now permits '. . . the offence and *one or more* offences associated with it' (emphasis supplied) to be taken into account when assessing seriousness and an analogous change to s6(2) CJA 91 under which the order or orders must now be the most suitable for the offender and the restrictions on liberty imposed on the offender by the particular order or orders must be '... commensurate with the seriousness of the offence or that offence and *one or more* offences associated with it ...' (emphasis supplied). This must be balanced with the suitability of the particular community order or orders for the offender.

The concept of 'restriction of liberty' is fundamental to the community sentence regime, as is the doctrine of 'suitability'. Both of these are variables according to the facts of the case and the individual offender—one consequence of which is the lack of any hierarchy or tariff already mentioned. Thus, eg a probation order with added conditions is not necessarily more, or less, onerous or intrusive as a sentence than a community service order or attendance at an attendance centre at a time which reduces the opportunity for leisure. It is the actual restrictions which must be commensurate with seriousness: the number of hours of community service, the extent of the requirements in a probation order, or the precise mix of different orders. Proportionality permitting, the total impact may be affected by the use of a fine or compensation in addition to a community sentence, as the law permits.

One attempt to deal with the variables involved in community sentences led to the issue of a joint paper by the Magistrates' Association, Justices' Clerks' Society and Association of Chief Officers of Probation, *Seriousness, Suitability and Restriction of Liberty* (Magistrates' Association, 1993) which is reproduced at the end of this work as *Appendix V*.

It can be objected that the lack of certainty concerning the weight of particular community sentences—exacerbated by the requirement to ensure that a particular community order is the most suitable for the offender—conflicts with the principle of proportionality. A similar difficulty arises in relation to probation orders and the probation aspect of combination orders in that further specific criteria relating to the use of these orders—rehabilitation, protection of the public or preventing offences—are in tension with the basic aim of a commensurate sentence: see generally *Chapter 8*. What must be borne in mind is that the starting point and primary consideration is the seriousness of the offence. Secondary sentencing considerations are common to all forms of sentence, *supra*: and see *Chapter 1(c) Judicial Guidance, ante*.

Custody—the 'so serious' test

Standard criteria were applied by the CJA 91 to custodial sentences, irrespective of the age of the offender or the legal power under which the sentence is passed. The main provisions are s1 to s5 CJA 91, discussed in *Chapter 7, Custody*. The use of custody depends on the seriousness of the offence or the need to protect the public from serious harm from the offender: s1(2)(a) and (b) CJA 91. Custody may also be used where the offender refuses to consent to a community sentence which requires that consent: s1(3) CJA 91.

'Custodial sentence' means: imprisonment where the offender is 21 years of age or over; or, if 15 to 20, detention in a young offender institution, or under s53 CYPA 1933, or custody for life under s8(2) CJA 82: s31(1) CJA 91. No restrictions attach where the sentence is 'fixed by law' (ie a life sentence for murder): s1(1) CJA 91. Partly suspended sentences were abolished by the CJA 91: see s5(2)(b) *ibid;* as were extended sentences of imprisonment: s5(2)(a). Ordinary suspended sentences of imprisonment continued: s22 PCCA 1973, as amended by s5(1) CJA 91, but with an enhanced test for their use, ie there must be 'exceptional circumstances': see *Chapter 7* and *Chapter 1(c), Judicial Guidance.* Suspended sentences are not available for offenders below the age of 21 years.

The approach adopted in the CJA 91 to custody mirrors that for community sentences—subject to a higher test of seriousness, the 'so serious' test. The CJA 93 amendments were, broadly speaking, analogous to those affecting community sentences.

Whereas under the original version of the 1991 Act the court could not pass a custodial sentence unless of opinion that '... the offence and *one other* offence associated with it ... was so serious that only such a sentence can be justified for the offence' (emphasis supplied): s1(2)(a)), the post-CJA 93 version of s1(2)(a) allows the offence and 'one or more' offences associated with it to be considered in determining whether the custody threshold has been reached.

Similarly, the length of a custody sentence must now be '... commensurate with the seriousness of the offence or the offence and *one or more* offences associated with it' (emphasis supplied): s2(2)(a) CJA 91 as amended by the CJA 93.

Mode of trial and committal for sentence

If a magistrates' court forms the opinion, after hearing a case, that a sentence beyond its own powers is necessary, it may commit to the Crown Court with a view to a greater sentence being imposed by that court. The committal must be on the basis of the seriousness of the offence (or the combined seriousness of that offence and one or more offences associated with it), or where the offence is a violent or sexual one *and the offender is aged 21 or over* (the CJ and PO Bill of 1994 removes this age limitation) on the basis that the court is satisfied that a sentence longer than it has the power to impose is necessary for the protection of the public from serious harm from the offender: s38 MCA 1980 (as initially substituted by s25 CJA 91 and replaced under the CJA 93): see *Chapter 7, Custody* and the references in this chapter to *National Mode of Trial Guidelines.*

Other considerations

The sentencing provisions depend on or are affected by a number of further considerations as follows:

Associated offences

Historically—in relation to the former s1(4A) CJA 82 as it applied to young offenders—appeal rulings clearly concluded that offences should be viewed individually, and without the flexibility even of a two offence rule: see eg *Hassan and Khan* (1989) 11 Cr App R (S) 148; *Roberts* (1987) 9 Cr App R (S); *Thompson* (1989) 11 Cr App (S) 245; *Davison* (1989) 11 Cr App R (S) 570. No aggregation was permitted. A rule had also developed under which, once seriousness was established, this inhibition was removed, at least so far as concurrent sentences for other offences (not necessarily meeting the seriousness criteria) were concerned: see eg *Pike* (1990) 12 Cr App R (S) 142; *Mussell and others* (1991) 12 Cr App R (S) 607. The CJA 91 thus broke new ground in introducing a 'two offence rule'. The CJA 93 abolished this limitation.

As already indicated, the relevant seriousness criteria now compel courts to view offences individually, but permit one or more associated offences to be placed into the balance.

This rule applies in relation to both the custody threshold and the community sentence threshold—and also to quantum, below. 'Associated offence' is defined in s31(2) CJA 91 as follows:

'(a) the offender is convicted of it in the proceedings in which he is convicted of the other offence, or (although convicted of it in earlier proceedings) is sentenced for it at the same time as he is sentenced for that offence; or (b) the offender admits the commission of it in proceedings in which he is sentenced for the other offence and requests the court to take it into consideration in sentencing him for that offence.': s31(2) CJA 91.

The same definition applies where any number of associated offences are taken into account in relation to the length of a custody sentence or to determine the precise restrictions on liberty in a community sentence. Note that the definition of associated offences includes offences taken into consideration.

'Other' offences

As already indicated, the basic rule is that other offences committed by the offender are not relevant when considering seriousness. This is subject to the following qualifications:

Seriousness based on several offences

For the purpose of deciding on the level of seriousness, the court is, in effect, constrained in taking account of other offences by the relevance of those other offences when viewed in combination with the current offence. In deciding whether the case is 'serious enough' to warrant a community sentence (s6(1) CJA 91) or whether a case is 'so serious' that only custody is justified (s1(2) CJA 91) a court is no longer limited by the former 'two offence rule', *supra*. But see the comments in *Chapter 1(b), Changes Made by the CJA 93*.

If a court decides that custody is justified, the length of sentence must—as a separate exercise—be determined by application of the same rule concerning multiple offences. Sentence length (or the restrictions of liberty contained in a community sentence) must be commensurate with the seriousness of the current offence and one or more offences associated with it. At this stage, the normal rules about consecutive and concurrent sentences apply. See also *Associated offences, post.*

The totality principle
Section 28 CJA 91 makes it clear that when a court passes consecutive or multiple sentences, the overall sentence should still be subject to the 'totality rule', ie not disproportionate to the inherent seriousness of the offences: see s28 CJA 91. For example, a person sentenced for several burglaries should not receive a total sentence more appropriate for armed robbery or attempted murder.

The offender's record
How does the offender's previous record fit with proportionality? The CJA 91 makes the seriousness of the offence the key issue. But the offender's record may have various effects. A poor record may aggravate the seriousness of the present offence: see *Chapter 4, Section 29 CJA 91.*

In that chapter it is argued that the present offence (or offences in combination) should act as a ceiling for the sentence within which the sentence may be increased—always provided that this is relevant to seriousness. Certain features of previous offences (or offences which the offender asks the court to take into consideration) may shed light on the seriousness of the present offence in some special way. For example, if a white defendant who is being sentenced for assaulting a black person already has previous convictions for criminal damage by spraying racist graffiti, this might justify the court in concluding that the present attack was racially motivated. A more serious view of the offence would be justified. Another example might be where other offences committed by a burglar indicate that the present offence is a professional rather than an opportunist one. In such cases the court must still sentence on the seriousness of the current offence but may take the previous conviction into account.

A good record may mitigate the final sentence, *post:* and see *Chapter 4.*

Aggravating and mitigating factors
In practice, courts must identify the *aggravating* and *mitigating* factors in each case. The court is required to consider '. . . all such information about the circumstances of an offence, including any aggravating or mitigating factors, as is available to it': s3(3) (custody), s7(1) (community sentences). This must include a pre-sentence report in certain prescribed circumstances: see *Information and Pre-Sentence Reports, post* and *Chapter 12* (but see the comments on the CJ and PO Bill of 1994 in that chapter).

The Magistrates' Association Sentencing Guidelines operate by the application of plus or minus factors which are applied to the norm or entry point contained in the guidelines. Judicial rulings reveal a host of individual factors which fall to be taken into account one way or the other: see *Chapter 1(c), Judicial Guidance.*

An important general provision is s28 CJA 91 which deals with mitigation, *post.* Mitigation may be on the basis of any matters which, in the opinion of the court, '... are relevant in mitigation of sentence'. This would include matters affecting the seriousness of the *offence* or matters relevant to the *offender*. The latter can always affect the final disposal. It is debatable whether personal considerations affecting the offender can affect the seriousness of the offence (cf *R v Doncaster Justices, ex p Boulding* (1991), *The Independent*, October 30). Initially, some commentators on the CJA 91 suggested that eg once the 'so serious' test in relation to custody in s1(2)(a) CJA 91 was satisfied the court would have no option but to sentence to custody. Section 28 counters this view as is now confirmed by legal authority: see the cases mentioned in Chapter 1(c), *Judicial Guidance* under the heading *'So serious' that only a non-custodial sentence can be justified.*

Mitigation generally

Section 28 CJA 91 states that courts may take account of any mitigating factors which they think relevant. The mitigation for a first offender obviously falls within this. The Act did not alter the time-honoured concession to first offenders. Conversely, the persistent offender can be sentenced more severely than the first offender—precisely because he or she has lost his or her mitigation for good character, but not more severely than is proportionate to the offence.

After assessing the seriousness of the offence, it is permissible for the court to move on and to consider any mitigating factors relating to the offender, for example his or her age, health, the fact that assistance was given to the police, or that some recompense has already been made to the victim. The court may not consider aggravating factors which are not relevant to the circumstances of the offence, whereas mitigating factors can be relevant to the offence or the offender: see *Chapter 1(c), Judicial Guidance.*

Section 28 is an aspect of the CJA 91 which appears to have attracted some misunderstanding. There is always power to reduce the sentence to correspond with circumstances which point to a lesser sentence. The provision is unaffected by later changes:

> '**28.**—(1) Nothing . . . shall prevent a court from mitigating an offender's sentence by taking into account any such matters as, in the opinion of the court, are relevant in mitigation of sentence.
> (2) Without prejudice to the generality of subsection (1) above, nothing . . . shall prevent a court—
> (a) from mitigating any penalty included in an offender's sentence by taking into account any other penalty included in that sentence; or
> (b) in a case of an offender who is convicted of one or more other offences, from mitigating his sentence by applying any rule of law as to the totality of sentences . . .'

The Court of Appeal has held that this extends to downgrading what might have been a custodial sentence to a community sentence: see the extract from the commentary on *Reynolds* [1993] Crim LR 467 mentioned in *Section (c) of Chapter 1, Judicial Guidance* under the heading *So serious that only custody can be justified.* Other cases on this aspect of sentencing are also mentioned in that section under the heading *Nature of section 28 mitigation.*

Mentally disordered offenders

In relation to mentally disordered offenders, s28(4) CJA 91 is quite specific as to the power to mitigate. The subsection provides that nothing shall be taken: '(a) as requiring a court to pass a custodial sentence, or any particular custodial sentence on a mentally disordered offender; or (b) as restricting any power (whether under the [Mental Health Act 1983] or otherwise) which enables a court to deal with such an offender in the manner it considers to be most appropriate in all the circumstances'.

Discount for a guilty plea

At common law an accused is entitled to a discount of up to one third of his or her sentence according to the time and the circumstances in which a guilty plea is entered in the case. The principle is scheduled to find statutory acknowledgement in the CJ and PO Bill of 1994 under which:

'(1) In determining what sentence to pass on an offender who has pleaded guilty to an offence in proceedings before that or another court a court shall take into account—
    (a) the stage in the proceedings for the offence at which the offender indicated his intention to plead guilty, and
    (b) the circumstances in which this indication was given.
(2) If, as a result of taking into account any matter referred to in subsection (1) above, the court imposes a punishment which is less severe than it would otherwise have done, it shall state in open court that it has done so.'

The provision leaves the amount of any discount as a matter for the court but requires the announcement, which would presumably become a feature of the vast majority of sentencing decisions, eg 'Fined £100 including discount for guilty plea'. The Magistrates' Association *Sentencing Guidelines, Appendix II, post* are based on a first time offender pleading not guilty and must be understood in the light of regular discounts.

Information and Pre-sentence Reports

The sentencing provisions are accompanied by procedural and other requirements requiring certain information to be taken into account before a sentence is passed. Thus, *inter alia*, courts have a duty to obtain a pre-sentence report in most cases before either a custodial sentence or most varieties of community order are used. *Pre-sentence Reports* are the subject matter of *Chapter 12*.

Proportionality in Practice

The process of decision making can be represented in three stages—first, to assess the seriousness of the type of offence in relation to offences generally; secondly to decide whether the offence is a more or less serious variety of the crime in question; and thirdly to transfer the decision on the relative seriousness of the offence to the statutory sentencing framework as outlined above.

Stage I: General levels of seriousness

The first stage is to assess the seriousness of the harm involved in the offence in relation to other offences—ie is pickpocketing more or less serious than shop thefts?; or reckless driving more or less serious than assault occasioning actual bodily harm?

These are questions at a general level. In *Stewart* (1987) 85 Cr App R 66, Lord Lane, Lord Chief Justice pointed the way by remarking that some offences are 'non-violent, non-sexual and non-frightening'. The White Paper drew a sharp distinction between violent offences and property offences which survived into the CJA 91 (as amended). As indicated *supra*, as an exception to the basic rule that sentences must be commensurate with seriousness, a custodial sentence for a sexual or violent offence can be used where the court is of opinion that 'only such a sentence would be adequate to protect the public from serious harm from the offender': s1(2)(b) CJA 91.

The Magistrates' Association *Sentencing Guidelines, supra,* contain instructions on 'How to assess the relative seriousness of each case; and how to arrive at a proportionate penalty'. A stated purpose of the guidelines is 'To improve consistency of approach in sentencing offenders aged 18 and over'. The introduction to the guidelines concludes with the point that '... the court must consider the proper exercise of its discretion in each case': see *Appendix II* to this work.

The *National Mode of Trial Guidelines* (Lord Chancellor's Department, 1989, 1993; also issued as *Practice Note (Mode of Trial Guidelines)* [1990] 1 WLR 1439, (1991) 92 Cr App R 142) indicate circumstances, largely seriousness based, in which magistrates should decline jurisdiction in favour of committal to the Crown Court for trial. These guidelines also emphasise the need for discretion in individual cases. The same stages of reasoning relevant to the sentencing decision are also relevant when a mode of trial determination is made. The magistrates' court must look at the relative seriousness of the offence in relation to its own sentencing powers and the greater sentencing powers of the Crown Court.

Both the *Sentencing Guidelines* and the *Mode of Trial Guidelines* treat offences at a general level, ie as theft, burglary, criminal damage. The former adopt the idea that there is a basic norm or an 'entry point' within the sentencing framework for an offence. This provisionally places it at a higher or lower level of seriousness than other criminal offences due to its general nature. Both sets of guidelines indicate in, broad terms, the situations in which a particular offence, eg assault, becomes more (and, in the case of the Magistrates' Association guidelines, less) serious of its kind.

Mode of trial decisions altered in line with the CJA 91 sentencing framework. The corresponding power to commit to the Crown Court, after conviction, for sentence is contained in s38 Magistrates' Courts Act 1980. Section 38 was amended by the CJA 91 to allow committal for sentence on the basis of either 'seriousness' in the case of offenders aged 18 or over, or either seriousness or the need to 'protect the public' from serious harm from the offender in the case of an offender aged 21. This provision was further revised by the CJA 93 in the light of the abolition of the 'two offence rule': see *Statutory Provisions, Appendix I, post*, and *Chapter 7, Custody;* and the CJ and PO Bill of 1994 removes the limitation to offenders aged 21 or over of the power to commit for sentence because of the need to protect the public from serious harm.

Initially it appeared that magistrates would be freer than they were before the 1991 Act to assume jurisdiction at a higher level of seriousness, or to risk the fact that a case might turn out to be more serious than first appeared once the full facts emerge, content in the knowledge that they now have power to commit for sentence to the Crown Court where their own powers (ie a maximum of six months' imprisonment or 12 months in the case of two either way offences) are insufficient. However, there are currently conflicting rulings of the higher courts on this point: see *Chapter 7*.

The mode of trial guidelines are reproduced in *Appendix IV*. They are largely 'seriousness' based, even in relation to sexual or violent offences. They are doubly useful in showing, in broad terms, those factors of particular offences which will make the case more or less serious, in whichever court the sentence is imposed. An example, indicating the circumstances in which magistrates should consider committing to the Crown Court for trial, reads as follows:

'THEFT AND FRAUD

1 Breach of trust by a person in a position of substantial authority, or in whom a high degree of trust is placed

2 Theft or fraud which has been committed or disguised in a sophisticated manner

3 Theft or fraud committed by an organised gang

4 The victim is particularly vulnerable to theft or fraud eg the elderly or infirm

5 The unrecovered property is of high value.'

Each page of the mode of trial guidelines carries the additional instruction: 'In general, cases should be tried summarily unless the court considers that one or more of the above features is present in the case and that its sentencing powers are insufficient'.

Stage II: Seriousness of individual offences

At the next stage the court is concerned with the precise, individual circumstances of the particular offence (or offences) before the court. Here, a court must decide whether the offence is a more or less serious variety of the crime in question. The court must look at the facts and identify any special features—any aggravating or mitigating factors in the offence which make it more or less serious than the norm.

Thus eg a relevant factor will be the defendant's culpability. Did he or she plan it, or was it impulsive? Was the offender provoked? Was the defendant affected by drink?

Stage III: Seriousness judged against the sentencing framework
The final stage is to transfer the decision on the relative seriousness of the offence to the sentencing framework as outlined above. Is the offence at a low level of seriousness, warranting only a financial penalty or even an absolute or conditional discharge? Or is it 'serious enough' to require a community sentence, or 'so serious' that even custody will need to be considered?

This is where the court's detailed assessment of the case will be crucial—not only in deciding what level to place it on, but also in determining the amount of a fine, the restrictions on liberty in a community order (in conjunction with the suitability of the particular community order or orders for the offender: *Chapter 8*), or the proper custodial term. The underlying and guiding principle through all these considerations is proportionality, *supra.*

Final adjustments
Once these three stages are complete, the court may need to make further adjustments to the penalty in the light of personal or other mitigation pursuant to s28 CJA 91, *supra,* to consider the overall effect of sentences passed at the same time so as to ensure that the total sentence is not out of all proportion and to give an appropriate discount for a timely guilty plea.

The process summarised

The sentencing process can be summarised in a sequence of questions which a court must ask itself in arriving to a decision. Where appropriate, this will be aided by a pre-sentence report: see *Chapter 12*:

- What is the general level of penalty for this kind of offence?

- How serious is this case compared with other offences of its type?

- What aggravating or mitigating factors apply to the case?

Seriousness and the sentencing framework
The progression through the sentencing framework, based on seriousness (proportionality) is then as follows

- In appropriate cases, the court should consider an absolute or conditional discharge or compensation order alone.

- Failing this, it should consider compensation and/or a fine. Preference must be given to compensation over a fine: s35 PCCA 73.

• If too serious for fining, a community sentence should then be considered.

• If 'serious enough' a community sentence is justified and it is then necessary to ask what restrictions on liberty are commensurate with the seriousness of the offence and which order or mix of orders is the most suitable for the offender.

• If the offence is too serious for a community sentence, ie 'so serious', then the court is directed towards custody

• If custody is justified, the court must decide how long the sentence should be.

• The court should then consider whether there are exceptional circumstances justifying suspension of the sentence (21 year olds and over: see *Chapter 7*)

• If a significantly greater punishment than six months is commensurate with seriousness, then the defendant should be committed to the Crown Court for sentence.

• Whatever the correct level of sentence as determined by the seriousness test the court may always mitigate the effects as discussed *supra*.

Reasons for Decisions

There are several other situations in which courts must announce reasons and make explanations. These are collated in *Chapter 4*.

Reasons must be given *inter alia* for custodial sentences. In the case of magistrates' courts (which are not courts of record) these must be entered in the court register and included in the warrant of commitment. Reasons are not required where the sentence is fixed by law (ie 'life' for murder). The rule is modified where the offender refuses consent to a community sentence requiring consent: see s1(3), (4) *ibid* and generally, *Chapter 4*.

With violent or sexual offences reasons must be given for the two separate aspects of the sentence. Reasons—which must be announced in open court and explained in 'ordinary language'—are required: (a) for using custody: s1(4) CJA 91; and (b) where a court passes a sentence which is *longer* than is commensurate with the seriousness of the offence: s2(3), *ibid*. As a matter of good practice, reasons for length of sentence should be recorded, albeit that there is no equivalent statutory duty in this regard (as there is in relation to the basic reasons for giving a custodial sentence).

4 Section 29 CJA 91

Section 29 CJA 91 governs the relevance *inter alia* of previous convictions and responses to previous sentences to the court's assessment of seriousness. This provision—rightly or wrongly—was at the very centre of public attention during the months following implementation of the Act. The principle of proportionality, so fundamental to the new sentencing framework, dictated a need to spell out that commensurate sentences meant that courts could not regard an offence as more serious because of the offender's previous convictions. But s29(2) provided a mechanism for courts which, correctly used and resourced, answered most of the criticisms levelled at the provision. What is more, the original version of s29 reflected the emerging jurisprudence—to which, ironically, it may be necessary to return following the changes contained in the CJA 93.

Previous Convictions at Common Law

Prior to the CJA 91, the general rule had been that, while previous convictions might reduce or eliminate the mitigation which could otherwise have reduced the proper sentence for the offence, a criminal record could not justify a more severe sentence disproportionate to the seriousness of the offence. An offender should not be 'sentenced for the offences which he has committed in the past and for which he has already been punished': *Queen* (1981) 3 Cr App R (S) 245. However, the Court of Appeal had also stated that an offender's record '. . . forms part of the matrix upon which he falls to be sentenced': *Bailey* (1988) 10 Cr App R (S) 231. In practice, the results of the latter principle had sometimes been difficult to distinguish from sentencing the offender on his or her record.

In several cases the Court of Appeal, even when reducing sentences after criticising judges for sentencing 'on the record', had nevertheless imposed penalties which still appeared disproportionate to the offences involved. For example, in *Galloway* (1979) 1 Cr App R (S) 311 the Court of Appeal reduced penalties imposed on an alcoholic who persistently shoplifted small items to consecutive sentences of 12 months, 12 months and six months (a total of two and a half years' imprisonment). In *Skidmore* (1983) 5 Cr App R (S) 17, sentences on a persistent offender for three offences of obtaining £20 by deception were reduced to a total of two years' imprisonment. In *Bailey, supra*, the Court of Appeal imposed reduced sentences on a persistent offender to 15 months' imprisonment for the shoplifting of nightdresses and three months' imprisonment for stealing cod fillets worth £12 from a hospital freezer.

It is difficult to envisage that these offences would have attracted custodial sentences at all in the absence of a persistent criminal record. A Home Office study of Crown Court sentencing found that in cases of theft of value under £200, 39 per cent of offenders received immediate prison sentences (*Sentencing Practice in the Crown Court*, Home Office Research Study No 103, 1988). In such cases imprisonment was in practice often a response to persistent minor offending in the past and could not be justified by the gravity of the offence for which the court was purporting to sentence. As the White Paper *Crime, Justice and Protecting the Public* (Cm 965, 1990), which led to the CJA 91, put matters:

> 'Injustice is more likely if courts do not focus on the seriousness of the offence before them when they sentence' (para. 2.19)

The sharper and more unambiguous focus on the seriousness of the current offence which the CJA 91 required was therefore welcome at that time. It became no longer possible for a court sentencing an offender to regard a previous record as 'part of the matrix upon which he falls to be sentenced' unless *either* it was a case of violent or sexual offending where custody could be justified 'to protect the public from serious harm' under section 1(2)(b) CJA 91 or it was a case where section 29(2) *post* could be applied.

The Original Version of s29

In its original form, s29 CJA 91 provided:

> '**29.**—(1) An offence shall not be regarded as more serious for the purpose of any provision of this Part by reason of any previous convictions of the offender or any failure of his to respond to previous sentences.
> (2) Where any aggravating factors of an offence are disclosed by the circumstances of other offences committed by the offender, nothing in this Part shall prevent the court from taking those factors into account for the purpose of forming an opinion as to the seriousness of the offence.'

This provision became the subject of extensive media comment and criticism. The provision is defended in the earlier books in this series and in the article 'In Defence of Section 29' by Paul Cavadino (156 JPN 470) reproduced in *Materials on the Criminal Justice Act 1991* (Waterside Press, 1992). That article points out that under the original s29 a court could not regard an offence as more serious eg simply because it was one of a series. Similarly a court could not regard an offence as more serious just because an offender had committed such an offence before (even many times before); but that—if the circumstances of other offences actually shed light on features of the current offence which made it more serious—a court could take this into account.

Even after the CJA 93, which reversed the effect of s29, it is not possible to by-pass some such reasoning process whereby the relevance of earlier offending to the sentence for the current offence is weighed. It remains to be seen whether the Court of Appeal, in interpreting the post-CJA 93 version of s29, will return to something approximating the old common law position, *supra*—or will hold that the position has changed. The latter seems unlikely, particularly as Lord Taylor, Lord Chief Justice, speaking extra-judicially, has stated that the earlier rules evolved by the Court of Appeal in this area remain valid: see *Chapter 1(c), Judicial Guidance, ante.* The CJA 93 allows previous convictions to be taken into account. It does not say what the effect of this may be. This remains a matter for the court—but Lord Taylor's remarks indicate that the court may legitimately take previous convictions into account only to the extent that the principles of 'progressive loss of mitigation' allow.

The practical effects
A practical effect of the original CJA 91 was that details of previous convictions needed to be made known to sentencers, but sentencers then had to be scrupulous in ensuring that such details were only taken into account in ways consistent with the Act's sentencing framework. Section 29(2) was permissive. It in no sense required courts to examine an offender's previous record, trawling for aggravating factors. Arguably, the subsection was designed to preserve the status quo. One reason for the demise of the original version was that the Crown Prosecution Service was unable to provide information on a regular basis concerning the circumstances of previous offences.

Section 29 CJA 91—The CJA 1993 Changes

Section 66 CJA 93 marks a U-turn in the treatment of previous convictions and responses to earlier sentences.

As already indicated, the first part of the original s29 stated that '... an offence shall not be regarded as more serious . . . by reason of any previous convictions of the offender'. This was represented by the media and also by some judges and magistrates as meaning that the law had been changed so that following the CJA 91 an offender's previous record was irrelevant to sentencing. Such contentions overlooked a number of matters all of which remain relevant following the amendments to s29 contained in the CJA 93. First, that interpretation overlooks s28(1) CJA 91 the effect of which is that a good previous record can mitigate. Second, Lord Taylor, Lord Chief Justice, stated in *Bexley* (1993) 14 Cr App R (S) that s29(1) embodied the common law principle 'that an offender who has been punished for offences committed in the past should not in effect be punished for them again when being sentenced for a fresh offence'. In fact, Lord Taylor stated that s29(1) went further: see *post*. Third, the original s29(2) CJA 91 permitted certain features of earlier offending to be taken into account. Properly construed, the original s29 was capable of meeting most of the objections put forward by its critics—but this is now history.

The new s29
The effect of s 66(6) CJA 93 is to substitute an entirely new s29 in the 1991 Act so that:

'. . . in considering the seriousness of the offence, the court may take into account any previous convictions of the offender . . . '.

It is debatable how far this alters the previous law. Even if the government's intention was that courts should be free to treat a bad record of previous convictions as an aggravating factor for sentencing purposes, that is not what these phrases in the new s29(1) actually say. (Government Ministers were in fact notably unforthcoming in Parliament in response to requests by the Opposition to clarify their intentions). The Court of Appeal has in many decisions stated that previous convictions should be taken into account: a good record mitigates, a repeat offender progressively loses mitigation, but the current offence should be regarded as setting a 'ceiling' beyond which the sentence cannot properly go: cf *Bexley, supra* and see D A Thomas, *Principles of Sentencing*, 2nd ed, 1979 at pp 41 to 44; M Wasik, *Emmins on Sentencing*, 2nd ed, 1993, at pp68 to 71. Lord Taylor CJ has also stated extra-judicially, since the CJA 93, that in his view these principles are preserved by the new s29(1): see *Chapter 1(b), ante.* One might therefore expect such an interpretation to be confirmed by the Court of Appeal in due course.

The old s29 had, in subsection (2), a limited form of 'escape clause' which allowed courts to take account of the 'circumstances' of previous offences where these revealed aggravating factors. This provision has been repealed (the new s29(2) deals with something else entirely, ie that where an offence is committed on bail this fact must be treated as an aggravating factor: see *Chapter 3*). The arrangements made to provide courts with details of previous offences left much to be desired (the Crown Prosecution Service faced a virtually impossible task in the absence of any information bank) and this may well have contributed to the demise of a provision that owed much to the concept of 'similar facts': see *DPP v Boardman* [1975] AC 421 and compare the examples given by Lord Taylor in *Bexley, supra.* The new s29 refers merely to 'previous convictions', but one would expect courts to consider any available information about their facts in order to assess their relevance.

The latest version of the Magistrates' Association *Sentencing Guidelines* (see *Appendix III* to this work) recommends '. . . that courts should clearly identify which convictions or failures are relevant for this purpose and then consider what the effect of such convictions or failures is in relation to seriousness.'

Somewhat oddly, there is now nothing in s29 to enable the court to take account of the circumstances of previous offences as opposed to the fact of a previous conviction. Section 3(3) CJA 91 still restricts courts, when determining the seriousness of an offence, to 'the circumstances of the offence' (ie the current offence). It directs courts not to consider 'information about the offender'. It can be argued that, almost perversely, details of previous convictions are inadmissible under s3(3), not being circumstances of the current offence. At the very least, s3(3) is now in tension with what would appear to be a straightforward interpretation of s29(1). Further, it can be argued that the circumstances in which the fact of previous conviction will be relevant is likely to be closely confined.

A new s29(4) inserted by s66(6) CJA 93 provides that a conviction in respect of which a probation order or conditional discharge was made before October 1992 (which would not otherwise be a conviction for the purposes of s29) is to be treated as a conviction for those purposes. The CJ and PO Bill of 1994 inserts a new s29(6) providing that a conviction in respect of which an absolute or conditional discharge order was made in or after October 1992 is to be treated as a conviction for those purposes.

Responses to previous sentences

The second change wrought by the new s29(1) concerns responses to previous sentences. The old s29(1) stated that an offence should not be regarded as more serious by reason of any failure of the offender to respond to previous sentences. The new s29(1), substituted by s66(6) CJA 93, provides that:

'. . . in considering the seriousness of an offence the court may take into account . . . any failure of [the offender] to respond to previous sentences.'

It is doubtful whether any court would be impressed by the logical argument that responses to previous sentences have nothing to do with the seriousness of the present offence—although it is, in fact, exceedingly difficult on a straightforward reading of the words of the subsection to see how they do—an argument which could be reinforced by reference to the distinction drawn in s3(3) CJA 1991 between the circumstances of this offence (admissible) and information about the offender (inadmissible). Whatever the niceties, Parliament clearly intended to reverse the effect and impact of the CJA 91.

The new s29(1) refers to 'responses to previous sentences': this implies that the offender must have been sentenced as least twice before: cf *R v Southwark Crown Court, ex p Ager* (1990) 12 Cr App R S 126. What counts as a 'sentence' for this purpose? The new s29(3) provides that a probation order or conditional discharge made before October 1992 (the commencement date of the CJA 91) is to be treated as a sentence. A probation order made since October 1992 clearly is a sentence: see s8 CJA 91. The CJ and PO Bill of 1994 inserts a new s29(5) providing that a conditional discharge made in or after October 1992 is also to be treated as a sentence for the purposes of s29.

However, the new s29(3) and the proposed s29(5) exclude absolute discharges and make no reference to the status of a compensation order made as the sole disposition on sentence: a point left open in *Ager, supra* and see generally concerning compensation *Chapter 9, post.*

What may be regarded as a 'response' to previous sentences? Two principal views have been advanced. The first and wider view is that any conduct following the imposition of the penalty may be regarded as a response. The second view is that only a breach of an existing sentence or the commission of a new offence during an existing sentence amount to responses. On the first view, not only is a breach of or failure in relation to a community order a 'response', but reconviction (and perhaps even other behaviour falling short of criminality or conviction) after the termination of such an order might also be such a 'response'. If the latter is indeed the true implication of the new s29(1), then the reference to 'response to previous sentences' may turn out to be of considerable importance in practice.

The practical effect can be illustrated by reference to *Bennett* [1994] Cr App R (S) 213. The offender was convicted of burglary, having broken into the house of someone who to his knowledge was away on holiday. He was apprehended before he stole anything. He had previous convictions for burglary and was subject to a probation order. In the Crown Court he was sentenced to six months detention for the burglary and, on revoking the probation order, to three months for the original offence. The Court of Appeal held that this particular house burglary was not so serious that only custody could be justified for it, and quashed the custodial sentences. The sentencer had wrongly referred to the offender's previous convictions and sentences when imposing custody.

Under the new s29(1), both these matters would become relevant to seriousness. Whether previous convictions for burglary would be sufficient to lift this non-frightening burglary over the custody threshold remains to be seen; if not, the 'failure to respond' to previous sentences, notably the commission of this offence during the currency of a probation order, might be regarded as sealing the offender's fate. A court would be free to take this into account, and it is possible that a custodial sentence could result. However, it seems likely that the Court of Appeal will reaffirm the principle that the facts of the present offence give rise to a 'ceiling' above which the sentence should not go—and the extra-judicial remarks of Lord Taylor, LCJ, cited in *Chapter 1(b) ante* indicate that the effect of both previous convictions and previous failures to respond must be seen as subject to this ceiling.

It is likely that the Crown Court will be dealing with more of these cases, since the basis on which a magistrates' court can commit for sentence under s38 Magistrates' Courts Act 1980 is unavoidably enlarged by the changes to the CJA 91 introduced by s66 CJA 93. *Any number* of associated offences can now be taken into account when assessing seriousness: s66(8) CJA 93 and see *Chapter 1, ante.*

In practice the notion of proportionality to the seriousness of the current offence, so fundamental to the scheme of the CJA 91, has been weakened. There is a risk that some courts may see the changes as an invitation to sentence 'on the record' without attention to the niceties and distinctions outlined above.

Use of the antecedent history
A suggested step by step procedure for the use of the antecedent history was incorporated in a *Justice of the Peace* editorial, 'Previous convictions', at 158 JPN 231.

Offending on bail
The new s29(2) concerns an entirely different matter. It takes the fact that an offence was committed whilst on bail for another charge and bases on this a requirement that '. . . the court shall treat the fact that it was committed in those circumstances as an aggravating factor.' There is no reference to considerations of relevance, comparative triviality or the like; parking on a yellow line whilst on bail for armed robbery appears to render the parking offence more serious. A government spokesman, however, gave a more flexible version of the purpose of the subsection: see *Chapter 1, ante.* The use of the mandatory word 'shall' in s29(2) CJA 93 seems to contradict the point made by Earl Ferrers, and it remains to be seen how far the courts will be able to exercise discretion in the application of the subsection.

5 Reasons for Decisions

Increasingly, courts are being required to give reasons for their decisions, particularly where these affect the liberty of the subject. This has been the case with magistrates' courts since the Bail Act 1976 imposed a duty to announce both the statutory ground for refusing bail *and* the reason in support. Another example—this time with victims of crime in mind—is s35 Powers of Criminal Courts Act 1973 (see *Chapter 9, post*) under which a magistrates' court must give reasons if it does not make a compensation order in circumstances where it has power to do so.

The Criminal Justice Act 1991 created several duties to give reasons and made the Crown Court subject to such duties for the first time. It is debatable whether the requirements go far enough. There seems to be no good reason why any restriction of liberty, not just custody, should not be explained in clear terms. Reason giving has a secondary effect over and above the process itself. It acts as a cross-check on the legality of a decision and ensures that the facts match and justify the conclusion. At various points the CJA 91 can be viewed as requiring greater openness in decision making. The sentencing framework encourages greater visibility of decision making in general—and the new parole and early release procedures in Part II CJA 91 are more open than hitherto (see *Chapter 12*).

Explanations in ordinary language
A formula has also emerged in modern Acts of Parliament under which—besides giving reasons proper—courts are required to explain their decisions 'in ordinary language'. This is again a feature of the CJA 91. It implies that there is a difference between legalistic compliance with the terms of a statute and the communication of a decision to an ordinary member of the public.

Situations where reasons or explanations are required
This chapter draws together the situations in which reasons or explanations must, as a matter of law, be given by courts under the terms of the CJA 91 (and associated provisions). The provisions are listed in the order in which they appear in statute. The statutory provisions are reproduced in full in *Appendix I* to this work.

Custody
When a court passes a custodial sentence, it is under a duty to state in *open court* that it is of opinion, either

- that the offence (or the combination of the offence and one or more offences associated with it) was *so serious* that only such a sentence can be justified; or
- in the case of a violent or sexual offence that only such a sentence would

be adequate to *protect the public* from serious harm from the offender; or
• that the offender has refused to consent to a community sentence which
requires that consent.

The court must also state 'why it is of that opinion': s1(4) CJA 1991. In
relation to the *seriousness* criterion, the explanation will, for example, need to
include some reference to previous convictions or responses where these have
been taken into account and particularly if these increase the seriousness of the
current offence pursuant to s29(1) CJA 91.

The requirement is modified where the offender refuses consent to a
community sentence which requires that consent and custody is imposed
pursuant to s1(3) CJA 91. The court may not be able to identify a statutory
ground for custody under s1(2) CJA 91, but there is a requirement to say why
custody has been imposed 'in any case' (ie because of the refusal, presumably).
The community sentences which require consent are identified in *Chapter 8*
(broadly speaking, all the adult forms of community sentence; but not
supervision orders, unless certain conditions are added, or attendance centre
orders: but see below).

Similarly, a modified form of reasons and an explanation will be needed
where a custodial sentence is imposed when an offender breaches a community
sentence and the court uses custody because he or she has 'wilfully and
persistently failed to comply' with the requirements of the particular order or
orders (a sentencing power which exists where the community order in question
required consent in the first place). The court may assume that the offender is
refusing consent to the order, the effect being to enable it to use custody under
s1(3), *supra*: see sched 2 CJA 91, para 3(2)(b) (magistrates' court), para 4(2)(b)
(Crown Court). (Attendance centre orders can result in a comparable resentencing
exercise due to a separate provision: see s18(5A) CJA 82 as inserted by s67(6)
CJA 91).

In all cases where reasons have to be given for custody, the court must go
on to explain to the offender in open court and in *ordinary language* why it is
passing a custodial sentence on him: s1(4)(b) CJA 91. Reasons are *not* required
(under this or the next following heading) where the sentence is fixed by law—ie
life imprisonment for murder (the original Bill exempted all offences triable only
on indictment but this was later amended): s1(1) CJA 91.

Subject to this exception, all the custodial sentencing provisions affecting
the giving of reasons apply to Crown Courts and magistrates' courts—the only
statutory distinction being a procedural one which requires magistrates' courts
(which unlike the Crown Court are not 'courts of record') to cause the reason
announced by the court to be entered in the court register and to be specified in
the warrant of commitment (ie the document addressed to the prison authorising
the carrying out of the sentence): s1(5), *ibid*. The provisions apply to all age
groups and all offenders.

Sentences longer than are commensurate with seriousness
Where a court passes a sentence in respect of a *violent* or *sexual* offence, under
the 'protection of the public' head and which is *longer* than is commensurate

114

with the seriousness of the offence and one or more offences associated with it, there is a duty to announce the reason for this in open court, and to explain the decision in ordinary language: s2(3) CJA 1991. There is no specific statutory duty to record this part of the reasons in the register, or warrant, although good practice dictates that the reason for the longer sentence should be written down. Possibly, it was envisaged that—due to its nature—the power is only likely to be exercised in the Crown Court: see, generally, *Chapter 3*. Where a longer sentence is imposed there are two sets of reasons to be announced and explained:

- the reason for imposing custody, ie the criterion, 'protection of the public', together with the explanation why the criterion is made out: s1(4) CJA 91, *supra*; and
- the reason why the court is imposing a sentence longer than is commensurate with the seriousness of the offence: s2(3) CJA 91.

Suspended sentences of imprisonment
Implicitly, reasons for custody must be given before a suspended sentence is used. Such a sentence can only be used *after* the court has concluded that custody is appropriate, ie that a criterion in s1(2)(a) or s1(2)(b) CJA 91 exists, or under s1(3), *ibid* (refusal of community sentence).

Section 5 CJA 91 inserted a new s22 PCCA 1973 which requires the court to be of opinion '... that the case is one in which a sentence of imprisonment would have been appropriate even without the power to suspend the sentence' (replacing a comparable provision). Under the CJA 91 there must be 'exceptional circumstances' to justify suspension: s22(2A): see *Chapters 1(c)* and *7*. The import of the suspended sentence must be explained to the offender in ordinary language, ie the offender's liability to the actual term of imprisonment fixed by the court (Crown Court: up to two years; magistrates' court: up to six months) if he or she commits another offence punishable by imprisonment during the 'operational period' of the suspension (one to two years): s22(4), *ibid*.

Probation order
The making of a probation order does not require the court to announce reasons in the strict sense, *supra*, but before such an order is made the effect of the order and the powers of the court on breach, and to review the order, must be explained to the offender 'in ordinary language': s2(3) PCCA 1973 (as substituted by s8 CJA 91). The same applies to combination orders (which are part probation order, part community service order: *Chapter 8*). Section 11(3) CJA 91 provides that the community service order and probation order provisions shall apply to the constituent parts of a combination order—the effect being that, procedurally speaking, each part of the order must be treated separately.

Curfew orders (not in force)
Section 12 CJA 91 requires the effect and import of a curfew order to be explained to the offender 'in ordinary language': s12(5) CJA 91. This would appear to extend to an explanation of electronic monitoring where used in

conjunction with a curfew.

Recall of long-term and life prisoners
Where a long term or life prisoner who has been released on licence is recalled to prison, s39(3) CJA 91 lays down a procedure whereby the prisoner may make written representations with respect to the recall. On return to prison, the prisoner must be informed of the reasons for the recall (ie those contained in the recommendation of the Parole Board: s39(1)) and the right to make representations. Whilst not a requirement of the CJA 91, open reporting and the giving of reasons are, where appropriate, features of the new scheme of parole and early release: see *Chapter 13, post.*

Parental bind-over
Where a youth court does not exercise its powers to bind over the parent or guardian of an offender below the age of 16 years the court must '... state in open court that it is not [satisfied, having regard to the circumstances of the case, that the exercise of the power to bind over the parent or guardian would be desirable in the interests of preventing the commission by the offender of further offences] and why it is not so satisfied': s58(1) CJA 91.

Note that *no* duty to bind over arises and *no* reasons are required where the offender is aged 16 or over, albeit the court has a discretion to bind over the parent or guardian: s58(1) and (2), *ibid.*

Detention at a police station
Where a custody officer authorises an arrested juvenile to be kept in police custody under s38(1) Police and Criminal Evidence Act 1984, the juvenile must be removed to local authority accommodation unless the custody officer certifies, for reasons stated in the certificate, that this is either impracticable or, where the arrested person has attained 15 years, that no secure accommodation is available and that other local authority accommodation would not be adequate to protect the public from serious harm from the juvenile: s38(6) and (6A) Police and Criminal Evidence Act 1984 as inserted by s59 CJA 91.

Remands of juveniles to prison or secure accommodation
Reasons and an explanation in ordinary language must be given for remands to local authority accommodation with a requirement of security: s23(6) CYPA 1969 (as inserted by s60 CJA 91); and an explanation in ordinary language where extra conditions are imposed on a remand without there being a condition of security: s23(8), *ibid.* The reasons must be entered in the court register and any warrant. Note that there will need to be cumulative reasons, ie for refusing bail *and* for relevant aspects of a remand to the local authority.

Conditional discharge
The duty to explain the effect of a conditional discharge to an offender before making such an order was re-enacted in the CJA 91 subject to a duty to explain 'in ordinary language' that if the offender commits another offence during the

period of the discharge he or she will be liable to be sentenced for the original offence: s1A(3) PCCA 73 (as inserted by sched 1 to the CJA 91): see *Appendix I, post.*

Compensation
Under s35(1) Powers of Criminal Courts Act 1973 magistrates' courts must give reasons for not awarding compensation in cases where they have power to make such an order. The original s18(7) CJA 91 explicitly protected the rule which requires preference to be given to compensation over a fine (see s35(4A) PCCA 73), so that it applied in relation to unit fines. No special statutory provision is contained in the post CJA 93 version of s18 and none would seem to be needed.

Supervision used as an alternative to custody
When a supervision order with a specified activities requirement is used as an alternative to a custodial sentence under s12D(1) Children and Young Persons Act 1969, the court must state that it is making the order instead of a custodial sentence; that it is satisfied that the offence (or the offence and one or more offences associated with it) was so serious that only such an order or a custodial sentence would be justified, or that only such an order or a custodial sentence would be adequate to protect the public from serious harm from the offender; and why it is so satisfied: s12D(1) CYPA 1969.

When the Crown Court makes such a statement, it must certify in the supervision order that it has made such a statement; and when a magistrates' court does so, it must certify in the supervision order that it has made such a statement and cause the statement to be entered in the court register: s12D(1A).

Secure training orders
The CJ and PO Bill of 1994 proposals in relation to secure training centres require a court to state that it is of opinion that the statutory conditions for such an order are made out. This is a somewhat muted requirement compared with that in relation to custody decisions, *supra*—but it should be borne in mind that reasons for imposing a custodial sentence will need to be given under the requirements of s1(4) CJA 91 already outlined. For the relevant details concerning secure training orders see the companion volume to this work *The Youth Court One Year Onwards.*

Discount for a guilty plea
Proposals in the CJ and PO Bill of 1994 concerning sentence discounts for pleas of guilty require a court—if it has imposed a less severe punishment as a result of its duty to take into account the time when and the circumstances in which a guilty plea was indicated by the offender—to 'state in open court that it has done so'. For the relevant provisions concerning discounts for guilty pleas see *Chapter 3, Sentencing Principles, ante.*

6 Avoiding Discrimination

Section 95 Criminal Justice Act 1991 states:

'95—. (1) The Secretary of State shall in each year publish such information as he considers expedient for the purpose of—
(a) enabling persons engaged in the administration of criminal justice to become aware of the financial implications of their decisions; or
(b) facilitating the performance by such persons of their duty to avoid discriminating against any persons on the ground of race or sex or any other improper ground.
(2) Publication under subsection (1) above shall be effected in such manner as the Secretary of State considers appropriate for the purpose of bringing the information to the attention of the persons concerned.'

This provision came into force in October 1991, ahead of the rest of the CJA 91. It should be noted that s95 goes beyond race: it explicitly includes sex discrimination whilst 'any other improper ground' would include eg discrimination on the grounds of religion, disability or sexual orientation.

Section 95 applies to all engaged in the criminal justice process, whether as judges, magistrates, administrators, police, Crown Prosecutors, probation officers, social workers and so on. The challenge is for those working within the system to make s95 a reality.

Publications
In pursuance of his statutory duty under s95 the Home Secretary published two booklets in September 1992, *Race and the Criminal Justice System* (Home Office, 1992) and *Gender and the Criminal Justice System* (Home Office, 1992). *Costs of the Criminal Justice System* (Home Office, 1992) was published in eight volumes in October 1992. All these booklets were distributed widely within the criminal justice system and copies of the first two booklets mentioned were sent to every member of the judiciary and every magistrate.

The Home Office also published a *Digest of Criminal Justice Information* (1991, Home Office Research and Statistics Department) of which some 30,000 copies were distributed. An updated version was issued in 1993.

Natural justice
The judicial oath and the rules of natural justice—which require courts to deal with people fairly, impartially and without bias—underpin the 'duty' in s95(1)(b) (see generally the commentary on natural justice in *Criminal Jurisdiction of Magistrates* by Brian Harris, ed Gibson, Kluwer, 11th Edn, p9). However, longstanding notions of treating people equally may, in a modern context, be more appropriately expressed as 'equal treatment' allowing for the differences between individuals.

118

The need for the provision

In the run up to the CJA 91 reports from organisations such as NACRO (*Black People and the Criminal Justice System*, 1986; *Race and Criminal Justice: A Way Forward*, 1989), the National Intermediate Treatment Federation (*Towards An Anti-racist Intermediate Treatment*,1985) and the Justices' Clerks' Society (*Dealing With Disadvantage*, 1989) and surveys by local probation services and social services departments focused attention on a developing cause for concern among the ethnic minority population in England and Wales: that there is a growing disparity in the proportions of black and white people in penal establishments; disproportionately high numbers of black people involved in the criminal justice process as defendants; and disproportionately small numbers as decision makers (judges, magistrates, Crown Prosecutors, probation officers and so on). During the House of Lords committee stage on the Bill on 21 March 1991, Lord Elton (a former Conservative Home Office Minister) said:

'I was a reluctant convert to the view that there appears to be an element of discrimination against ethnic minority offenders in our criminal processes. In his reply, I ask my noble friend to consider what are the social effects of that. The fabric of our society is only sustainable if the mass of society consents to the criteria on which justice is administered. If a particular discrete, identifiable and self-identifiable sector of that society believes that there is a system of justice which is just for other people but not just for them, whether or not that belief is well founded, the effects upon our society as a whole will be very damaging because those people will see the judicial system not as a means of maintaining law and order but as a means of keeping 'them' down and 'us' up. That is a recipe for internecine warfare and is very dangerous'.

To understand the strength of feeling among many members of ethnic minorities, it is necessary to appreciate the widespread and mounting concern about the disproportionate number of black people in the prison system. Since 1985, the Home Office has published figures showing the proportion of prisoners in each ethnic group. In 1992 the proportion of prisoners from racial minorities was 16 per cent compared with 12.5 per cent in 1985. Over the same period, the proportion of women prisoners from ethnic minorities rose from 17 per cent to 26 per cent. In contrast, 5.9 per cent of the population of England and Wales are from ethnic minorities.

The evidence contains disturbing indications that black people who commit offences are more likely to end up in prison than comparable white offenders: for example, Home Office statistics on the racial composition of the prison population show that black people entering prison have on average fewer previous convictions than white prisoners.

In 1991 the then available evidence from official statistics and research was summarised in *NACRO Briefing* No 77 *Race and Criminal Justice* (January 1991). The sources cited included a number of research studies indicating that young black men are more likely to be stopped by the police than young white men (a similar small proportion of stops leading to prosecution in each case); that young black people are less likely to be cautioned and more likely to be prosecuted than comparable white offenders; and that black defendants are more likely to be remanded in custody than white defendants. Such factors as differences in the seriousness of the alleged offences could not account for all the identified disparities.

The evidence from the studies on sentencing summarised in the same *NACRO Briefing* was contradictory. Some suggested that offenders were equally likely to receive custodial sentences whatever their ethnic origin. For example, the Home Office Research Study, *Sentencing Practice in the Crown Court* (No 103, Moxon, HMSO, 1988)—which examined the cases of 2077 offenders sentenced at 18 Crown Courts—found that differences in the use of custody between racial groups could apparently be accounted for by differences in their offences and criminal history. There was, however, a highly significant and disturbing difference in the extent to which social inquiry reports ('SIRs') were prepared on different ethnic groups.

Twenty-two per cent of white defendants had no SIR compared with 37 per cent of black and Asian defendants. Part of the reason for this difference stemmed from differences in relation to plea. Eighteen per cent of whites, 24 per cent of Asians and 29 per cent of black defendants pleaded 'not guilty' and reports were prepared in 51 per cent of contested cases compared with 82 per cent of guilty plea cases. However, substantial differences remained in the extent to which reports were provided for different racial groups *after* allowing for plea. For current practice see *Chapter 12, Pre-sentence Reports, post.*

Other studies had found that black people are sent to prison more often and with fewer previous convictions. For example, a study by Dr Barbara Hudson of the Middlesex probation service, published in 1989, surveyed sentencing in magistrates' courts and Crown Courts in eight Greater London boroughs (*Discrimination and Disparity: The Influence of Race on Sentencing*, New Community, Vol 16, No 1). The study was carried out over a three year period and covered 8,000 sentencing decisions. A significantly higher proportion of Afro-Caribbean offenders received custodial sentences than white offenders for common types of offence. For example, 50 per cent of white offenders and 75 per cent of Afro-Caribbean offenders convicted of assault causing actual bodily harm received custodial sentences. For burglary the proportions were 49 per cent and 64 per cent respectively. Factors related to the nature of offences and characteristics of offenders explained part of the difference, but some discriminatory effects remained after these were taken into account.

The Home Office booklet on race
The Home Office booklet *Race and Criminal Justice* (1992) said in part:

'At present there is only limited information available on any part of this subject. Research findings to date have been patchy in their coverage. Both statistics and research findings, however, provide evidence which supports the concerns which have been expressed about differential treatment of Afro-Caribbeans (that is, people of West Indian or African origin), although they do not at present show that there is any comparable cause for concern about the treatment of members of other ethnic groups. Nor should any differences which

120

appear to exist in the treatment of members of different ethnic groups be taken to demonstrate that improper discrimination has necessarily taken place: these differences need to be interpreted in the light of many different social and legal factors, including the pattern of offending by members of different ethnic groups. . .

—Afro-Caribbeans are significantly more likely than whites to be stopped by the police even when other relevant factors such as age and employment are taken into account (source: British Crime Survey, Skogan 1990). These differences may partly reflect variations in the extent to which 'stop' powers are used generally in different police areas.

—In London, arrest rates were proportionately higher for Afro-Caribbeans than for whites even when age was taken into account. For Asians there was little or no difference (Metropolitan Police figures for 1983 analysed in Home Office Statistical Bulletin (HOSB) 5/89 and in Walker 1988, 1989).

This finding was replicated in Leeds in 1987. However, the researchers found that in that city it was in areas with smaller ethnic minority populations that arrest rates for Afro-Caribbeans were proportionately higher. On the other hand, in areas where the ethnic minority populations were larger than average, white people were proportionately more likely to be arrested (source: Walker et al, 1990).

—Ethnic minorities are charged with different offences from whites and from each other (source: Prison Statistics published annually by HMSO and reported on in HOSB 17/86; Metropolitan Police figures: HOSB 5/89; 6/89, Walker, 1988, 1989).

This may reflect different patterns of offending but could also reflect differences in charging practices. . .

—Afro-Caribbeans are more likely than whites to be remanded in custody before trial. The proportion of male remand prisoners in 1990 who were of Afro-Caribbean origin (12 per cent) was greater than the proportion of sentenced prisoners (10 per cent). The type of offence with which they were charged only partly explains this difference; and a higher proportion of Afro-Caribbeans who have spent time in custody on remand were subsequently acquitted (sources: HOSB 17/86, HOSB 6/89. Walker, 1988, 1989). Analysis of data from one local area in 1984-85 found that magistrates were twice as likely to remand Afro-Caribbeans in custody as whites even when seriousness of offence and other relevant factors were taken into account. They were almost three times as likely to grant bail to Asians as to white people (source: Macleod, 1990).

—Afro-Caribbeans are more likely than whites to be tried at the Crown Court. This is partly because they are more likely to be charged with indictable-only offences. They are also more likely to be tried at the Crown Court in triable either-way cases. Afro-Caribbean defendants themselves are more likely to elect Crown Court trial. Local studies in Leeds showed that magistrates were also more likely to have declined jurisdiction in such cases. However, this may not be true of other areas (sources: Brown and Hullin, Jefferson et al, Shallice and Gordon).

—The Metropolitan Police data show that Afro-Caribbean and Asian males are more likely to be acquitted of the charges against them at both magistrates' courts and the Crown Court. In Leeds Crown Court, Afro-Caribbeans were again more likely to be acquitted than whites; but Asians were more likely to be found guilty. In London, Afro-Caribbeans were also more likely to have their cases withdrawn at magistrates' courts because of lack of evidence against them (sources: HOSB 6/89, Walker 1988, 1989, Walker et al, 1990). . .

'Between 1986 and 1990 the proportion of sentenced prisoners who came from ethnic minorities rose every year. However, it fell slightly in 1991. Afro-Caribbeans in particular are very heavily over represented in prison. In 1986 they made up 8 per cent of sentenced male prisoners and 12 per cent of sentenced female prisoners. By 1990 these figures had increased to 10 per cent for males and 24 per cent for females. This apparently dramatic rise for women may be accounted for by an increase in those convicted of drug smuggling, many of whom are foreign nationals.

—Several factors help to explain apparent differences in the use of custody and in sentence lengths for members of ethnic minority groups including offence, plea, court of trial (and of sentence) and previous convictions. It is also possible that these differences may be partly explained by general differences between areas in the use of custody rates. . .

'Specific research studies show that ethnic minorities are less likely to receive probation orders (sources: HOSB 6/89, Brown and Hullin, Mair, Moxon, Voakes and Fowler, Walker, 1989). In the case of Afro-Caribbeans this may be partly owing to the greater likelihood of their pleading 'not-guilty'. Until the Criminal Justice Act 1991, this meant that they were less likely to have been the subject of a social inquiry report. . .

'Once the courts have passed sentence, the prison service is responsible for the allocation of prisoners. Disproportionate numbers from the ethnic minorities serve their sentences in closed conditions: for instance 16 per cent of West Indian/African sentenced adults were in Category B closed training prisons compared with 11 per cent of all ethnic groups in 1990. Differences in categorisation in part reflect differences in offence type and sentence lengths.'

More recent studies

Research published in 1992 by Dr Roger Hood, Director of the Centre for Criminological Research at Oxford University, examined the sentences passed in 3,317 cases heard by the Crown Court in the West Midlands—at Dudley, Coventry, Birmingham, Warwick and Stafford during 1989. (*Race and Sentencing: A Study in the Crown Court*, Clarendon Press 1992; *A question of judgement: summary of 'Race and Sentencing'*, Commission for Racial Equality, 1992). Overall, black males were 17% more likely to receive a custodial sentence than white males. Even after controlling for 15 key variables relating to the seriousness of the offence and other legally relevant factors, Dr Hood found that black people had a five to eight per cent greater overall chance of going to prison. In cases of medium gravity, where judges had a greater discretion than in the most serious cases, the difference was 13%.

There were significant differences between the courts examined. In Dudley black offenders in the Crown Court had a 23% higher chance of receiving a custodial sentence than white offenders when the key variables had been allowed for; at Warwick and Stafford black people were also considerably more likely to receive a prison sentence; but at Birmingham Crown Court there was no significant difference between the various ethnic groups in relation to the likelihood of custody. The study estimated:

'Eighty per cent of the over-representation of black men in the prison population was due to the disproportionate number of them appearing before the Crown Courts (reflecting, of course, decisions made at all previous stages of the criminal justice process) and the seriousness of their cases. The remaining 20% ... could only be explained as a result of differential treatment by the courts and other factors influencing the use of custody and the severity of the sentences they received. One third of this "race effect" was due to the higher proportion sentenced to custody and two-thirds to the higher proportion of black offenders pleading not guilty and the longer prison terms they got as a result ... It would not need very many courts to behave as the Dudley courts and the courts at Warwick and Stafford appear to have done for it to have a considerable disproportionate effect on the racial composition of the prison population.'

The study also found that significantly higher proportions of black (42%) and Asian (43%) offenders were sentenced without a social inquiry report being available to the court, compared with 28% of white offenders. This was partly because more black and Asian defendants had indicated that they intended to plead not guilty; but even those pleading guilty were significantly less likely to have a report than white offenders.

There were also significant racial disparities in the distribution of non-custodial sentences. After taking account of the factors influencing the severity of the sentence, it was found that black adults were given sentences higher up the 'tariff' than whites, especially among those sentenced at the Dudley courts. They were more likely than whites to receive a suspended prison sentence; less likely to have been given a community service or probation order; less likely to be recommended for probation; and, even when recommended for probation, less likely to get it than white offenders. These differences were concentrated among cases in the medium risk of custody band. Among young offenders whose cases fell within this band, black offenders were more likely than whites to get a community service order or to be sent to an attendance centre, and less likely to be placed on probation. The study observed:

'The evidence supports the contention that black offenders receive sentences which are higher up the "tariff" of penalties than do whites and, therefore, put at more risk of getting a prison sentence should they re-appear on fresh charges.'

A higher proportion of black people (26%) than white (20%) had been refused bail. An analysis was undertaken to see if this was because the criteria used to decide between bail and custody had not been applied equally. It was estimated, after taking into account all the available relevant factors likely to lead to refusal of bail, that there was a 16% greater probability of black offenders being remanded in custody.

Also in 1992, the Commission for Racial Equality published a study entitled 'Cautions v Prosecutions' which examined cautioning and prosecution decisions in respect of juveniles in seven police force areas. This found that:

'In the majority of forces, proportionately more ethnic minority young people—and particularly Afro-Caribbeans—were referred for prosecution than white young people; in inner-city areas the difference was very substantial indeed. The widespread police view that such differentials would indicate that, on average, ethnic minority young people were committing more serious offences was not borne out. Statistical controls for 'offence-type' (such as burglary, robbery, etc) suggested that this factor played a very small part in explaining the differences in prosecution rates. Controls for the number of past offences also suggested that this was not the main explanation.'

One police force had analysed the number of cases in which young people admitted the offence and found that only half as many young Afro-Caribbeans admitted the offence as young whites—a relevant consideration as cautioning is precluded if the offence is not admitted (as is any discount for a guilty plea: see *Chapter 3, ante*).

A study by Imogen Brown and Roy Hullin, published in 1993, of contested bail applications coming before Leeds magistrates during a six month period during 1989 found no difference between the proportion of white and Afro-Caribbean defendants who were remanded in custody when the prosecution opposed bail. However, there was evidence to suggest that the Crown Prosecution Service opposed bail in a higher proportion of cases involving black defendants than white defendants. The authors commented:

'... if a larger proportion of ethnic minority defendants make bail applications which are opposed, and are thereafter remanded in custody by magistrates in the same proportion as white defendants, there will be an imbalance in the overall remand picture.' ('Contested Bail Applications: The Treatment of Ethnic Minority and White Offenders', [1993] Crim L R 107).

Finally, a paper prepared for the Royal Commission on Criminal Procedure by Marian Fitzgerald, *Ethnic Minorities and the Criminal Justice System* (HMSO, 1993), reviewed the key findings from research. She concluded:

'The research available addresses many of the concerns which have been raised by ethnic minorities about their experience of criminal justice. It does not do so definitively, however, and many gaps remain. Yet Hood adds weight to the evidence already accumulated which strongly suggests that, even where differences in social and legal factors are taken into account, there are ethnic differences in outcomes which can only be explained in terms of discrimination.'

Progress in implementing race policies
According to a report published by the National Association for the Care and Resettlement of Offenders, progress by criminal justice agencies in implementing race equality policies has been 'slow and patchy'. The report, 'Race Policies Into Action' (NACRO, 1992), examines how far the courts, the legal professions, the prison service and the probation service have put into

action policies to promote racial equality. It concludes:

'Although written equal opportunities policies have now been adopted by all the criminal justice agencies, far more still needs to be done to implement the statements made on paper, so that race equality becomes a reality in day-to-day practice.'

Nonetheless, a range of current initiatives taken by criminal justice agencies to promote equality in their operations were identified and commented on in the report, including:

• The Lord Chancellor's Department and the Home Office have issued guidance to courts, requiring them to develop policies and working practices to ensure equality of treatment for people of all races. The Judicial Studies Board has established an Ethnic Minorities Advisory Committee. Its chairman, Mr. Justice Brooke, has adopted a prominent role in speaking to judges and magistrates, and in the public arena, about the need to improve the way the courts deal with people from the ethnic minorities. (An extract from his address to the Justices' Clerks' Society in Cambridge in 1992 is reproduced in *Materials on the Criminal Justice Act 1991*, Waterside Press, 1992.)

• The Law Society and the Bar have established Race Relations Committees. The Law Society has a code of practice on racial discrimination governing service delivery, acceptance of instructions, instructions to barristers and employment matters. The Bar Council has adopted a detailed race equality policy, which it estimates should result in at least 5% of members of each chambers being drawn from ethnic minorities. In October 1992, *Bar News* (No 47) carried the announcement that two equal opportunities officers had been appointed, stating that: 'The equal apportunities officers will provide advice to chambers on good equal opportunities practice and on implementing the recommendations of the Bar's Race Equality Policy and the recently adopted Maternity Guidelines'.

• The professional organisations involved in the probation service have taken steps to promote racial equality in every aspect of the service's work, including the production of policy statements and practice guidance. Area probation services have produced equal opportunities policy statements, given special responsibility for race relations to staff members of chief officer grade, and introduced monitoring of the service's court reports and other areas of practice to ensure that they are non-discriminatory. Section 95 is also taken account of in *National standards, post*.

• The prison service has developed a particularly comprehensive race relations policy. In individual prisons race relations liaison officers have been appointed and race relations management teams established to implement the service's policies. A race relations manual was launched in 1991 setting out detailed policies on monitoring, access to facilities, work, education and training, allocation of accommodation, religion, diet, discipline matters, racially derogatory language, complaints of racial

125

discrimination, and contacts with ethnic minority organisations outside prison.

• The Justices' Clerks' Society has published a wide-ranging document designed to promote equality entitled *Dealing With Disadvantage* and set up a working group, 'Black People in Magistrates' Courts' which is due to report in September 1994.

Gender and criminal justice

The particularly high proportion of women prisoners from racial minorities (26 per cent in 1992 compared with 17 per cent in 1985) lends weight to a growing sense that the impact of decisions relating to women *in general* give cause for concern. The fact that fewer women are formally caught up in the criminal justice process has tended to lead to the relative invisibility of this aspect. While the available evidence does not show that women are systematically discriminated against in the criminal justice process—eg in Dr. Hood's study women were less likely to be sentenced to custody than men—the evidence indicates that the women who *are* imprisoned have often been harshly dealt with in comparison with equivalent male offenders.

Home Office figures show that 53 per cent of women in prison have two or fewer previous convictions compared with 23 per cent of male prisoners and that, overall, female prisoners have committed less serious offences than the male prison population. A report by HM Inspectorate of Probation, *Women Offenders and Probation Service Provision* (Home Office 1991), helped to indicate some of the reasons for these figures. Members of the Inspectorate team read a total of 303 SIRs on women in six prisons which they visited. These had been prepared by the probation service for sentencing courts. The Inspectorate said:

'In certain cases custody could be viewed as inevitable because of the nature of the offence, for instance serious violence and drug trafficking. In other instances such as persistent petty theft, small scale fraud, possession of drugs for personal use and minor assault, custody might not have been inevitable and it was therefore found useful to analyse the data in these cases, which constituted 174 (57 per cent) of the total sample of 303 ... the principal recommendations were for straight probation. Given that all these women were subsequently sent to prison ... it seems reasonable to ask why the options of a residence requirement (in a hostel) or schedule 11 4A and 4B were not brought to the attention of the courts more frequently or why courts had not asked about the availability and suitability of community service' (para 5.5).

On community service orders specifically, the Inspectorate said of the SIRs it had read: 'All the community service schemes seen during this inspection had at least a modicum of child minding provision and in some cases quite adequate facilities, yet a number of reports read in the six prisons referred ... to the unsuitability of a mother for community service. Reports on women who had subsequently been incarcerated had statements such as: 'The ages of her children mean she is not suitable for community service'; 'As a single parent with two small children she is not suitable for community service'; 'Community service, regrettably, is not a viable option in view of her responsibilities as a mother'. In all these cases the woman had been sent to prison and in some she was from an area which was known to have child minding facilities' (para 5.6).

Although 'some excellent SIRs were seen in prisons' (para 6.10), the Inspectorate's summary of its analysis of SIRs commented: 'Many SIRs lacked confidence and punch. Community service in particular seemed not to be in the consciousness of report writers as a disposal suitable for women. Probation orders without requirements and suspended prison sentences were the most frequently recommended disposals found in reports on imprisoned women. The sparsity of constructive recommendations to courts for community service, hostels and probation orders with schedule 11 4A and 4B requirements was of concern to Inspectors and to prison probation staff involved in the examination of the reports' (para 5.20). It seems clear, therefore, that many imprisoned women have not been seriously considered for community service orders, probation hostels or probation centre programmes, and are therefore failing to benefit from a number of community penalties which are widely used for men. It is a particularly disturbing irony that women may be considered less suitable for community service because they have to care for young children, and so end up in prison with devastating results for their children's welfare.

The probation service has taken these findings seriously and many probation areas have since been working hard to eliminate discriminatory approaches from their pre-sentence reports. Current probation policy, practice and initiatives were usefully summarised in *Provision for Women* by Marie Edmonds (Somerset Probation Service, November 1993), based on responses from 51 of the 55 probation areas in England and Wales.

The value of monitoring
It is important to see the role of monitoring as wider than that of avoiding discrimination. Monitoring and evaluation is an essential element in ensuring that the aims of any institution, agency or project are being achieved by its activities, and for identifying areas of concern and establishing future targets. The specific requirements of s95(1)(b) CJA 91 monitoring should thus not be seen as separate from such good practice. The real task is to monitor the experience of all people in the criminal justice process, deriving, as required, comparative data on the treatment of black people, women, people with disabilities and further groups which might be at a disadvantage in the absence of such interest.

In relation to race, the Metropolitan Police monitor arrests by ethnic group; many police forces monitor decisions to caution or to refer cases for prosecution; and the use of 'stop and search' powers has been monitored nationally since April 1993. A national system for race and ethnic monitoring was introduced in the probation service in October 1992 on the basis of a negotiated agreement with probation service organisations. It currently extends to pre-sentence reports, probation, community service and combination orders, through-care cases and bail information schemes. The prison service records the ethnic origin of all prisoners and publishes information regularly. While this represents considerable progress, there is still a long way to go before a comprehensive system of ethnic monitoring of decisions at all stages of the criminal justice system is in place.

Costs of criminal justice

Section 95 CJA 91 also obliges the Secretary of State to publish data concerning the financial implications of decisions taken within the criminal justice process: see the provisions of s95 at the start of this chapter. 'Costs and the Criminal Justice System 1991', Volume 1 (HMSO), published in October 1992 looks at the Crown Court in England and Wales in 1990-91. Volumes 2-8 examine magistrates' courts. The pubications give an indication *inter alia* of the average cost of imprisonment, community service and decisions to grant bail. Average sentence lengths for various crimes are broken down into regions.

7 Custodial Sentences

The CJA 91 sets out criteria and procedures for the use of custodial sentences. These provisions have their roots in s1(4) and (4A) CJA 82 (as amended by s123 CJA 88) which contained restrictions on custodial sentences for *young offenders*, ie those below 21 years of age. Subsections (4) and (4A) were repealed by s101(2) and sched 13 CJA 91.

Under the CJA 91, standard restrictions on custodial sentences apply to *all* offenders, regardless of age. Custodial sentencing must be considered within the framework created by Part I CJA 91—including in particular the strengthened regime and provisions for enforcement of *Community Sentences* (*Chapter 8*) and the 'continuum' created by Part II CJA 91 which deals with *Parole and Early Release of Prisoners* (*Chapter 13:* and see, in this context, the *Practice Statement* of Lord Taylor LCJ reproduced under the heading *Length of custodial sentence* in this chapter *post*).

It is fundamentally important in relation to custody sentences to bear in mind that two aspects fall to be considered, ie whether a custody threshold has been reached and, if so, how long the sentence should be—always assuming that there is no 'offender mitigation' (see s28 CJA 91) to downgrade the matter to one for which a community sentence can be used instead.

Sentences to which the criteria apply

The restrictions apply to all custody sentences regardless of the status of the offence or the place of trial, ie whether summary or indictable, and whether tried by magistrates or on indictment, except where the penalty is fixed by law (ie life imprisonment for murder. Thus, the criteria *do* apply to *discretionary* life sentences, whatever the offence): s1(1) CJA 91.

The term 'custodial sentence' is defined in s31 CJA 91:

- 'a sentence of imprisonment' in the case of a person aged 21 or over
- 'detention in a young offender institution' for people below 21
- Sentences 'under s53 CYPA 1933' imposed on juveniles convicted in the Crown Court of 'grave crimes'
- 'a sentence of custody for life under s8(2) [CJA 82]' (people aged 18 years of age and over only: see s63(5) CJA 91).

Under proposals contained in the CJ and PO Bill of 1994, a secure training order is specifically stated to be a 'custodial sentence' for the purpose of s1 to s4 CJA 91 thereby making that order subject to the general restrictions and procedures discussed in this chapter as well as those contained in the substantive provisions relating to that particular order: see *Chapter 10*.

Excluded from the definition are committals or attachment for contempt: s31(1) CJA 91, eg under the Contempt of Act 1981.

Three routes to custody

At the point of sentence there are three avenues to custody: two grounds—(i) the 'so serious' test in s1(2)(a) CJA 91 and (ii) the 'protection of the public from serious harm from the offender' test in s1(2)(b) CJA 91—and what amounts to a default provision contained in s1(3) CJA 91, ie that the offender has refused to consent to a community sentence which requires such consent.

Section 1(2) and s1(3) CJA 91 (as amended by the CJA 93) provide:

'**1.—** . . . (2) Subject to subsection (3) below, the court shall not pass a custodial sentence on the offender unless it is of the opinion—
(a) that the offence, or the combination of the offence and one or more offences associated with it, was so serious that only such a sentence can be justified for the offence; or
(b) where the offence is a violent or sexual offence, that only such a sentence would be adequate to protect the public from serious harm from him.
(3) Nothing in subsection (2) above shall prevent the court from passing a custodial sentence on the offender if he refuses to give his consent to a community sentence which is proposed by the court and requires that consent.'

At the enforcement stage—quite separate and apart from these 'primary' tests—custody is a possibility where an offender fails to comply with a community sentence: see *Breach of community sentence* (*Chapter 8*), fails to pay a fine: see *Fines and Compensation* (*Chapter 9*) or breaches his or her post custody licence: see *Parole and Early Release of Prisoners* (*Chapter 13*).

Seriousness of the offence

The first criterion prevents a court from passing a custodial sentence unless it is of the opinion that the offence itself (or one or more offences associated with it) is so serious that *only* custody can be justified (a variant, though seemingly a stricter test, than that in relation to young offenders under the repealed s1(4) and (4A) CJA 1982, ie 'so serious that a non-custodial sentence cannot be justified').

There is no absolute measure of seriousness, which is a question of fact in each case. However, the Court of Appeal has given a number of helpful pointers and this guidance summarised in *Chapter 1(c)*, *Judicial Guidance, ante*. Readers are also referred to the general comments on *Seriousness* in *Chapter 3, Sentencing Principles* and to the Magistrates' Association *Sentencing Guidelines* reproduced in *Appendix II post*.

Unless the penalty—from a 'commensurate' (or 'proportionate') standpoint—is beyond the scope of a community sentence then it is wrong to use custody under this particular head.

'Associated offence' is defined in s31(1) CJA 91: *see Statutory Provisions, Appendix I, post* and under the next heading *Offences in combination*.

In forming its opinion the court must take account of certain *Information, post*. The words '. . . *only* such a sentence can be justified' must be read in the light of s28(1) CJA 91 under which mitigation serves to downgrade what might have been a custody sentence to a community sentence in appropriate circumstances: see the cases cited under the heading *'So serious' that only custody can be justified* in *Chapter 1(c), Judicial Guidance, ante.*

Offences in combination

The seriousness criterion compels courts to view offences individually, but permits *one or more* other offences to be placed into the balance. There has been something of an unusual progression in this regard.

In relation to the former s1(4) and (4A) CJA 82 the appeal rulings clearly established that offences should be viewed individually, and without even the flexibility of a two offence rule: see eg *Hassan and Khan* (1989) 11 Cr App R (S) 148; *Davison* (1989) 11 Cr App R (S) 570. Then, under the original version of s1 CJA 91, seriousness had to be judged on the basis of a maximum of two associated offences. It is now open to a court to consider 'one or more'— in effect any number of offences—in combination, s66(1) CJA 93 having abrogated the 'two offence rule' in favour of that set out in s1(2)(a) CJA 91 *supra*. This is not to say that courts are obliged to aggravate seriousness *ad infinitum*. The better view is probably that associated offences should have only a marginal effect on the seriousness of each other, although everything will depend on the circumstances. The principles would appear to be not dissimilar to those in relation to *Previous convictions*, see *Chapter 4, ante*. A degree of relevance should be present. The totality principle also comes into play.

Section 31(2) defines 'associated offence' as follows:

'(a) the offender is convicted of it in the proceedings in which he is convicted of the other offence, or (although convicted of it in earlier proceedings) is sentenced for it at the same time as he is sentenced for that offence; or (b) the offender admits the commission of it in proceedings in which he is sentenced for the other offence and requests the court to take it into consideration in sentencing him for that offence.'

Broadly speaking, then, an associated offence is any offence for which the offender is being sentenced at the same time as the current offence (except for breaches of earlier orders): see *Chapter 1(c), Judicial Guidance*. The term specifically includes offences taken into consideration ('t.i.cs').

The provision in s1(2)(a) CJA 91 concerning 'one or more offences' (ie the custody threshold test) now equates with the test for the *Length of custodial sentences* in s2(2)(a) CJA 91 (see under that heading, *post*).

It has always been the case that *any number* of associated offences could be taken into account 'in combination' when considering the length of a custodial sentence as opposed to whether the custody threshold has been reached.

Previous convictions

Previous convictions can be taken into account in arriving at a decision on seriousness in accordance with s29(1) CJA 91: see *Chapter 4, ante*. Where the offence was committed on bail then this fact must be treated as an aggravating factor s29(2): but see the comments concerning this outwardly inflexible rule in *Chapter 1, Changes Made by the CJA 93*.

Protection of the public

The second criterion for a custodial sentence reflects the principle that a distinction should be drawn between offences against property and offences against the person: see *Chapter 3, Sentencing Principles*. It applies only to violent or sexual offences and only in relation to custody decisions (whereas 'commensurate' sentences are also a feature of the criteria for community sentences).

Section 1(2)(b) CJA 91 (which is unaffected by any subsequent changes) allows custody to be used if the court is of opinion:

'... where the offence is a violent or sexual offence, that only such a sentence would be adequate to protect the public from serious harm from [the offender]'.

It should be noted that the provision is directed towards public protection not punishment of the offender and that it is prospective in nature, ie any such sentence must contemplate future risk, not the the degree of harm caused by past behaviour (in contrast to the 'seriousness' limb, *supra*). That behaviour, however, may well be a reliable indicator of the extent of the risk to the public if a custody sentence is not used. Note also the use of the words 'serious harm' (a question of fact but defined in s31 CJA 91, see *Serious harm, post*) and that the protection criterion is aimed directly at the offender who is being sentenced through the fact of custody—ie using this criterion to justify a sentence designed to deter other people from offending would be improper.

Sentences for violent or sexual offences may be passed under either criterion.

Sexual or violent offences

'Sexual offence' and 'violent offence' are defined in s31(1) CJA 91. These key definitions are as follows:

violent offence—'... an offence which leads, or is intended or likely to lead, to a person's death or to physical injury to a person, and includes an offence which is required to be charged as arson [ie damage by fire: see s1(3) Criminal Damage Act 1971] (whether or not it would otherwise fall within this definition)';

sexual offence—'... an offence under the Sexual Offences Act 1956, the Indecency with Children Act 1960, the Sexual Offences Act 1967, section 54 of the Criminal Law Act 1977 or the Protection of Children Act 1978, other than— (a) an offence under section 12 or 13 of the Sexual Offences Act 1956 which would not be an offence but for section 2 of the Sexual Offences Act 1967; (b) an offence under section 30, 31 or 33 to 36 of the said Act of 1956; and (c) an offence under section 4 or 5 of the said Act of 1967'. Broadly speaking, the list includes most statutory sexual offences except those concerned with prostitution and certain consenting acts between homosexuals.

In *Robinson* (1993) 14 Cr App R (S) 448, the Court of Appeal was asked to rule on whether the offence of attempted rape was a 'sexual offence' or a 'violent offence' for the purposes of the Act. The Court said that section 31(1) of the CJA 91 defined the term by reference to a number of specific statutory provisions, including the Sexual Offences Act 1956. Attempted rape, like any other attempt, was charged as an offence contrary to the Criminal Attempts Act 1981; this statute was omitted from the statutory provisions included in the definition of a 'sexual offence' in the CJA 91. Section 57 of the Sexual Offences Act 1956 provided for the prosecution and punishment of rape and attempted rape as well as other sexual offences, and in sched 2 to the Act rape and attempted rape were listed together in the column marked 'offence'. The Court therefore concluded that attempted rape was an offence under the 1956 Act for the purpose of specifying the court's statutory powers of sentence. Although the offence was indicted under the Criminal Attempts 1981, it was properly regarded as an offence 'under' the Sexual Offences Act 1956. In those circumstances the Court had concluded that attempted rape came within the definition of 'sexual offence' for the purposes of the CJA 91.

The Court observed that the definition of 'violent offence' did not require that the physical injury should be serious. In the present case the victim was likely to suffer and did in fact suffer physical injury as a direct result of the offence of attempted rape, and it was therefore a 'violent offence' for the purpose of the CJA 91.

An article by Dr David Thomas in *Sentencing News*, Issue 1, January 26, 1993 commented:

'While this decision resolves the problem of the status of attempted rape, it has limitations—the reasoning of the Court is clearly applicable only to those attempts which are mentioned specifically in Schedule 2 to the Sexual Offences Act 1956 ... Schedule 2 specifically mentions attempted rape, attempted unlawful intercourse, attempting to procure a woman to have sexual intercourse by threats, attempted intercourse with a defective, attempted incest, attempting to cause prostitution and attempted procuration, but in relation to attempted buggery, only attempted buggery of a boy under 16, a woman or an animal is mentioned. It seems to follow that attempted buggery of a male over 16 is not a "sexual offence" for the purposes of CJA 1991, s31.'

The CJ and PO Bill of 1994 substitutes for the definition of a 'sexual offence' in s31(1) of the CJA 91 the following definition:

'(a) an offence under the Sexual Offences Act 1956, other than—
(i) an offence under section 12 or 13 of that Act which would not be an offence but for section 2 of the Sexual Offences Act 1967, or
(ii) an offence under section 30, 31 or 33 to 36 of that Act;
(b) an offence under section 128 of the Mental Health Act 1959;
(c) an offence under the Indecency with Children Act 1960;
(d) an offence under section 9 of the Theft Act 1968 of burglary with intent to commit rape;
(e) an offence under section 54 of the Criminal Law Act 1977;
(f) an offence under the Protection of Children Act 1978;
(g) an offence under section 1 of the Criminal Law Act 1977 of conspiracy to commit any of the offences in paragraphs (a) to (f) above;

(h) an offence under section 1 of the Criminal Attempts Act 1981 of attempting to commit any of those offences;

(i) an offence of inciting another to commit any of those offences.'

Serious harm

The meaning of 'protecting the public from *serious harm*' is defined in s31(3) CJA 91 as meaning: '... protecting members of the public from death or serious injury, whether physical or psychological, occasioned by further such offences committed by [the offender]'.

Application of the public protection criterion

Several points can be noted concerning the protection of the public criterion in s1(2)(b) CJA 91. First, as already indicated the provision is *prospective* in nature, looking to future risk. In contrast, s1(2)(a) CJA 91 requires a court to look to *past* conduct when viewing seriousness (there may be other, forward looking, *offender* based factors which affect the ultimate sentence, but the seriousness test itself concerns past behaviour).

It is *not* the present offence which must cause serious harm. An offender can receive a custodial sentence within s1(2)(b) notwithstanding that the present offence is neither serious enough to qualify for custody under s1(2)(a) nor one which causes serious harm itself. It is also implicit in s1(4)(a) CJA 91 (which requires a court to give *reasons* for a custodial sentence) that what may justify such a sentence is an amalgam of seriousness under s1(2)(a) and the need for protection under s1(2)(b).

The 'two offence rule' of the original s1(2)(a) CJA 91 in relation to seriousness never applied to s1(2)(b); or to s2(3), *ibid, post* (length of sentence). Neither did the original version of s29 CJA 91 (inadmissibility of previous convictions). This former distinction serves to indicate that the main purpose of the criterion was always to enable courts to pass custodial sentences on sexual or violent offenders who pose risks evidenced by a previous history of similar offences which indicates that they are a continuing danger to the public. The potential relevance of medical reports under s4 CJA 91 to this criterion cannot be overstated.

For cases on the use of this criterion, see *Chapter 1(c), Judicial Guidance.*

Refusal to accept a community sentence

The third basis for custody provided for in s1(3) CJA 91 is as follows:

'... Nothing ... shall prevent the court from passing a custodial sentence on the offender if he refuses to give his consent to a community sentence which is proposed by the court and requires that consent.'

This replaced the less direct power in s1(4A)(a) CJA 82 under which it was permissible to use custody where the offender '. . . has a history of failure to respond to non-custodial penalties and is unable or unwilling to respond to them'. The existence of s1(3) CJA 91 means that custodial sentences can, *ex hypothesi*, be used at a lower level of seriousness than is commensurate with

134

that of the offence under s1(2)(a), *ibid*, or where the need for public protection is not sufficiently high to justify the use of s1(2)(b), *ibid*.

This result is not automatic. It may be that another community sentence should be tried. On failure, without reasonable excuse, to comply with a community sentence which initially required consent, the court may not only re-sentence but '... may assume, in the case of an offender who has wilfully and persistently failed to comply ... that he has refused to give his consent to a community sentence which has been proposed by the court and requires that consent': sched 2 CJA 91, para 3(2)(b) (magistrates' court); para 4(2)(b) Crown Court. The effect is that s1(3) CJA 91 will then apply.

Length of custodial sentences

The statutory test for the *length* of a custodial sentence is contained in s2 CJA 91. The section provides that where a court passes a custodial sentence, other than one fixed by law (ie a mandatory life sentence):

'... the custodial sentence shall be—(a) for such term (not exceeding the permitted maximum) as in the opinion of the court is commensurate with the seriousness of the offence, or the combination of the offence and one or more offences associated with it; or (b) where the offence is a violent or sexual offence, for such longer term (not exceeding the permitted maximum) as in the opinion of the court is necessary to protect the public from serious harm from the offender': s2(1), (2) CJA 92.

Concerning sentence length, the Carlisle Committee indicated that some downwards re-appraisal would be necessary in the light of what are now the *Parole and Early Release* provisions of Part II CJA 1991: see *Chapter 13*. This was confirmed on 1 October 1992 (the day on which the sentencing and early release provisions of the Criminal Justice Act 1991 were implemented), by the Lord Chief Justice, Lord Taylor of Gosforth PC, who issued a *Practice Statement* concerning the relevance to sentencing decisions of the new rules governing early release.

The statement said (in part):

'Where the sentence of the court is less than four years the Secretary of State will be under a duty to release the prisoner after he has served one half of his sentence. Thus, where the sentence is three years, 18 months will be served. This is significantly longer than would normally have been served before the new provisions came into force. Furthermore, on release the prisoner will in effect be subject to a continuing suspended sentence. If between his release and the end of the period covered by the original sentence, he commits any offence punishable by imprisonment, he will be liable to serve the balance of the original sentence outstanding at the date of the fresh offence.

'For determinate sentences of four years or longer the Secretary of State will have a continuing but reduced element of discretion on release. Prisoners will be released on licence after serving two thirds of the sentence. Whereas hitherto they became eligible for parole after serving one third of the sentence, they will

135

not now become eligible until they have served half. The "at risk" provisions following release will be the same for long term as for short term prisoners.

'It is therefore vital for all sentencers in the Crown Court to realise that sentences on the "old" scale would under the "new" Act result in many prisoners actually serving longer in custody than hitherto.

'It has been an axiomatic principle of sentencing policy until now that the court should decide the appropriate sentence in each case without reference to questions of remission or parole. I have consulted the Lords Justices presiding in the Court of Appeal Criminal Division and we have decided that a new approach is essential.

'Accordingly, from October 1, 1992, it will be necessary, when passing a custodial sentence in the Crown Court, to have regard to the actual period likely to be served, and as far as practicable to the risk of offenders serving substantially longer under the new regime than would have been normal under the old. Existing guideline judgements should be applied with these considerations in mind.

'I stress however that, having taken the above considerations into account, sentencers must, of course, exercise their individual judgement as to the appropriate sentence to be passed and nothing in this statement is intended to restrict that independence.'

In *Cunningham* (1993) 14 Cr App R (S) 444 Lord Taylor LCJ said:

'The Practice Direction does not require an arithmetically precise calculation to be made. Its object was to give general guidance by alerting sentencers to the changed regime of early release and requiring them to have regard to the possible effects of passing sentences after October 1992 of the same length as those they would have passed before.... It should be stressed that where the the length of a custodial sentence is challenged, this Court will be concerned as to whether the term is appropriate under the criteria of the 1991 Act. It is unlikely to be moved by nice arithmetical comparisons between periods under the old and new regimes.'

Committal for sentence

The mode of trial provisions contained in the s19 *et al* Magistrates' Courts Act 1980 and associated provisions were amended by sched 8 CJA 91 so that they apply only to persons aged *18 and over*.

The power of magistrates to commit to the Crown Court for sentence was similarly altered by means of a substituted s38 MCA 1980 which expressly refers to 'persons not less than 18 years old': see s25 CJA 91. Section 38(1) MCA 1980 (as amended by the CJA 93) provides:

'**38.**—(1) This section applies where on the summary trial of an offence triable either way . . . a person who is not less than 18 is convicted of the offence.
(2) If the court is of opinion—

136

(a) that the offence or the combination of the offence and one or more offences associated with it was so serious that greater punishment should be inflicted for the offence than the court has power to impose; or

(b) in the case of a violent or sexual offence committed by a person who is not less than 21 years old, that a sentence of imprisonment for a term longer than the court has power to impose is necessary to protect the public from serious harm from him,

the court may, in accordance with section 56 of the Criminal Justice Act 1967, commit the offender in custody or on bail to the Crown Court for sentence in accordance with the provisions of section 42 of the Powers of Criminal Courts Act 1973.'

Where, in the case of an either way offence dealt with summarily, it transpires that an offence, or the combination of the offence and one or more offences associated with it, is more serious than is commensurate with the six months' imprisonment which magistrates have power to impose (12 months where there are two or more either way offences), they may thus commit to the Crown Court for sentence: s38(2)(a) *supra*.

Offences taken into consideration ('t.i.c.') are 'associated offences' (s31(2) CJA 91) and may thus justify committal for sentence, as was the case before the CJA 91: cf, eg *Vallet* [1951] 1 All ER 231 (albeit that the emphasis has shifted to the effect that such offences have when the statutory seriousness formula in s1(2)(a) CJA 91 is applied to a given case). 'Character and antecedents' as such ceased to be a basis for committal under the CJA 91 but previous convictions may now affect seriousness: s29(1) CJA 91. It could be argued that seriousness and character overlapped to some extent for the purposes of committal for sentence under the pre-CJA 91 law—close to which the CJA 93 amendments may well, in overall effect, have returned matters: cf *R v Doncaster Justices, ex p Goulding* (1991), *The Independent*, October 30; 156 JP 681 (discussed at 155 JPN 745).

The power to commit for sentence can also be exercised where there is a need for the public to be protected from serious harm from the offender for longer than six months, but only, in this instance, where the offender is *21 years of age or over*: s38(2)(b) MCA 1980, as substituted. (The CJ and PO Bill of 1994 removes the limitation to those aged 21).

Mode of trial decisions, ie decisions by magistrates as to whether summary trial or trial in the Crown Court is more appropriate, are unavoidably affected by s38. However, conflicting rulings of the Divisional Court indicate how fraught with difficulty this area of the law can become in its practical application. In *R v Manchester City Magistrates' Court, ex p Kaymanesh* (1994), *The Times*, March 3 (Balcombe LJ and Schieman J), it was held that when justices are considering whether to commit to the Crown Court for sentence it remains the position, post-CJA 91, that they should normally only use their powers under s38 where new material has come to light since the time of the original mode of trial decision—ie magistrates must be careful to give full attention to any seriousness factors affecting mode of trial at the time of the decision whether or not to assume summary jurisdiction (as to which see the *National Mode of*

137

Trial Guidelines, reproduced in *Appendix IV* to this work). However, a differently constituted court held that the decision to accept jurisdiction and the decision to commit were 'different stages' so that there is nothing illogical in a court forming different views of seriousness at each stage: *R v Dover Justices, ex p Pamment* (1994), *The Times*, March 3 (Kennedy LJ and Scott Baker J) and see the *Sheffield* case mentioned *post* where the court (constituted of the same judges) reached an identical conclusion. Notwithstanding, magistrates' courts should 'think carefully' before accepting jurisdiction: *ibid*. Whilst the *Manchester case, supra*, is more in keeping with the position historically, it may well take a ruling of the House of Lords to resolve matters. (On this point see also the article 'Considering Whether to Commit for Sentence' at 158 JPN 265).

Once magistrates have committed for sentence, the Crown Court has no power to remit the case back to the magistrates' court except where the committal is bad on its face: *R v Sheffield Crown Court, ex p DPP* (1994), *The Times*, March 3.

Corporations can be committed for sentence (though obviously not for custodial sentences). Schedule 3 MCA 1980, para 5, which previously prevented this, was abolished by s25(2) CJA 91.

Information and procedures
The court is required to consider certain matters before reaching a decision about custody or the length of custody. These are:

'... (a) all such information about the circumstances of the *offence* (including any *aggravating* or *mitigating* factors) as is available to it ... and (b) ... [in relation to the protection of the public criterion *only*] may take into account any information about the *offender* which is before it': s3(3) CJA 91 (italics supplied).

So far as the facts of cases are concerned, much will depend on what information the Crown Prosecution Service (or other prosecutor) places before the court, also defence advocates and other agencies (see eg *Pre-sentence reports, post*). Aggravating and mitigating factors—including s28 CJA 91 mitigation are discussed in *Chapter 3, General Principles*.

Pre-sentence reports
The legal position and the practice in relation to *Pre-sentence Reports* is discussed in *Chapter 13*. Pre-sentence reports have a key role in the information gathering and sentencing process. Certain provisions of the CJA 91 apply specifically to custodial sentences. Thus *before* any decision can be taken as to whether either of the criteria for custody in s1(2) CJA 91 is made out or on the length of a custodial sentence under s2(2) CJA 91 the court must obtain and consider a pre-sentence report: s3(1) CJA 91—except where the offence or any other offence associated with it is triable *only on indictment* and provided that, in the circumstances, the court is of the opinion that a pre-sentence report is unnecessary: s3(2).

The exception applies in relation to offences triable only on indictment, a restricted category of very serious matters where custody must normally be a reasonable presumption. There is nothing to prevent a report in such cases. The Crown Court *is* under a duty to obtain reports in relation to other custody sentences: s3(2), *supra*; and on an appeal against a custodial sentence: s3(4) CJA 91.

The court's duty to obtain a report '. . . *before* forming any such opinion' as is contained in s3(1), *supra*, emphasises that there should be no provisional decision making ahead of the report being received. The timely production of reports and a preparedness on the part of courts to indicate factors which are likely to be relevant to the particular sentencing decision, albeit that this may need to be in broad terms, can do much to assist preparation of an effective PSR.

The PSR regime—including the national standard for PSRs—is set out in *Chapter 12*.

No custodial sentence is invalidated by the failure of a court to obtain a pre-sentence report, although any court on an appeal against such a sentence must obtain and consider a report if none was obtained by the court below: s3(4) CJA 91; similarly the appeal court must consider any reports which *were* obtained originally: *ibid*. A 'pre-sentence' report is defined in s 3(5) as a report *in writing* which:

'... (a) with a view to assisting the court in determining the most suitable method of dealing with an offender, is made or submitted by a probation officer or by a social worker of a local authority social services department; and (b) contains information as to such matters, presented in such manner, as may be prescribed by rules made by the Secretary of State.'

The Criminal Justice and Public Order Bill of 1994 contains provisions which, if enacted, would enable courts to dispense with PSRs where this is deemed 'unnecessary'. The provision would apply in a modified form to offenders under the age of 18: see *Chapter 10*.

Medical reports
There are special additional requirements concerning reports in relation to mentally disordered offenders. Section 4 CJA 91 provides: '(1) Subject to subsection (2) below, in any case where section 3(1) above applies [ie the duty to obtain a pre-sentence report] and the offender *is* or *appears* to be mentally disordered, the court *shall* obtain and consider a medical report before passing a custodial sentence other than one fixed by law' (italics supplied). This subsection does *not* apply where the sentence is fixed by law (ie life for murder) or if, in the circumstances of the case, the court is of the opinion that it is *unnecessary* to obtain a medical report. The question *When is a report unnecessary?* is discussed in *Chapter 12*.

It should be noted that the exception is of general application to all offences, in contrast to that in s3(2) CJA 91, *supra*, concerning pre-sentence reports, which applies solely to offences triable only on indictment. There is a comparable savings provision to that in s3(4) CJA 91 so that failure to obtain a medical report does not invalidate a sentence, but any appellate court must obtain and consider such a report: s4(4) CJA 91.

Reasons for custodial sentences

Where the court passes a custodial sentence it is placed under two duties by s1(4) CJA 91. First it must '... (a) ... state in open court that it is of the opinion that either or both of [the statutory criteria] apply and why it is of that opinion'. It must then '... (b) ... explain to the offender in open court and in *ordinary language* why it is passing a custodial sentence on him'. The obligation to give reasons applies to a decision to use custody following a refusal to accept a community sentence, but in an appropriately modified form, since there is no statutory criterion to identify: see s1(4)(b). The requirement to explain in ordinary language applies to *all* custody situations.

In the case of a magistrates' court (which is not a court of record) the reason stated must be specified in the warrant of commitment and entered in the court register: s1(5) CJA 91. Whilst courts should be meticulous to observe this requirement, it is suggested that the requirement goes to the form of the decision and not its substance so that it is 'directory' rather than 'mandatory'. It is unlikely that failure to observe s1(5) would invalidate the decision. It is suggested that it would not, and that reasons which existed at the time could be announced and explained at a later time in the event of a mistake resulting in their not being given originally. It might be otherwise where no proper reasons existed. Section 142 MCA 1980 (power to rectify mistakes) might be used within the 28 days envisaged by that section.

Extra reasons for longer sentences

Where a court passes a custodial sentence for a term *longer* than is commensurate with the seriousness of the offence, or the combination of the offence and one or more offences associated with it, the court must '... (a) state in open court that it is of opinion that [s2(2)(b) CJA 91, *supra*] applies and why it is of that opinion'.

As with reasons for imposing custody, the court must also '... explain to the offender in ordinary language why the sentence is for such a term': s2(3)(b). An indeterminate sentence of the Crown Court is treated as a longer sentence for this purpose: s 2(4).

Suspended sentences

The CJA 91 retained but adjusted the suspended sentence of imprisonment by amending s22 PCCA 1973 to read as follows:

'... (2) A court shall not deal with an offender by means of a suspended sentence unless it is of the opinion—

(a) that the case is one in which a sentence of imprisonment would have been appropriate even without the power to suspend the sentence; and

(b) that the exercise of that power can be justified by the *exceptional* circumstances of the case' (italics supplied).

140

Section 22(2A) CJA 91 provides that:

'A court which passes a suspended sentence on any person for an offence shall consider whether the circumstances of the case are such as to warrant *in addition* the imposition of a fine or the making of a compensation order' (italics supplied).

This power existed before the CJA 91 which created a *duty* to consider exercising it. Compensation must be given preference over a fine: s35(1) PCCA 73. The court should reach a decision on custody without any regard to the fact that the power to suspend exists. It should then, and *only* then, apply the test in s22(2)(b), *supra*.

There CJA 91 narrowed the basis for suspension to 'exceptional circumstances' a term which has been interpreted very restrictively: see *Chapter 1(c), Judicial Guidance, ante*.

Young offenders, ie those aged below 21, continue to be ineligible for suspended sentences. There is a prohibition on making a probation order in respect of another offence for which the offender is before the court: s22(3) PCCA 73.

In the Crown Court, a suspended sentence supervision order can be made in respect of a single offence: s26 PCCA 73.

Partly suspended and extended sentences
The CJA 91 abolished extended sentences of imprisonment and partly suspended sentences: s5(2) CJA 1991.

8 Community Sentences

The Criminal Justice Act 1991 made significant changes to the structure, range, terminology and thinking behind community penalties. One purpose was to promote community sentences as realistic and demanding punishments in their own right—so that courts would be more confident in dealing with a range of offences and offenders by this means rather than custody.

The key to this expansion lies in the fact that community sentences involve significant 'restriction of liberty', albeit in the community and varying in intrusiveness into the offender's life according to the precise order or orders made by the court. The CJA 91 also enhanced the worth of community sentences by providing more powers for the enforcement of orders and National Standards for various aspects of probation work serve to support this form of disposal. The words 'community *sentence*' appeared in statute for the first time in the 1991 Act. Section 6 CJA 91 as amended by s66(4) CJA 93 provides:

> '**6.**—(1) A court shall not pass a community sentence . . . which consists of one or more community orders, unless it is of opinion that the offence, or the combination of the offence and one or more offences associated with it, was serious enough to warrant such a sentence.
>
> (2) . . . where a court passes a community sentence—
> (a) the particular order or orders comprising or forming part of the sentence shall be such as in the opinion of the court is, or taken together, are, the most suitable for the offender; and
> (b) the restrictions on liberty imposed by the order or orders shall be such as in the opinion of the court are commensurate with the seriousness of the offence, or the combination of the offence and one or more offences associated with it.'

Correct use of community sentences thus involves matching restriction of liberty to the seriousness of the offence—in accordance with the proportionate, or 'commensurate' approach to sentencing of the Act. The order or orders involved must also be the most suitable for the offender. In practice much depends on the information available to the court, notably that contained in a pre-sentence report: see *Chapter 12*. The relevant provisions are contained principally in s6 to s16 CJA 91: see *Appendix I, post*.

The test in s6(2)(b) concerning the extent of restrictions on liberty is comparable to that for *length* of custody in s2(2)(a) CJA 91. The test in s6(2)(a), *ibid*, must be applied in conjunction with any specific critera contained in independent statutory provisions affecting individual community orders, eg s2 PCCA 73 (probation); s11 CJA 91 (combination order), *post*.The tests in s6(2) combine *suitability* of a particular order for the *offender*, because, for example, the order might provide support and supervision which could assist the offender to avoid offending in the future or to make reparation, with a commensurate sentence measured against the restrictions on liberty involved.

Community sentencing trends prior to the CJA 91

The trend in the years leading up to the CJA 91 was towards greater use of community based orders such as probation (with or without extra conditions) and community service. The CJA 91 sought to reinforce this momentum. Court of Appeal rulings confirm the extent to which existing community orders were already acknowledged as a sound disposal at relatively high levels of seriousness. An extreme example is *Grant* (1990) 12 Cr App R (S) 441 where an offence of malicious wounding resulting in two broken teeth and the need for seven stitches was described by the Court of Appeal as 'tailor made' for community service where the accused was of previous good character and stood to lose both his home and regular employment if sentenced to custody.

Terminology

It should be noted that the terms used by the CJA 91 are 'community *sentence*', ie the umbrella term for this form of disposal, and 'community *order*', which refers to the particular order (eg probation, community service, attendance centre) which is used by the court—alone or in conjunction with further community orders or financial penalties to form the community sentence. Community sentences may be combined with each other and/or with financial penalties— fines and compensation—for the same offence. There is an exception affecting *Combination orders,* see under that heading *post.*

A note on restriction of liberty

In one sense all sentences involve restriction of the offender's liberty to a degree. Even a fine restricts the offender's ability to spend as he or she wishes and thereby limits choice. Community orders are specifically intended to place restrictions on the liberty of offenders and community sentences thus occupy an increasingly strategic role in sentencing. It is important to recognize that the impact eg of a particular requirement in a probation order may vary according to the individual—although this aspect should not be overplayed.

Some orders may be generally more demanding than others, eg a combination order (certainly if it involves a significant number of hours' community service and with extra probation requirements) would clearly be more onerous than a straight probation order with no conditions attached to it. Generally, however, the decision will be more subtle than this and will need to take account of the degree to which an individual's freedom is curtailed by a particular order or mix of orders. The Magistrates' Association has, in conjunction with the Justices' Clerks' Society and the Association of Chief Officers of Probation, published a paper on *Seriousness, Suitability and Restriction of Liberty:* see *Appendix V* to this work.

Alternatives to custody disappear

A consequence of the proportionate approach to sentencing is that 'alternatives to custody'—as community orders have been labelled in the past—disappear. The 'alternative to custody' approach to sentencing involved courts in using community penalties in circumstances where the court had first decided that custody might be the appropriate sentence, but then stepped back to use a community alternative instead.

This contorted reasoning is redundant under the CJA 91. All community orders are now sentences in their own right. The intention is that they should be sufficiently onerous in themselves to be used for all but the more serious offences. The one exception and anomaly is the retention of an existing power in relation to supervision orders for juveniles where 'specified activities' requirements are made, when the court may stipulate that the order was made instead of custody: see s12D CYPA 1933 discussed in the companion volume to this work *The Youth Court One Year Onwards*.

Community orders
The range of community orders which may be included in a community sentence is set out in s6(4) CJA 91 as follows:

- *Probation*: s2 PCCA 73 (substituted by s8, s9 CJA 91) (16 and over);
- *Community service*: s14 PCCA 73 (amended by s10 CJA 91) (16 and over);
- *Combination order*: s11 CJA 91, a new order combining probation and community service, as a consequence of which probation and community service cannot themselves be combined with one another: s6(3) CJA 91. (16 and over);
- *Curfew orders*: s12 CJA 91, a new order, which will be capable of being combined with electronic monitoring: s13, *ibid* ('tagging'), as and when this facility becomes available (16 and over). NB that curfews did not come into force with the main part of the Act in October 1992;
- *Supervision orders*: s7(7) and s12 CYPA 91 (largely unaffected) (10 to 17 years inclusive);
- *Attendance centre orders*: s17 CJA 82 (as amended by s67 CJA 91) (10 to 20 years inclusive).

Distinctive features of each of these orders are described in this chapter (apart from the supervision order—which is dealt with in *Chapter 10, post* and in greater detail in *The Youth Court One Year Onwards*).

Information and pre-sentence reports
In selecting a community sentence, the court *must*, under s7(1) CJA 91, take into account all relevant information about the circumstances of the offence, including factors which might *aggravate* or *mitigate* seriousness (note also the effect of s28 CJA 91 (general mitigation provision) and s29(1) CJA 91 (admissibility of previous convictions and responses: *Chapter 3*).

Under s7(2) CJA 91, the court *may* in relation to s6(2)(a) (suitability of a community order or orders for the *offender*) take into account any information about the offender which is before it. This latter requirement is, in effect, transformed into a *duty* in relation to those community orders where a pre-sentence report is a legal prerequisite to the order. Under s7(3) CJA 91 a pre-

144

sentence report must be obtained *before* certain kinds of community order are made. Section 7 CJA 91 provides:

7.—(1) In forming any such opinion as is mentioned in [s6(1) CJA 91 or s6(2)(b) CJA 91, *supra*] a court shall take into account all such information about the circumstances of the offence (including any aggravating or mitigating factors) as is available to it.

(2) In forming any such opinion as is mentioned in subsection (2)(a) of that section, a court may take into account any information about the offender which is before it.

(3) A court shall obtain and consider a pre-sentence report before forming any such opinion as to the suitability for the offender of one or more of the following orders, namely—

(a) a probation order which includes additional requirements authorised by Schedule 1A to the 1973 Act;

(b) a community service order;

(c) a combination order; and

(d) a supervision order which includes requirements imposed under section 12, 12A, 12AA, 12B or 12C of the Children and Young Persons Act 1969 ("the 1969 Act").

However, no community sentence which consists of or includes such an order as is mentioned in s7(3) CJA 91 is invalidated by the failure of a court to comply with that subsection, but any court on an appeal against such a sentence— '. . . (a) shall obtain a pre-sentence report if none was obtained by the court below; and (b) shall consider any such report obtained by it or by that court.'

'Pre-sentence report' is defined in s3(5) CJA 91 as a report *in writing* from a probation officer or social worker containing information of a kind which may be specified in rules made by the Secretary of State. Under the CJA 91, pre-sentence reports (PSRs) replaced the former social inquiry reports (SIRs) and are more sharply focused on matters outlined in National Standards such as the nature of the offence and the programme which the probation service or social services can provide if the court is minded to make a community sentence. It is essential that lawyers understand how report writers approach their information based task of writing reports. A useful publication is *Pre-sentence Reports: A Guide for Probation Officers and Social Workers* (NACRO, revised edition 1993).

Proposals contained in the CJ and PO Bill of 1994 would give courts a discretion to dispense with pre-sentence reports where these are deemed to be unnecessary.

Community sentence threshold—the 'serious enough' test
As indicated *supra,* before passing any community sentence, the court must be satisfied that the offence, or the offence and one or more offences associated with it, is serious enough to warrant this: 6(1) CJA 91.

There is no absolute standard of seriousness which will warrant a community sentence. This is a matter of fact and judgment for the court. Given the range and flexibility of community orders, it is likely that courts will find that individual orders or mixes of orders can be used in a variety of situations and for offences of differing levels of seriousness. This lack of any defined hierarchy of community orders—or tariff—recognizes the wide scope which community sentences provide for the construction of commensurate penalties and the effective use of restrictions on liberty in individual cases.

However, if the offence is one which can adequately be dealt with by a fine or a discharge, the test in s6(1), *supra*, will not be satisfied.

Note that there is no 'protection of the public' criterion in relation to community sentences (ct *Custody, Chapter 7*: but see the separate criteria for probation orders and the probation aspect of combination orders, *post*, which contain a similar, though lesser, test which goes to 'suitability' as opposed to 'seriousness').

The extent of restriction of liberty

It should be emphasised that the question 'How much restriction of liberty should a community sentence impose?' must be answered separately once the threshold test has been satisfied. Decisions concerning the degree of restriction of liberty are analogous to those concerning the length of a custody sentence: see *Chapter 7, ante.*

Provisional indications of seriousness

An area of practice which has caused difficulty is that affecting whether courts can legitimately give non-binding indications of seriousness/sentence when calling for a PSR. In *Materials on the Criminal Justice Act 1991* (Waterside Press, 1992) we proffered the following view, which has also found favour with the Magistrates' Association and the Justices' Clerks' Society: see the joint paper on *Seriousness, Suitability and Restriction of Liberty: Appendix V, post.*

'Should courts indicate seriousness/sentence levels when requesting a report?

Some courts have objected that they should not indicate levels of seriousness or likely sentence because this might fetter their discretion when it comes to deciding on sentence when the report, along with all the other sentencing information, is eventually received. The argument appears to rely on cases such as *Gillam* (1980) 2 Cr App R (S) 267; *Millwood* (1982) 4 Cr App R (S) 281; and *Rennes* (1985) 7 Cr App R (S) 343. In *Gillam* it was held that where a court adjourns a case after conviction for the purpose of obtaining a report in order to ascertain the offender's suitability for community service and the report shows the offender to be suitable for such an order, the court ought to make it because otherwise a feeling of injustice might be aroused. In *Rennes* it was held that the principle applies equally where the magistrates commit to the Crown Court for sentence, the latter being equally bound. However, it has been held to be otherwise where the sentencer makes clear that he or she expects a custodial sentence to be imposed and does 'not create in the mind of anyone present in court the expectation of a non-custodial sentence' : see *Horton and Alexander*

(1985) 7 Cr App R (S) 299.

It is submitted that these rulings must now be viewed in the light of the CJA 91 with its clear imperative for the report writer to consider seriousness as part of the reporting process. Unless the court is free to indicate broad levels of seriousness/sentence on the basis of the information available at the time of the request, then there is real risk that the framework envisaged by the Act will be placed in jeopardy. In any event, a clear form of words used by the court and which makes it clear that the final sentencing decision remains to be made in the light of all available information would appear to cover the situation.

The following is the announcement made to an offender at one court when a PSR is requested:

ON WHAT WE HAVE HEARD SO FAR WE HAVE FORMED THE OPINION THAT A FINE OR A DISCHARGE IS UNLIKELY TO MATCH WITH THE SERIOUSNESS OF YOUR OFFENCE(S). WE ARE THEREFORE ADJOURNING YOUR CASE SO THAT A PRE-SENTENCE REPORT CAN BE PREPARED BY THE PROBATION SERVICE.

WE MUST POINT OUT THAT THE MAGISTRATES WHO DEAL WITH YOUR CASE WILL NOT BE BOUND BY OUR VIEWS OR ANY SUGGESTION IN THE REPORT ABOUT HOW YOUR CASE SHOULD BE DEALT WITH.

It is submitted that, where possible, courts ought also to indicate which two offences [since the CJA 93 'which offences'] appear to be the most serious ['. . . are relied upon for this provisional conclusion']: see s1(2)(a) CJA 91, s6(1) CJA 91.'

Since the above was written, the case of *Woodin* (1994) 15 Cr App R (S) 307 has held that, when a court adjourns for a PSR which is mandatory under s3(1) CJA 91 without warning the offender that a custodial sentence is likely, this does not entitle the offender to believe that a community sentence will be imposed. However, there is nothing in the judgment which discourages the practice of giving non-binding indications of seriousness. As the editor of *Justice of the Peace* wrote in an article discussing the implications of *Woodin* at 158 JPN 163:

'. . . it is surely bad sentencing practice to adjourn a case leaving the defendant, his advocate and the probation officer "in limbo". In our respectful submission there is nothing in the statutory framework which prevents the court from giving its provisional view as to seriousness—even if that view is based solely on the prosecution case.'

Probation order

Sections 8 and 9 CJA 1991 and Part II of sched 1, *ibid*, re-enacted with modifications and rearrangements the previous probation order provisions of the PCCA 1973, which dealt with probation orders. Three substantive changes were made to the existing law governing probation orders:

• The *minimum age* at which an offender may be placed on probation was lowered from 17 years to 16 years.

• The probation order was turned into a *sentence* of the court, rather than an order made 'instead of sentencing' the offender. This reflects the increasing use of the probation order as a penalty for persistent offenders, and for those who might otherwise be sent to prison; together with the fact that compliance with the terms of a probation order, *a fortiori* one with extra conditions, places considerable restrictions on the liberty of the offender. This new status also enables probation to be combined with a financial penalty or other community order as part of a community sentence for a single offence (except for community service: s6(3) *supra*). Section 8(2) CJA 91 repeals the effect of s13 PCCA 73 on a probation order (but not on a discharge) so that convictions resulting in probation count as *convictions* for all purposes.

• The criteria for making a probation order were more clearly defined. Previously, a probation order could be made if the court considered this 'expedient' in the circumstances. Section 2(1) PCCA 73 (as substituted by s8 CJA 91) inserted the following specific criteria for making a probation order: the court must be of the opinion that: '. . . supervision of the offender by a probation officer is desirable in the interests of - (a) securing the rehabilitation of the offender; or (b) protecting the public from harm from him or preventing the commission by him of further offences'.

The new provisions also clarified the obligations on the offender to keep in touch with his or her supervising officer and to notify any change of address: s2(6) PCCA 73 (as substituted).

The National Standard for probation orders, issued in 1992 by the Home Office, Department of Health and the Welsh Office, said that probation order supervision

'. . . should generally entail establishing a professional relationship, in which to advise, assist and befriend the offender with the aim of:

• securing the offender's co-operation and compliance with the probation order and enforcing its terms;
• challenging the offender to accept responsibility for his or her crime and its consequences;
• helping the offender to resolve personal difficulties linked with offending and to acquire new skills; and
• motivating and assisting the offender to become a responsible and law-abiding member of the community.'

Probation order with additional requirements

Section 9 CJA 91 together with Part II of Schedule 1, *ibid*, re-enacted with modifications those provisions of the PCCA 1973 dealing with additional requirements in probation orders. The requirements which may be included were set out in a substituted s3(1) and sched 1A PCCA 73. Additional requirements may be included 'during the whole or any part of the probation order' (but see the schedule for exact details) if this is in the interests of securing rehabilitation, protecting the public from harm from the offender, or preventing the commission by the offender of further offences (ie the same criteria as for the making of probation orders). Section 3(2), *ibid*, provides that the payment of sums by way of damages for injury or compensation for loss may not be included as requirements. Thus, failure to make payments under a compensation order cannot amount to breach of probation order.

The new schedule 1A PCCA 1973 sets out five types of additional requirements which may be included in a probation order. These relate to residence, activities, attendance at a probation centre, treatment for a a mental condition and treatment for drug or alcohol dependency. Provision is also made to enable longer and more intensive supervision of offenders given probation for *sexual* offences.

(i) *Residence*: The Act preserved the previous power to include requirements about where the offender should live.

(ii) *Activities*: The Act also preserved, without significant change, the power of courts to require offenders who are given probation orders to participate or refrain from participating in specified activities, and to report to a specified person at a specified place for a total of up to *60 days* in the aggregate.

(iii) *Probation centres*: Offenders could already be required to attend a day centre run by the probation service for up to *60 days* in total. Under para 3 of sched 1A, day centres were renamed 'probation centres', thereby better indicating their purpose and reflecting the provision of evening activities at centres. The Home Secretary's approval is required for the operation of a probation centre. The Home Office is thus able to ensure that centres operate to National Standards for such establishments.

(iv) *Sexual offences*: Paragraph 4 of sched 1A provided for offenders convicted of *sexual* offences to be required to participate in specified activities or to attend a probation centre without this being limited to the 60 days for other offenders. This is to allow the probation service an opportunity to work with sex offenders over an extended period to tackle their offending, and with the aims of reducing the risk of further sexual offences and protecting the public.

(v) *Treatment for mental condition*: sched 1A, para 5, continued existing powers of courts to require an offender whose mental condition requires and is susceptible to treatment, but not such as to warrant a hospital order, to submit to suitable medical treatment as a requirement of probation.

(vi) *Drug and alcohol dependency*: para 6 of sched 1A provided, for the first time, for offenders who are dependent on, or who misuse *drugs* or *alcohol*, to be required to undergo treatment for their condition, where this is associated with their offending, as an additional requirement of probation. The provisions are analogous to those for offenders with a mental condition. The offender can be required to submit for treatment only if a 'suitably qualified person' satisfies the court that the offender is dependent on or misuses drugs or alcohol, that this contributed in some way to the offence committed, and that the offender's condition requires, or may respond to treatment. The suitably qualified person may be a medical practitioner, *or* a person who, though not medically qualified, has *experience of working with people who misuse drugs or alcohol* and is able to provide suitable treatment of a high standard. This treatment may be either residential or non-residential, at an institution or under supervision of such person as may be specified.

Community service orders
Section 10 CJA 91 made three substantive changes to the law relating to community service orders. Under the previous s14, 15 and 17 PCCA 1973, a court could 'instead of dealing with [the offender] in any other way' require the offender to perform unpaid work in the community. The first change was the removal of the words 'instead of dealing with him in any other way'. This was to enable community service to be brought fully within the new sentencing framework of Part I CJA 91. Community service had evolved, in practice and in many areas of the country, as an 'alternative to custody' (a concept made redundant by the commensurate sentencing approach). The offence must be imprisonable: s14(1) PCCA 73.

Secondly, the provisions relating to community service for 16 year olds were brought into line with those for offenders aged 17 and over: s14(1A) PCCA 73 (as amended by s10 CJA 91). This meant that the maximum number of hours rose from 120 to 240 for 16 year olds. The provisions also reflected the fact that facilities for 16 year olds (as for older offenders) to perform community service are now available in all parts of the country, so that there is no longer a need for a court to establish that the Home Secretary has notified them that suitable arrangements exist for offenders of this age. Finally, a new provision was added concerning the offender's duty to report to the relevant supervising officer as and when required. This would *inter alia* enable the officer to hold a disciplinary interview with an offender who had failed to comply with the order before deciding whether to initiate court proceedings for a breach.

The National Standard for community service orders states that:

'The main purpose of a CSO is to reintegrate the offender into the community through:

• positive and demanding unpaid work, keeping to disciplined requirements; and
• reparation to the community by undertaking socially useful work which, if possible, makes good damage done by offending.'

Combination order
Section 11 CJA 91 created a new order, the combination order, which combines elements of both probation and community service. While, in general, community orders can be combined in any permutation to make up a community sentence, the combination order is the only way in which it is permissible to combine probation and community service: see s6(3) CJA 91. However, there is nothing to stop the combination order itself from being combined *with other community orders*, or with financial penalties where desirable (always remembering the high level of restriction on liberty that this would entail). The official Home Office view is that the combination order is intended for offenders who courts believe should make some reparation to the

150

community, through a community service order, and who also need probation supervision to tackle problems that underlie their offending and thus reduce the risk of further offending in the future.

Under s11(1) CJA 91, a combination order can be given to any offender aged *16 or over* who is convicted of an offence punishable with imprisonment. The maximum duration of the probation element is three years; minimum 12 months. (It is intended that, whenever a combination order is made, probation supervision should continue for at least as long as the community service work is performed, and the 12 months' minimum is to allow for this, even in cases where the court gives the maximum number of community service hours which is permissible under a combination order). The limits of the community service component are 40 to 100 hours (ct the normal upper limit of 240 hours in a freestanding community service order).

The National Standard for combination orders says:

'Given the considerable restriction on liberty inherent in a combination order, such an order will be appropriate for amongst the most serious offenders likely to be given a community sentence.... In practice, this may well mean that combination orders feature most frequently in Crown Court rather than magistrates' court cases' (para. 7).

It states that a combination order is likely to be most appropriate for an offender who has committed an offence which is amongst the most serious for which a community sentence may be imposed; has clearly identified areas of need that have contributed to the offending and which can be dealt with by probation supervision; and has a realistic prospect of completing such an order. The standard adds:

'Amongst those offenders who might **not** be well suited to a combination order would be those whose lifestyle is particularly chaotic, for example, as a result of drug or alcohol misuse, and who might therefore have particular difficulty in keeping to a programme of CS work; or offenders with well-ordered lifestyles who have little need of (or alternatively little prospect of responding to) probation supervision. Combination orders that include demanding additional requirements within the probation element are particularly onerous and are likely to be difficult to complete, especially for younger offenders.' (para. 9).

Curfew orders
Section 12 CJA 91 created a new species of order, the curfew. In conjunction with this, s13, *ibid*, provided for such orders to be electronically monitored ('tagging'). The offence need not be imprisonable. The courts may make a curfew order *without* imposing an electronic monitoring requirement, but may not order electronic monitoring on its own. Curfew orders will be available for any offender aged *16 or over*. The order will require the offender to be at the place specified in the order for the period specified in it. The place will normally be the offender's residence, though it can be any place: but see s12(6), *ibid*. The maximum number of hours in a day during which a curfew can operate is

12 hours, and the minimum is *2 hours*. The curfew may not operate for more than six months. Different lengths of time for different days, and different places, can be specified in the order, to take account of the circumstances of the offender. The maximum curfew of 12 hours in a day does not have to be specified in one block, but can be broken into several shorter periods.

Under s12(3) CJA 91, the court, in making the order, is required, so far as practicable, to avoid conflict with the offender's religious beliefs, the requirements of other community orders to which the offender is subject, and interference with the times at which the offender works or attends school or other educational establishment. A designated person must be made responsible for monitoring the offender's whereabouts during the curfew period: s12(4), *ibid*; and the court must explain the effects of the curfew order to the offender in ordinary language: s12(5), *ibid. Before* making the order, the court must obtain and consider relevant information about the places to be specified in the order, including information about the attitude of persons likely to be affected by the order, eg the offender's partner or parents: s12(6), *ibid.* It is envisaged that facilities under s13 CJA 91 for the electronic monitoring of the whereabouts of offenders given curfew orders will be made through contracts placed by the Secretary of State with private sector concerns. Under s 13, courts will not be able to impose electronic monitoring requirements unless they have been notified that such arrangements have been made for the area concerned. [The likely arrangements are that where the offender's whereabouts are to be electronically monitored, the offender will be required to wear on his or her ankle or wrist a small electronic device from which signals will be transmitted to a monitoring station, and which will alert the monitoring station if the offender leaves the premises to which the curfew order confines him. On receipt of such an alert, the monitoring station will initiate the steps necessary to check physically whether the offender has breached the terms of his or her curfew order and report the matter, so that consideration can be given to proceedings for breach of the requirements of the order.]

The CJ and PO Bill of 1994 amends s12 CJA 91 to allow the area by area introduction of curfew orders with electronic monitoring. The Bill's financial memorandum says: '. . . it is planned to conduct pilot trials of curfew orders with electronic monitoring at a total cost of £1.375 million.'

Supervision orders
Consistent with the policy of making the full range of adult and juvenile community orders available for both *16 and 17 year olds*, the Act made supervision orders available for 17 year olds (thus making the full age range for this order 10 to 17 inclusive). This is one effect of s68 CJA 91. The main supervision order provisions are contained in s7(7) and s12 CYPA 69 which, the new age limits apart, stand unaffected. This leaves the anomaly of s12D CYPA 69 (supervision as an alternative to custody). However, section 66 CJA 91 and sched 7 revised and replaced s15 CYPA 1969 to bring the provisions governing the variation and discharge of supervision orders broadly into line with the principles underlying sched 2 for the *Enforcement of community*

orders generally: see under that heading, *post*. They also took account of the introduction of the unit fine scheme; the increased maximum fines under the Act; and the effects of the Children Act 1989. The 1989 Act abolished care orders in criminal proceedings and added a power to add a residence requirement to a supervision order. There was some simplification of the relevant provisions.

The National Standard for supervision orders states that such an order

'. . . should entail establishing a professional relationship, in which to advise, assist and befriend the offender with the aim of:

• enabling and encouraging the child or young person to understand and accept responsibility for his or her behaviour and its consequences;
• helping the child or young person to resolve personal difficulties linked with offending and to acquire new skills; and
• securing the child or young person's co-operation and compliance with the supervision order and enforcing its terms.'

It observes that an important issue when considering a 16 year old for supervision is whether to propose a supervision or probation order in a pre-sentence report, and comments:

'While both a supervision order and a probation order are intended to assist an offender to become more responsible and to keep out of trouble, the clearest distinguishing feature is that the supervision order is also intended to help a young person to develop into an adult, whereas a probation order is more appropriate for someone who is already emotionally, intellectually, socially and physically an adult. Since many 16 and 17 year olds are still very much in the stage of transition into adulthood, the supervision order may often in practice be the more suitable form of supervision.'

Attendance centre orders

Section 67 CJA 91 made several changes to the existing law concerning attendance centre orders by:

• removing the restriction which prevented an attendance centre order being made, in normal circumstances, on an offender who had previously received a custodial sentence. This restriction was inconsistent with the Act's commensurate approach to sentencing, ie sentences should be determined by the seriousness of the offence rather than the offender's previous record.
• bringing the maximum number of hours' attendance that can be ordered for a 16 year old offender into line with that for 17 year olds (in keeping with the general policy of treating 16 and 17 year olds as a distinct group, 'near adults'). As a result, the new maxima are: *under 16*: normally 12 hours, but up to 24 hours if the court considers that 12 hours is inadequate in the circumstances of the case; *age 16 to 20*: up to 36 hours.
• bringing the procedures for enforcement of orders broadly into line with those for the enforcement of other community penalties (as set out in

Schedule 2 CJA 91): s19(5A) CJA 82 as inserted by s67(6) CJA 91.

Enforcement of community orders
Section 14 and sched 2 CJA 91 set out the powers of courts to deal with breaches of requirements of community orders (except supervision orders: see s15 CYPA 69 as substituted by s66 and sched 7 CJA 91); and attendance centre orders: s18 and 19 CJA 82 as amended by s67(2) to (6) CJA 91), and to discharge, or vary or revoke such orders (where applicable), and to substitute other sentences which could have been imposed at the time when the order was made. These replaced, with significant changes, s5, s6, s16, s17, and sched 1 PCCA 1973. Section 16 and sched 3 CJA 91 made corresponding provision for cases where a community order is made by a court in one part of the United Kingdom but the offender resides in another.

The purpose of the new provisions governing the enforcement of community penalties is to provide a clearer, more coherent and more consistent set of arrangements. As a general rule, all types of community order are now enforceable under comparable procedures. Credit must be given for that part of a community sentence which has been completed. All this lends strength to the new system of community sentences, the new sentencing framework and the commensurate approach. It is also a reason why, with some confidence, courts should be more prepared to try community sentences whenever possible.

The new provisions also make a clear distinction between failure to comply with the requirements of a community order, and the commission of a further offence during the currency of the order. The latter is not to be regarded in itself as a breach of the terms of the order, as is made clear by paragraph 5(1) of Schedule 2 CJA 91. Again, this reflects the view that community orders are punishments *in their own right* and are not equivalent to a conditional discharge whose terms are breached automatically if the offender commits a further offence. However, the new s29 CJA 91 substituted by s66(6) CJA 93 (see *Chapter 4*) enables courts to take into account the failure to respond to the previous sentence when assessing the seriousness of the new offence. The provisions give the courts full powers to deal effectively, but in different ways, with both breaches of the requirements of orders and with new offences committed during the currency of orders.

The relevant changes re enforcement summarised
The main changes introduced by Schedule 2 to the CJA 91 compared with the equivalent provisions of the Powers of Criminal Courts Act 1973, are:

- provision is made for the enforcement of combination orders. In so far as they include probation supervision, they are to be enforced as probation orders, and insofar as they include community service, they are to be enforced as community service orders: para 12.
- paragraphs 3 and 6 set out the powers which magistrates and the Crown Court respectively have to deal with breaches of the requirements of community orders of all kinds which they have made. In all cases, a fine

154

not exceeding £1,000 may be imposed, to be determined as a level 3 fine in accordance with the unit fine scheme. Up to 60 hours' community service may be imposed (provided this does not take the offender beyond the maximum 240 hours for which he or she may be liable at any one time, or beyond 100 hours in the case of a combination order). If the offender is under 21, the court may impose an attendance centre order for breach of a probation order. Finally, where the breach is a *serious* one, the court may decide to revoke the order and impose a different penalty for the original offence, as if it had just convicted the offender of it. In imposing a new penalty, the court is required, under paragraph 3(2)(a) and 4(2)(a), to take into account the extent to which the offender has so far complied with the requirements of the original order.

• if, however, the offender has *wilfully* and *persistently* failed to comply with the requirements of a community order, the court may assume that he or she has refused to give consent to the community sentence concerned: paras 3(2)(b); 4(2)(b). This exposes the offender to liability to a custodial sentence pursuant to s1(3) CJA 91.

• Part III of sched 2 deals with the court's powers to revoke a community order. The circumstances in which an order can be revoked include (but are not restricted to) a conviction for a further offence—but see *Breach of community sentences by reoffending* in *Chapter 1(c), ante*—or the fact that the offender has made good progress and is responding satisfactorily to supervision. When revoking an order, the court may deal afresh with the offence in respect of which the order was made, dealing with the offender in any manner in which it could have done if the offender had just been convicted of it (taking account of the extent to which he or she has complied with the requirements of the order).

9 Fines and Compensation

The Criminal Justice Act 1993 abolished unit fines, at least in so far as the statutory version of that method is concerned (see the *Note* at the end of this chapter). The Criminal Justice Act 1993 substituted a new s18 CJA 91 which establishes a flexible approach to means related fines—free from the high level of prescription which probably served, more than anything else, to undermine the statutory unit fines scheme. The CJA 93 preserves certain rules introduced by the CJA 91, the most significant of these being the power to increase fines on account of the means of the offender (along with the power to decrease fines for the less well off which existed prior to the CJA 91). Section 18(5) CJA 91 as amended provides that the new duty to 'take into account the circumstances of the case, including the financial curcumstances of the offender so far as they are known, or appear, to the court' pursuant to s18(3) applies:

'. . . whether taking into account the financial circumstances of the offender has the effect of increasing or reducing the amount of the fine.'

The power to order a statement of means (renamed 'financial circumstances order') on pain of penalties for non-compliance or for providing false information—introduced by the CJA 91—is also retained: see s20 CJA 91 as amended, *post*. A freshly inserted s20(1A) allows a magistrates' court to make a financial circumstances order once a written plea of guilty has been notified to the court pursuant to s12 MCA 1980

Parents or guardians of offenders below the age of 18 years are, following the CJA 93, subject to the full force of s20 in respect of financial circumstances orders made where the court proposes to exercise its powers under s55 CYPA 1933, ie to order the parent or guardian to pay the fine of a child or young person.

The unit fines scheme applied only in the magistrates' court. Identical provisions now apply to fines in both the Crown Court and the magistrates' court (subject to a maximum fine in this court of £5,000—according to five levels on the 'standard scale', ie level 1: £200; 2: £500; 3: £1,000; 4: £2,500; 5: £5000).

Setting the amount of a fine

Under s18 CJA 91 (as substituted by the CJA 93) fines are a flexible product of seriousness and financial circumstances. There are no precise statutory rules for either of these assessments—such as existed in relation to unit fines (see *Introduction to the Criminal Justice Act 1991*, Waterside Press, 1992). Questions concerning how the two sides of the seriousness/financial circumstances equation interact, and what weight is given to particular factors, in a given case are left to the discretion of the court. Sentencers are left free to construct their own approach. The new statutory framework is as follows:

'**18.**—(1) Before fixing the amount of any fine, a court shall inquire into the financial circumstances of the offender.

(2) The amount of any fine fixed by a court shall be such as, in the opinion of the court, reflects the seriousness of the offence.

(3) In fixing the amount of any fine, a court shall take into account the circumstances of the case including, among other things, the financial circumstances of the offender so far as they are known, or appear to the court.'

Seriousness

The word 'commensurate' (which appeared in the original s18 CJA 91) has been omitted from the post-CJA 93 fining provisions. Instead, fines must 'reflect' the seriousness of the offence: s18(2) CJA 1991. The word 'reflect' probably has less rigid connotations than 'commensurate', something which serves to reinforce the somewhat looser formula in s18(1) to (3), *supra*, under which less precise calculations on either side of the seriousness/means equation seem to be permissible.

Section 18(1) refers to 'the seriousness of the offence', thereby avoiding the 'associated offences' formula common to custody and community sentences: see *Chapter 3*. On the face of things, this could be taken as an indication that all fines must be assessed individually, regardless of other offences for which the offender stands to be sentenced—but this would be to ignore both s28(1) CJA 91 (general mitigation provision) and the totality principle: see *Chapter 3*. The offender's financial circumstances, *post*, are bound to act as a further restraining factor in many instances.

Financial circumstances

So far as the offender's own financial position is concerned, the court is under a duty:

• to inquire into the offender's financial circumstances before fixing the amount of the fine: s18(1) CJA 91, *supra;* and

• to take into account the circumstances of the case including the 'financial circumstances' of the offender so far as they are known or appear to the court: s18(3), *supra*.

The duty to inquire is not absolute: see s18(4) CJA 91 reproduced under the heading *Absence of financial information, post*. This is also confirmed by the words 'so far as they are known or appear' in s18(3). The court has a discretion to make a financial circumstances order under s20 CJA 93, *post*. It remains good practice, *semble*, for courts to continue with pre-CJA 93 practices under which means forms were distributed with summonses and, in some instances, charge sheets. The temptation for courts not to adjourn post-conviction is obvious and seemingly the remainder of the fining provisions will not discourage courts from proceeding on whatever information is, or is not, known about the offender's financial circumstances. Under the non-statutory unit fines pilot projects which preceded the CJA 91, some support for the contention that an offender who fails to provide financial details forfeits the right to any reduction on the average fine exists in *Higgins* (1988) 10 Cr App R (S) 144.

The court is free to decide, within its discretion under s18(1) to (3) and in individual cases, what effect financial circumstances should have on the fine. The statutory terminology is now 'financial circumstances' as opposed to 'means' (discerned under the former unit fines scheme via 'disposable weekly income'). Little may turn on the new terminology except, perhaps, where the offender has financial resources other than income, or conversely where a low 'cash flow' belies the fact that the offender also has no real personal expenses to meet (but see the case law concerning family resources below). Financial circumstances arguably includes potential earnings: cf Lewis [1985] Crim LR 121.

The Magistrates' Association *Sentencing Guidelines* reproduced in *Appendix II, post* are set by reference to 'average means nationally' by which is meant £200 per week net: letter to *The Magistrate*, Vol 50, No 3, at p 60. As a high proportion of sentenced offenders are unemployed (62 per cent of people sentenced for indictable offences in a recent Home Office survey of nine magistrates' courts), courts using the guidelines will need to make full use of their discretion to reduce fines for those on low incomes if we are not to see swingeing increases in the level of fines imposed on such offenders in comparison with the unit fine scheme and a corresponding increase in the rate of default.

Certain common law rules re-emerge in so far as they are not inconsistent with the new regime. One of these is the rule (not strict) that '. . . Save in exceptional circumstances a fine should normally be capable of being paid within 12 months or thereabouts': *Hewitt* (1971) 55 Cr App R 433; *Knight* (1980) 2 Cr App R (S) 82; *Owen* [1984] Crim LR 436; *Nunn* (1984) 5 Cr App R (S) 203.

The ruling in *Olliver* (1989) 11 Cr App R (S) 10 cast doubt on the 12 months principle, although most commentators have suggested that, in extending the limit up to three years, the *Olliver* case—which also concerned compensation, for which a longer payment period may be in order—did no more than reflect the existing rule that the normal limit of 12 months may be exceeded in exceptional circumstances.

An aspect of the pre-CJA law which may be acutely relevant in view of the use of the words 'financial circumstances' is the rule that fines are a punishment which is personal to the offender and are not intended to impact on other people, eg those of a spouse, partner or family member: see *Baxter* [1974] Crim LR 611; *Charalambous* [1985] Crim LR 328.

Absence of financial information

Special provisions apply where an offender has been convicted in his or her absence pursuant to section 11 or 12 Magistrates' Courts Act 1980 (non-appearance of accused and written pleas of guilty, respectively). Under s18(4) where an offender:

'**18.**—(4) . . . (b) . . .
(i) has failed to comply with an order under section 20 (1) below [ie to disclose his or her financial circumstances']; or
(ii) has otherwise failed to co-operate with the court in its inquiry into his financial circumstances . . . and the court considers that it has insufficient information to make a proper determination of the financial circumstances of the offender, it may make such determination as it thinks fit.'

Analogous provisions apply where the parent or guardian of a child or young person has failed to provide details of his or her financial circumstances or otherwise failed to cooperate: s18(4)(c) CJA 91.

The effect in both instances is that a court may estimate an offender's means. In practice it is likely that the court will apply some regular tariff or guideline fine where there is no other information to go on. A problem is that such approaches are likely to have a 'ripple effect'. Once a regular guideline is applied to those who do not respond there will be a tendency to avoid treating offenders who have taken the trouble to provide financial information more severely. The dilemma appears to be insoluble and this could lead to a standardisation of fines by application of the 'norm' or 'tariff'—with lower fines being imposed only where offenders' financial circumstances show them to be very impoverished. By the same token, unusually high fines are likely to be reserved for the patently wealthy.

Statements of financial circumstances and offences

The CJA 91 places a statutory duty on offenders to provide information about their financial circumstances: s20(1). This duty only arises following an order made *on conviction.*

The maximum penalty for failure, without reasonable excuse, to comply with an order under s20(1) is a level 3 fine.

A person who '. . . in furnishing any statement in pursuance of an order under subsection [20(1)] . . . (a) makes a statement which he knows to be false in a material particular; (b) recklessly furnishes a statement which is false in a material particular; or (c) knowingly fails to disclose any material fact . . .' is liable to a level 4 fine and/or 3 months imprisonment: s20(3).

The former unit fines rules placed a duty on justices' clerks to 'make arrangements' for the service of means inquiry forms on defendants (and, where appropriate, the parents or guardians of juvenile defendants). This duty was removed as a consequence of the CJA 93 with the disappearance of the old s18 CJA 91 which contained rule making powers in this regard conferred on the Lord Chancellor.

Section 20 CJA 91 (as amended) provides as follows:

20.—(1) Where a person has been convicted of an offence, the court may, before sentencing him, make a financial circumstances order with respect to him.

(1A) Where a magistrates' court has been notified in accordance with section 12(2) of the Magistrates' Courts Act 1980 that a person desires to plead guilty without appearing before the court, the court may make a financial circumstances order with respect to him.

159

(1B) Before exercising its powers under section 55 of the Children and Young Persons Act 1933 against the parent or guardian of any person who has been convicted of an offence, the court may make a financial circumstances order with respect to the parent or (as the case may be) the guardian.

(1C) In this section "a financial circumstances order" means, in relation to any person, an order requiring him to give to the court, within such period as may be specified in the order, such a statement of his financial circumstances as the court may require.

Consequential amendments are made to s20(2) and (3) whereby the words 'financial circumstances order' are substituted for references to 'an order under subsection (1) above'. The Lord Chancellor can no longer prescribe the means form; s20(5) CJA 91 under which he could *inter alia* do so ceases to have effect: see para 2(3) of sched 3 to CJA 1993.

The power in s20(1A) enables a court to make an order before conviction once a written plea of guilty has been received by the court administration. The power to make such an order has been delegated to clerks under the Justices' Clerks' Rules. The CJ and Public Order Bill provides that the offence would be committed by failure to comply with an 'official request' made at this stage.

Remission of fines
Fresh powers to remit fines, ie cancel their effect in whole or in part, result from the CJA 93. Paragraph 3 of sched 3 to the 1993 Act substitutes a new s21 CJA 91 as follows:

21.—(1) This section applies where a court has, in fixing the amount of a fine, determined the offender's financial circumstances under section 18(4) above.

(2) If, on subsequently inquiring into the offender's financial circumstances, the court is satisfied that had it had the results of that inquiry when sentencing the offender it would—

(a) have fixed a smaller amount; or

(b) not have fined him,

it may remit the whole or any part of the fine.

(3) Where under this section the court remits the whole or part of any fine after a term of imprisonment has been fixed under section 82(5) of the Magistrates' Courts Act 1980 (issue of warrant of commitment in default) or section 31 of the Powers of Criminal Courts Act 1973 (powers of the Crown Court in relation to fines), it shall reduce the term by the corresponding proportion.

(4) In calculating any reduction required by subsection (3) above, any fraction of a day shall be ignored.

Default
One consequence of the new provisions is that s22 CJA 1991 which dealt with default in paying fines under the original s18 (when the periods of imprisonment in default were linked to units as opposed to cash) ceases to have effect: para 4 of sched to the 3 CJA 93. Periods of imprisonment in default are now governed by the tables in s31(3A) PCCA 1973 and para 1 of sched 4 to the MCA 1980 as amended by s23(1) CJA 91: see *Statutory Provisions* in *Appendix I, post*.

Offenders below the age of 18 cannot be committed to prison or other forms of custody in default of payment of a financial penalty: s1 CJA 1982.

Parents and guardians

A revised s57(3) and s57(4) CJA 1991 are substituted by para 5 of sched 3 to deal with the responsibility of parents or guardians for the fines of children and young persons. The new provisions are as follows:

'(3) For the purposes of any order under that section made against a parent or guardian of a child or young person—
(a) sections 18 and 21 above; and
(b) section 35(4)(a) of the 1973 Act (fixing amount of compensation order),
shall have effect (so far as applicable) as if any references to the financial circumstances of the offender, or (as the case may be) to the means of the person against whom the compensation order is made, were a reference to the financial circumstances of the parent or guardian.
(4) For the purposes of any such order made against a local authority (as defined for the purposes of the Children Act 1989)—
(a) section 18(1) above, and section 35(4)(a) of the 1973 Act, shall not apply, and
(b) section 18(3) above shall apply as if the words from "including" to the end were omitted.'

Other changes

The old s19 CJA 91 which allowed certain non-unit fines to be increased or decreased according to the means of the offender ceases to have effect, having become redundant: see s65(2) CJA 1993. All fines are now within the ambit of s18(5) *supra*. Ancillary amendments are made by sched 3 to the 1993 Act: see s65(3) CJA 1993.

All the changes apply in relation to offenders convicted (but not sentenced) before the date on which the provisions of the CJA 93 relating to fines came into effect: s65(4) *ibid* (ie 20 September 1993).

The amendments in sched 3 include the cessation of various fining provisions in other statutes which had been made referable to the original s18 CJA 91 and changes to s20 CJA 91, *supra,* dealing with statements of financial circumstances and offences.

See also *Deductions from income support, post.*

Compensation

Arguably, the extent to which compensation to victims of crime is ordered by courts is directly related to two things: sensitivity by courts to the interests of victims; and the extent of the financial information about defendants which courts have before them. Forms containing details of financial circumstances therefore facilitate improved use of compensation orders.

By law, compensation must be given preference over a fine: s35(4A) PCCA 73. The original version of s18 CJA 91 contained a provision emphasising that this rule remained unaffected: s18(7)(a) CJA 91 (now repealed). The position is now dealt with exclusively in s35(1) PCCA 73 which states:

'... a court shall give reasons, on passing sentence, if it does not make [a compensation] order in a case where this section empowers it to do so'.

Section 35 also enables the court to order payment of compensation as a *sentence* in its own right. Since the CJA 91 magistrates have power to award compensation for personal injury, loss or damage of up to £5,000 (sched 4 CJA 91).

For general guidance to magistrates' courts see the Magistrates' Association *Sentencing Guidelines, Appendix II post* and the extracts from Home Office circular 53/1993 reproduced at the end of this chapter.

Deductions from income support
Under s24 CJA 91, a system was introduced for recovering fines, other penalties and compensation by means of attachment of state benefits. The method applies where magistrates enforce their own penalties, or where they enforce those imposed by the Crown Court under s32 PCCA 1973 and s41 Administration of Justice Act 1970. The benefits which may be attached are income support under the Social Security Act 1986, whether standing alone or together with unemployment, sickness or invalidity benefit, retirement pension, or severe disablement allowance paid at the same time.

The court may apply to the Secretary of State for sums payable to be deducted from the offender's entitlements. The rules provide that the court must hold a means enquiry before a request is made. They also contain a formula for determining the level at which deductions can be made (around £2 a week at the time of writing).

Present Department of Social Security regulations provide that deductions for housing, fuel or water debts may not exceed five per cent of the personal allowance for a single claimant aged 25 or over and deductions for a combination of such debts may not exceed 15 per cent. Deductions for fines will be subject to the same overall maximum. If the defaulter does not receive enough benefit to cover all deductions, other debts rank ahead of those for fines and compensation. The power to apply for attachment extends to certain other financial penalties and costs by virtue of s24(4) CJA 91.

Small refinements were added by the CJA 93 and others are contained in the CJ and PO Bill 1994—including provision for attachment following a transfer of fine order from one court to another.

Regulations
The Fines (Deductions from Income Support) Regulations 1992 SI 2182 provide for deductions to be made from income support where a fine or compensation order has been imposed upon a person by a court. The Regulations further provide that where an application to make such deductions is received by the Secretary of State the application shall be referred to an adjudication officer. The officer must determine whether there is sufficient income support to allow such deductions to be made and, where other deductions are being made from income

162

support, the priority of deductions for fines and compensation orders in relation to those deductions. Provision is also made by regulation 7 for deductions to be made in respect of one application at a time and that the Secretary of State should not make deductions unless the offender is 18 or over when the application is made. The provisions also establish circumstances in which deductions should cease and what order of priority should be given to multiple applications in respect of one offender.

Payment of deductions is to be made at intervals of 13 weeks by the Secretary of State to the court. Provision is also made for appeals by the offender from the decision of the adjudication officer to the Social Security Appeal Tribunal and for further appeal by the offender and the adjudication officer to the Social Security Commissioners and from there by the debtor, adjudication officer and the Secretary of State to the Court of Appeal.

Incidental provision is made for setting aside decisions, correcting decisions, the withdrawal of applications, time limits for making appeals and applications and service of notices. The Regulations themselves—which of necessity are long and complex in order to cover this extensive framework of legal requirements, rights and appeals—are summarised in Home Office circular 74/1992 issued on 1 September 1992 and reproduced in *Materials on the Criminal Justice Act 1991* (Waterside Press, 1992).

Home Office Circular 53/1993

Compensation in the Criminal Courts

1. This circular updates the previous guidance on the use of compensation orders given in Home Office Circulars 85/1988 and 86/1988 and gives advice on a number of points which have arisen since their publication. It also draws attention to the findings of recent Home Office research and provides updated guidance on levels of compensation in personal injury cases.

2. Section 104 of the Criminal Justice Act 1988 amended Section 35 of the Powers of Criminal Courts Act 1973 to emphasise the requirement for courts to consider compensation in every case involving personal injury, loss or damage by requiring them, on passing sentence, to give reasons where no compensation order was made. The research study assessed the impact of this, and related measures in the Act. It showed there had been a significant increase in the use of compensation orders. But it also showed that some courts appeared not to be aware of the priority to be given to compensation, nor of the requirement to consider making a compensation order in every appropriate case.

3. The main findings of the study were as follows:

i) Both magistrates' courts and the Crown Court imposed compensation orders in substantially more cases after the 1988 Act came into force, particularly for personal injury. Use remained lower at the Crown Court, where it was used for 17% of offences falling within the relevant categories compared with 39% of those dealt with at magistrates' courts.

ii) Courts frequently imposed a fine or costs even though the compensation order had been reduced due to the offender's lack of means. This appears to contravene the statutory requirement to give preference to compensation over a fine where the offender lacks the means to pay both. (See s.35(4A) of the Powers of the Criminal Courts Act 1973, as inserted by s.67 of the Criminal Justice Act 1982).

iii) The recording of reasons for not making an order rose from 52 per cent to 72 per cent with the 1988 Act. The most common reason for not awarding compensation (see table below) was that it had not been specifically sought (although application on behalf of the victims is not in fact required).

Reason	% cases where given as sole or partial reason
Not sought	63%
Custodial sentence	18%
Insufficient means	17%
Loss made good/property recovered	16%
Inadequate information	10%
Alternative recourse	8%
Other	15%

iv) The possibility of making a compensation order was sometimes dismissed in favour of civil action, even though for many victims this might be impractical.

v) The approach to the use of compensation orders for different offences varied widely between courts, both as to whether an order should be made, and in amounts awarded.

vi) Amounts awarded in more serious injury cases were generally well below the levels suggested in the guidelines appended to Home Office Circular 85/1988 (although this to some extent reflects the finding that in 73 per cent of cases where an order was reduced 'insufficient means' was recorded as the sole or partial reason).

vii) There was wide divergence of views on how to assess compensation, if at all, for items of sentimental or uncertain financial value.

viii) The number of cases involving uninsured vehicles in which compensation was awarded quadrupled but remained very small (about 350 out of more than 200,000 cases involving uninsured drivers).

4. Against the background of these findings courts may wish to consider the following points.

Information about loss

5. The study showed that sentencers were often hampered in making compensation orders by lack of information about the victim's loss or injury. New measures have, however, been introduced which should help to overcome that difficulty. Since October 1992 the police have been asking all victims for details of their losses or injuries etc. which are recorded on Form MG19. This information is then passed to the Crown Prosecution Service to enable them to supply it to the court. If this information is not presented to the court it should be asked for so that the court can be better able to discharge its duty to consider making a compensation order, whether or not there has been a request by the prosecution or the victim.

Priority of compensation orders

6. Under section 67 of the Criminal Justice Act 1982 courts may order payment of

compensation either instead of, or in addition to, dealing with the offender in any other way. A compensation order may therefore be used as a sentence on its own. Where, because the offender lacks the means to pay both, the court has to choose between a compensation order and a fine or other financial penalty, the court is required to give preference to compensating the victim (as fully as possible). Courts should not therefore reduce a compensation order in order to impose another financial penalty. (Section 35(4A) Powers of Criminal Courts Act 1973.)

Civil Redress

7. Although civil action may provide a means of redress, for many victims it will be too costly or uncertain for other reasons. It may also prolong the memory of the incident. Civil action may of course be the only means of obtaining a judgement for the full damages appropriate in all the circumstances. But the sentencing court need not rule out making a compensation order solely because the full value of recompense appropriate could only be established in civil proceedings. It may still be in the victim's interests to make a compensation order for at least as much as is clearly supported by the evidence. For example, if there is medical evidence that the offender broke the victim's nose, but the final medical outcome is uncertain, a compensation order might be considered of at least the value of a simple nasal fracture. In the event of a subsequent successful action for damages the civil court would be able to take into account any sums paid in pursuance of a compensation order. If no order is made but the offender is sentenced to another financial penalty for the offence, his ability to pay any civil damages subsequently awarded to the victim may be reduced.

8. If the court wishes to make a compensation order but requires fuller evidence of the loss or injury, it may be appropriate to ask the prosecution to obtain it (unless the victim has already been asked, but has failed to provide it, or has indicated that he or she does not wish the matter to be considered). Such action should not, however, conflict with the general principle that compensation orders are more normally used in the more clear cut and simple cases and are not always suitable where there are complex issues about the extent of loss or injury.

Stating and recording reasons for not making an order

9. Courts are reminded that section 35 of the Powers of Criminal Courts Act 1973 as amended by section 104 of the Criminal Justice Act 1988 requires them, on passing sentence, to give reasons for not making an order where they could have done so. These reasons must be given in open court and, in magistrates' courts, recorded in the register (Magistrates' Courts Rules 1981 rule 66 (10A)). The Research Study found that courts recorded their reasons in about 72% of cases in 1988-89, compared with 52% in 1987-88. This increase is encouraging, but is still some way from full compliance.

Compensation for Distress and Anxiety

10. Compensation may be ordered for distress and anxiety - for example, caused by threats - and for mental as well as physical injury (see Bond v Chief Constable of Kent [1983] All ER 456). The assessment of compensation in such cases is not always easy, but some factors which can be taken into account are any medical or other help required, the length of any absence from work and a comparison with the suggested levels of compensation for physical injury.

165

Items of Sentimental Value
11. Similarly in the case of stolen or damaged items of sentimental value or where the value can no longer be ascertained, it may be possible to draw commonsense comparisons with other property losses and the likely effect on the victim. The fact that an exact value cannot be established should not necessarily deter courts from attempting to assess compensation and from making an order: victims will otherwise take away the impression that their losses have been ignored.

Uninsured losses in road traffic cases
12. Courts are reminded that the Criminal Justice Act 1988 removed some restrictions on compensation in road traffic cases (see HO Circular 86/1988, paragraph 25). Courts may make compensation orders in any case where injury, loss or damage results from an offence involving a motor vehicle in the control of the offender, provided that the offender is uninsured in respect of such injury, loss and damage and that compensation is not payable under the Motor Insurers' Bureau (MIB) arrangements.

13. In respect of property damage, claimants must always pay the first £175 of any successful claim to MIB. To this extent at least, therefore, a victim's property losses will not be met by MIB. Successful injury claims are paid in full. Where the victim has applied to MIB for compensation it will therefore be necessary, if it is proposed to make a compensation order, to establish from MIB the nature, amount and terms of payment and the amount paid, and to arrange for all payments to be passed to MIB in the event of them awarding compensation. In this way the possibility of double payment of compensation to the victim will be avoided. Because such enquiries may take some time to deal with they should be put in hand at the earliest opportunity. (The address of the Motor Insurers' Bureau is 152 Silbury Boulevard, Central Milton Keynes, MK9 1NB; telephone 0908 240000).

14. Compensation may also be ordered for the victim's loss of or reduction of preferential insurance rates (no-claims bonus).

Period of payment
15. Wherever possible the period of payment should not be more than 12 months. However, the Court of Appeal in Olliver and Olliver (1989 (11) Cr. App. R.(S)10), in considering the maximum period over which fines and compensation orders might normally be paid, said that there was nothing wrong with the period of payment being longer than one year, provided that it was not an undue burden and too severe a punishment, having regard to the nature of the offence and the offender. The court indicated that even a three year payment period might not be inappropriate in certain cases.

Guidelines for compensation in personal injury cases
16. The annex to this circular updates guidance on compensation in personal injury cases. It is based on awards currently made by the Criminal Injuries Compensation Board. The Board bases its awards on common law damages. Guidance on the assessment of common law damages for a wider range of more serious injuries can be found in a recent publication by the Judicial Studies Board, "Guidelines on the Assessment of General Damages in Personal Injury Cases" (ISBN: 1 85431 243 X, published by Blackstone Press, price £14.95).

17. In considering whether to make a compensation order in more serious cases of injury the courts should disregard the possibility that the victim might expect to receive compensation under the Criminal Injuries Compensation Scheme. Where any award is made under the scheme it will be abated to reflect the amount of compensation received from other sources.

Criminal Justice Act 1991
18. Courts are reminded that under the 1991 Act the maximum compensation order which the magistrates' courts may impose for any one offence was raised from £2,000 to £5,000. The Act also empowered courts to make attachments to offenders' social security benefits.

Liaison with recipients of compensation
19. An order for compensation is one of the few tangible ways in which victims can see that their interests have been taken into account by the criminal justice system. It is accordingly important for courts with the responsibility for collecting or enforcing compensation to remember that the public perception of the effectiveness of the system as a whole will be affected by the way in which this task is discharged. Best practice guidance on the handling of the write-off of compensation orders has already been issued (Best Practice Advisory Group Bulletin: Fine Enforcement Part II, issued September 1992). The Magistrates' Courts Rule covering the procedure for obtaining views of victims was modified earlier this year to take account of their special position. Justices' clerks may now wish to review their existing procedures for notifying and keeping victims informed of progress in the recovery of compensation where this has been awarded.

Survey of Local Fining Practices

There are indications of efforts by magistrates' courts to achieve structured outcomes following the CJA 93. Many courts continue to operate extra-statutory unit fine schemes or a 'unit approach' within the framework set by the new s18 CJA 91. The validity of these practices was expressly confirmed by David Maclean MP, Minister of State at the Home Office, when the 1993 Bill was before the House of Commons. The following is a provisional summary of responses received to a survey of magistrates' courts by the Justices' Clerks' Society conducted between October 1993 and May 1994.

Using unit fines (or a close variant thereof):
Bradford
Calderdale
Cumbria
Hampshire (apart from Southampton)
Kennet
Montgomeryshire
North Oxfordshire
Swansea and Lliw Valley
Wiltshire (generally except Salisbury)
Woodspring (Weston-super-Mare)

Courts describing themselves as using a 'unit approach'
Cornwall (except East Cornwall)
Coventry (but using 'gravity factors')
Furness and District
Lanbaurgh East (Cleveland)
North Sefton (based on 'days income')
Salisbury (sub titled 'Income Related Assessment Scheme')
Solihull
Tynedale
Wigan (moderated against M A guidelines)

Magistrates' Association guidelines (or local version)
Canterbury and St Augustine, Faversham and Sittingbourne, Thanet
Dorset
Berkshire
Bristol
Cirencester, Fairford and Tetbury
Ealing
Gloucester
Newport, Gwent
North Staffordshire
Port Talbot
Richmond on Thames
Somerset
Southampton
Stockport
Taunton Deane and West Somerset
Warwickshire
West London

Other methods
Bath (matrix)
Bexley ('standard fines' plus four 'means categories')
East Cornwall (matrix)
Hounslow (banded approach)
North Yorkshire (banded approach based on M A guidelines)
Rochdale, Middleton and Heywood ('pre-CJA 91 practices')
Sedgemoor and Mendip (sliding scale applied to M A guidelines)
West Midlands (various hybrid approaches including some 'unit based')

10 The Youth Court in Outline

This chapter provides an overview of the youth court and associated provisions by way of a general introduction. Readers requiring a specialist treatment of this topic are referred to the companion volume to this work *The Youth Court One Year Onwards* which deals in detail with the items noted at the end of this chapter.

Background

The youth court replaced the former juvenile court in October 1992 under the provisions of the CJA 91—and deals with offenders aged 10 to 17 years inclusive (as opposed to 10 to 16 as was the case with the juvenile court). These and other developments must be considered alongside key aspects of the Children Act 1989 (which took effect a year sooner in October 1991).

The 'care order in criminal proceedings' was abolished by the 1989 Act, having fallen into virtual disuse in the 1980s. The Children Act provided the court with the power to impose a supervision order with a condition of residence (of up to six months: see s12AA CYPA 69 as inserted by s108(4) and sched 12 Children Act 1989). This sentencing option is only available where *inter alia* the young person has been convicted of a serious offence which was committed during the currency of an existing supervision order. The court must be satisfied that the home circumstances of the child or young person have contributed to the offending behaviour.

It should also be noted that the Children Act 1989 gives statutory recognition to the need to avoid prosecution (a somewhat similar intent in the CYPA 1969 remained unimplemented). Local authorities are required to take reasonable steps to reduce the need to bring criminal proceedings against children and young persons (ie following the CJA 91 people below the age of 18): sched 2, para 7(a)(ii) to the 1989 Act. This endorses the practice of the police and the Crown Prosecution Service over recent years, ie in using prosecution as a last resort. This approach must now be considered *inter alia* in the context of the Home Office circular on 'The Cautioning of Offenders' (HOC 18/94) published in March 1994 and reproduced in *Appendix III* to this work.

Welfare

Many of the approaches and practices to emerge in relation to youth justice arise from the 'welfare' orientation to young people: a recognition that most young people will grow out of crime and that exposure to the courts is likely to retard that process (*Growing Out of Crime: The New Era*, Andrew Rutherford, Waterside Press, 1992).

A fundamental duty on the court and others to act in the interests of the welfare of young people exists in s44 CYPA 1933 and survives all subsequent legislation concerning this age group. The Crown Prosecution Service has accepted this duty as a basis for decision making with respect to juveniles (as a result of undertakings made during the passage of the Prosecution of Offenders Act 1985). It is essential to recognize the continuing vitality of a principle enshrined in statute almost 60 years ago.

Outline of the youth court jurisdiction under the CJA 91

There is no overall body of law applicable to the youth court. Rather, the jurisdiction is a mixture of separate legal and practice changes over a number of years—the combined effect of which is to create a different ethos from that in the adult court. The principal developments of recent times (all of which are subject to the welfare principle, *supra*) can be summarised as follows. The CJA 91:

• renamed the 'juvenile court' as the 'youth court': s70 CJA 91.
• extended the jurisdiction so that the youth court and not the magistrates' court deals with people under 18 (not under 17 as previously): s68 and sched 8, *ibid*.
• gave youth court magistrates new sentencing powers (Part III CJA 91) to be exercised within the new overall sentencing framework (*Chapter 1*) along with a new scheme of post-custody supervision (*Chapter 13*).
• followed the principle that sentencing of young people should be governed by individual 'maturity' (this chapter *post*).
• re-directed the existing emphasis on parental responsibility (something built on in the CJ and PO Bill of 1994)
• created a fresh impetus by making 17 year olds subject to the ethos of the former juvenile court—precipitating new practice based strategies via 'action plans' and multi-agency co-operation.

Development of sentencing criteria
The sentencing criteria in Part I CJA 91 (as amended by the CJA 93) apply to offenders of *all* ages. The criteria for passing a custodial sentence contained in s1(2) CJA 91 are similar (though with important differences) to the former criteria governing the use of custody for offenders under 21 contained in s1(4) and s1(4A) CJA 82 (repealed by the CJA 91). These criteria helped to bring about a reduction in custodial sentences on juvenile offenders between 1982 and 1991, when the number of such sentences fell from 7,400 to 1,900. The White Paper, *Crime Justice and Protecting the Public*, proposed the extension of similar criteria to all offenders:

'The Criminal Justice Act 1982 set out the circumstances in which courts could give custodial sentences to offenders under 21. These requirements were refined in the Criminal Justice Act 1988. The provisions reflected the widespread view that, so far as possible, young offenders should not be sentenced to custody, since this is likely to confirm them in a criminal career. Since 1983, the number of offenders under 17 sentenced to custody has been halved and there has been no discernible increase in the number of offences committed by juveniles. In the last year, there has been a significant drop in the number of young adults aged 17 to 20 sentenced to custody ... A more consistent approach to sentencing young offenders has emerged from the Court of Appeal's guidance on interpreting the legislation' (paras 3.6, 3.9).

The historical origin of the custody criteria in the CJA 91 means that those criteria have special significance for the youth court age range. Sentencing criteria now span out to encompass custody and community sentences. The general sentencing changes including those brought about subsequently by the CJA 93 and mentioned throughout this book apply to the youth court age group—with the exception of certain specific items such as suspended sentences (over 21s only) or ordinary mode of trial decisions (adults only) which are reserved to an older age group and any special modifications such as lower overall limits on the length of custody or on the amount of any fine, *post*.

Fines on juvenile offenders
The statutory unit fines system applied to young people in a modified form but this is now replaced by the general fining criteria in the new s18 CJA 93 subject to overall cash fining limits set by the 1991 Act, ie £250 in the case of a person aged 10 to 14 inclusive; £1,000 above that age: see also *Parental responsibility*, *post*.

The position of 16 and 17 year olds
The White Paper, *supra*, said of offenders aged 16 and 17:

'The Government proposes major changes in arrangements for dealing with young offenders aged 16 and 17. As teenagers approach adulthood, their parents' responsibility for them is reduced. Young people should begin to take more responsibility for the consequences of their own decisions and actions. They are at an intermediate stage between childhood and adulthood. The arrangements for dealing with offenders of this age should reflect this' (para 8.14).

A flexible approach
The idea was that 16 and 17 year olds should be dealt with as 'near adults' and that there should be greater flexibility in the overall sentencing arrangements for this age group. As a result, the law governing custodial sentencing of 17 year olds was brought into line with that which applied to 16 year olds under existing legislation.

Section 63 of the CJA 91 *reduced* the maximum term of detention in a young offender institution for an offender aged 17 to 12 months, and Schedule 8 to the Act brought 17 year olds within the ambit of s53 CYPA 1933 under which longer terms of detention can be ordered by the Crown Court in respect of certain 'grave crimes'.

The full range of community penalties previously available for 16 year olds was retained and extended to 17 year olds.

The CJ and PO Bill of 1994 proposes new increased limits of detention in a young offender institution and widens the ambit of s53 CYPA 1933.

171

Maturity of the offender
Also under the CJA 91, 16 year olds became eligible for community penalties or maxima previously applicable and restricted to those aged 17 and over, ie in relation to probation, community service and attendance centre orders. The purpose of these arrangements was to allow courts to select the most suitable sentence according to the maturity and circumstances of the offender and the precise arrangements available locally. The overall effect was as follows:

• the youth court can give either a probation order or a supervision order to a 16 or 17 year old
• the maximum number of hours of work that can be imposed in a community service order is 240 hours for offenders aged 16 and 17 (the former maximum for 16 year olds was 120 hours)
• both 16 and 17 year olds can be ordered to attend an attendance centre for up to 36 hours (the maximum formerly applicable to 17 to 20 year olds. The maximum re 16 year olds was 24 hours)
• combination orders introduced by s11 CJA 91 and curfew orders introduced by s12 CJA 91 (not yet brought into force) are available for 16 and 17 year olds as well as adults.

Parental responsibility
The White Paper *supra* placed considerable emphasis on parental responsibility. Under Part III CJA 91, courts may require the parents or guardians of 16 year olds and 17 year olds to attend court or to pay any financial penalties imposed on their child. Similarly, the court may bind over the parents or guardians of offenders aged 16 and 17 to take proper care of and to exercise proper control over the offender. (The CJ and PO Bill of 1994 empowers the court also to bind over the parent or guardian to ensure that the minor complies with the requirements of a community sentence). However, the court is not placed under a duty to consider exercising these powers, in contrast to the position in relation to offenders below the age of 16.

With these younger offenders the court *must* exercise its powers to require parents or guardians to attend court or to pay any financial penalty imposed unless the parents or guardians cannot be found or it would be unreasonable; and it must bind over the parent or guardian if it is satisfied that this would be desirable in the interests of preventing further offending.

Parents or guardians who are ordered to pay the fines of their children are assessed on the basis of their *own* means, not that of the child.

Apart from responsibilities introduced by the Children Act 1989, *supra*, there were new responsibilities under the CJA 91 for local authorities. Where a child is in care or accommodated by a local authority and the authority has parental responsibility, it can be ordered to pay fines and compensation imposed on the child or young person. The position post-CJA 93 is that a local authority may be ordered to pay these fines without reference to any means test or special provisions concerning the value of the fine (in contrast to the position under the original CJA 91).

Service delivery

It was generally acknowledged as necessary for social services departments and probation services in each area to prepare agreed local plans for dealing with 16 and 17 year olds—the non-statutory term 'Action Plan' being applied to this idea. In summary, action plans include arrangements for providing pre-sentence reports, for carrying out community orders made by courts and for supervising 16 and 17 year old offenders released from custody. A joint Home Office and Department of Health circular on young offenders and the youth court was issued 1992 of which the following is an extract:

'Close liaison is an essential pre-requisite for the provision of good service to the courts and effective work with young offenders ... The new provisions for dealing with 16 and 17 year old offenders bring together elements of both the juvenile and adult court systems, for which there are separate practices and procedures. Their implementation will need to be carefully planned locally, in order to make the best use of opportunities and resources for constructive work with offenders in this age group and to avoid conflicts in objectives and working methods, duplication of effort, or failure to provide necessary support' (para 13).

The circular indicated that, where the boundaries of the probation service and social services departments are the same, the Chief Probation Officer should initiate the joint planning process; but where probation service boundaries contain more than one social services department, responsibility for initiating the process lies with the Director of Social Services.

A feature of the juvenile justice experience since 1980 is the extent to which the relevant agencies have been prepared to work together to form policies generally and to create forums for ideas, eg concerning crime prevention, prosecution policies, cautioning of offenders and the kind of community resources which might be made available for services to courts. In some instances, juvenile court magistrates have become involved in this process in an advisory or consultative capacity. The success of such initiatives laid the foundations of the wider multi-agency co-operation which has emerged within the criminal justice process as a whole (as to which cf eg: the Criminal Justice Consultative Council; Area Consultative Committees; Home Office Special Conferences; multi-agency training; bail information schemes; 'duty psychiatrist' schemes; initiatives in relation to 'young adult offenders' (formerly those aged 17 to 20 inclusive). The youth court thus inherited a sound tradition.

Guilty plea in the absence of the defendant

Section 12 MCA 1980 was amended by sched 11 CJA 91 so as to enable a person who has reached the age of 16 to enter a plea of guilty in writing, in the youth court, where the procedure envisaged by s12 has been adopted by the prosecutor: see new s12(1A). Section 12 is affected by proposals in the CJ and PO Bill (notably a provision which allows courts to deal with written plea cases at any time within 28 days of the return date of the summons without giving notice of adjournment).

The youth court in perspective after the CJA 91
In an article published in *The Magistrate* just prior to the inauguration of the youth court, David Faulkner, formerly Deputy Under-Secretary of State at the Home Office with responsibility for criminal justice policy—and now a Fellow of St John's College and Senior Research Associate at the Oxford Centre for Criminological Research—wrote that the task facing practitioners '. . . will continue to demand creativity and imagination, and a special ethos of the kind which has distinguished the juvenile court in the past'. David Faulkner offered thoughts about the developing role of lay justices in the youth court and its changing social, legal, professional and administrative environment. It looked at the social context, traced the development of a number of themes which came together in the Children Act 1989 and the Criminal Justice Act 1991, and discussed some of the implications for those who work in the youth court or who are associated with it. The remainder of that article is reproduced in *Materials on the Criminal Justice Act 1991* (Waterside Press, 1992).

Youth court trends after the CJA 91
The available information about trends in the sentencing of young offenders and remand decisions in relation to young defendants is summarised in *Chapter 1(d) ante.*

The Criminal Justice and Public Order Bill of 1994
The Bill proposes significant changes to the sentencing powers of the courts in relation to juvenile offenders and introduces other new procedures. These are summarised at the end of *Chapter 1(b), ante.*

The Youth Court One Year Onwards
The companion volume to this work which deals with sentencing and practice in relation to the youth court age group includes sections on: *General Principles, The Changing Policy Context, Jurisdiction, Age Ranges, Parental Responsibility, Procedures, Remands, Custody, Community Sentences, Fines and Compensation, Pre-sentence Reports* and *Inter-agency Co-operation,* together with a *Table of Sentences* and relevant *Statutory Provisions.*

11 Young Adult Offenders

A main theme of penal policy and practice to emerge from the 1980s is that many of the advances made with regard to juveniles (see *The Youth Court in Outline, Chapter 10*) are also relevant in relation to young adult offenders, ie those aged 18 to 20 years of age inclusive.

With the extension of the jurisdiction of the youth court to include 17 year olds under the CJA 91 it became important not to lose sight of the fact that special considerations of age still attach to young adults. This was underlined by the *Code of Practice for the Crown Prosecution Service* (1986).

In 1988 the government, in noting with approval the general reduction in the level of sentences imposed on juveniles, stated that it was '... reasonable to look to a significant drop in the number of young adults sentenced to custody': *Punishment, Custody and the Community* (1988, Cm 424, p 7). Later the same year, the Home Office urged probation areas to establish 'Action Plans', in collaboration with other criminal justice agencies, to encourage 'punishment in the community' for this older age group.

Special Provisions Affecting Young Adults

There are several distinctive features in the law concerning the sentencing of young adults compared with the sentencing of people aged 21 or over, or in some instances those below the age of 18:

No power to suspend sentences
The power in s22 Powers of Criminal Courts Act 1973 to suspend custodial sentences was removed in relation to people below the age of 21 by the CJA 82. The absence of such a power serves to concentrate the mind of the sentencer on the special character of custody.

Minimum and maximum sentences
In contrast to the one year limit on custodial sentences for offenders below the age of 18 (s1B CJA 82 as amended by s63 CJA 91: to be altered to two years by the CJ and PO Bill of 1994) the maximum term of a custodial sentence for a young adult offender is the same as that for a person aged 21 or over; but there is a special *minimum* sentence, applicable to either sex, of 21 days: s1A(4A) CJA 82 as inserted by s63 CJA 91.

Life sentences
A sentence of custody for life under s8(2) CJA 82 can only be imposed on a person aged 18 to 20 following the CJA 91 (formerly 17 to 20): s8(2), *ibid*, as amended by s63(5) CJA 91. Except where a sentence of custody for life is fixed by law, the usual restrictions on custodial sentences in s1(2) CJA 91 apply: see *Chapter 7, ante* and the definition of 'custodial sentence' in s31(1) CJA 91.

Detention for default or contempt
Detention (as opposed to imprisonment for full adults) for default (eg non-payment of fine) or contempt can only be ordered in the case of a person aged 18 to 20 following the CJA 91. This particular form of detention is specifically excluded from the definition of 'custodial sentence' in s31(1) CJA 91, so that the restrictions and procedures in s1 to 4, *ibid*, do not apply. Whereas a person *below* the age of 18 cannot be sent to custody for non-payment of fine, or eg cannot be detained for refusal to be bound over (*Veater v Glennon* (1981) 72 Cr App R 331, [1981] Crim LR 563), a person aged 18 to 20 can be: s9 CJA 82 and cf *Howley v Oxford* (1985) 81 Cr App R 246, 149 JP 363.

Case law
Restrictions on custodial sentences which, until the CJA 91, applied only to persons aged below 21, now apply, in their new form, to offenders of whatever age: *Chapter 7, ante.* However, historically speaking, statutory approaches to young adults have a greater affinity with those relating to the younger age group than with those which affect full adults of 21 years of age or over. Sections 1(4) and (4A) CJA 1982 (repealed by sched 13 to the CJA 91) applied equally to all those below 21.

By far the largest proportion of the case law on the sentencing of offenders below the age of 21 concerns appeals by offenders aged 17 to 20 (the previous age band for 'young adults'). The nature of the appellate system is such that cases heard by youth courts only rarely lead to direct rulings by the higher courts on sentencing matters whereas appeals by young adults from sentencing decisions in the Crown Court lead to authoritative rulings of the Court of Appeal. The effect has been that principles stated in these young adult appeal cases have 'cascaded downwards' and been applied, by analogy, in the juvenile and youth courts to the younger age group.

The nature of custody for young adults
Within the Prison Service, the status of young adults is recognised in their placement in young offender institutions for persons aged 15 to 20: cf s1C CJA 82 which (as amended by s63(4) CJA 91) provides *inter alia* that those serving sentences of detention in a young offender institution shall be held in a young offender institution unless the Home Secretary 'from time to time' directs that they shall be held in a prison or remand centre. The CJ and PO Bill of 1994 extends this provision to young adults serving sentences of custody for life. When they are not held in a young offender institution, but placed in a prison, efforts are made to ensure that young offenders are kept separate from adults. This principle dates from the Prevention of Crime Act 1908 which established the borstal system.

Attendance centre
Apart from custodial sentencing, the only sentence available for those aged 18 to 20 which is not also available for adults is an attendance centre order, not

exceeding 36 hours (the same as for offenders aged 16 and 17 following the CJA 91): s17 CJA 82 as amended by s67 CJA 91.

Mode of trial and committal for sentence
All persons aged 18 or over are subject to the mode of trial procedures contained in s19 MCA 1980, *et al.* However, persons below the age of 21 cannot be committed to the Crown Court for sentence under the 'protection of the public' limb of s38 MCA 1980 as amended by s25 CJA 91 and the CJA 93 (this restriction is removed by the CJ and PO Bill of 1994). They can be so committed under the 'seriousness' limb of s38: see further *Chapter 3, Sentencing Principles* under the heading *Committal to the Crown Court for sentence.*

Post-custody supervision
A special scheme of post-custody supervision applies to all offenders *under 22* released from a sentence of detention in a young offender institution or under s53 CYPA 33: *Chapter 13, post.* Such people may be supervised by a social worker or a probation officer: s43(5) CJA 91.

Section 65 CJA contains special arrangements for the supervision of all such offenders on release. These preserve the previous arrangements under which they receive a minimum of three months' compulsory supervision (subject to this not extending beyond the 22nd birthday). In relation to this age group, the post-custody supervision arrangements apply even in relation to sentences of less than 12 months (cf full adults).

The anomaly of remands
All defendants aged *17 or over* remain subject to adult remand powers.

Section 53 CYPA 1933
Section 53 CYPA 91 (detention for 'grave crimes') does not apply to offenders aged 18 or over: see s68 and sched 8 CJA 91.

12 Pre-sentence Reports

The pre-sentence report (PSR) occupies a strategic position under the provisions of the CJA 91. The Act provided that the court must consider a PSR before passing a custodial sentence other than one fixed by law: s3(1). The only exception is where the offence, or an associated offence, is triable *only* on indictment and the court considers a PSR unnecessary: s3(2). The court must also consider a PSR before making a probation order with any of the additional requirements contained in Schedule 1A to the PCCA 73 (inserted by Schedule 1 to the CJA 91); a community service order; a combination order; or a supervision order containing requirements imposed under section 12, 12A, 12AA, 12B or 12C of the CYPA 69: s7(3). Failure to obtain a PSR does not invalidate the sentence, but on appeal the court considering the appeal must obtain a report: s3(4), 7(4).

Definition of 'pre-sentence report'
The CJA 91 defines a pre-sentence report as follows: '... a report in writing which ... (a) with a view to assisting the court in determining the most suitable method of dealing with the offender, is made or submitted by a probation officer or by a social worker of a local authority social services department; and which (b) contains information as to such matters, presented in such manner as may be prescribed by rules made by the Secretary of State': s3(5).

The purpose of a report
As the definition of a pre-sentence report makes clear, the essential purpose of a PSR is to assist the court in determining 'the most suitable method of dealing with the offender': s3(5)(a). **When contemplating a custodial sentence,** the court must consider a PSR before forming an opinion on whether the criteria for passing a custodial sentence or for the length of the sentence are satisfied: s3(1). **When contemplating a community sentence** the court must consider a PSR before forming an opinion as to its suitability for the offender: s7(3); and s7(1) requires a court considering a community sentence to take into account all information available to it about the circumstances of the offence when deciding on seriousness, which would include such information in a PSR.

Information contained in a report may also be relevant to s28 CJA 91 which enables a court, having decided on the seriousness of the offence, to take into account other mitigating factors and reduce the sentence if appropriate.

In addition to the above statutory provisions governing PSRs as such, reports on young offenders must be written against the background of welfare considerations implicit in both the CYPA 1933 and the Children Act 1989, as to which see *Chapter 10, ante.*

Why was the 1991 law on PSRs necessary?
The principal reason for requiring courts to consider a PSR before passing a

custodial sentence was summarised in the White Paper, *Crime, Justice and Protecting the Public* (1990), as follows:

'The purpose of requiring the courts to consider a report by the probation service when a custodial sentence is contemplated will be to provide the court with detailed information about how the offender could be punished in the community, so that option can be fully considered.' (para 3.10)

Before the Criminal Justice Act 1991, many offenders pleading not guilty in Crown Courts were sentenced to custody without a social inquiry report. (Where a guilty plea was known in advance, reports were normally prepared.) A report prepared for the Association of Chief Officers of Probation entitled 'How Do You Plead?' (1989) looked at all 'not guilty' cases at Crown Courts on the Midland and Oxford circuit between May and October 1988. Fifty-nine per cent of offenders **sentenced to immediate custody** who pleaded not guilty (or entered a plea of guilty at a late stage) had no social inquiry report.

This was disturbing enough in itself. It was even more disturbing in view of the evidence showing that this disproportionately disadvantaged black offenders: see eg the findings of Home Office Research Study 103 'Sentencing Practice in the Crown Court' (David Moxon, 1988), summarised in *Chapter 6, ante.*

The CJA 91 therefore sought to ensure that PSRs would be prepared on the vast majority of offenders in all racial groups before they could be sentenced to custody or to any of the more intensive community orders.

The content of reports

The Home Secretary has the power to specify in statutory rules both the contents and the manner of presentation of pre-sentence reports: s3(5)(b) CJA 91. To date, however, no statutory rules have been made. Instead a National Standard for pre-sentence reports was produced in 1992 by the Home Office, the Department of Health and the Welsh Office alongside various National Standards for the supervision of offenders in the community. The National Standard for PSRs is reproduced in *Materials on the Criminal Justice Act 1991* (Waterside Press, 1992).

The National Standard was complemented by training materials produced for the Home Office by the National Association for the Care and Resettlement of Offenders (NACRO) in 1992 and revised in 1993. The NACRO publication 'Pre-Sentence Reports: A Handbook for Probation Officers and Social Workers' (1993 revised edition) is a useful summary for practitioners of guidance to current best practice in the preparation of PSRs. A revised National Standard was in preparation at the time of going to press: the Home Office aims to publish revised standards in the autumn of 1994.

The current guidance to report writers indicates that PSRs should be divided into four main sections:

(i) Introduction
This should specify briefly the sources used in preparing the report (documents seen, people interviewed and agencies consulted); the extent of the report writer's

knowledge of, and number of interviews with, the defendant and others; and steps taken to verify information. Any significant information which was not available to the writer should be specified.

(ii) Analysis of current offence(s)
This section should contain an analysis of the current offence (or offences) and the circumstances leading up to it. It should include information about **aggravating** or **mitigating** features of the offence which will help the court to assess its seriousness. (However, it is **not** normally appropriate to use the words 'aggravating' and 'mitigating').

This section should include an assessment of the context in which the offence occurred; the actual damage/harm/cost of the offending including (where there is a personal victim) the impact on the victim; the offender's motivation, view of and attitude to the offence, attitude to the victim, any expressed remorse or guilt, and any expressed desire to make reparation/compensation; and any special circumstances (eg family crisis, alcohol, drugs, physical or mental health problems) which were **directly relevant** to the offending.

Analysing the offence does not mean simply reporting the prosecution version, followed by the defendant's version, without comment. It means presenting the report writer's analysis, following a consideration of all the versions of the offence. The analysis should reflect an integrated approach, looking at both the offence and the offender's motivation, with the aim of helping the sentencer to understand **why** the offender committed this particular offence at this time.

(iii) Relevant information about the offender
If the offender has no previous convictions, this should be stated. Otherwise the report should evaluate patterns of offending to date in the light of the personal and social factors which have contributed to them. It is not necessary to include full details of the defendant's criminal history, which will be available to the court from the prosecution; it is an analysis of the **pattern** of offending which is important. Where appropriate, the period of time since the most recent previous conviction should be included.

The report should discuss earlier disposals including an assessment of positive and negative results. It should refer to successful completions of probation, supervision, community service and combination orders, suspended sentence supervision orders and after-care licences. Where these were not completed, the writer should assess whether there were nevertheless any partial successes on which future sentences could build, eg improvements in attitude, personal growth, a lengthening of time between convictions, reduced seriousness of offending.

This section should include any personal or social information about the offender **which is relevant to past offending, to the likelihood or otherwise of reoffending or to a proposed community sentence.** Relevant considerations could include the offender's domestic situation, family and peer group relationships, finances/budgeting, employment status, housing, training or education, use of leisure, social skills, medical and psychiatric considerations, gambling, alcohol or drug problems, local environment (including any relevant cultural factors), sexual problems, aggression, racism. **However, this information should be included only if it is relevant to past offending, to the likelihood or otherwise of further offending or to an appropriate community sentence.** Information about positive aspects of the offender's life or attitudes will often be relevant to an overall assessment of the likelihood of reoffending. The report should refer also to any positive action taken by the offender (eg in relation to employment or education) since the offence was committed. This section may also include information on mitigating factors unrelated to the offence which the court may see as justifying a reduction in sentence.

Where the current offence is a violent or sexual one, the report writer should consider whether there is a risk to the public of serious harm to the offender. If so, he or she should consider whether a community sentence of any kind could reduce the risk and refer to this as appropriate in the next section of the report.

The material in this section is highly relevant to assessing suitability for particular community sentences. This section should therefore, where appropriate, pave the way for a well reasoned proposal for a community sentence.

(iv) Conclusion
The conclusion should flow from the rest of the report. Unless the offence is so serious that a lengthy custodial sentence is inevitable, or not serious enough to justify a community sentence, this section should propose a community sentence which contains a degree of restriction on liberty matching the seriousness of the offence. When the court has asked for other options to be considered, or where a discussion of any other options seems appropriate, the writer should briefly give reasons for regarding other options as unsuitable. Where appropriate, the proposed length of the order should be stated. **The report should not make a firm recommendation** to the sentencer. The proposal should inform the court of what could best be done with the offender if the court was minded to pass a community sentence.

Where the proposed sentence is a probation order, supervision order or combination order, the report should contain an outline of the supervision plan agreed with the offender. When any community sentence is proposed, there should be a description of the purposes and desired outcomes of the proposed sentence, the methods to be used, a timetable with targets for achieving the programme's objectives, the frequency of contact by the probation service, social services or other agencies responsible for any part of the programme, where the work will take place (if appropriate), and the likely effect on dependants. It should spell out the likely impact on offending and the steps to be taken if the offender does not comply.

When any community sentence requiring consent is proposed, the report should state that the offender is willing to comply and is clear about the consequences of failure to comply. It is legitimate to include any available local information on the success rate of the proposed programme. The description of the proposed programme should make clear (i) the degree of restriction of liberty involved and (ii) how the disposal would help to tackle the behaviour which led to the offence.

Where custody is a likely option, this should be acknowledged and discussed. Where the offender is at risk of a custodial sentence, it is legitimate to refer to any possible adverse effects of custody for the offender and for other people (eg on attitudes, relationships, family, dependants, employment, training, education, accommodation, likelihood of reoffending etc). It is **not** appropriate to refer to likely **positive** effects of custody relating to treatment of the offender: under the sentencing criteria in the Criminal Justice Act 1991 these are not legitimate considerations justifying a custodial sentence. Where custody appears inevitable, the report may appropriately refer to considerations which the court may regard as relevant to the length of sentence.

The new section 29 and pre-sentence reports

The new s29 CJA 91, substituted by s66(6) CJA 93, empowers courts considering the seriousness of an offence to 'take into account any previous convictions of the offender or any failure of his to respond to previous sentences'. However, it would **not** normally be appropriate (as well as being confusing) for PSR writers to include information about the offender's previous record in the section of the PSR concerned with the current offence. In some cases a previous record will be relevant to the seriousness of the current offence; but in others it will not. It is for the court rather than the PSR writer to make this decision. The new draft National Standard on pre-sentence reports, issued for comment in March 1994, says (in relation to the section of the PSR which concerns the current offence):

'Where there is a specific feature of the offence which appears to conform to a pattern of previous offending which could be relevant to the court's judgement as to its seriousness (eg targeting vulnerable victims), it is appropriate to refer to this in this section. **Otherwise, discussion of offending history should take place in the following section of the report.'** (Emphasis added).

In effect, the draft National Standard indicates that PSR writers should include information about the previous record in the section on 'relevant information about the offender' **unless** it reveals the kind of aggravating factor of the current offence similar to those which could have fallen within the original s29(2).

Selecting proposals in a PSR

It is for the court, not the PSR writer, to make a definitive decision on the seriousness of the offence. However, when considering what proposal to make in a PSR in line with the statutory sentencing criteria, the report writer **mentally** has to go through a three stage process:

• First, form a view in broad terms of how serious the offence is

- Second, assess what type of sentence is the most suitable for the offender.
- Third, ensure that the proposed sentence contains an appropriate degree of restriction on liberty.

In going through this process, the writer should bear in mind that, having decided on the seriousness of the offence, the court can also take into account any mitigating factors unrelated to the offence and can reduce the sentence from the level which the seriousness of the offence would justify: s28(1) CJA 91.

How can report writers avoid unnecessary tension and misunderstanding with courts in this process? PSR writers can be assisted in forming an opinion of the seriousness of the offence if judges and magistrates give a 'preliminary and non-binding view of seriousness': as to which see *Chapter 8*. This view is 'preliminary' because a consideration of information contained in the PSR could alter that view; but such an indication of the court's provisional view can help PSR writers to avoid making what courts might regard as wholly unrealistic proposals. The Justices' Clerks' Society and the Magistrates' Association have expressed the view that is it desirable that courts should indicate their provisional view of seriousness and possible sentence when requesting a PSR.

Where there is an adjournment to obtain a PSR, report writers should therefore seek such advice from the court. The court adjourning for a PSR must phrase any such statement carefully to avoid giving an unfairly misleading message to the defendant. Wrongly phrased, such a message could legally tie the court's hands as to future sentence by, for example, creating a 'legitimate expectation' of a community sentence by the defendant. However, such problems can be avoided by the use of an appropriate form of words such as that cited under the heading *Provisional indications of seriousness* in *Chapter 8*.

The language of the report must not suggest that the writer is usurping the sentencer's function by making a definitive assessment of seriousness. But in order to propose a community sentence with an appropriate degree of restriction of liberty, the writer must first form a view of how serious the offence is. This view will be formed **in the PSR writer's own mind** and he or she will use it to assist in selecting an appropriately targeted proposal. If there has been no preliminary non-binding indication of seriousness from a magistrates' court, report writers should bear in mind that the Magistrates' Association's guidelines may provide the starting point for the court's consideration of sentence.

Having formed a view of the offence, the report writer may have concluded that the offence was not serious enough to justify a community sentence. If it is serious enough, he or she must then assess what type of sentence is the most **suitable** for the offender. The most important element in 'suitability' is the likely effectiveness of the sentence in preventing further offending. Factors which may be relevant in assessing the suitability for the offender of a particular sentence or order include:

- the risk of reoffending and the likely seriousness of further offences;
- the need and scope for intervention, including help with particular problems as part of a programme to reduce offending (eg alcohol, drugs, aggression, sexual offending, social skills, employment, accommodation,

training or education, finances, budgeting);
- the need for work to confront offending behaviour;
- the need for psychiatric treatment;
- the maturity (or stage of development) of the offender;
- the composition of groups in any group activity to which referral is being considered;
- previous experience of this particular sentence;
- whether the sentence stands a realistic prospect of completion by the offender.

On the last point, the White Paper *Crime, Justice and Protecting the Public* (1990) stressed that the courts should be 'realistic as well as demanding' in the requirements they place on offenders:

'The lifestyle of many offenders, especially young adults, is often disorganised and impulsive, particularly if they drink too much or are addicted to drugs. The probation service will have a duty to ensure that difficulties of this kind are made known to the court. Each order should be tailored both to the seriousness of the offence and the characteristics of the offender. A comparatively short order may make more severe demands on some offenders than more severe orders would on others.' (para. 4.9)

It is therefore legitimate to refer in a PSR to factors which make compliance with a particular order or requirement more onerous for some individuals than for others.

In addition to assessing suitability, the report writer must ensure that his or her preferred community sentence proposal contains a degree of restriction on liberty commensurate with the seriousness of the offence. This is not, of course, an exact science. For example, the number of **hours** involved in different **types** of sentence cannot be directly compared. In assessing the degree of restriction on liberty, it is necessary to consider the content of the activity as well as its duration: for example, supervision programmes involving confrontation of offenders' attitudes and behaviour can be very intensive and 'restrictive'.

Restrictions on liberty can operate in a number of ways. Attendance centre and community service orders require offenders to give up **time and effort** and thereby restrict them from undertaking other activities. Probation and supervision orders require this as well, but also require offenders to make **changes in their lives** which will reduce the likelihood of reoffending. Combination orders bring together the restrictions imposed by community service orders and probation.

The joint discussion paper of March 1993
In March 1993 a discussion paper entitled 'Community Sentences and Restriction on Liberty' was produced by the Magistrates' Association, the Association of Chief Officers of Probation and the Justices' Clerks' Society. This made the following observations of relevance to probation and supervision

orders:

- Much activity and effort needs to be undertaken by the offender between meetings if the supervision is to achieve its objectives. The demands of the order are much greater than the number of hours' formal contact suggest
- Orders are often made in the expectation of considerable changes to the offender's behaviour—for example:

—In tackling drug or alcohol abuse, dealing with cravings and building a new way of life
—In addressing violent offending, adopting more constructive ways of handling frustration and dealing with other people
—Changing a lifestyle on giving up theft
—Probation centre and specified activity programmes require offenders to face a great many challenges to their way of life and most offenders do not experience them as an easy option: indeed, many recidivists say they are much more demanding than custody
—A requirement to live in a hostel is a substantial restriction of liberty. It involves being subject to the rules of the hostel, which affect all aspects of everyday life
—In some cases 'straight' probation and supervision orders involve offenders in substantial elements of work or programmes which in other cases would form part of a formal requirement.

Among the observations made by the joint discussion paper were the following:

'A disorganised offender may find the completion of a short community service order to be much more restricting than a longer order would be for a well organised individual.'

'A probation order, made in the expectation that the recipient will tackle a drug dependency problem, will make huge demands in terms of altering an established way of life.'

These quotations illustrate ways in which, in some cases, apparently less restrictive sentences (e.g. a short community service order or a straight probation order) can in fact make heavy demands on offenders. In these circumstances, such orders could legitimately be seen by courts as commensurate with the seriousness of an offence which would otherwise merit a more severe sentence, and it is legitimate for PSR writers to refer to such considerations in their reports.

Quality assurance
The National Standard for PSRs states that Chief Probation Officers and Directors of Social Services should establish quality assurance procedures adapted to suit the range of circumstances in their area:

'... for example, court and field teams and arrangements for the youth court; the individual circumstances of each offence and offender, including appropriate action to ensure anti-discriminatory practice and the urgency with which different reports should be prepared. Quality can be ensured through training and selection of staff; local practice guidance; procedures for internal monitoring and inspection agreed with HM Inspectorate of Probation and, where appropriate, equivalent arrangements for inspection by the social services inspectorates; and review of individual PSRs before submission to the sentencer by the writer, a colleague or line manager, eg to ensure that proposals for community sentences are realistic and appropriate in relation to seriousness, that PSRs do not stereotype the offender, and that in general reports are crisp, clear, easy to understand and relevant.' (para. 35).

Among the features of reports to which quality assurance procedures of any kind should address themselves are:

—whether reports comply with National Standards
—sources used for reports
—the format and structure of reports
—whether proposals for community sentences are realistic, appropriate, clearly explained, and supported by the body of reports
—whether reports contain racist or sexist language, stereotypes, negative images of women or black people, other types of stereotyping or improper discriminatory comment or inferences
—relevance of information included in reports
—overall balance of reports including positive and negative impressions
—whether reports comply with important points of agency policy
—use of jargon in reports.

The aim of quality assurance is to **improve practice,** not to criticise or demoralise report writers. In practice, the existence of quality assurance procedures can **motivate** probation officers and social workers to improve the standard of reports by paying careful attention to these issues when preparing PSRs.

Defendant's access to reports
Section 46(1) PCCA 73 requires a copy of the PSR to be given to an adult defendant, or to his or her counsel or solicitor. Section 46(2) provides that, where the defendant is under 17 and is unrepresented, a copy need not be given to him or her but must be given to the parents or guardian if they are present in court.

Youth courts are required by Rule 10(3) and (4) of the Magistrates' Courts (Children and Young Persons) Rules 1992 to make any written report available to:

(a) the defendant's legal representative;
(b) the defendant's parent or guardian, if present;

(c) the defendant, unless the court directs that this is impracticable because of his or her age or understanding or undesirable, in which case the defendant should normally be told the substance of any material information.

The above provisions are statutory requirements; but good practice requires that report writers go further than this and ensure that all defendants are given a copy of the report.

Procedures in courts

The National Standard on pre-sentence reports emphasised that at the Crown Court there was a need to ensure that there were as few and as short adjournments as possible for PSRs to be prepared. Pilot trials in five Crown Court centres before the implementation of the CJA 91 had demonstrated that, given effective co-operation between all paticipants, it was possible for the probation service to provide an effective report-writing service for a broad range of cases, including preparation of some reports on the day they were requested. The findings of the trials were summarised in a joint circular 'Pre-Sentence Reports—Pilot Trials in the Crown Courts' issued by the Home Office, Lord Chancellor's Department and Crown Prosecution Service in May 1992: this is reproduced in *Materials on the Criminal Justice Act 1991* (Waterside Press, 1992).

The National Standard said that, in preparing reports for the Crown Court, the objective should be:

• to avoid as far as possible adjournments for reports, by preparing PSRs in advance of trial whenever there is sufficient notice of a guilty plea to the principal charge;
• where an adjournment for a PSR is necessary, to prepare the report as expeditiously as possible (especially where the offender is remanded in custody, the trial judge wishes the report to be available quickly and there is any other reason for urgency) consistent with the requirements of the standard;
• to seek to operate these arrangements on a basis of mutual understanding with the judiciary and others in the criminal justice systen, respecting both trial judges' wishes and the professional advice of report writers as to the length of time needed for reports to be prepared to the requirements of the standard.

The standard included a model agreement or 'statement of preferred practice' to be adopted by local probation services and Crown Courts. This stated that pre-trial PSRs would be prepared where there was a plea of guilty, or a plea of guilty to the more serious offence in a mixed plea, at the point of committal; or when the probation service was given sufficient notice of a change of plea before the Crown Court hearing. Where an offender is convicted and a PSR has not been prepared, the model statement provided that:

'... the judge should ask for a probation officer to be called (if not already present in court) to advise how quickly a PSR could be prepared. Unless the probation officer is already able to advise the judge, the case should be briefly stood down so that the probation officer may assess the situation and report back as to how quickly it appears that a satisfactory PSR can be written in accordance with the requirements of the probation service National Standard. That time can vary considerably from case to case: the probation service will seek to write each report as expeditiously as possible, particularly where the defendant is in custody or the report is otherwise needed urgently. In appropriate cases only, this may be later the same day, but in other cases considerably longer may be required. Once the officer has reported back, the date should be set for the PSR to be available and sentencing to take place.'

The model statement of preferred practice is reproduced in full in *Materials on the Criminal Justice Act 1991* (Waterside Press, 1992). Statements of preferred practice were duly adopted by probation services and Crown Courts around the country, and probation services increased the size of their Crown Court teams to enable these arrangements to work efficiently.

The National Standards observed that arrangements in magistrates' courts and youths courts were different from those in the Crown Court, most significantly because it would normally be impracticable to provide dedicated PSR-writing teams in magistrates' courts and youth courts and therefore to respond very quickly to requests for short notice reports. It continued:

'Nevertheless, all reports should be prepared as expeditiously as possible— particularly, for example, in more straightforward cases and those where the offender is remanded in custody awaiting sentence.'

The National Standard on pre-sentence reports and the model statement of preferred practice for the Crown Court are reproduced in *Materials on the Criminal Justice Act 1991* (Waterside Press, 1992).

Changes made by the 1994 Bill
The CJ and PO Bill of 1994 substantially weakens the mandatory requirements of the CJA 91 to obtain PSRs before passing custodial sentences or certain community sentences. It allows courts to dispense with a PSR in these situations if they consider that it is 'unnecessary' to obtain a report. This is identical to the provision which currently applies to custodial sentences passed for offences triable only on indictment: it would apply also to custodial sentences passed for summary and either-way offences and to the community sentences in relation to which the CJA 91 made PSRs mandatory. Where the offender is aged under 18, the Bill provides that a court can decide that a report is 'unnecessary' only if the offence is indictable-only or it has considered a previous PSR obtained in respect of the offender.

When is a report unnecessary?
If the changes proposed in the CJ and PO Bill of 1994 survive the Bill's passage through Parliament, the circumstances in which courts may dispense with a PSR when they consider that a report is 'unnecessary' will take on greatly increased significance.

The terms of s3(2) CJA 91, which currently empowers a court to dispense with a pre-sentence report when sentencing for offences triable only on indictment when the court considers that a report is 'unnecessary', are similar to those of s2(3) CJA 1982 relating to young offenders (repealed by the 1991 Act). Section 2(2) required courts to obtain a social inquiry report before imposing a custodial sentence on a young offender; but s2(3) stated that this did not apply '... if, in the circumstances of the case, the court is of the opinion that it is unnecessary to obtain a social inquiry report'. A similarly worded provision and exception applied to the imposition of a prison sentence on an adult offender who had not already served one: see s20 and 20A PCCA 1973 (again repealed and replaced by the 1991 Act).

There has been relatively little judicial guidance on the circumstances making a social inquiry report unnecessary. The unreported case of *Griffiths* (1984), heard in the High Court on February 14 of that year, concerned a 19 year old offender who was given a three months' detention centre order without a social inquiry report. Watkins LJ said:

> '... It may well be that had the judge taken the precaution which Parliament bids every judge in this sort of circumstance to do, he would still have imposed the sentence which he did upon this appellant. But this court, because of the judge's failure adequately to inform himself, has come to the conclusion that, bearing in mind the contents of the social inquiry report which is before us, we have no alternative but to quash the sentence imposed'.

In the case of *Massheder* (1983) 5 Cr App R (S) 442, a 15 year old defendant admitted being concerned with others in an offence of arson involving criminal damage valued at over £5,000. No social inquiry report had been prepared because of industrial action and the then practice of social services not to prepare reports in circumstances where no finding of guilt had been recorded. The trial judge described this as a 'disgraceful situation'. Despite an offer from a representative from social services, he refused to adjourn. He imposed 18 months' detention under s53 CYPA 1993. On appeal, Macpherson J stated that:

> '... the whole purpose of obtaining a report is to give help and balance to the consideration of all available courses open to the court. In this case, in spite of the difficulty, the matter should have been adjourned to see whether a report was produced'.

Varying sentence to a supervision order, he added: '... If the case had been adjourned and a report like the one before us had been obtained, we feel it is likely that the judge would have been affected and perhaps persuaded by it as we have been.' It is submitted that a pre-sentence report could be regarded as 'unnecessary' only where the court is sure that, whatever it contained, it would make no difference to the sentence imposed (including sentence *length*). The circumstances in which this can be predicted with certainty must be comparatively few.

13 Parole and Early Release of Prisoners

The CJA 91 introduced the most far-reaching overhaul of arrangements for the early release of sentenced prisoners since the introduction of the parole system in England and Wales in 1968 (under the Criminal Justice Act 1967). The changes largely followed (although not entirely) the proposals made in Lord Carlisle's inquiry which reported in November 1988: *The Parole System in England and Wales: Report of the Review Committee*, Cm 532. The Carlisle Committee sought to reduce the disparity between the length of sentences imposed and served. The Act's scheme was based on a distinction between prisoners sentenced to short and long sentences with the latter being defined as sentences of four years or more (Carlisle had recommended that the dividing line be sentences of *over* four years). Under the Act, the framework for early release from prison (which applies to those sentenced on or after 1 October 1992) was revised as follows:

• remission (in its previous form and under which prisoners were formerly released, subject to good behaviour, after serving one-third of their sentence) was abolished
• all prisoners would spend at least half their sentences in prison
• additional days in prison could be ordered for misconduct (replacing the system of loss of remission for offences against prison discipline)
• short sentence prisoners (ie persons serving sentences of under four years) would spend 50 per cent of their sentence in prison. Release would then be *automatic* (subject to additional days ordered for misconduct).
• for prisoners serving sentences of four years or more, a discretionary system of parole would remain
• all prisoners sentenced to imprisonment of one year or more would be supervised on release until the three-quarters point of their sentences (in the case of sex offenders, courts could order supervision to continue until the end of the sentence)
• all prisoners would be *at risk* of being returned to prison to serve the remainder of their sentence if convicted of a further imprisonable offence committed before the end of the sentence
• the Secretary of State could direct the Parole Board as to matters to be taken into account by it in discharging its functions: see *Secretary of State and the Parole Board, post.*

The CJA 91 stressed the continuum between life in prison and in the community. 'To provide the best opportunity to prevent reoffending, what prisoners do in prison must be related to and lead to the arrangements for their supervision on release': *Custody, Care and Justice: The Way Ahead for the Prison Service in England and Wales* (1991, Cm 1647, p 10). This required close co-operation between prisons and the probation service. In September 1991, the government announced that it would enshrine the need for co-operation between the two services in *National Standards* for the supervision of offenders by the probation service before and after release. A National Standard on 'Supervision Before and After Release from Custody' was published in August 1992 by the Home Office, Department of Health and Welsh Office. This was followed in 1993 by a 'National Framework for the Throughcare of Offenders in Custody to Completion of Supervision in the Community', published by the Home Office following consultation with the prison and probation services.

Comparison with previous rules for release
Part II of the CJA 1991 altered the rules governing the proportion of a sentence which is actually to be spent in custody and the position of prisoners on release. Previously it was possible for an offender to be released on parole after serving one-third of his or her sentence. As a result of the system of remission, all determinate sentence prisoners (ie those serving a fixed term) were released from prison free of any restriction whatsoever after serving two-thirds of their sentence (except where they lost remission through misbehaviour). The changes are summarised in the chart at the end of the chapter. Prisoners sentenced before the provisions came into force retain previous entitlements.

Secretary of State and the Parole Board
The Parole Board still exists to discharge certain functions set out in the Act, principally in relation to long-term prisoners and lifers, *post*. The Board is required to advise the Secretary of State in connection with any matter referred to it by him which is connected with the early release or recall of prisoners: s32(2) CJA 91. The way in which the Board must act in arriving at decisions and the power of the Secretary of State to regulate this process are set out in s32, *ibid*. In particular, the Secretary of State may give the Board directions as to matters to be taken into account when making recommendations. In giving such directions, he must have regard to: (a) the need to *protect the public* from *serious harm* from offenders; and (b) the desirability of *preventing* the commission by them of further *offences* and of *securing* their *rehabilitation* (s32(6), *ibid*).

The directions made by the Home Secretary under this section stated:

'The decision whether or not to recommend parole should focus primarily on the risk to the public of a further offence being committed at a time when the offender would otherwise be in prison. This should be balanced against the benefit, both to the public and the offender, of early release back into the

191

community under a degree of supervision which might help rehabilitation and so lessen the risk of reoffending in the future ...

'Before recommending parole, the Parole Board should be satisfied that:

a) the longer period of supervision that parole would provide is likely to reduce the risk of further imprisonable offences being committed. In assessing the risk to the community, a small risk of violent offending is to be treated as more serious than a larger risk of non-violent offending;
b) the offender has shown by his attitude and behaviour in custody that he is willing to address his offending and has made positive efforts and progress in doing so;
c) the resettlement plan will help to ensure the offender's rehabilitation.' (paras 1.1, 1.3)

These directions apply to prisoners sentenced *before or after* 1 October 1992. They were intended to be more stringent than the previous criteria for parole and in June 1992 the then Home Secretary, Kenneth Clarke, therefore abolished the 'restricted policy' (which permitted parole for offenders serving sentences of over five years for offences involving violence, sex, arson or drug trafficking only if there were exceptional circumstances or for a short period near the end of the sentence). The Report of the Parole Board for 1992 commented:

'We believe that paragraph 1.3 represents a somewhat tougher line than hitherto and, taken with the introduction of an automatic period of supervision, may result in proportionately fewer recommendations for release, notwithstanding the abolition of the restricted policy.'

Schedule 5 CJA 91 dealt with membership of the Board, terms of appointment, remuneration and allowances. The Board continues to have four statutory categories of person among its membership. A duty is imposed on the Board: '... as soon as practicable after the end of each year [to] make to the Secretary of State a report on the performance of its functions during the year; and the Secretary of State shall lay a copy of the report before Parliament': sched 5, para 6.

Early Release

There are three forms of release: 'automatic unconditional release', 'automatic conditional release' (ACR) and 'discretionary conditional release' (DCR: or parole). The arrangements operate as follows:

Short-term prisoners
A short-term prisoner is defined as 'a person serving a sentence of imprisonment for a term of less than four years' : s33(5) CJA 91. Under s33(1), *ibid*, as soon

as a short-term prisoner has served one half of his or her sentence, the Secretary of State must release him or her, either: (a) unconditionally, if the term imposed did not exceed 12 months; or (b) on licence, if the term imposed was 12 months or more. The licence then expires at the end of three-quarters of the original term imposed: s33(3), *ibid.* (It should be noted that the term 'unconditionally' in practice means 'unsupervised': even prisoners released from sentences of under 12 months remain liable to serve the remainder of their sentence if convicted of another imprisonable offence committed before the end of the sentence.)

In relation to a short-term prisoner under the age of 18 years, the rules are marginally different in that the Secretary of State is required to release such detainees unconditionally if the term is *12 months or less*, and on licence if sentenced to a term of *more than 12 months*: s43(4) CJA 91. However, all such prisoners released from sentences of 12 months or less are subject to a period of three months' supervision under the separate provisions of s65 CJA 91 (supervision of young offenders after release): see *Young offenders, post.*

Long-term prisoners (not including lifers)

A long-term prisoner is defined as 'a person serving a sentence of imprisonment for a term of four years or more': s 33(5) CJA 91. As soon as a long-term prisoner has served two-thirds of his sentence, the Secretary of State must release him or her on licence: s33(2), *ibid*, which will then remain in force until the time at which the prisoner would have served three-quarters of the original term, but for his or her release: s33(3), *ibid.* A long-term prisoner *may* be released on licence at any time between one-half and two-thirds of his sentence if the Parole Board recommends release on licence to the Home Secretary. Section 50, *ibid*, empowers the Secretary of State to specify by statutory instrument categories of prisoner whose release may be authorised by the Parole Board without reference to the Home Secretary. The government decided initially to delegate to the Board the power to make the final decision on the release of prisoners serving less than seven years.

The government has also decided that, when prisoners given determinate sentences on or after 1 October 1992 come up for review, their dossiers will be disclosed and the Parole Board will give reasons for its decisions.

Life sentence prisoners

The power to release a prisoner serving a mandatory life sentence remains as it was before the CJA 91 in that the Parole Board may make such a recommendation to the Secretary of State who must consult with the Lord Chief Justice and if possible the trial judge. The Secretary of State may then authorise his release on licence. This licence must remain in force until his death (although the condition of supervision may be cancelled). For changes in the system concerning discretionary life sentences, see *Discretionary life sentences, post.*

Compassionate release
There are discretionary powers to release any prisoner on licence if the Secretary of State is satisfied, in *exceptional circumstances*, that he should be released on compassionate grounds: s36 CJA 91. But he must consult the Parole Board before doing so in the case of long-term or life prisoners.

Release on licence
This is a release with conditions. There will always be a condition to be supervised by a probation officer. Further conditions may also be specified as the Parole Board (in discretionary conditional release cases) or the prison governor (in automatic conditional release cases) thinks fit. In relation to a person released on licence who is under the age of 22 years, supervision may be carried out by a social worker from a local authority social services department or a probation officer: s43(5) CJA 91, s65(1), *ibid*.

Annex 8.A of the National Standard on 'Supervision Before and After Release from Custody' contains a list of extra conditions which can be included in licences. These are:

i. to attend upon a duly qualified psychiatrist/psychologist/medical practitioner.
ii. not to engage in any work or other organised activity involving young people.
iii. to live at a specified place and not to leave to live elsewhere without the prior approval of the supervising officer.
iv. not to reside in the same household as any child under a specified age.
v. not to approach or communicate with specified persons without prior approval.
vi. to comply with requirements imposed by the supervising officer to address the offender's problems in relation to alcohol/drug/sexual/gambling/solvent abuse/anger/debt/offending behaviour problems.

Misbehaviour after release on licence
Before the CJA 91, failure to comply with the conditions of a licence was not an offence; it was dealt with by the Parole Board rather than the courts. The new code of sanctions for misbehaviour depends on the type of sentence, as follows:

Short-term prisoners
Section 38(1) CJA 91 created an offence of 'breach of licence conditions'. This is punishable in the magistrates' court with a fine not exceeding level 3, ie 10 units. Section 38(2) CJA 91 gave the magistrates' court power when convicting a person of the above offence (whether or not it passes any other sentence on him) to suspend the licence for a period *not exceeding* 6 months; and to order his recall to prison for the period during which the licence is suspended. Once the licence is suspended, the person is liable to be detained and is otherwise deemed

to be unlawfully at large.

Long-term prisoners and lifers
Section 39 CJA 91 gave the Secretary of State power to revoke a licence and to recall the offender to prison if recommended to do so by the Board. Where it appears expedient in the public interest to recall a prisoner, the Secretary of State may do so before any recommendation by the Board is practicable. A prisoner recalled under this provision has the right to be informed of the reasons for this, and to make representations. These must be referred by the Secretary of State to the Board. The Board then has a discretion to *direct* immediate release in the case of a discretionary life sentence prisoner, or *recommend* immediate release in the case of any other person.

Alongside the directions to the Parole Board about the criteria for release of determinate sentence prisoners, the Home Secretary has also given directions concerning the recall of long-term prisoners released on licence. These also provide that 'a small risk of violent offending is to be treated as more serious than a larger risk of non-violent offending'.

Power to return short-term and long-term prisoners to prison
Section 40 CJA 91 contained power for a court dealing with the commission by a person of an offence punishable with imprisonment during his licence to return him or her to prison for the whole or any part of the original term. This power exists whether the conviction for the new offence occurs *before* or *after* the date on which he or she would have served the full sentence but for release. The court dealing with the new offence possesses this power whether or not it passes sentence for the new offence. The return to prison may run from the date of the court's order and be equal in length to the period between the commission of the new offence and the date when he or she would have served the sentence in full but for release. Magistrates' courts are restricted to returning an offender for a period of up to six months, but they can commit to the Crown Court for sentence in accordance with s42 PCCA 1973, ie with a view to his or her return for a longer period. Any period imposed under this section can be served concurrently with or consecutive to the sentence for the new offence according to the order of the court. A return to prison operates as a sentence of imprisonment for the purpose of subsequent entitlements to early release.

Guidance on the operation of these provisions was given to courts in Home Office Circular 104/1992, 'Criminal Justice Act 1991: Role of the Magistrates' Courts in Breach of Licence Conditions by Short-Term Prisoners and their Conviction During Currency of Original Sentences': reproduced in *Materials on the Criminal Justice Act 1991* (Waterside Press, 1992).

Fine defaulters
Where a person is sentenced to imprisonment for non-payment of fines etc, the

defaulter is released unconditionally without a licence after serving half the sentence where the term is less than twelve months, or after two-thirds if the term is 12 months or more: s45 CJA 91.

Young offenders

People sentenced to detention in a young offender institution are bound by the same rules in relation to parole and early release as those sent to prison except that supervision may be by a social worker, *supra*. The same applies to detention under s53 CYPA 1933 and custody for life under s8 CJA 1982: s43(2) CJA 91. In relation to s53 of the 1933 Act ('grave crimes'), s43(1) CJA 91 brought those sentenced under that provision into line with other inmates. Previously, all such detainees serving determinate sentences had no formal entitlement to parole (although the Home Secretary could refer their cases to the Parole Board at any time if he saw fit) and any time spent on remand was not counted towards the sentence. All offenders under the age of 22 when released from a sentence of detention in a young offender institution or under s53 CYPA 33 are subject to a minimum three months' compulsory supervision (subject to this not going beyond the 22nd birthday): see, generally, in relation to young offenders, *Chapters 9* and *10, ante*.

Sexual offenders

Section 44 CJA 91 empowered a court sentencing a sexual offender to custody to order that supervision on release will continue until the end of the sentence instead of to the three-quarters point. A court must have regard to the need to protect the public from serious harm from offenders, and the desirability of preventing the commission by them of further offences and of securing their rehabilitation.

Deportees

Section 46 CJA 91 provided that prisoners who are liable to be removed from the United Kingdom at the end of their sentence would not be subject to post-release supervision by a probation officer (thereby removing an obstacle to their immediate deportation on release). The Home Secretary is empowered by s46(1), *ibid*, to release long term prisoners who are liable to removal from the United Kingdom without a recommendation from the Parole Board at any time between the one-half and two-thirds point of the sentence. Deportees serving less than four years will be released automatically and deported at the half-way point of the sentence.

Extradited offenders

Section 47 CJA 91 provided that, where an offender has spent time in custody abroad awaiting extradition to the United Kingdom, a court passing a custodial sentence may order that a specified period of time (not exceeding the time spent in custody abroad) shall be deducted from the length of time which the prisoner will spend in custody. This specified period operates to reduce the time spent in custody in the same way as does a period spent on remand in custody. (The position previously was that the sentencer could make allowance in the sentence itself for the fact that time spent in custody abroad did not count towards the sentence).

Discretionary life sentences
Section 34 CJA 91 provided that when an offender is given a discretionary life sentence (ie one which is not mandatory by law) the court may order that, after he has served a specified part of the sentence, the Parole Board shall have power to order his release on licence, ie not simply to make a recommendation to the Home Secretary as previously, if it is satisfied that the prisoner's continued confinement 'is no longer necessary for the protection of the public'. The period specified by the court—often referred to as the 'tariff' element in the sentence—must take into account the seriousness of the offence (or the combination of the offence and other associated offences) *and* the effect of the rules relating to parole and early release on the proportion of a determinate sentence which is actually served in custody. The period should therefore be between one-half and two-thirds of the length of the determinate sentence which, if it had not passed a life sentence, the court would have considered commensurate with the seriousness of the offence. Section 34 does not require the judge to specify a period in every case. However, *Practice Direction (Crime: Life Sentences)* [1993] 1 WLR 223 stated that: '. . . the judge should do so, save in the very exceptional case where the judge considers that the offence is so serious that detention for life is justified by the seriousness of the offence alone, irrespective of the risk to the public. In such a case, the judge should state this in open court when passing sentence.' In order to comply with the decision of the European Court of Human Rights in *Thynne, Wilson and Gunnell* (1990) that discretionary lifers have the right to periodic reviews of their detention by a 'court', the Parole Board follows a judicial procedure in these cases. In the House of Commons on 25 June 1991, Mrs Angela Rumbold MP, Minister of State at the Home Office, said:

'... the prisoner would be entitled to have his continued detention after the term set by the trial judge reviewed by an independent body having the status of a court for the purposes of the European Court of Human Rights. We propose that the body should be the Parole Board, operating under a special set of procedures which would be laid down in the rules made by the Secretary of State ... We intend that the panel of the Parole Board which will consider discretionary life sentence cases will be chaired by a judge who is a member of the Board, and one of its members will be a psychiatrist. The prisoner will be entitled to appear before the panel and be legally represented. If the panel concludes that the prisoner's continued detention is no longer necessary to protect the public, the Parole Board will direct the Secretary of State to release him.' (Hansard, cols. 903-4).

The Parole Board Rules 1992 stipulated that when considering the cases of discretionary lifers the Board would sit in panels of three known as 'discretionary lifer panels.' The Rules state that the chairman of each panel must hold judicial office but do not otherwise specify the composition of panels. However, criteria were set out for the Chairman of the Board in a letter from the Home Secretary. These criteria stipulated that panels would be chaired by High Court judges where cases involve: terrorist offences; attempted murder or wounding of a police or prison officer; the sexual assault or mutilation *and* killing of a child; serial rape; manslaughter following release from prison on a previous manslaughter sentence; offences giving rise to multiple life sentences. Otherwise, a circuit judge or recorder may take the chair.

The second member will generally be a psychiatrist. But, if there is conclusive medical evidence that no serious concern exists about the prisoner's state of mind at the time of the offence or subsequently during imprisonment, a psychologist or probation officer may be appointed. The third member will be a lay member, a criminologist, or a psychologist or probation officer (where not already the second member). The Rules provide that the prisoner has the right to attend the hearing; to be represented, to apply for others to attend, to hear and question other parties' evidence; to call authorised witnesses; to make pre-hearing representations (which may include professional reports and other written evidence); and, with very rare exceptions, to see reports on himself or herself which are submitted to the Board. The majority decision of the panel will prevail. Their decision will be recorded in writing and given, with reasons, to the parties within seven days of the hearing.

When the Home Secretary refers a recall case to the Board under s39(4) of the Act, the case will be considered by a panel under the procedures set out in the Rules only when the prisoner makes representations against recall.

The CJA 91 did not alter the system in relation to those serving *mandatory* life sentences for murder. The 'tariff' element in these cases continues to be determined by the Home Secretary following a consideration of recommendations by the trial judge and the Lord Chief Justice. However, as a result of the House of Lords decision in *Secretary of State for the Home Department, ex p Doody* [1993] 3 WLR 154, mandatory lifers have been given the right to a more open system including the right to know the trial judge's recommendation, the right to make representations to the Home Secretary and the right to be given the reasons for any departure from the judicial recommendation by the Home Secretary or the junior minister to whom the decision is delegated. It has also been decided that mandatory lifers being considered by the Parole Board will be able to see their dossiers and will be given reasons for the Board's decisions.

The need to re-assess sentence lengths

The early release and parole provisions of Part II CJA 91 meant that a larger proportion of each sentence would be served in custody (in many cases), and that there would be longer 'at risk' periods and stronger powers of return and recall.

The Carlisle Report, *supra*, stated that its proposed scheme 'should provide the springboard for a thorough re-assessment of present sentencing levels. We therefore recommend that the implementation of our proposals should be accompanied by a determined attempt on the part of the government and the judiciary to secure a corresponding reduction in sentencing at all levels ... [We] are quite clear that it would be an unbalanced approach and add undesirably to the overall quantum of punishment to enhance the meaning of sentences in the way we propose without at the same time working for a reduction in present tariffs, which have evolved within a quite different framework': *The Parole System in England and Wales: Report of the Review Committee, supra*, pp 72-73.

Adult Parole/Release Schemes

(determinate sentences of one year or more)

Eligibility	Old scheme	New scheme
One year up to 4 years	Parole selection after one third of sentence (taking into account remand time) or 6 months after sentence passed, whichever is the longer; then annual	Automatic conditional release ('ACR') on licence after 50% of the sentence (remand time to count).
Four years and upwards	reviews until release on parole or at two-thirds of sentence (subject to loss of remission).	Parole selection after 50% of the sentence with annual reviews until release on parole or at two-thirds.
Structure	Local Review Committees 'LRCs' at the prison consider each case. Parole Board has second view on more serious cases (generally those serving more than four years). Home Secretary decides but may only grant parole on the basis of a positive Parole Board or LRC recommendation.	LRCs abolished. Parole Board (comprised of statutory and independent members) decides on parole for those serving between 4 and less than 7 years. Home Secretary decides on the basis of Parole Board recommendation for those serving 7 years or more.
Release criteria	Balance of risk versus benefit. Parole Board have developed 6 criteria. Home Secretary's restricted policy applies allowing only very limited parole to those serving sentences of over 5 years for offences of violence, sexual offences, arson and drug offences.	Risk based criteria (with heavy emphasis on risk of serious harm) based on policy directions from the Home Secretary to the Parole Board.
Supervision	Only those granted parole lasting to two-thirds EDR ('earliest date of release').	*All* supervised from date of release to 75% point (for some sex offenders to 100% subject to judicial order at time of sentence).

Eligibility	Old scheme	New scheme
Recall	By Home Secretary or Parole Board. From date of recall to EDR (minimum 30 days).	By Home Secretary or Parole Board for those on parole; by magistrates' court for those on ACR. For a period to be specified (a maximum of six months for magistrates' court decisions) but not beyond the 75% point. Courts can also fine up to level 3 on the standard scale.
Remission	Subject to good behaviour, one-third: ie at two-thirds of sentence all prisoner liability ends.	Abolished but replaced by 'additional days awarded' in the event of bad behaviour; last 25% of sentence may be re-activated by the court if a further imprisonable offence is committed.
	Deportees considered on same basis as others.	Deportees have similar early release entitlements to others, but are not considered by the Parole Board and are not supervised on release.
	Secrecy: no feedback to prisoners.	Open reporting and the giving of reasons are features of the new scheme. This is not a statutory requirement but was promised by Ministers during the passing of the legislation.

We are indebted to Mrs V V R Harris, Head of DSP2 Division, Home Office *Life Sentence Section & Parole Unit* for this chart which was first published at a Home Office *Special Conference* on the CJA 91.

Part III

Appendices

Appendix I Statutory Provisions

Reproduced below are the main sentencing provisions resulting from the CJA 91 and subsequent amendments relevant to this work—in chronological order and with annotations or explanations as appropriate.

Powers of Criminal Courts Act 1973

Absolute and conditional discharge

1A.—(1) Where a court by or before which a person is convicted of an offence (not being an offence the sentence for which is fixed by law) is of opinion, having regard to the circumstances including the nature of the offence and the character of the offender, that is is inexpedient to inflict punishment, the court may make an order either—

(a) discharging him absolutely; or

(b) if the court thinks fit, discharging him subject to the condition that he commits no offence during such period, not exceeding three years from the date of the order, as may be specified in the order.

(2) An order discharging a person subject to such a condition is in this Act referred to as 'an order for conditional discharge', and the period specified in any such order as 'the period of the conditional discharge'.

(3) Before making an order for conditional discharge the court shall explain to the offender in ordinary language that if he commits another offence during the period of conditional discharge he will be liable to be sentenced again for the original offence.

(4) Where, under the following provisions of this Part of this Act, a person conditionally discharged under this section is sentenced for the offence in respect of which the order for conditional discharge was made, that order shall cease to have effect.

(5) [Power of Secretary of State to alter maximum period in s1A(1)(b) *supra*.]
[Section 1A PCCA 1973 as inserted by s8(3) and Schedule 1 CJA 1991]

Commission of further offence by person conditionally discharged

1B.—(1) If it appears to the Crown Court, where that court has jurisdiction in accordance with subsection (2) below, or to a justice of the peace having jurisdiction in accordance with that subsection, that a person in whose case an order for conditional discharge has been made—

(a) has been convicted by a court in any part of Great Britain of an offence committed during the period of conditional discharge; and

(b) has been dealt with in respect of that offence,

that court or justice may, subject to subsection (3) below, issue a summons requiring that person to appear at the place and time specified therein or a warrant for his arrest.

(2) Jurisdiction for the purposes of subsection (1) above may be exercised —

(a) if the order for conditional discharge was made by the Crown Court, by that court;

(b) if the order was made by a magistrates' court, by a justice acting for the petty sessions area for which that court acts.

(3) A justice of the peace shall not issue a summons under this section except on information and shall not issue a warrant under this section except on information in writing and on oath.

(4) A summons or warrant issued under this section shall direct the person to whom it relates to appear or to be brought before the court by which the order for conditional discharge was made.

(5) If a person in whose case an order for conditional discharge has been made by the Crown Court is convicted by a magistrates' court of an offence committed during the period of conditional discharge, the magistrates' court—

(a) may commit him to custody or release him on bail until he can be brought or appear before the Crown Court; and

(b) if it does so, shall send to the Crown Court a copy of the minute or memorandum of the conviction entered in the court register, signed by the clerk of the court by whom the register is kept.

(6) Where it is proved to the satisfaction of the court by which an order for conditional discharge was made that the person in whose case the order was made has been convicted of an offence committed during the period of conditional discharge, the court may deal with him, for the offence for which the order was made, in any manner in which it could deal with him if he had just been convicted by or before that court of that offence.

(7) If a person in whose case an order for conditional discharge has been made by a magistrates' court—

(a) is convicted before the Crown Court of an offence committed during the period of conditional discharge; or

(b) is dealt with by the Crown Court for any such offence in respect of which he was committed for sentence to the Crown Court,

the Crown Court may deal with him, for the offence for which the order was made, in any manner in which the magistrates' court could deal with him if it had just convicted him of that offence.

(8) If a person in whose case an order for conditional discharge has been made by a magistrates' court is convicted by another magistrates' court of any offence committed during the period of conditional discharge, that other court may, with the consent of the court which made the order, deal with him, for the offence for which the order was made, in any manner in which the court could deal with him if it had just convicted him of that offence.

(9) Where an order for conditional discharge has been made by a magistrates' court in the case of an offender under eighteen years of age in respect of an offence triable only on indictment in the case of an adult, any powers exercisable under subsection (6), (7) or (8) above by that or any other court in respect of the offender after he has attained the age of eighteen years shall be those which would be exercisable if that offence were an offence triable either way and had

205

been tried summarily.

(10) For the purposes of this section the age of an offender at a particular time shall be deemed to be or to have been that which appears to the court after considering any available evidence to be or to have been his age at that time. [Section 1B PCCA 1973 as inserted by s8(3) and Schedule 1 CJA 1991]

Effect of discharge

1C.—(1) Subject to subsection (2) below and to section 50(1A) of the Criminal Appeal Act 1968 and section 108(1A) of the Magistrates' Courts Act 1980, a conviction of an offence for which the order is made under this Part of this Act discharging the offender absolutely or conditionally shall be deemed not to be a conviction for any purpose other than—

(a) the purposes of the proceedings in which the order is made and of any subsequent proceedings which may be taken against the offender under the following provisions of this Act; and

(b) the purposes of section 1(2)(bb) Children and Young Persons Act 1969.

(2) Where the offender was of or over eighteen years of age at the time of his conviction of the offence in question and is subsequently sentenced under this Part of this Act for that offence, subsection (1) above shall cease to apply to the conviction.

(3) Without prejudice to the preceding provisions of this section, the conviction of an offender who is discharged absolutely or conditionally under this Part of this Act shall in any event be disregarded for the purposes of any enactment or instrument which—

(a) imposes any disqualification or disability upon convicted persons; or

(b) authorises or requires the imposition of any such disqualification or disability.

(4) The preceding provisions of this section shall not affect—

(a) any right of any offender discharged absolutely or conditionally under this Part of this Act to rely on his conviction in bar of any subsequent proceedings for the same offence; or

(b) the restoration of any property in consequence of the conviction of any such offender; or

(c) the operation, in relation to any such offender, of any enactment or instrument in force at the commencement of this Act which is expressed to extend to persons dealt with under section 1(1) of the Probation of Offenders Act 1907 as well as to convicted persons.

(5) In this section 'enactment' includes an enactment contained in a local Act and 'instrument' means an instrument having effect by virtue of an Act. [Section 1C PCCA 1973 as amended by s8(3) and Schedule 1 CJA 1991]

NOTE Conditional discharges made before 1 October 1992 (start of CJA 91) are 'sentences' and 'convictions' for the purposes of s29 CJA 91, *post*: s29(3), (4).

Probation orders

2.—(1) Where a court by or before which a person of or over the age of sixteen years is convicted of an offence (not being an offence for which the sentence is fixed by law) is of opinion that the supervision of the offender by a probation officer is desirable in the interests of—

(a) securing the rehabilitation of the offender; or

(b) protecting the public from harm from him or preventing the commission by him of further offences,

the court may make a probation order, that is to say, an order requiring him to be under the supervision of a probation officer for a period specified in the order of not less than six months nor more than three years.

For the purposes of this subsection the age of a person shall be deemed to be that which it appears to the court to be after considering any available evidence.

(2) A probation order shall specify the petty sessions area in which the offender resides or will reside; and the offender shall, subject to paragraph 12 of Schedule 2 to the Criminal Justice Act 1991 (offenders who change their residence), be required to be under the supervision of a probation officer appointed for or assigned to that area.

(3) Before making a probation order, the court shall explain to the offender in ordinary language—

(a) the effect of the order (including any additional requirements proposed to be included in the order in accordance with section 3 below);

(b) the consequences which may follow under Schedule 2 to the Criminal Justice Act 1991 if he fails to comply with any of the requirements of the order; and

(c) that the court has under that Schedule power to review the order on the application of either the offender or the supervising officer,

and the court shall not make the order unless he expresses willingness to comply with its requirements.

(4) The court by which a probation order is made shall forthwith give copies of the order to a probation officer assigned to the court, and he shall give a copy—

(a) to the offender;

(b) to the probation officer responsible for the offender's supervision; and

(c) to the person in charge of any institution in which the offender is required by the order to reside.

(5) The court by which such an order is made shall also, except where it itself acts for the petty sessions area specified in the order, send to the clerk to the justices for that area—

(a) a copy of the order; and

(b) such documents and information relating to the case as it considers likely to be of assistance to a court acting for that area in the exercise of its functions in relation to the order.

(6) An offender in respect of whom a probation order is made shall keep in touch with the probation officer responsible for his supervision in accordance with such instructions as may from time to time be given by that officer and shall notify him of any change of address.

(7) The Secretary of State may by order direct that subsection (1) above shall be amended by substituting, for the minimum period specified in that

subsection, such period as may be specified in the order.

(8) An order under subsection (7) above may make in paragraph 13(2)(a)(ii) of Schedule 2 to the Criminal Justice Act 1991 any amendment which the Secretary of State thinks necessary in consequence of any substitution made by the order. [Section 2 PCCA 1973 as substituted by s8 CJA 1991]

NOTE Probation orders made before 1 October 1992 (start of CJA 91) are 'sentences' and 'convictions' for the purposes of s29 CJA 91, *post*: s29(3), (4).

Additional requirements which may be included in such orders
3.—(1) Subject to subsection (2) below, a probation order may in addition require the offender to comply during the whole or any part of the probation period with such requirements as the court, having regard to the circumstances of the case, considers desirable in the interests of—
   (a) securing the rehabilitation of the offender; or
   (b) protecting the public from harm from him or preventing the commission by him of further offences.
(2) Without prejudice to the power of the court under section 35 of this Act to make a compensation order, the payment of sums by way of damages for injury or compensation for loss shall not be included among the additional requirements of a probation order.
(3) Without prejudice to the generality of subsection (1) above, the additional requirements which may be included in a probation order shall include the requirements which are authorised by Schedule 1A to this Act.
[Section 3 PCCA 1973 as substituted by s9 CJA 91]

7. [Section 7 PCCA 1973 ceased under the CJA 91, being re-enacted with modifications by s1A and s1B PCCA 73 *supra:* see s8(3) CJA 1991]

8. [Section 8 PCCA 1973 ceased so far as it related to discharges, being re-enacted with modifications by s1B and s1C PCCA 73, *supra*: s8(3) CJA 1991]

9. [Section 9 PCCA 1973 ceased along with s7 PCCA 1973 *supra*]

13. ['Effect of probation and discharge'. Section 13 ceased: re probation under s8(2) CJA 1991; re conditional discharges it was replaced by s1B and s1C PCCA 73: s8(3) CJA 1991. See also s29(3), (4) CJA 91, *post*]

Community service orders in respect of offenders
14.—(1) Where a person of or over sixteen years is convicted of an offence punishable with imprisonment, the court by or before which he is convicted may (subject to subsection (2) below) make an order (in this Act referred to as "a community service order") requiring him to perform unpaid work in accordance with the subsequent provisions of this Act.

The reference in this subsection to an offence punishable with imprisonment shall be construed without regard to any prohibition or restriction imposed by or under any enactment on the imprisonment of young offenders.

(1A) [This subsection substitutes for paragraph (b), the words '(b) not more than 240'. The effect is to make this the maximum number of hours for all offenders aged 16 years and upwards].

(2) A court shall not make a community service order in respect of any offender unless the offender consents and the court, after hearing (if the court thinks it necessary) a probation officer or social worker of a local authority social services department, is satisfied that the offender is a suitable person to perform work under such an order.

(2A) Subject to paragraphs 3 and 4 of Schedule 3 to the Criminal Justice Act 1991 (reciprocal enforcement of certain orders) a court shall not make a community service order in respect of an offender unless it is satisfied that provision for him to perform work under such orders which exist in the petty sessions area in which he resides or will reside ...

(4) [The former reference to 'section 17(5) of this Act' (change of residence) becomes a reference to 'Part IV of Schedule 2 to the Criminal Justice Act 1991', *post*]

(5) [Similarly, the reference in s14(5)(b) to 'section 16' (breach of community service order) becomes a reference to 'Part II of Schedule 2 to [the CJA 91]' and that in s14(5)(c) to 'section 17' (amendment and revocation) becomes a reference to 'Parts III and IV of [that Schedule]'.] ... ...

[Section 14 PCCA 1973 as amended by s10 CJA 1991 and sched 11 *ibid*]

NOTE Sched 2 CJA 91 'Enforcement, etc of Community Orders': see *post*.

Obligations of persons subject to community service orders

15. [A new s15(1)(a) was inserted by the CJA 91 which requires offenders to: '(a) keep in touch with the relevant officer in accordance with such instructions as he may from time to time be given by that officer and notify him of any change of address'. In s15(2) 'paragraph 15 of Schedule 2 to the Criminal Justice Act 1991' [Enforcement] replaced 'section 17' (amendment etc)].

[Section 15 PCCA 1973 as amended by s10 CJA 1991 and sched 11]

Suspended sentences of imprisonment.

22.—(1) Subject to subsection (2) below, a court which passes a sentence of imprisonment for a term of not more than two years for an offence may order that the sentence shall not take effect unless, during a period specified in the order, being not less than one year or more than two years from the date of the order, the offender commits in Great Britain another offence punishable with imprisonment and thereafter a court having power to do so orders under section 23 of this Act that the original sentence shall take effect; and in this Part of this Act "operational period", in relation to a suspended sentence, means the period so specified.

(2) A court shall not deal with an offender by means of a suspended sentence unless it is of the opinion—

(a) that the case is one in which a sentence of imprisonment would have been appropriate even without the power to suspend the sentence; and

(b) that the exercise of that power can be justified by the exceptional circumstances of the case.

(2A) A court which passes a suspended sentence on any person for an offence shall consider whether the circumstances of the case are such as to warrant in addition the imposition of a fine or the making of a compensation order.

(3) A court which passes a suspended sentence on any person for an offence shall not make a probation order in his case with respect to another offence of which he is convicted by or before the court or for which he is dealt with by the court.

(4) On passing a suspended sentence the court shall explain to the offender in ordinary language his liability under section 23 of this Act if during the operational period he commits an offence punishable by imprisonment.

(5) [Repealed]

(6) [Effect on other enactments].

[Section 22 PCCA 1973 with s22(2), (2A) as substituted by s5(1) CJA 91].

NOTES S22(2)(a) 'would have been appropriate' The court should thus reach a decision on custody without regard to the power to suspend, by applying the criteria and procedures in s1 to s3 CJA 91. The court should only then apply the test in s22(2)(b). S22(2)(b) The basis for suspension was narrowed by the CJA 91 to 'exceptional circumstances'—a term which has been applied restrictively: see the cases noted in *Chapter 1(c)* of this work, *Judicial Guidance*. S22(2A) 'consider . . fine or . . compensation' This *duty* was created by the CJA 91. Preference must be given to compensation over a fine: s35(1) PCCA 73: *Chapter 9*.

Schedule 1A [inserted by Part II of sched 1 CJA 91]

ADDITIONAL REQUIREMENTS IN PROBATION ORDERS

Requirements as to residence

1.—(1) Subject to sub-paragraphs (2) and (3) below, a probation order may include requirements as to the residence of the offender.

(2) Before making a probation order containing any such requirement, the court shall consider the home surroundings of the offender.

(3) Where a probation order requires the offender to reside in an approved hostel or any other institution, the period for which he is so required to reside shall be specified in the order.

Requirements as to activities

2.—(1) Subject to the provisions of this paragraph, a probation order may require the offender—

(a) to present himself to a person or persons specified in the order at a place or places so specified;

(b) to participate or refrain from participating in activities specified in the order—

(i) on a day or days so specified; or

(ii) during the probation period or such proportion of it as may be so specified.

(2) A court shall not include in a probation order a requirement such as is mentioned in sub-paragraph (1) above unless—

(a) it has consulted a probation officer; and

(b) it is satisfied that it is feasible to secure compliance with the requirement.

(3) A court shall not include in a probation order a requirement such as is mentioned in sub-paragraph (1)(a) above or a requirement to participate in activities if it would involve the co-operation of a person other than the offender and the probation officer responsible for his supervision, unless that other person consents to its inclusion.

(4) A requirement such as is mentioned in sub-paragraph (1)(a) above shall operate to require the offender—

(a) in accordance with instructions given by the probation officer responsible for his supervision, to present himself at a place or places for not more than 60 days in the aggregate; and

(b) while at any place, to comply with instructions given by, or under the authority of, the person in charge of that place.

(5) A place specified in an order shall have been approved by the probation committee for the area in which the premises are situated as providing facilities suitable for persons subject to probation orders.

(6) A requirement to participate in activities shall operate to require the offender—

(a) in accordance with instructions given by the probation officer responsible for his supervision, to participate in activities for not more than 60 days in the aggregate; and

(b) while participating, to comply with instructions given by, or under the authority of, the person in charge of the activities.

(7) Instructions given by a probation officer under sub-paragraph (4) or (6) above shall, so far as practicable, be such as to avoid any interference with the times, if any, at which the offender normally works or attends a school or other educational establishment.

Requirements as to attendance at probation centre

3.—(1) Subject to the provisions of this paragraph, a probation order may require the offender during the probation period to attend at a probation centre specified in the order.

(2) A court shall not include such a requirement in a probation order unless—

(a) it has consulted a probation officer; and

(b) it is satisfied—

(i) that arrangements can be made for the offender's attendance at a centre; and

(ii) that the person in charge of the centre consents to the inclusion of the requirement.

(3) A requirement under sub-paragraph (1) above shall operate to require the offender—

(a) in accordance with instructions given by the probation officer responsible for his supervision, to attend on not more than 60 days at the centre specified in the order; and

(b) while attending there to comply with instructions given by, or under the authority of, the person in charge of the centre.

(4) Instructions given by a probation officer under sub-paragraph (3) above shall, so far as practicable, be such as to avoid any interference with the times, if any, at which the offender normally works or attends a school or other education establishment.

(5) References in this paragraph to attendance at a probation centre include references to attendance elsewhere than at the centre for the purpose of participating in activities in accordance with instructions given by, or under the authority of, the person in charge of the centre.

(6) The Secretary of State may make rules for regulating the provision and carrying on of probation centres and the attendance at such centres of persons subject to probation orders; and such rules may in particular include provision with respect to hours of attendance, the reckoning of days of attendance and the keeping of attendance records.

(7) In this paragraph 'probation centre' means premises—

(a) at which non-residential facilities are provided for use in connection with the rehabilitation of offenders; and

(b) which are for the time being approved by the Secretary of State as providing facilities suitable for persons subject to probation orders.

Extension of requirements for sexual offenders

4.—(1) If the court so directs in the case of an offender who has been convicted of a sexual offence—

(a) sub-paragraphs (4) and (6) of paragraph 2 above; and

(b) sub-paragraph (3) of paragraph 3 above,

shall each have effect as if for the reference to 60 days there were substituted a reference to such greater number of days as may be specified in the direction.

(2) In this paragraph 'sexual offence' has the same meaning as in Part I of the Criminal Justice Act 1991.

Requirements as to treatment for mental condition etc.

5.—(1) This paragraph applies where a court proposing to make a probation order is satisfied, on the evidence of a duly qualified medical practitioner approved for the purposes of section 12 Mental Health Act 1983, that the mental condition of the offender—

(a) is such as requires and may be susceptible to treatment; but

(b) is not such as to warrant the making of a hospital order or guardianship order within the meaning of that Act.

(2) The probation order may include a requirement that the offender shall submit, during the whole of the probation period or during such part of that period as may be specified in the order, to treatment by or under the direction of a duly qualified medical

practitioner with a view to the improvement of the offender's mental condition.

(3) The treatment required by any such order shall be such one of the following kinds of treatment as may be specified in the order, that is to say—

(a) treatment as a resident patient in a mental hospital;

(b) treatment as a non-resident patient at such institution or place as may be specified in the order; and

(c) treatment by or under the direction of such duly qualified medical practitioner as may be so specified;

but the nature of the treatment shall not be specified in the order except as mentioned in paragraph (a), (b) or (c) above.

(4) A court shall not by virtue of this paragraph include in a probation order a requirement that the offender shall submit to treatment for his mental condition unless it is satisfied that arrangements have been made for the treatment intended to be specified in the order (including arrangements for the reception of the offender where he is to be required to submit to treatment as a resident patient).

(5) While the offender is under treatment as a resident patient in pursuance of a requirement of the probation order, the probation officer responsible for his supervision shall carry out the supervision to such extent only as may be necessary for the purpose of revocation or amendment of the order.

(6) Where the medical practitioner by whom or under whose direction an offender is being treated for his mental condition in pursuance of a probation order is of the opinion that part of the treatment can be better or more conveniently given in or at an institution or place which—

(a) is not specified in the order; and

(b) is one in or at which the treatment of the offender will be given by or under the direction of a duly qualified medical practitioner,

he may, with the consent of the offender, make arrangements for him to be treated accordingly.

(7) Such arrangements as are mentioned in sub-paragraph (6) may provide for the offender to receive part of his treatment as a resident patient in an institution or place notwithstanding that the institution or place is not one which could have been specified for that purpose in the probation order.

(8) Where any such arrangements as are mentioned in sub-paragraph (6) above are made for the treatment of the offender—

(a) the medical practitioner by whom the arrangements are made shall give notice in writing to the probation officer responsible for the supervision of the offender, specifying the institution or place in or at which the treatment is to be carried out; and

(b) the treatment provided for by the arrangements shall be deemed to be treatment to which he is required to submit in pursuance of the probation order.

(9) Subsections (2) and (3) of section 54 of the Mental Health Act 1983 shall have effect with respect to proof for the purposes of sub-paragraph (1) above of an offender's mental condition as they have effect with respect to proof of an offender's mental condition for the purposes of section 37(2)(a) of that Act.

(10) In this paragraph 'mental hospital' means a hospital within the meaning of the Mental Health Act 1983 or mental nursing home within the meaning of the Registered Homes Act 1984, not being a special hospital within the meaning of the

213

National Health Service Act 1977.

Requirements as to treatment for drug or alcohol dependency

6.—(1) This paragraph applies where a court proposing to make a probation order is satisfied—

(a) that the offender is dependent on drugs or alcohol;

(b) that his dependency caused or contributed to the offence in respect of which the order is proposed to be made; and

(c) that his dependency is such as requires and may be susceptible to treatment.

(2) The probation order may include a requirement that the offender shall submit, during the whole of the probation period or during such part of that period as may be specified in the order, to treatment by or under the direction of a person having the necessary qualifications or experience with a view to the reduction or elimination of the offender's dependency on drugs or alcohol.

(3) The treatment required by any such order shall be such one of the following kinds of treatment as may be specified in the order, that is to say—

(a) treatment as a resident in such institution or place as may be specified in the order;

(b) treatment as a non-resident in or at such institution or place as may be so specified; and

(c) treatment by or under the direction of such person having the necessary qualifications or experience as may be so specified;

but the nature of the treatment shall not be specified in the order except as mentioned in paragraph (a), (b) or (c) above.

(4) A court shall not by virtue of this paragraph include in a probation order a requirement that the offender shall submit to treatment for his dependency on drugs or alcohol unless it is satisfied that arrangements have been made for the treatment intended to be specified in the order (including arrangements for the reception of the offender where he is to be required to submit to treatment as a resident).

(5) While the offender is under treatment as a resident in pursuance of a requirement of the probation order, the probation officer responsible for his supervision shall carry out the supervision to such extent only as may be necessary for the purpose of the revocation or amendment of the order.

(6) Where the person by whom or under whose direction an offender is being treated for dependency on drugs or alcohol in pursuance of a probation order is of the opinion that part of the treatment can be better or more conveniently given in or at an institution or place which—

(a) is not specified in the order; and

(b) is one in or at which the treatment of the offender will be given by or under the direction of a person having the necessary qualifications or experience,

he may with the consent of the offender, make arrangements for him to be treated accordingly.

(7) Such arrangements as are mentioned in sub-paragraph (6) above may provide for the offender to receive part of his treatment as a resident in an institution or place notwithstanding that the institution or place is not one which could have been

specified for that purpose in the probation order.

(8) Where any such arrangements as are mentioned in sub-paragraph (6) above are made for the treatment of an offender—

(a) the person by whom the arrangements are made shall give notice in writing to the probation officer responsible for the supervision of the offender, specifying the institution or place in or at which the treatment is to be carried out; and

(b) the treatment provided for by the arrangements shall be deemed to be treatment to which he is required to submit in pursuance of the probation order.

(9) In this paragraph the reference to the offender being dependent on drugs or alcohol includes a reference to his having a propensity towards the misuse of drugs or alcohol, and references to his dependency on drugs or alcohol shall be construed accordingly.

[Schedule 1A Powers of Criminal Courts Act 1973 as inserted by Part II of sched 1 CJA 91]

Magistrates' Courts Act 1980

Committal for sentence on summary trial of offence triable either way

38.—(1) This section applies where on the summary trial of an offence triable either way (not being an offence as regards which this section is excluded by section 33 above) a person who is not less than 18 is convicted of the offence.

(2) If the court is of opinion—

(a) that the offence or the combination of the offence and one or more offences associated with it was so serious that greater punishment should be inflicted for the offence than the court has power to impose; or

(b) in the case of a violent or sexual offence committed by a person who is not less than 21 years old, that a sentence of imprisonment for a term longer than the court has power to impose is necessary to protect the public from serious harm from him,

the court may, in accordance with section 56 of the Criminal Justice Act 1967, commit the offender in custody or on bail to the Crown Court for sentence in accordance with the provisions of section 42 of the Powers of Criminal Courts Act 1973.

(3) Paragraphs (a) and (b) of subsection (2) above shall be construed as if they were contained in Part I of the Criminal Justice Act 1991.

(4) The preceding provisions of this section shall apply in relation to a corporation as if—

(a) the corporation were an individual who is not less than 18 years old; and

(b) in subsection (2) above, paragraph (b) and the words 'in custody or on bail' were omitted.

[Section 38 Magistrates' Courts Act 1980 as substituted by s25 CJA 91 and amended by s66(8) CJA 93]

NOTES S38(1) 'Subject to section 33' Section 33 MCA 1980 excludes the operation of s38 in relation to 'summary' criminal damage. S38(2)(a) 'greater punishment' magistrates' courts can impose sentences of up to six months for each either way offence to a total of 12 months in aggregate: MCA 1980. Section 38(2)(a) operates by reference to seriousness and is, in effect, parasitic on s1 CJA 91, *post*. It follows that previous convictions and responses can be taken into account: s29(1) CJA 91, *post*. Under the pre-CJA 91 law the test for committal was whether the offender's 'character and antecedents' indicated greater punishment than the magistrates' court could impose. The CJA 93 returns the law to a comparable, though not identical, position: *Chapter 7*. S38(2)(b) Note that the alternative test for committal to the Crown Court in relation to violent or sexual offences is based on the need to protect the public from serious harm. S38(3) One effect is that s31 CJA 91 (definitions), *post*, applies. S38(4) Note that s25(2) CJA 91 amended sched 3 MCA 1980, para 5 (provisions relating to committal to the Crown Court for sentence) so that there is no longer a bar to committing a corporation for sentence.

Criminal Justice Act 1991: Part I

POWERS OF COURTS TO DEAL WITH OFFENDERS

Restrictions on imposing custodial sentences

1.—(1) This section applies where a person is convicted of an offence punishable with a custodial sentence other than one fixed by law.

(2) Subject to subsection (3) below, the court shall not pass a custodial sentence on the offender unless it is of the opinion—

(a) that the offence, or the combination of the offence and one or more offences associated with it, was so serious that only such a sentence can be justified for the offence; or

(b) where the offence is a violent or sexual offence, that only such a sentence would be adequate to protect the public from serious harm from him.

(3) Nothing in subsection (2) above shall prevent the court from passing a custodial sentence on the offender if he refuses to give his consent to a community sentence which is proposed by the court and requires that consent.

(4) Where a court passes a custodial sentence, it shall be its duty—

(a) in a case not falling within subsection (3) above, to state in open court that it is of the opinion that either or both of paragraphs (a) and (b) of subsection (2) above apply and why it is of that opinion; and

(b) in any case, to explain to the offender in open court and in ordinary language why it is passing a custodial sentence on him.

(5) A magistrates' court shall cause the reason stated by it under subsection (4) above to be specified in the warrant of commitment and to be entered in the register.

[Section 1 Criminal Justice Act 1991 as amended by s66(1) CJA 1993]

NOTES S1(2)(a) '... the offence and one or more offences associated with it' The CJA 93 abolished the former 'two offence rule': see *Chapter 1(b)*.

'**associated with it**' ie seriousness must be assessed by reference to associated offences only for the purpose of determining whether only custody can be justified. 'Associated offence' is defined in s31(2) CJA 91, *post* and see the cases noted in *Chapter 1(c), Judicial Guidance*. Under s29(1) CJA 91 (as amended by the CJA 93), previous convictions and failures to respond to previous sentences may be taken into account in assessing the seriousness of the current [associated] offences as envisaged by section 1(2)(a). The seriousness threshold test in s1(1) CJA 91 and that for *length* of sentence in 2(2) CJA 91 are now in line—in that both refer to 'one or more' associated offences. Under the original s1(1) the court was restricted to *two* associated offences for the purposes of the custody threshold . The test for *length* of sentence under the original CJA 91 merely referred to 'other' associated offences. '**commensurate**' This indicates the underlying aim of proportionality in sentencing. '**so serious**' see *Chapters 3 and 7*. S1(2)(b) Although s29 CJA 91 (admissibility of previous convictions etc) does not apply to the protection of the public test for custody, previous convictions are admissible under s3(3)(b) *post* in relation to the prediction of risk of serious harm to the public. '**violent offence**': defined in s31(1) CJA 91 *post*. '**sexual offence**': defined in s31(1) CJA 91 *post* by reference to a list of statutory offences. Broadly speaking, the list includes all statutory sexual offences except those concerning prostitution and certain consenting homosexual acts. Attempts are within the definition: see *Chapter 1(c), Judicial Guidance*. S1(3) '**consent**' All community sentences capable of being imposed on adults require consent, but not attendance centre orders (under 21) or supervision orders (under 18) unless with certain added conditions: see *Chapter 8*. It would be wrong to offer a disproportionate community sentence with the aim of triggering a refusal—and thus a custodial sentence under s1(3).

Length of custodial sentences.

2.—(1) This section applies where a court passes a custodial sentence other than one fixed by law.

(2) The custodial sentence shall be—

(a) for such term (not exceeding the permitted maximum) as in the opinion of the court is commensurate with the seriousness of the offence, or the combination of the offence and one or more offences associated with it; or

(b) where the offence is a violent or sexual offence, for such longer term (not exceeding the permitted maximum) as in the opinion of the court is necessary to protect the public from serious harm from the offender.

(3) Where the court passes a custodial sentence for a term longer than is commensurate with the seriousness of the offence, or the combination of the offence and one or more offences associated with it, the court shall—

(a) state in open court that it is of the opinion that subsection (2)(b) above applies and why it is of that opinion; and

(b) explain to the offender in ordinary language why the sentence is for such a term.

(4) A custodial sentence for an indeterminate period shall be regarded for the purposes of subsections (2) and (3) above as a custodial sentence for a term longer than any actual term.

[Section 2 Criminal Justice Act 1991 as amended by s66(2) CJA 1993]

NOTES S2(2)(a) In assessing *length* of a sentence, the court can have regard to the present offence and 'one or more' others, ie *any number* of offences provided they are associated (as defined in s31(2) CJA 91, *post*). **'commensurate'** This indicates the underlying aim of proportionality in sentencing. **S2(2)(b) 'violent offence'**: defined in section 31(1) CJA 91 *post*. **Sexual offence**: defined in section 31(1) CJA 91, *post*, by reference to a list of statutory offences. **'serious harm'** is defined in s31(3) CJA 91 post. **S2(3) 'longer than'** Note the court's duty to give extra reasons where the sentence for a violent or sexual offence is longer than is commensurate with seriousness, ie the basic reason for using custody, pursuant to s1(4) CJA 91; and a reason under this subsection: see *Chapter 5*.

Procedural requirements for custodial sentences.

3.—(1) Subject to subsection (2) below, a court shall obtain and consider a pre-sentence report before forming any such opinion as is mentioned in subsection (2) of section 1 or 2 above.

(2) Where the offence or any other offence associated with it is triable only on indictment, subsection (1) above does not apply if, in the circumstances of the case, the court is of the opinion that it is unnecessary to obtain a pre-sentence report.

(3) In forming any such opinion as is mentioned in subsection (2) of section 1 or 2 above a court—

(a) shall take into account all such information about the circumstances of the offence or (as the case may be) of the offence and the offence or offences associated with it (including any aggravating or mitigating factors) as is available to it; and

(b) in the case of any such opinion as is mentioned in paragraph (b) of that subsection, may take into account any information about the offender which is before it.

(4) No custodial sentence which is passed in a case to which subsection (1) above applies shall be invalidated by the failure of a court to comply with that subsection but any court on an appeal against such a sentence—

(a) shall obtain a pre-sentence report if none was obtained by the court below; and

(b) shall consider any such report obtained by it or by that court.

(5) In this Part "pre-sentence report" means a report in writing which—

(a) with a view to assisting the court in determining the most suitable method of dealing with an offender, is made or submitted by a probation officer or by a social worker of a local authority social services department; and

(b) contains information as to such matters, presented in such manner, as may be prescribed by rules made by the Secretary of State.

[Section 3 Criminal Justice Act 1991 as amended by s66(3) CJA 1993]

NOTES

S3(1) 'pre-sentence report': defined in s3(5). The exception under which courts need not obtain a report applies in the Crown Court in relation to offences triable *only* on indictment. That court is under a duty to obtain and consider reports in other cases: s3(1); and on appeal: s3(4) (cf s4(4); s7(4), *post*). Note that proposals in the CJ and PO Bill of 1994 would confer a discretion on courts whether to ask for a PSR:

see *Chapter 12.* 'before forming any such opinion' There should thus be no provisional decision making. But the court will need to make some assessment of the risk of custody etc in order to know whether to ask for a report. It follows that the report should address those matters affecting the offence which the court will have to consider in relation to s1(2)(a) or (b) CJA 91, ie *seriousness* and *protection of the public:* see *Chapter 7, Custody;* as well as the most suitable method of dealing with the *offender:* s3(5)(a) and see *Chapter 12, Pre-sentence Reports.* '... subsection (2) of section 1 or 2 above' ie before deciding on custody or the length of custody. 'associated with it' Associated offence' is defined in s31(2) CJA 91. S3(2) 'unnecessary' see *When is a report unnecessary?: Chapter 12.* S3(3)(a) 'aggravating or mitigating factors' Apart from the facts of the offence under consideration, note also the effect of s28 CJA 91 (general mitigation provision), s29(1) CJA 91 (effect of previous convictions and responses to sentences) and s29(2) CJA 91 (offending on bail an aggravating factor). S3(3)(b) Note that courts must consider both the *offence* and the *offender.* 'about the offence ... as is available to it' Much depends on what information the Crown prosecutor, the defence and others place before the court. S3(5) 'pre-sentence report' Note that reports must be *in writing.* This does not prevent a 'standdown' written report, or a 'standdown' oral report in situations where a PSR is not required by law—should this be appropriate. See also the comments concerning procedures for obtaining expedited reports in *Chapter 12.* S3(5)(b) content and style can be prescribed by regulation. No regulations have been made as at the time of writing. *National Standards* fill this void.

Additional requirements in the case of mentally disordered offenders.

4.—(1) Subject to subsection (2) below, in any case where section 3(1) above applies and the offender is or appears to be mentally disordered, the court shall obtain and consider a medical report before passing a custodial sentence other than one fixed by law.

(2) Subsection (1) above does not apply if, in the circumstances of the case, the court is of the opinion that it is unnecessary to obtain a medical report.

(3) Before passing a custodial sentence other than one fixed by law on an offender who is or appears to be mentally disordered, a court shall consider—

(a) any information before it which relates to his mental condition (whether given in a medical report, a pre-sentence report or otherwise); and

(b) the likely effect of such a sentence on that condition and on any treatment which may be available for it.

(4) No custodial sentence which is passed in a case to which subsection (1) above applies shall be invalidated by the failure of a court to comply with that subsection, but any court on an appeal against such a sentence—

(a) shall obtain a medical report if none was obtained by the court below; and

(b) shall consider any such report obtained by it or by that court.

(5) In this section—

"duly approved", in relation to a registered medical practitioner, means approved for the purposes of section 12 of the Mental Health Act 1983 ("the 1983 Act") by the Secretary of State as having special experience in the diagnosis or treatment of mental disorder;

"medical report" means a report as to an offender's mental condition made or submitted orally or in writing by a registered medical practitioner who is duly approved.

(6) Nothing in this section shall be taken as prejudicing the generality of section 3 above.

[Section 4 Criminal Justice Act 1991]

Restrictions on imposing community sentences

6.—(1) A court shall not pass a community sentence, that is to say, a sentence which consists of one or more community orders, unless it is of opinion that the offence, or the combination of the offence and one or more offences associated with it, was serious enough to warrant such a sentence.

(2) Subject to subsection (3) below, where a court passes a community sentence—

(a) the particular order or orders comprising or forming part of the sentence shall be such as in the opinion of the court is, or taken together are, the most suitable for the offender; and

(b) the restrictions on liberty imposed by the order or orders shall be such as in the opinion of the court are commensurate with the seriousness of the offence, or the combination of the offence and one or more offences associated with it.

(3) In consequence of the provisions made by section 11 below with respect to combination orders, a community sentence shall not consist of or include both a probation order and a community service order.

(4) In this Part "community order" means any of the following orders, namely—

(a) a probation order;

(b) a community service order;

(c) a combination order;

(d) a curfew order;

(e) a supervision order;

(f) an attendance centre order.

[Section 6 Criminal Justice Act 1991 as amended by s66(4) CJA 93]

Procedural requirements for community sentences.

7.—(1) In forming any such opinion as is mentioned in subsection (1) or (2)(b) of section 6 above, a court shall take into account all such information about the circumstances of the offence or (as the case may be) of the offence and the offence or offences associated with it (including any aggravating or mitigating factors) as is available to it.

(2) In forming any such opinion as is mentioned in subsection (2)(a) of that section, a court may take into account any information about the offender which is before it.

(3) A court shall obtain and consider a pre-sentence report before forming any such opinion as to the suitability for the offender of one or more of the

following orders, namely—

(a) a probation order which includes additional requirements authorised by Schedule 1A to the 1973 Act;

(b) a community service order;

(c) a combination order; and

(d) a supervision order which includes requirements imposed under section 12, 12A, 12AA, 12B or 12C of the Children and Young Persons Act 1969 ("the 1969 Act").

(4) No community sentence which consists of or includes such an order as is mentioned in subsection (3) above shall be invalidated by the failure of a court to comply with that subsection, but any court on an appeal against such a sentence—

(a) shall obtain a pre-sentence report if none was obtained by the court below; and

(b) shall consider any such report obtained by it or by that court.

[Section 7 Criminal Justice Act 1991 as amended by s66(5) CJA 93]

Orders combining probation and community service

11.—(1) Where a court by or before which a person of or over the age of sixteen years is convicted of an offence punishable with imprisonment (not being an offence for which the sentence is fixed by law) is of the opinion mentioned in subsection (2) below, the court may make a combination order, that is to say, an order requiring him both—

(a) to be under the supervision of a probation officer for a period specified in the order, being not less than twelve months nor more than three years; and

(b) to perform unpaid work for the number of hours so specified, being in the aggregate not less than 40 nor more than 100.

(2) The opinion referred to in subsection (1) above is that the making of a combination order is desirable in the interests of—

(a) securing the rehabilitation of the offender; or

(b) protecting the public from harm from him or preventing the commission by him of further offences.

(3) Subject to subsection (1) above, Part I of the 1973 Act shall apply in relation to combination orders—

(a) in so far as they impose such a requirement as is mentioned in paragraph (a) of that subsection, as if they were probation orders; and

(b) in so far as they impose such a requirement as is mentioned in paragraph (b) of that subsection, as if they were community service orders.

[Section 11 Criminal Justice Act 1991]

Curfew orders

12.—(1) Where a person of or over the age of sixteen years is convicted of an offence (not being an offence for which the sentence is fixed by law), the court by or before which he is convicted may make a curfew order, that is to say, an order requiring him to remain, for periods specified in the order, at a place so specified.

(2) A curfew order may specify different places or different periods for different days, but shall not specify—

(a) periods which fall outside the period of six months begining with the day on which it is made; or

(b) periods which amount to less than 2 hours or more than 12 hours in any one day.

(4) A curfew order shall include provision for making a person responsible for monitoring the offender's whereabouts during the periods specified in the order; and a person who is made so responsible shall be of a description specified in an order made by the Secretary of State.

(5) Before making a curfew order, the court shall explain to the offender in ordinary language—

(a) the effect of the order (including any additional requirements proposed to be included in the order in accordance with section 13 below);

(b) the consequences which follow under Schedule 2 to this Act if he fails to comply with any of the requirements of the order; and

(c) that the court has under that Schedule power to review the order on the application either of the offender or of the supervising officer,

and the court shall not make the order unless he expresses his willingness to comply with its requirements.

(6) Before making a curfew order, the court shall obtain and consider information about the place proposed to be specified in the order (including information as to the attitude of persons likely to be affected by the enforced presence there of the offender).

(7) The Secretary of State may by order direct—

(a) that subsection (2) above shall have effect with the substitution, for any period there specified, of such period as may be specified in the order; or

(b) that subsection (3) above shall have effect with such additional restrictions as may be so specified.

[Section 12 Criminal Justice Act 1991]

NOTE: Sections 12 and 13 are not in force but the Secretary of State has announced an intention to authorise their use in test areas of the country when s12 has been amended by the CJ and PO Bill of 1994.

Electronic monitoring of curfew orders

13.—(1) Subject to subsection (2) below, a curfew order may in addition include requirements for securing the electronic monitoring of the offender's whereabouts during the curfew periods specified in the order.

(2) A court shall not make a curfew order which includes such requirements unless the court—

(a) has been notified by the Secretary of State that electronic monitoring arrangements are available in the area in which the place proposed to be specified in the order is situated; and

(b) is satisfied that the necessary provisions can be made under those arrangements.

222

(3) Electronic monitoring arrangements made by the Secretary of State under this section may include entering into contract with other persons for the electronic monitoring by them of the offender's whereabouts.
[Section 13 Criminal Justice Act 1991]

Enforcement etc of community orders
14.—(1) Schedule 2 to this Act (which makes provision for dealing with failures to comply with the requirements of certain community orders, for amending such orders and for revoking them with or without the substitution of other sentences) shall have effect.
(2) [Repeals of the former enforcement provisions in the PCCA 1973].
[Section 14 Criminal Justice Act 1991]

Regulation of community orders
15.—(1) The Secretary of State may make rules for regulating—
(a) the supervision of persons who are subject to probation orders;
(b) the arrangements to be made under Schedule 3 to the 1973 Act for persons who are subject to community service orders to perform work under those orders and the performance by such persons of such work;
(c) the monitoring of the whereabouts of persons who are subject to curfew orders (including electronic monitoring in cases where arrangements for such monitoring are available); and
(d) without prejudice to the generality of paragraphs (a) to (c) above, the functions of the responsible officers of such persons as are mentioned in those paragraphs.
(2) Rules under subsection (1)(b) above may in particular -
(a) limit the number of hours of work to be done by a person on any one day;
(b) make provision as to the reckoning of hours worked and the keeping of work records;
(c) make provision for the payment of travelling and work expenses in connection with the performance of work.
(3) In this Part "responsible officer" means—
(a) in relation to an offender who is subject to a probation order, the probation officer responsible for his supervision;
(b) in relation to an offender who is subject to a community service order, the relevant officer within the meaning of section 14(4) of the 1973 Act; and
(c) in relation to an offender who is subject to curfew order, the person responsible for monitoring his whereabouts during the curfew periods specified in the order.
(4) This section shall apply in relation to combination orders—
(a) in so far as they impose such a requirement as is mentioned in paragraph (a) of subsection (1) of section 11 above, as if they were probation orders; and
(b) in so far as they impose such a requirement as is mentioned in paragraph (b) of that subsection, as if they were community service orders.
[Section 15 Criminal Justice Act 1991]

Reciprocal enforcement of certain orders

16.—(1) Schedule 3 to this Act shall have effect for making provision for and in connection with—

(a) the making and amendment in England and Wales of community orders relating to persons residing in Scotland and Northern Ireland; and

(b) the making and amendment in Scotland or Northern Ireland of corresponding orders relating to persons residing in England and Wales.

[Section 16 Criminal Justice Act 1991]

NOTE: Schedule 3 is not reproduced in this work.

Increase of certain maxima

17.—(1) In section 37 (standard scale of fines) of the Criminal Justice Act 1982 ("the 1982 Act") and section 289G of the Criminal Procedure (Scotland) Act 1975 (corresponding Scottish provision), for subsection (2) there shall be substituted the following subsection—

"(2) The standard scale is shown below—

Level on the scale	Amount of Fine
1	£200
2	£500
3	£1,000
4	£2,500
5	£5,000".

(2) Part I of the Magistrates' Courts Act 1980 ("the 1980 Act") shall be amended as follows—

(a) in section 24(3) and (4) (maximum fine on summary conviction of young person for indictable offence) and section 36(1) and (2) (maximum fine on conviction of young person by magistrates' court), for "£400" there shall be substituted "£1,000";

(b) in section 24(4) (maximum fine on summary conviction of child for indictable offence) and section 36(2) (maximum fine on conviction of child by magistrates' court), for "£100" there shall be substituted "£250"; and

(c) in section 32(9) (maximum fine on summary conviction of offence triable either way), for "£2,000" there shall be substituted "£5,000";

and in section 289B(6) of the Criminal Procedure (Scotland) Act 1975 (interpretation), in the definition of "prescribed sum", for "£2,000" there shall be substituted "£5,000".

(3) Schedule 4 to this Act shall have effect as follows—

[Increase in maximum fines for individual matters: not reproduced in this work].

(e) [Repealed by sched 3, para 1(1) and sched 6, part I CJA 1993]

[Section 17 Criminal Justice Act 1991 as amended by the CJA 1993]

Fixing of fines

18.—(1) Before fixing the amount of any fine, a court shall inquire into the financial circumstances of the offender.

(2) The amount of any fine fixed by a court shall be such as, in the opinion of the court, reflects the seriousness of the offence.

(3) In fixing the amount of any fine, a court shall take into account the circumstances of the case including, among other things, the financial circumstances of the offender so far as they are known, or appear, to the court.

(4) Where—

(a) an offender has been convicted in his absence in pursuance of section 11 or 12 of the Magistrates' Courts Act 1980 (non-appearance of the accused),

(b) an offender—

(i) has failed to comply with an order under section 20(1) below; or

(ii) has otherwise failed to cooperate with the court in its inquiry into his financial circumstances, or

(c) the parent or guardian of an offender who is a child or young person—

(i) has failed to comply with an order under section 20(1B) below; or

(ii) has otherwise failed to cooperate with the court in its inquiry into his financial circumstances,

and the court considers that it has insufficient information to make a proper determination of the financial circumstances of the offender, it may make such determination as it thinks fit.

(5) Subsection (3) above applies whether taking into account the financial circumstances of the offender has the effect of increasing or reducing the amount of the fine.

[Section 18 Criminal Justice Act 1991 as substituted by s65(1) CJA 1993]

NOTES Section 18(1) 'before fixing the amount of any fine' It is not specified how the court will inquire into the financial circumstances of the offender (contrast unit fines)—but see the power to order a statement of financial circumstances in s20, *post*. Financial circumstances must be taken into account 'among other things': s18(3). Note the 'escape' provision in s18(4). S18(2) The fine must 'reflect' seriousness, which arguably has less rigid connotations than the word 'commensurate' which appears in s1 and s6 CJA 91, *supra*—and which appeared in the original version of s18: S18(5)

Statements as to offenders' means

20.—(1) Where a person has been convicted of an offence, the court may, before sentencing him, make a financial circumstances order with respect to him.

(1A) Where a magistrates' court has been notified in accordance with section 12(2) of the Magistrates' Courts Act 1980 that a person desires to plead guilty without appearing before the court, the court may make a financial circumstances order with respect to him.

(1B) Before exercising its powers under section 55 of the Children and Young Persons Act 1933 against the parent or guardian of any person who has been convicted of an offence, the court may make a financial circumstances order with respect to the parent or (as the case may be) the guardian.

(1C) In this section a 'financial circumstances order' means, in relation to any person, an order requiring him to give to the court, within such period as may be specified in the order, such a statement of his financial circumstances as the court

225

may require.

(2) A person who without reasonable excuse fails to comply with a financial circumstances order shall be liable on summary conviction to a fine not exceeding level 3 on the standard scale.

(3) If a person in furnishing any statement in pursance of a financial circumstances order—

(a) makes a statement which he knows to be false in a material particular;

(b) recklessly furnishes a statement which is false in a material particular; or

(c) knowingly fails to disclose any material fact,

he shall be liable on summary conviction to imprisonment for a term not exceeding three months or a fine not exceeding level 4 on the standard scale or both.

(4) Proceedings in respect of an offence under subsection (3) above may, notwithstanding anything in section 127(1) of the [Magistrates' Courts Act 1980] (limitation of time), be commenced at any time within two years of the date of the commission of the offence or within six months from its first discovery by the prosecutor, whichever period expires earlier.

(5) [Repealed. Power to make rules prescribing the form in which statements are to be furnished in pursuance of orders under subsection (1) above]

[Section 20 Criminal Justice Act 1991 as amended by sched 3, para 2 and sched 6, part I CJA 1993]

NOTES **Section 20(1)** This power arises only *on conviction*. There is nothing to prevent courts seeking information in advance—and this was formerly encouraged by Home Office administrative advice to courts (and by Rule 3 Magistrates' Courts (Unit Fines) Rules 1992 SI 1856—now redundant). Compare also the Home Office letter to courts of 16 April 1991. **S20(2)** and **(3)** A suggestion is made in *Chapter 9* concerning the practical means whereby proceedings can be brought: see under the heading *Penalties for failure to furnish information*. Note that parents or guardians can now commit offences created by s20 in respect of fines imposed on their children (they did not under the original s20 CJA 91, an ommission corrected by the CJA 93).

Remission of fines fixed under section 18

21.—(1) This section applies where a court has, in fixing the amount of a fine, determined the offender's financial circumstances under section 18(4) above.

(2) If, on subsequently inquiring into the offender's financial circumstances, the court is satisfied that had it had the results of that inquiry when sentencing the offender it would—

(a) have fixed a smaller amount; or

(b) not have fined him,

it may remit the whole or part of the fine.

(3) Where under this section the court remits the whole or part of a fine after a term of imprisonment has been fixed under section 82(5) of the Magistrates' Court 1980 (issue of warrant of commitment for default) or section 31 of the Powers of Criminal Courts Act 1973 (powers of Crown Court in relation to fines), it shall reduce the term by the corresponding proportion.

(4) In calculating any reduction required by subsection (3) above, any fraction

of a day shall be ignored.
[Section 21 Criminal Justice Act 1991 as substituted by sched 3, para 3 CJA 1993]

NOTE Section 21(1) applies to all fines fixed by reference to s18(4) CJA 91, ie where the court has acted in default of financial information under that provision.

Default in other cases
23.—(1) In the Tables in section 31(3A) of the [PCCA 1973] and paragraph 1 of Schedule 4 to the [MCA 1980] (maximum periods of imprisonment for default in paying fines etc.), for the entries relating to amounts not exceeding £5,000 there shall be substituted the following entries—

"An amount not exceeding £200	7 days
An amount exceeding £200 but not exceeding £500	14 days
An amount exceeding £500 but not exceeding £1,000	28 days
An amount exceeding £1,000 but not exceeding £2,500	45 days
An amount exceeding £2,500 but not exceeding £5,000	3 months"

(2) [Table for Scotland].

(3) In Schedule 16 (repeals) to the [CJA 1988], the entry relating to subsection (8) of section 41 of the Administration of Justice Act 1970 shall cease to have effect; and that subsection (discretion of Crown Court to specify extended period of imprisonment in default of payment of compensation) shall have effect as if that entry had not been enacted.
[Section 23 Criminal Justice Act 1991]

NOTE The reference to 'other cases' originally served distinguished the above from the special default rules relating to unit fines.

Recovery of fines etc by deduction from income support
24.—The Secretary of State may by regulations provide that where a fine has been imposed on an offender by a magistrates' court, or a sum is required to be paid by a compensation order which has been made against an offender by such a court, and (in either case) the offender is entitled to income support—
(a) the court may apply to the Secretary of State asking him to deduct sums from any amounts payable to the offender by way of income support, in order to secure the payment of any sum which is or forms part of the fine or compensation; and
(b) the Secretary of State may deduct sums from any such amounts and pay them to the court towards satisfaction of any such sum.
(2) [Power to make regulations]
(3) In subsection (1) above—
(a) the reference to a fine having been imposed by a magistrates' court includes a reference to a fine being treated, by virtue of section 32 of the 1973 Act, as having been so imposed; and
(b) the reference to a sum being required to be paid by a compensation order which has been made by a magistrates' court includes a reference to a sum

which is required to be paid by such an order being treated, by virtue of section 41 of the Administration of Justice Act 1970, as having been adjudged to be paid on conviction by such a court.

(4) In this section—

"fine" includes—

(a) a penalty imposed under section 8(1) or 18(4) of the Vehicles (Excise) Act 1971 or section 102(3)(aa) of the Customs and Excise Management Act 1979 (penalties imposed for certain offences in relation to excise licences);

(b) an amount ordered to be paid, in addition to any penalty so imposed, under section 9, 18A or 26A of the said Act of 1971 (liability to additional duty);

(c) an amount ordered to be paid by way of costs which is, by virtue of section 41 of the Administration of Justice Act 1970, treated as having been adjudged to be paid on conviction by a magistrates' court;

"income support" means income support within the meaning of the Social Security Act 1986, either alone or together with any unemployment, sickness or invalidity benefit, retirement pension or severe disablement allowance which is paid by means of the same instrument of payment;

"prescribed" means prescribed by regulations made by the Secretary of State.

(5) [Adjustments relating to Scotland]

[Section 24 Criminal Justice Act 1991]

NOTES Section 24(3) a fine 'being treated ... as having been so imposed' ie a fine imposed by the Crown Court: see s32 PCCA 73. S24(1)(a) '... may apply to the Secretary of State asking him' Attachment of state benefits can only occur following a *request* by the court and subject to the *discretion* of the Secretary of State.

Savings for mitigation and mentally disordered offenders

28.—(1) Nothing in [Part I of the CJA 91] shall prevent a court from mitigating an offender's sentence by taking into account any such matters as, in the opinion of the court, are relevant in mitigation of sentence.

(2) Without prejudice to the generality of subsection (1) above, nothing in [Part I of the CJA 91] shall prevent a court—

(a) from mitigating any penalty included in an offender's sentence by taking into account any other penalty included in that sentence; or

(b) in a case of an offender who is convicted of one or more other offences, from mitigating his sentence by applying any rule of law as to the totality of sentences.

(3) [Repealed by sched 6, part I CJA 1993]

(4) Nothing in [Part I CJA 91] shall be taken—

(a) as requiring a court to pass a custodial sentence, or any particular custodial sentence, on a mentally disordered offender; or

(b) as restricting any power (whether under the [Mental Health Act 1983] or otherwise) which enables a court to deal with such an offender in the manner it considers to be most appropriate in all the circumstances.

[Section 28 Criminal Justice Act 1991 as amended by the Criminal Justice Act 1993]

NOTES s28(1) is of general application and seemingly unfettered—subject to relevance in an individual case. For a catalogue of mitigatory features: see *Chapter 1(c), Judicial Guidance.* s28(3) This repealed provision concerned mitigation of unit fines. s28(4)(b) There must be a medical report before any decision on custody can be made unless the court considers this unnecessary: s4 CJA 91.

Effect of previous convictions etc

29.—(1) In considering the seriousness of any offence, the court may take into account any previous convictions of the offender or any failure of his to respond to previous sentences.

(2) In considering the seriousness of any offence committed while the offender was on bail, the court shall treat the fact that it was committed in those circumstances as an aggravating factor.

(3) A probation order or conditional discharge order made before 1st October 1992 (which, by virtue of section 2 or 7 of the Powers of Criminal Courts Act 1973, would otherwise not be a sentence for the purposes of this section) is to be treated as a sentence for those purposes.

(4) A conviction in respect of which a probation order or conditional discharge order was made before that date (which, by virtue of section 13 of that Act, would otherwise not be a conviction for those purposes) is to be treated as a conviction for those purposes.

[Section 29 Criminal Justice Act 1991 as substituted by s66(6) CJA 1993]

NOTES S29(1) The original version of s29(1) prevented a sentence from being increased beyond what was commensurate with the seriousness of the present offence. The prohibition did not apply in relation to s1(2)(b) CJA 91 ('protection of the public'). Indeed, previous convictions may be one indicator of the risk of future serious harm to the public from an offender: see *Chapters 3 and 7.* The present s29(1) reverses the prohibition on taking account of previous conviction in relation to the seriousness of the present offence. **s29(2)** The effect of this provision under which the court is required to regard an offence committed on bail as more serious is considered in *Chapter 4, Section 29 CJA 91.* **s29(3)** and **(4)** These provisions are necessary to counteract the effect of ss2, 7 and 13 PCCA 1973 under which probation orders and conditional discharges did not rank as sentences or convictions. No mention is made of absolute discharges (but see the CJ and PO Bill of 1994, which provides that a conviction resulting in an absolute discharge order in or after October 1992 shall be treated as a conviction for the purposes of s29), or of compensation used as a sentence in its own right. Arguably, such outcomes escape the effect of s29(1) although this argument is less convincing re compensation which can be viewed as akin to a fine.

Interpretation of Part I

31.— In this Part—

"attendance centre order" means an order under section 17 [Criminal Justice Act 1982];

"combination order" means an order under section 11 [CJA 91];

"community order" has the meaning given by s6(4) [CJA 91];

"community sentence" has the meaning given by s6(1) [CJA 91];

"curfew order" means an order under s12 [CJA 91];

"custodial sentence" means—

(a) in relation to an offender of or over the age of twenty-one years, a sentence of imprisonment; and

(b) in relation to an offender under that age, a sentence of detention in a young offender institution or under section 53 of the Children and Young Persons Act 1933 ("the 1933 Act"), or a sentence of custody for life under section 8(2) of the 1982 Act;

"mentally disordered", in relation to any person, means suffering from a mental disorder within the meaning of the [Mental Health Act 1983];

"pre-sentence report" has the meaning given by section 3(5) [CJA 91];

"responsible officer" has the meaning given by section 15 (3) [CJA 91];

"sentence of imprisonment" does not include a committal or attachment for contempt of court;

"sexual offence" means an offence under the Sexual Offences Act 1956, the Indecency with Children Act 1960, the Sexual Offences Act 1967, section 54 of the Criminal Law Act 1977 or the Protection of Children Act 1978, other than—

(a) an offence under section 12 or 13 of the Sexual Offences Act 1956 which would not be an offence but for section 2 of the Sexual Offences Act 1967;

(b) an offence under section 30, 31 or 33 to 36 of the said Act of 1956; and

(c) an offence under section 4 or 5 of the said Act of 1967;

"violent offence" means an offence which leads, or is intended or likely to lead, to a person's death or to physical injury to a person, and includes an offence which is required to be charged as arson (whether or not it would otherwise fall within this definition).

(2) For the purposes of this Part, an offence is associated with another if—

(a) the offender is convicted of it in the proceedings in which he is convicted of the other offence, or (although convicted of it in earlier proceedings) is sentenced for it at the same time as he is sentenced for that offence; or

(b) the offender admits the commission of it in the proceedings in which he is sentenced for the other offence and requests the court to take it into consideration in sentencing him for that offence.

(3) In this Part any reference, in relation to an offender convicted of a violent or sexual offence, to protecting the public from serious harm from him shall be construed as a reference to protecting members of the public from death or serious personal injury, whether physical or psychological, occasioned by further such offences committed by him.

[Section 31 Criminal Justice Act 1991]

Part II EARLY RELEASE OF PRISONERS

The Parole Board

32.—(1) There shall continue to be a body to be known as the Parole Board ("the Board") which shall discharge the functions conferred on it by this Part.

(2) It shall be the duty of the Board to advise the Secretary of State with respect to any matter referred to it by him which is connected with the early release of prisoners.

(3) The Board shall deal with cases as respects which it makes recommendations under this Part on consideration of—

(a) any documents given to it by the Secretary of State; and

(b) any other oral or written information obtained by it,

and if in any particular case the Board thinks it necessary to interview the person to whom the case relates before reaching a decision, the Board may authorise one of its members to interview him and shall consider the report of the interview made by that member.

(4) The Board shall deal with cases as respects which it gives directions under this Part on consideration of all such evidence as may be adduced before it.

(5) Without prejudice to subsections (3) and (4) above, the Secretary of State may make rules with respect to the proceedings of the Board, including provision authorising cases to be dealt with by a prescribed number of its members or requiring cases to be dealt with at prescribed times.

(6) The Secretary of State may also give to the Board directions as to the matters to be taken into account by it in discharging any functions under this Part; and in giving any such directions the Secretary of State shall in particular have regard to—

(a) the need to protect the public from serious harm from offenders; and

(b) the desirability of preventing the commission by them of further offences and of securing their rehabilitation.

(7) Schedule 5 to this Act shall have effect with respect to the Board.

[Section 32 Criminal Justice Act 1991]

Duty to release short-term and long-term prisoners

33.—(1) As soon as a short-term prisoner has served one-half of his sentence, it shall be the duty of the Secretary of State—

(a) to release him unconditionally if that sentence is for a term of less than twelve months; and

(b) to release him on licence if that sentence is for a term of twelve months or more.

(2) As soon as a long-term prisoner has served two-thirds of his sentence, it shall be the duty of the Secretary of State to release him on licence.

(3) As soon as a short-term or long-term prisoner who—

(a) has been released on licence under subsection (1)(b) or (2) above or section 35 or 36(1) below; and

(b) has been recalled to prison under section 38(2) or 39(1) below,

would (but for his release) have served three-quarters of his sentence, it shall be the duty of the Secretary of State to release him unconditionally.

(4) Where a prisoner whose sentence is for a term of less than twelve months

has been released on licence under section 36(1) below and recalled to prison under section 38(2) below, subsection (3) above shall have effect as if for the reference to three-quarters of his sentence there were substituted a reference to one-half of that sentence.

(5) In this Part—

"long-term prisoner" means a person serving a sentence of imprisonment for a term of four years or more;

"short-term prisoner" means a person serving a sentence of imprisonment for a term of less than four years.

[Section 33 Criminal Justice Act 1991]

NOTE S33(1) to (4) Other provisions are substituted re young offenders committed or detained for contempt under s9 CJA 82: see s45 CJA 91, *post*.

Duty to release discretionary life prisoners

34.—(1) A life prisoner is a discretionary life prisoner for the purposes of this Part if—

(a) his sentence was imposed for a violent or sexual offence the sentence for which is not fixed by law; and

(b) the court by which he was sentenced for that offence ordered that this section should apply to him as soon as he had served a part of his sentence specified in the order.

(2) A part of a sentence so specified shall be such part as the court considers appropriate taking into account—

(a) the seriousness of the offence, or the combination of the offence and other offences associated with it; and

(b) the provisions of this section as compared with those of section 33(2) above and section 25(1) below.

(3) As soon as, in the case of a discretionary life prisoner—

(a) he has served the part of his sentence specified in the order ("the relevant part"); and

(b) the Board has directed his release under this section,

it shall be the duty of the Secretary of State to release him on licence.

(4) The Board shall not give a direction under subsection (3) above with respect to a discretionary life prisoner unless—

(a) the Secretary of State has referred the prisoner's case to the Board; and

(b) the Board is satisfied that it is no longer necessary for the protection of the public that the prisoner should be confined.

(5) A discretionary life prisoner may require the Secretary of State to refer his case to the Board at any time—

(a) after he has served the relevant part of his sentence; and

(b) where there has been a previous reference to the Board, after the end of the period of two years beginning with the disposal of that reference; and

(c) where he is also serving a sentence of imprisonment for a term, after he has served one-half of that sentence;

and in this subsection "previous reference" means a reference under subsection

(4) above or section 39(4) below made after the prisoner had served the relevant part of his sentence.

(6) In determining for the purpose of subsection (3) or (5) above whether a discretionary life prisoner has served the relevant part of his sentence, no account shall be taken of any time during which he was unlawfully at large within the meaning of section 49 of the Prison Act 1952 ("the 1952 Act").

(7) In this Part "life prisoner" means a person serving one or more sentences of life imprisonment; but—

(a) a person serving two or more such sentences shall not be treated as a discretionary life prisoner for the purposes of this Part unless the requirements of subsection (1) above are satisfied as respects each of those sentences; and

(b) subsections (3) and (5) above shall not apply in relation to such a person until after he has served the relevant part of each of those sentences.

[Section 34 Criminal Justice Act 1991]

Power to release long-term and life prisoners

35.—(1) After a long-term prisoner has served one-half of his sentence, the Secretary of State may, if recommended to do so by the Board, release him on licence.

(2) If recommended to do so by the Board, the Secretary of State may, after consultation with the Lord Chief Justice together with the trial judge if available, release on licence a life prisoner who is not a discretionary life prisoner.

(3) The Board shall not make a recommendation under subsection (2) above unless the Secretary of State has referred the particular case, or the class of case to which that case belongs, to the Board for its advice.

[Section 35 Criminal Justice Act 1991]

Power to release prisoners on compassionate grounds

36.—(1) The Secretary of State may at any time release a prisoner on licence if he is satisfied that exceptional circumstances exist which justify the prisoner's release on compassionate grounds.

(2) Before releasing a long-term or life prisoner under subsection (1) above, the Secretary of State shall consult the Board, unless the circumstances are such as to render such consultation impracticable.

[Section 36 Criminal Justice Act 1991]

Duration and condition of licence

37.—(1) Subject to subsection (2) below, where a short-term prisoner is released on licence, the licence shall, subject to any suspension under section 38(2) below or, as the case may be, any revocation under section 39(1) or (2) below, remain in force until the date on which he would (but for his release) have served three-quarters of his sentence.

(2) Where a prisoner whose sentence is for a term of less than twelve months is released on licence under section 36(1) above, subsection (1) above shall have effect as if for the reference to three-quarters of his sentence there were

substituted a reference to one-half of that sentence.

(3) Where a life prisoner is released on licence, the licence shall, unless previously revoked under section 39(1) or (2) below, remain in force until his death.

(4) A person subject to a licence shall comply with such conditions (which shall include on his release conditions as to his supervision by a probation officer) as may for the time being be specified in the licence; and the Secretary of State may make rules for regulating the supervision of any description of such persons.

(5) The Secretary of State shall not include on release, or subsequently insert, a condition in the licence of a long-term or life prisoner, or vary or cancel any such condition, except—

(a) in the case of the inclusion of a condition in the licence of a discretionary life prisoner, in accordance with recommendations of the Board; and

(b) in any other case, after consultation with the Board.

(6) For the purposes of subsection (5) above, the Secretary of State shall be treated as having consulted the Board about a proposal to include, insert, vary or cancel a condition in any case if he has consulted the Board about the implementation of proposals of that description generally or in that class of case.

(7) The power to make rules under this section shall be exercisable by statutory instrument which shall be subject to annulment in pursuance of a resolution of either House of Parliament.

[Section 37 Criminal Justice Act 1991]

NOTE S37(1) to (3) Other provisions are substituted in the case of young offenders committed or detained under s9 CJA 82: see s45 CJA 91, *post*.

Breach of licence conditions by short-term prisoners

38.—(1) A short-term prisoner—

(a) who is released on licence under this Part; and

(b) who fails to comply with such conditions as may for the time being be specified in the licence,

shall be liable on summary conviction to a fine not exceeding level 3 on the standard scale.

(2) The magistrates' court by which a person is convicted of an offence under subsection (1) above may, whether or not it passes any other sentence on him—

(a) suspend the licence for a period not exceeding six months; and

(b) order him to be recalled to prison for the period during which the licence is so suspended.

(3) On the suspension of the licence of any person under this section, he shall be liable to be detained in pursuance of his sentence and, if at large, shall be deemed to be unlawfully at large.

[Section 38 Criminal Justice Act 1991]

NOTE S38(1) and (2) These provisions have considerable implications for courts (including the posssibly of co-ordinated approaches to recall as between courts and the Parole Board) and in relation to information generally. There is scope for multi-agency liaison.

Recall of long-term and life prisoners while on licence.

39.—(1) If recommended to do so by the Board in the case of a long-term or life prisoner who has been released on licence under this Part, the Secretary of State may revoke his licence and recall him to prison.

(2) The Secretary of State may revoke the licence of any such person and recall him to prison without a recommendation by the Board, where it appears to him that it is expedient in the public interest to recall that person before such a recommendation is practicable.

(3) A person recalled to prison under subsection (1) or (2) above—

(a) may make representations in writing with respect to his recall; and

(b) on his return to prison, shall be informed of the reasons for his recall and the right to make representations.

(4) The Secretary of State shall refer to the Board—

(a) the case of a person recalled under subsection (1) above who makes representations under subsection (3) above; and

(b) the case of a person recalled under subsection (2) above.

(5) Where on a reference under subsection (4) above the Board—

(a) directs in the case of a discretionary life prisoner; or

(b) recommends in the case of any other person,

his immediate release on licence under this section, the Secretary of State shall give effect to the direction or recommendation.

(6) On the revocation of the licence of any person under this section, he shall be liable to be detained in pursuance of his sentence and, if at large, shall be deemed to be unlawfully at large.

[Section 39 Criminal Justice Act 1991]

Convictions during currency of original sentences

40.—(1) This section applies to a short-term or long-term prisoner who is released under this Part if—

(a) before the date on which he would (but for his release) have served his sentence in full, he commits an offence punishable with imprisonment; and

(b) whether before or after that date, he is convicted of that offence ("the new offence").

(2) Subject to subsection (3) below, the court by or before which a person to whom this section applies is convicted of the new offence may, whether or not it passes any other sentence on him, order him to be returned to prison for the whole or any part of the period which—

(a) begins with the date of the order; and

(b) is equal in length to the period between the date on which the new offence was committed and the date mentioned in subsection (1) above.

(3) A magistrates' court—

(a) shall not have power to order a person to whom this section applies to be returned to prison for a period of more than six months; but

(b) may commit him in custody or on bail to the Crown Court for sentence in accordance with section 42 of the 1973 Act (power of the Crown Court to sentence persons convicted by magistrates' courts of indictable offences).

(4) The period for which a person to whom this section applies is ordered under subsection (2) above to be returned to prison—

(a) shall be taken to be a sentence of imprisonment for the purposes of this Part;

(b) shall, as the court may direct, either be served before and be followed by, or be served concurrently with, the sentence imposed for the new offence; and

(c) in either case, shall be disregarded in determining the appropriate length of that sentence.

[Section 40 Criminal Justice Act 1991]

NOTES Section **40** introduces the 'at risk' concept, whereby anyone committing an imprisonable offence between release and the 100 per cent point of their sentence can be returned to custody by the court. S40(2) empowers the court dealing with the new offence to order the offender to be returned to custody to serve all or part of the balance of the original sentence outstanding at the time the fresh offence *was committed*. S40(4) allows courts to order this period to be served consecutively to—or concurrently with—any fresh sentence.

Remand time to count towards time served

41.—(1) This section applies to any person whose sentence falls to be reduced under section 67 of the Criminal Justice Act 1967 ("the 1967 Act") by any relevant period within the meaning of that section ("the relevant period").

(2) For the purpose of determining for the purposes of this Part—

(a) whether a person to whom this section applies has served one-half or two-thirds of his sentence; or

(b) whether such person would (but for his release) have served three-quarters of that sentence,

the relevant period shall, subject to subsection (3) below, be treated as having been served by him as part of that sentence.

(3) Nothing in subsection (2) above shall have the effect of reducing the period for which a licence granted under this Part to a short-term or long-term prisoner remains in force to a period which is less than—

(a) one-quarter of his sentence in the case of a short-term prisoner; or

(b) one-twelfth of his sentence in the case of a long-term prisoner.

[Section 41 Criminal Justice Act 1991]

NOTE S41(1) **'reduced under s67 of the Criminal Justice Act 1967'** S67 CJA 1967 sets out 'relevant periods' by which custodial sentences must be reduced, eg time spent in police detention or in custody on remand.

Additional days for disciplinary offences

42.—(1) Prison rules, that is to say rules made under section 47 of the 1952 Act, may include provision for the award of additional days—

(a) to short-term or long-term prisoners; or

(b) conditionally on their subsequently becoming such prisoners, to prisoners on remand,

who (in either case) are guilty of disciplinary offences.

(2) Where additional days are awarded to a short-term or long-term prisoner, or to a person on remand who subsequently becomes such a prisoner, and are not remitted in accordance with prison rules—

(a) any period which he must serve before becoming entitled to or eligible for release under this Part; and

(b) any period for which a licence granted to him under this Part remains in force,

shall be extended by the aggregate of those additional days.

[Section 42 Criminal Justice Act 1991]

Young offenders

43.—(1) Subject to subsections (4) and (5) below, this Part applies to persons serving sentences of detention in a young offender institution, or determinate sentences of detention under section 53 of the 1933 Act, as it applies to persons serving equivalent sentences of imprisonment.

(2) Subject to subsection (5) below, this Part applies to persons serving—

(a) sentences of detention during Her Majesty's pleasure or for life under section 53 of the 1933 Act; or

(b) sentences of custody for life under section 8 of the 1982 Act,

as it applies to persons serving sentences of imprisonment for life.

(3) References in this Part to prisoners (whether short-term, long-term or life prisoners), or to prison or imprisonment, shall be construed in accordance with subsections (1) and (2) above.

(4) In relation to a short-term prisoner under the age of 18 years to whom subsection (1) of section 33 above applies, that subsection shall have effect as if it required the Secretary of State—

(a) to release him unconditionally if his sentence is for a term of twelve months or less; and

(b) to release him on licence if that sentence is for a term of more than twelve months.

(5) In relation to a person under 22 years who is released on licence under this Part, section 37(4) above shall have effect as if the reference to supervision by a probation officer included a reference to supervision by a social worker of a local authority social services department.

[Section 43 Criminal Justice Act 1991]

Sexual Offenders

44.—(1) Where, in the case of a long-term or short-term prisoner—

(a) the whole or any part of his sentence was imposed for a sexual offence; and

(b) the court by which he was sentenced for that offence, having had regard to the matters mentioned in section 32(6)(a) and (b) above, ordered that this section should apply, sections 33(3) and 37(1) above shall each have effect as if for the reference to three-quarters of his sentence there were substituted a reference to the whole of that sentence.

[Section 44 Criminal Justice Act 1991]

Fine defaulters and contemnors

45.—(1) Subject to subsection (2) below, this Part (except sections 35 and 40 above) applies to persons committed to prison or to be detained under section 9 of the 1982 Act—

(a) in default of payment of a sum adjudged to be paid by a conviction; or

(b) for contempt of court or any kindred offence,

as it applies to persons serving equivalent sentences of imprisonment; and references in this Part to short-term or long-term prisoners, or to prison or imprisonment, shall be construed accordingly.

(2) In relation to persons committed as mentioned in subsection (1) above, the provisions specified in subsections (3) and (4) below shall have effect subject to the modifications so specified.

(3) In section 33 above, for subsections (1) to (4) there shall be substituted the following subsections -

"(1) As soon as a person committed as mentioned in section 45(1) below has served the appropriate proportion of his term, that is to say -

(a) one-half, in the case of a person committed for a term of less than twelve months;

(b) two-thirds, in the case of a person committed for a term of twelve months or more,

it shall be the duty of the Secretary of State to release him unconditionally.

(2) As soon as a person so committed who -

(a) has been released on licence under section 36(1) below; and

(b) has been recalled under section 38(2) or 39(1) below,

would (but for his release) have served the appropriate proportion of his term, it shall be the duty of the Secretary of State to release him unconditionally."

(4) In section 37 above, for subsections (1) to (3) there shall be substituted the following subsection—

"(1) Where a person committed as mentioned in section 45(1) below is released on licence under section 36(1) above, the licence shall, subject to—

(a) any suspension under section 38(2) below; or

(b) any revocation under section 39(1) below,

continue in force until the date on which he would (but for his release) have served the appropriate proportion of his term; and in this subsection 'appropriate proportion' has the meaning given by section 33(1) above."

[Section 45 Criminal Justice Act 1991]

[Persons liable to removal from the United Kingdom 46.- Not reproduced. **Persons extradited to the United Kingdom 47.**— Not reproduced (but see outline in main text). **Life prisoners transferred to England and Wales 48.**— Not reproduced.]

Alteration by order of relevant proportion of sentences

49.—(1) The Secretary of State may by order made by statutory instrument provide—

(a) that references in section 33(5) above to four years shall be construed as references to such other period as may be specified in the order;

(b) that any reference in this Part to a particular proportion of a prisoner's sentence shall be construed as a reference to such other proportion of a prisoner's sentence as shall be so specified.

(2) An order under this section may make such transitional provisions as appear to the Secretary of State necessary or expedient in connection with any provision made by the order.

(3) No order shall be made under this section unless a draft of the order has been laid before and approved by resolution of each House of Parliament.

[Section 49 Criminal Justice Act 1991]

Interpretation of Part II

51.— (1) In this Part—

"the Board" means the Parole Board;

"discretionary life prisoner" has the meaning given by section 34 above (as extended by section 43(2) above);

"life prisoner" has the meaning given by section 34(7) above (as extended by section 43(2) above);

"long-term prisoner" and "short-term prisoner" have the meanings given by section 33(5) above (as extended by sections 43(1) and 45(1) above);

"sentence of imprisonment" does not include a committal in default of payment of any sum of money, or for want of sufficient distress to satisfy any sum of money, or for failure to do or abstain from doing anything required to be done or left undone.

"sexual offence" and "violent offence" have the same meanings as in Part I of this Act.

(2) For the purposes of any reference in [Part II CJA 91], however expressed, to the term of imprisonment to which a person has been sentenced or which, or part of which, he has served, consecutive terms and terms which are wholly or partly concurrent shall be treated as a single term.

(3) Nothing in [Part II CJA 91] shall require the Secretary of State to release a person who is serving—

(a) a sentence of imprisonment for a term; and

(b) one or more sentences of imprisonment for life,

unless and until he is entitled under this Part to be released in respect of each of those sentences.

(4) Subsections (2) and (3) of section 31 above shall apply for the purposes of this Part as they apply for the purposes of Part I of this Act.

[Section 51 Criminal Justice Act 1991]

NOTE S51(1) 'sexual offence' and 'violent offence' see s31(1) CJA 91 *supra.*

Part III

[Relevant extracts from Part III CJA 1991 which applies to 'Children and Young Persons' are reproduced in the companion volume to this work *The Youth Court One Year Onwards*. Note, however, s57 which contains new provisions and amendments (to s55 CYPA 1933, in particular) concerning the liability of parents, guardians and local authorities for financial penalties imposed on young people. This provision is further amended by the CJA 93. The position is noted, in outline, in *Chapter 9, Fines and Compensation*. A detailed treatment and the statutory provisions themselves are contained in *Chapter 7* of *The Youth Court One Year Onwards*].

Part V

FINANCIAL AND OTHER PROVISIONS

Information for financial and other purposes

95.—(1) The Secretary of State shall in each year publish such information as he considers expedient for the purpose of—

(a) enabling persons engaged in the administration of criminal justice to become aware of the financial implications of their decisions; or

(b) facilitating the performance by such persons of their duty to avoid discriminating against any persons on the ground of race or sex or any other improper ground.

(2) Publication under subsection (1) above shall be effected in such manner as the Secretary of State considers appropriate for the purpose of bringing the information to the attention of the persons concerned.

[Section 95 Criminal Justice Act 1991]

NOTES S95(1) 'persons engaged in the administration of criminal justice' The words are not qualified—but would apply to judges, magistrates, police, Crown Prosecutors, probation officers, social workers etc. **'duty to avoid discrimination'** ie under the general law or rules of natural justice.

Grants by probation committees

97.—In Schedule 3 to the PCCA 1973 (the probation service and its functions), after paragraph 12 there shall be inserted the following paragraph—

"*Payment of grants in prescribed cases*

12A.— A probation committee may, in prescribed cases, make such payments to such persons as may be prescribed."

Schedule 2 [CJA 91]

ENFORCEMENT ETC. OF COMMUNITY ORDERS

PART I: PRELIMINARY

1.—(1) In this schedule "relevant order" means any of the following orders, namely, a probation order, a community service order and a curfew order; and "the petty sessions area concerned" means—

(a) In relation to a probation or community service order, the petty sessions area for the time being specified in the order; and

(b) In relation to a curfew order, the petty sessions area in which the place for the time being specified in the order is situated.

(2) Subject to sub-paragraph (3) below, this Schedule shall apply in relation to combination orders—

(a) in so far as they impose such a requirement as is mentioned in paragraph (a) of subsection (1) of section 11 of this Act, as if they were probation orders; and

(b) in so far as they impose such a requirement as is mentioned in paragraph (b) of that subsection, as if they were community service orders.

(3) In its application to combination orders, paragraph 6(3) below shall have effect as if the reference to section 14(1A) of the 1973 Act were a reference to section 11(1) of this Act.

PART II: BREACH OF REQUIREMENT OF ORDER
Issue of summons or warrant

2.—(1) If at any time while a relevant order is in force in respect of an offender it appears on information to a justice of the peace acting for the petty sessions area concerned that the offender has failed to comply with any of the requirements of the order, the justice may—

(a) issue a summons requiring the offender to appear at the place and time specified in it; or

(b) if the information is in writing and on oath, issue a warrant for his arrest.

(2) Any summons or warrant issued under this paragraph shall direct the offender to appear or be brought before a magistrates' court acting for the petty sessions area concerned.

Powers of magistrates' court

3.—(1) If it is proved to the satisfaction of the magistrates' court before which an offender appears or is brought under paragraph 2 above that he has failed without reasonable excuse to comply with any of the requirements of the relevant order, the court may deal with him in respect of the failure in any one of the following ways, namely—

(a) it may impose on him a fine not exceeding £1,000;

(b) subject to paragraph 6(3) to (5) below, it may make a community service order in respect of him.

(c) where the relevant order is a probation order and the case is one to which section 17 of the 1982 Act applies, it may make an order under that section requiring him to attend at an attendance centre; or

(d) where the relevant order was made by a magistrates' court, it may revoke the order and deal with him, for the offence in respect of which the order was made, in any manner in which it could deal with him if he had just been convicted by the court of the offence.

(2) In dealing with an offender under sub-paragraph (1)(d) above, a magistrates' court—

(a) shall take into account the extent to which the offender has complied with the requirements of the relevant order; and

(b) may assume, in the case of an offender who has wilfully and persistently failed to comply with those requirements, that he has refused to consent to a community sentence which has been proposed by the court and requires that consent.

(3) Where a relevant order was made by the Crown Court and a magistrates' court has power to deal with the offender under sub-paragraph (1)(a), (b) or (c) above, it may instead commit him to custody or release him on bail until he can be brought or appear before the Crown Court.

(4) A magistrates' court which deals with an offender's case under sub-paragraph (3) above shall send to the Crown Court—

(a) a certificate signed by a justice of the peace certifying that the offender has failed to comply with the requirements of the relevant order in the respect certified in the certificate; and

(b) such other particulars of the case as may be desirable;

and a certificate purporting to be so signed shall be admissible as evidence of the failure before the Crown Court.

(5) A person sentenced under sub-paragraph (1)(d) above for an offence may appeal to the Crown Court against the sentence.

Powers of Crown Court

4.—(1) Where by virtue of paragraph 3(3) above an offender is brought or appears before the Crown Court and it is proved to the satisfaction of the court that he has failed to comply with any of the requirements of the relevant order, that court may deal with him in respect of the failure in any one of the following ways, namely—

(a) it may impose on him a fine not exceeding £1,000;

(b) subject to paragraph 6(3) to (5) below, it may make a community service order in respect of him;

(c) where the relevant order is a probation order and the case is one to which section 17 of the 1982 Act applies, it may make an order under that section requiring him to attend at an attendance centre; or

(d) it may revoke the order and deal with him, for the offence in respect of which the order was made, in any manner in which it could deal with him if he had just been convicted before the court of the offence.

242

(2) In dealing with an offender under sub-paragraph (1)(d) above, the Crown Court—

(a) shall take into account the extent to which the offender has complied with the requirements of the relevant order; and

(b) may assume, in the case of an offender who has wilfully and persistently failed to comply with those requirements, that he has refused to consent to a community sentence which has been proposed by the court and requires that consent.

(3) In proceedings before the Crown Court under this paragraph any question whether the offender has failed to comply with the requirements of the relevant order shall be determined by the court and not by the verdict of a jury.

Exclusions

5.—(1) Without prejudice to paragraphs 7 and 8 below, an offender who is convicted of a further offence while a relevant order is in force in respect of him shall not on that account be liable to be dealt with under paragraph 3 or 4 above in respect of a failure to comply with any requirement of the order.

(2) An offender who is required by a probation order to submit to treatment for his mental condition, or his dependency on drugs or alcohol, shall not be treated for the purposes of paragraphs 3 or 4 above as having failed to comply with that requirement on the ground only that he has refused to undergo any surgical, electrical or other treatment if, in the opinion of the court, his refusal was reasonable having regard to all the circumstances.

Supplemental

6.—(1) Any exercise by a court of its powers under paragraph 3(1)(a), (b) or (c) or 4(1)(a) or (b) above shall be without prejudice to the continuance of the relevant order.

(2) Section 18 of the Act shall apply for the purposes of paragraph 3(1)(a) above as if the failure to comply with the requirement were a summary offence punishable by a fine not exceeding level 3 on the standard scale; and a fine imposed under that paragraph or paragraph 4(1)(a) above shall be deemed for the purposes of any enactment to be a sum adjudged to be paid by a conviction.

(3) The number of hours which an offender may be required to work under a community service order made under paragraph 3(1)(b) or 4(1)(b) above

(a) shall be specified in the order and shall not exceed 60 in the aggregate; and

(b) where the relevant order is a community service order, shall not be such that the total number of hours under both orders exceeds the maximum specified in section 14(1A) of the 1973 Act.

(4) Section 14(2) of the 1973 Act and, so far as applicable—

(a) the following provisions of that Act relating to community service orders; and

(b) the provisions of this Schedule so far as relating,

shall have effect in relation to a community service order under paragraph 3(1)(b) or 4(1)(b) above as they have effect in relation to a community service order in respect of the offender.

(5) Where the provisions of this Schedule have effect as mentioned in sub-

paragraph (4) above, the powers conferred by those provisions to deal with the offender for the offence in respect of which the community service order was made shall be construed as powers to deal with the offender for the failure to comply with the requirements of the relevant order in respect of which the community service order was made.

PART III: REVOCATION OF ORDER
Revocation of order with or without resentencing

7.—(1) This paragraph applies where a relevant order is in force in respect of any offender and, on the application of the offender or the responsible officer, it appears to a magistrates' court acting for the petty sessions area concerned that, having regard to circumstances that have arisen since the order was made, it would be in the interests of justice—

(a) that the order should be revoked; or

(b) that the offender should be dealt with in some other manner for the offence in respect of which the order was made.

(2) The court may—

(a) if the order was made by a magistrates' court -

(i) revoke the order; or

(ii) revoke the order and deal with the offender, for the offence in respect of which the order was made, in any manner in which it could deal with him if he had just been convicted by that court of the offence; or

(b) if the order was made by the Crown Court, commit him to custody or release him on bail until he can be brought or appear before the Crown Court.

(3) The circumstances in which a probation order may be revoked under sub-paragraph 2(a)(i) above shall include the offender's making good progress or his responding satisfactorily to supervision.

(4) In dealing with an offender under sub-paragraph 2(a)(ii) above, a magistrates' court shall take into account the extent to which the offender has complied with the relevant order.

(5) An offender sentenced under sub-paragraph 2(a)(ii) above may appeal to the Crown Court against sentence.

(6) Where the court deals with an offender's case under sub-paragraph (2)(b) above, it shall send to the Crown Court such particulars of the case as may be desirable.

(7) Where a magistrates' court proposes to exercise its powers under this paragraph otherwise than on the application of the offender, it shall summon him to appear before the court and, if he does not appear in answer to the summons, may issue a warrant for his arrest.

(8) No application may be made by the offender under sub-paragraph (1) above while an appeal against the relevant order is pending.

8.—(1) This paragraph applies where an offender in respect of whom a relevant order is in force—

(a) is convicted of an offence before the Crown Court; or

(b) is committed by a magistrates' court to the Crown Court for sentence and is brought or appears before the Crown Court; or

(c) by virtue of paragraph 7(2)(b) above is brought or appears before the Crown Court.

(2) If it appears to the Crown Court to be in the interests of justice to do so, having regard to circumstances which have arisen since the order was made, the Crown Court may—

(a) revoke the order; or

(b) revoke the order and deal with the offender, for the offence in respect of which the order was made, in any manner in which it could deal with him if he had just been convicted by or before the court of the offence.

(3) The circumstances in which a probation order may be revoked under subparagraph (2)(a) above shall include the offender making good progress or him responding satisfactorily to supervision.

(4) In dealing with an offender under sub-paragraph (2)(b) above, the Crown Court shall take into account the extent to which the offender has complied with the requirements of the relevant order.

Revocation of order following custodial sentence

9.—(1) This paragraph applies where—

(a) an offender in respect of whom a relevant order is in force is convicted of an offence before a magistrates' court other than a magistrates' court acting for the petty sessions area concerned; and

(b) the court imposes a custodial sentence on the offender.

(2) If it appears to the court, on the application of the offender or the responsible officer, that it would be in the interests of justice to do so having regard to circumstances that have arisen since the order was made, the court may—

(a) if the order was made by a magistrates' court, revoke it; and

(b) if the order was made by the Crown Court, commit the offender in custody or release him on bail until he can be brought or appear before the Crown Court.

(3) Where the court deals with an offender's case under sub-paragraph (2)(b) above, it shall send to the Crown Court such particulars of the case as may be desirable.

10.— Where by virtue of paragraph 9(2)(b) above an offender is brought or appears before the Crown Court and it appears to the Crown Court to be in the interests of justice to do so, having regard to circumstances which have arisen since the relevant order was made, the Crown Court may revoke the order.

Supplemental

11.—(1) On the making under this Part of this Schedule of an order revoking a relevant order, the clerk to the court shall forthwith give copies of the revoking order to the responsible officer.

(2) A responsible officer to whom in accordance with sub-paragraph (1) above copies of a revoking order are given shall give a copy to the offender and to the person in charge of any institution in which the offender was required by the order to

reside.

PART IV: AMENDMENT OF THE ORDER
Amendments by reason of change of residence

12.—(1) This paragraph applies where, at any time while a relevant order is in force in respect of an offender, a magistrates' court acting for the petty sessions area concerned is satisfied that the offender proposes to change, or has changed, his residence from that petty sessions area to another petty sessions area.

(2) Subject to sub-paragraphs (3) and (4) below, the court may, and on the application of the responsible officer shall, amend the relevant order by substituting the other petty sessions area for the area specified in the order or, in the case of a curfew order, a place in that other area for the place so specified.

(3) The court shall not amend under this paragraph a probation or curfew order which contains requirements which, in the opinion of the court, cannot be complied with unless the offender continues to reside in the petty sessions area concerned unless, in accordance with paragraph 13 below, it either—

(a) cancels those requirements; or

(b) substitutes for those requirements other requirements which can be complied with if the offender ceases to reside in that area.

(4) The court shall not amend a community service order under this paragraph unless it appears to the court that provision can be made for the offender to perform work under the order under the arrangements which exist for persons who reside in the other petty sessions area to perform work under such orders.

Amendment of requirements of probation or curfew order

13.—(1) Without prejudice to the provisions of paragraph 12 above, but subject to sub-paragraph (2) below, a magistrates' court for the petty sessions area concerned may, on the application of the offender or the responsible officer, by order amend a probation or curfew order—

(a) by cancelling any requirement of the order; or

(b) by inserting in the order (either in addition to or in substitution for any such requirement) any requirement which the court could include if it were then making the order.

(2) The power of a magistrates' court under sub-paragraph (1) above shall be subject to the following restrictions, namely—

(a) The court shall not amend a probation order—

(i) by reducing the probation period, or by extending that period beyond the end of three years from the making of the original order; or

(ii) by inserting in it a requirement that the offender shall submit to treatment for his mental condition, or his dependency on drugs or alcohol, unless the amending order is made within three months after the date of the original order; and

(b) the court shall not amend a curfew order by extending the curfew periods beyond the end of six months from the date of the original order.

(3) In this paragraph and paragraph 14 below, references to the offender's dependency on drugs or alcohol include references to his propensity towards the

misuse of drugs or alcohol.

Amendment of certain requirements of probation order

14.—(1) Where the medical practitioner or other person by whom or under whose direction an offender is being treated for his mental condition, or his dependency on drugs or alcohol, in pursuance of any requirement of a probation order—
(a) is of the opinion mentioned in sub-paragraph (2) below; or
(b) is for any reason unwilling to continue to treat or direct the treatment of the offender,
he shall make a report in writing to that effect to the responsible officer and that officer shall apply under paragraph 13 above to a magistrates' court for the petty sessions area concerned for the variation or cancellation of the requirement.

(2) The opinion referred to in sub-paragraph (1) above is—
(a) that the treatment of the offender should be continued beyond the period specified in that behalf in the order;
(b) that the offender needs different treatment, being treatment of a kind to which he could be required to submit in pursuance of a probation order;
(c) that the offender is not susceptible to treatment; or
(d) that the offender does not require further treatment.

Extension of community service order

15.— Where—
(a) a community service order is in force in respect of any offender; and
(b) on the application of the offender or the responsible officer, it appears to a magistrates' court acting for the petty sessions area concerned that it would be in the interests of justice to do so having regard to circumstances which have arisen since the order was made,
the court may, in relation to the order, extend the period of twelve months specified in section 15(2) of the 1973 Act.

Supplemental

16.— No order may be made under paragraph 12 above, and no application may be made under paragraph 13 or 15 above, while an appeal against the relevant order is pending.

17.—(1) Subject to sub-paragraph (2) below, where the court proposes to exercise its powers under this Part of this Schedule, otherwise than on the application of the offender, the court—
(a) shall summon him to appear before the court; and
(b) if he does not appear in answer to the summons, may issue a warrant for his arrest;
and the court shall not amend a relevant order under this Part of this Schedule unless the offender expresses his willingness to comply with the requirements of the order as

amended.

(2) This paragraph shall not apply to an order cancelling a requirement of a relevant order or reducing the period of any requirement, or substitiuting a new petty sessions area or a new place for the one specified in the relevant order.

18.—(1) On the making under this Part of this Schedule of an order amending a relevant order, the clerk to the court shall forthwith—

(a) if the order amends the relevant order otherwise than by substitiuting a new petty sessions area or a new place for the one specified in the relevant order, give copies of the amending order to the responsible officer;

(b) if the order amends the relevant order in the manner excepted by paragraph (a) above, send to the clerk to the justices for the new petty sessions area or, as the case may be, for the petty sessions area in which the new place is situated—

(i) copies of the amending order; and

(ii) such documents and information relating to the case as he considers likely to be of assistance to a court acting for that area in exercising its functions in relation to the order;

and in a case falling within paragraph (b) above the clerk to the justices for that area shall give copies of the amending order to the responsible officer.

(2) A responsible officer to whom in accordance with sub-paragraph (1) above copies of an order are given shall give a copy to the offender and to the person in charge of any institution in which the offender is or was required by the order to reside.

[Schedule 2 to the Criminal Justice Act 1991]

NOTE Schedule 3 to the Act (not reproduced) contains provisions concerning reciprocal enforcement and transfer of certain orders relating to community sentences, ie probation orders, community service orders and combination orders, as between England, Scotland and Northern Ireland. Readers are referred to the statute for this detailed information.

Schedule 5 [Extracts]

THE PAROLE BOARD

1. The Board shall consist of a chairman and not less than four other members appointed by the Secretary of State.

2. The Board shall include among its members—

(a) a person who holds or has held judicial office;

(b) a registered medical practitioner who is a psychiatrist;

(c) a person appearing to the Secretary of State to have knowledge and experience of the supervision and after-care of discharged prisoners; and

(d) a person appearing to the Secretary of State to have made a study of the causes of delinquency or the treatment of offenders.

[3, 4, 5]

6. The Board shall as soon as practicable after the end of each year make to the Secretary of State a report on the performance of its functions during that year; and

248

the Secretary of State shall lay a copy of the report before Parliament.
[Schedule 5 to the Criminal Justice Act 1991: invoked by s32(7) (extracts)]

Schedule 12

TRANSITIONAL PROVISIONS AND SAVINGS
Custodial and community sentences

1. Each of sections 1 to 13 of this Act shall apply in relation to offenders convicted (but not sentenced) before the commencement of that section as it applies in relation to offenders convicted after that commencement.
2. Neither subsection (2) of section 8 of this Act, nor the repeal by this Act of section 13 of the 1973 Act, shall affect the operation of section 13 in relation to persons placed on probation before the commencement of that subsection or, as the case may be, that repeal.
3. An establishment which immediately before the commencement of Part II of Schedule 1 to this Act is a day centre within the meaning of section 4B of the 1973 Act shall be treated as if, immediately after the commencement, it had been approved by the Secretary of State as a probation centre within the meaning of paragraph 3(7) of Schedule 1A to that Act.
4. Paragraph 6 of Schedule 11 to this Act shall apply in relation to offenders convicted (but not sentenced) before the commencement of that paragraph as it applies to offenders convicted after that commencement.

Community orders: supplemental

5.—(1) Paragraphs 3 and 4 of Schedule 2 to this Act shall apply in relation to pre-existing failures to comply with the requirements of probation orders or community service orders as if, in sub-paragraph (1)(a), for "£1,000" there were substituted "£400".

(2) In this paragraph "pre-existing", in relation to either of those paragraphs, means occuring before the commencement of that paragraph.

Financial penalties

6. None of sections 17 to 20 of this Act shall apply in relation to offences committed before the commencement of that section.

Increase in certain penalties

7. Neither of subsections (3) and (4) of section 26 of this Act shall apply in relation to offences committed before the commencement of that subsection.

Early release: general

8.—(1) In this paragraph and paragraphs 9 to 11 below—
"existing licensee" means any person who, before the commencement of Part II of this Act, has been released on licence under section 60 of the 1967 Act and whose licence under that section is in force at that commencement;
"existing prisoner" means any person who, at that commencement, is serving a

custodial sentence;
and sub-paragraphs (2) to (7) below shall have effect subject to those paragraphs.

(2) Subject to sub-paragraphs (3) to (7) below, Part II of this Act shall apply in relation to an existing licensee as it applies in relation to a person who is released on licence under this Part; and in its application to an existing prisoner, or to an existing licensee who is recalled under section 39 of this Act, that Part shall apply with the modifications made by those sub-paragraphs.

(3) Section 40 of this Act shall not apply in relation to an existing prisoner or licensee.

(4) In relation to an existing prisoner whose sentence is for a term of twelve months, section 33(1) of this Act shall apply as if that sentence were for a term of less than twelve months.

(5) In relation to an existing prisoner or licensee whose sentence is for a term of—
(a) more than twelve months; and
(b) less than four years or, as the case may require, such other period as may for the time being be referred to in s33(5) of the Act,
Part II of this Act shall apply as if he were or had been a long-term rather than a short-term prisoner.

(6) In relation to an existing prisoner or licensee whose sentence is for a term of more than 12 months—
(a) section 35(1) of this Act shall apply as if the reference to one half of his sentence were a reference to one-third of that sentence or six months, whichever is the longer; and
(b) sections 33(3) and 37(1) of this Act shall apply as if the reference to three-quarters of his sentence were a reference to two-thirds of that sentence.

(7) In relation to an existing prisoner or licensee—
(a) whose sentence is for a term of more than twelve months; and
(b) whose case falls within such class of cases as the Secretary of State may determine after consultation with the Parole Board,
section 35(1) of this Act shall apply as if the reference to a recommendation by the Board included a reference to a recommendation by a local review committee established under section 59(6) of the 1967 Act.

(8) In this paragraph "custodial sentence" means—
(a) a sentence of imprisonment;
(b) a sentence of detention in a young offender institution;
(c) a sentence of detention (whether during Her Majesty's pleasure, for life or for a determinate term) under section 53 of the 1933 Act; or
(d) a sentence of custody for life under section 8 of the 1982 Act.

9.— (1) This paragraph applies where, in the case of an existing life prisoner, the Secretary of State certifies his opinion that, if—
(a) section 34 of this Act had been in force at the time when he was sentenced; and
(b) the reference in subsection (1)(a) of that section to a violent or sexual offence the sentence for which is not fixed by law were a reference to any offence the sentence for which is not so fixed,
the court by which he was sentenced would have ordered that that section should apply to him as soon as he had served a part of his sentence specified in the certificate.

(2) In a case to which this paragraph applies, Part II of this Act except section 35(2) shall apply as if—
(a) the existing life prisoner were a discretionary life prisoner for the purposes of

250

that Part; and

(b) the relevant part of his sentence within the meaning of section 34 of this Act were the part specified in the certificate.

(3) In this paragraph "existing life prisoner" means a person who, at the commencement of Part II of this Act, is serving one or more of the following sentences, namely—

(a) a sentence of life imprisonment;

(b) a sentence of detention during Her Majesty's pleasure or for life under section 53 of the 1933 Act; or

(c) a sentence of custody for life under section 8 of the 1982 Act.

(4) A person serving two or more such sentences shall not be treated as a discretionary life prisoner for the purposes of Part II of this Act unless the requirements of sub-paragraph (1) above are satisfied as respects each of those sentences; and subsections (3) and (5) of section 34 of this Act shall not apply in relation to such a person until after he has served the relevant part of each of those sentences.

10. Prison rules made by virtue of section 42 of this Act may include provision for applying any provisions of Part II of this Act, in relation to any existing prisoner or licensee who has forfeited any remission of his sentence, as if he had been awarded such number of additional days as may be determined by or under the rules.

Early release of young persons detained under 1933 Act

11. In relation to an existing prisoner or licensee whose sentence is a determinate sentence of detention under section 53 of the 1933 Act—

(a) Part II of this Act shall apply as if he were or had been a life rather than a long-term prisoner;

(b) section 35(2) of this Act shall apply as if the requirement as to consultation were omitted; and

(c) section 37(3) of this Act shall apply as if the reference to his death were a reference to the date on which he would (but for his release) have served the whole of his sentence.

Early release of prisoners serving extended sentences

12.— (1) In relation to an existing prisoner or licensee on the passing of whose sentence an extended sentence certificate was issued—

(a) section 33(3) of this Act shall apply as if the duty to release him unconditionally were a duty to release him on licence; and

(b) section 37(1) of this Act shall apply as if the reference to three-quarters of his sentence were a reference to the whole of that sentence.

(2) In this paragraph "extended sentence certificate" means a certificate issued under section 28 of the 1973 Act stating that an extended term of imprisonment was imposed on an offender under that section.

Early release of fine defaulters and contemnors

13. Part II of this Act shall apply in relation to any person who, before the commencement of that Part, has been committed to prison or to be detained under section 9 of the 1982 Act—

(a) in default of payment of a sum adjudged to be paid by a conviction; or

(b) for contempt of court or any kindred offence,

as it applies in relation to any person who is committed after that commencement.

14. [*Responsibilities of parent or guardian*: see *The Youth Court One Year Onwards*]

Attendance centre orders

21.—(1) Subsection (2) of section 67 of this Act shall not apply in relation to attendance centre orders made before the commencement of that section.

(2) Subsection (4) of that section shall not apply in relation to pre-existing failures to attend in accordance with an attendance centre order or pre-existing breaches of rules made under section 16(3) of the 1982 Act.

(3) In this paragraph "pre-existing" means occuring or committed before that commencement.

NOTE Para 21(1) Section 67(2) CJA 91 inserts a new s18(4A) CJA 82 so as to empower courts, on discharging an attendance centre order, to sentence afresh for the original offence.

22 to 25 [*see The Youth Court One Year Onwards*].

Supplemental

24.— For the purposes of this Schedule proceedings for an offence shall be regarded as having begun as follows—

(a) in the case of an offence triable only summarily, when a plea is entered;

(b) in the case of an offence triable only on indictment, when the magistrates' court begins to inquire into the offence as examining magistrates;

(c) in the case of an offence triable either way, when the magistrates' court determines to proceed with the summary trial of the offence or, as the case may be, to proceed to inquire into the offence as examining justices.

Criminal Justice Act 1991 (Commencement No.1) Order SI 1991 2208 [Extract - Summarised]

Readers are referred to the above statutory instrument, to which the following information serves as a reminder. Schedule 1: Provisions effective 14 October 1991: s60(3), s99(1) (part), s100 and sched 11 (part), s101(1) and sched 12 (part), s102, para 36 of sched 11, para 23 of sched 12. Schedule 2: Provisions effective 25 October 1991: s26(3) (part), s101(1) and sched 12 (part), para 7 of sched 12. Schedule 3: Provisions effective 31 October 1991: s26(4), (5), s73, s74, s80 to 91, s92(1), s93 to 96, s98, s100 and sched 11 (part), s101(2) and sched 13 (part), sched 10, sched 11 (part), sched 13 (part).

Criminal Justice Act 1991 (Commencement No.2) Order [Scotland] SI 2706 Not reproduced.

Appendix II Note on the Magistrates' Association Sentencing Guidelines

In September 1993 the Magistrates' Association produced an updated version of its *Sentencing Guidelines* to coincide with the implementation of the 1993 changes to CJA 1991 *supra*. The guidelines, which apply to offenders aged 18 and over, stipulate 'entry points'—ie types of sentence which should first be considered for different types of offence. It is emphasised that the guidelines 'are only starting points for discussion of individual sentences'. They relate to cases 'of average seriousness' and magistrates may increase the severity of the sentence if the offence has aggravating factors, or reduce it if there are mitigating factors either of the offence itself or of a personal kind relating to the offender. The entry points are 'based on a first-time offender pleading not guilty' and a timely guilty plea 'may be regarded as a mitigating factor for which a sentencing discount of approximately one-third might be given.' The guidelines are reproduced in full below.

The guidelines state that when 'protection of the public from serious harm' is involved in relation to violent or sexual offences, this 'will usually be a reason for committing to the Crown Court for sentence.'

When the guidelines were published, widespread concern was expressed that many magistrates might assume that, when the 'entry point' was custody, the court could not regard such mitigating factors as a timely guilty plea as justifying the use of community penalty instead of a custodial sentence in an appropriate case—only as justifying a reduction in the length of a custodial sentence of up to one-third.

Such an interpretation would be inconsistent with the principle which has been repeatedly emphasised in Court of Appeal judgments since the Criminal Justice Act 1991 that, even when an offence taken on its own is 'so serious' that only a custodial sentence can be justified, the court may still mitigate the sentence—where appropriate passing a community sentence instead of custody—by reason of mitigating factors relating to the offender (of which one example is a timely plea of guilty).

If magistrates did not have this discretion to 'move down' from custody, some aspects of the 'Sentencing Guidelines' would be considerably more severe than the approach of the Court of Appeal. An example is the 'entry point' for driving while disqualified. In *Crawford* (1993) 14 Cr App R (S) 782 a sentence of one month's imprisonment for driving while disqualified was quashed by the Court on the ground that, as this was the first such offence and without aggravating features, it was not one which warranted a sentence of imprisonment. Yet the Magistrates' Association guidelines state that the 'entry point' for driving while disqualified—for an offence of 'average seriousness' committed by a first offender—is custody. The two approaches can be reconciled; but only if it is borne in mind that the 'entry point' assumes a not guilty plea and that a timely plea of guilty or other mitigation enables magistrates in such a case, where the circumstances justify it, to impose a community sentence instead.

In an article in *The Times* of 21 September 1993, Bryan Gibson, legal adviser to the Magistrates' Association's Sentencing of Offenders Committee, acknowledged that:

' ... the new guidelines look harsher. In the language of practitioners, sentencing has moved "up tariff", especially for offences of violence, house burglary, criminal deception or those involving hard drugs.'

He warned that:

'Wrongly used—if too little account is taken of these items that make an offence less serious, or of personal mitigation affecting an individual offender—the guidelines could escalate sentencing, with serious cost implications, and undermine much progressive community-based work.'

A similar point could be made in relation to the guideline fines contained in the document, which relate to offences of average seriousness committed by first offenders. For example, the guideline fine for shoplifting is £280; for abstracting electricity £270; for television licence evasion £180; and for driving with no insurance £570. A letter to *The Magistrate*, vol 50, no 3, discloses that the guideline fines were set by reference to average earnings of £200 per week net.

Although the guidelines advise magistrates to 'increase or decrease the amount according to the financial circumstances of the offender', given that most offenders in magistrates' courts are unemployed (62% of those sentenced for indictable offences in a recent Home Office survey of nine magistrates' courts), fines would need to be greatly reduced from the suggested starting points to avoid swingeing increases in fines following the abolition of the unit fine scheme.

The guidelines are advisory only. Those courts which prefer to continue operating their own voluntary 'unit fine' systems remain free to do so after the CJA 93. David Maclean MP, Minister of State at the Home Office, told the House of Commons on 29 June 1993:

'I have no objection to magistrates adopting an informal unit model if they find it helpful in setting a fine—for example, in reaching a starting point from which they can use their discretion to depart to reach a just result' (col. 915)

Similarly, when the Criminal Justice Act 1993 was in Committee on 17 June 1993, Alun Michael MP asked the Minister:

'Will courts be able to operate the type of system that they operated in the four successful pilot projects under the proposals?' (cols. 251-2).

David Maclean replied:

'There is nothing to stop the courts operating their own voluntary pilot schemes, but, at the end of the day, the statute applies. They must decide on a sentence that takes into account the seriousness of the offence and the offender's ability to pay. They are free to use informal yardsticks or schemes to help them to decide what is a just sentence' (col. 252).

254

In his address to the NACRO Annual General Meeting on 11 November 1993, the Lord Chief Justice, Lord Taylor acknowledged that anxieties had been expressed that magistrates would be reluctant to move away from the 'entry point', but expressed the hope that this was `an unworthy piece of scepticism'. He said:

'When you find, for example "House burglary: entry point, custody", I know that some of you are concerned that that will be a red light to the magistrate and that anything that is further down the page may not make much further impact. I hope that that is an unworthy piece of scepticism because the whole point of the guidelines is that they are only a guide. They give you a starting point. After that the magistrate has to consider the matters which may aggravate the instant offence as against the average, the matters which may mitigate it as against the average, and—looking at the case as a whole—consider whether, although the entry point may be custody, this is a case where a non-custodial sentence may be appropriate.'

The guidelines are reproduced in this work by kind permission of the Magistrates' Association. Blank pages are not reproduced but the original numbering system is retained.

This edition of the Magistrates' Association Sentencing Guidelines has been produced in consultation with Stipendiary Magistrates and the Justices' Clerks' Society. Grateful thanks go to all those involved in this unique collaboration.

The Sentencing Guidelines are issued with the blessing of the Lord Chancellor and the Lord Chief Justice. The Guidelines are endorsed by the Justices' Clerks' Society.

Mrs J D H Rose
Chairman of Council

THE MAGISTRATES' ASSOCIATION

SENTENCING GUIDELINES

CONTENTS

Introduction and User Guide

This guide deals with criminal offences which come before magistrates' courts frequently. A structure is provided to suggest:—

— how to assess the relative seriousness of each case, and
— how to arrive at a commensurate penalty

Magistrates should always remember that the guidelines are *only* starting points for discussion of individual sentences. The guide gives a number of entry points for thinking and discussion. The guidelines deal with offenders of 18 years of age and over.

Entry Points

For all types of case, including road traffic cases, the guide provides entry points, not finishing points. The term 'entry point' has been used to give a guide for an offence of 'average' seriousness. Justices will have to consider whether the particular case before them is of average seriousness or whether there are specific aggravating or mitigating circumstances which make it more serious or less serious than the average offence of that type. Having considered the seriousness of the offence, the justices will have to consider any personal mitigating factors and decide whether any such factor(s) enable them to change the kind of penalty which the offence would otherwise merit.

The responsibility for the sentence is that of the justices and it is they who must assess each case judicially having regard to (a) the circumstances of the particular offence and (b) the circumstances of the particular offender.

Where the entry point is a fine the guideline fine is that which is regarded as appropriate for an offence of average seriousness. It follows that the bench when considering an individual case will have to decide whether there are particular features of the case which either aggravate or mitigate the seriousness of the offence and, if it is, whether the level of the fine should be above or below the guideline. Having considered the seriousness of the offence the Bench will then have to consider any personal mitigation and, assuming that a fine is still the appropriate penalty, they must then consider the offender's means. If of below average means, the amount should be reduced to a level which the offender can realistically be expected to pay and, if of above average means, there is a presumption that the fine should be increased.

The guideline sentences represent a broad consensus of view and are based on a first-time offender pleading not-guilty. A timely guilty plea may be regarded as a mitigating factor for which a sentencing discount of approximately one-third might be given. The precise discount a court should allow must depend upon the facts of the case. An early admission of guilt where an offence would otherwise be undetected should attract a substantial discount; on the other hand, a last minute guilty plea when faced with witnesses may attract only a nominal discount. The existence of relevant previous offences and/or failures to respond to previous sentences may be regarded as aggravating factors.

Means forms

The means form is no longer a statutory requirement but before fixing the amount of any fine the court must enquire into the financial circumstances of the offender. If there is insufficient information to make a proper determination, the court may make such determination as it thinks fit.

The Association is aware that there are many local means forms in existence and suggests that courts build on these. However, as a general guide means forms should be as simple to complete as possible and in line with a broad approach to income and other financial resources. In order to encourage defendants to complete the means form, it is suggested that the form carries a simple warning, for example:

IF YOU DO NOT FILL IN THE FORM YOU MAY BE FINED MORE HEAVILY THAN YOU CAN AFFORD

Penalties

The fine imposed is determined by the court to be commensurate with the seriousness of the offence(s) before the court. The amount of the fine shall not exceed the upper limit for the level of offence ie.—

For a level 1 offence — £200
For a level 2 offence — £500
For a level 3 offence — £1000
For a level 4 offence — £2500
For a level 5 offence — £5000

The offence

Each page deals with a separate offence. The process is:—

How serious is the case compared with other offences of this type?

— Consider the various 'seriousness indicators'
— Remember that these lists are not comprehensive and other factors may be important in individual cases
— Previous convictions or failure to respond to previous sentences may be taken into account in considering the seriousness of the present offence. It is recommended that courts should clearly identify which convictions or failures are relevant for this purpose and then consider what the effect of such convictions or failures is in relation to seriousness.
— Consider all aggravating or mitigating factors. Remember that the fact that an offence was committed whilst the offender was on bail should be treated as an aggravating factor.

Note that when there are several offences, the overall sentence should be kept in proportion to the totality of the offending behaviour with which the court is dealing

If in any doubt seek advice from the clerk.

Mode of trial

If the offence is triable either way, the seriousness indicators are relevant to the mode of trial decision but see the National Mode of Trial Guidelines which provide more comprehensive information (available from the Lord Chancellor's Department)

The offender

After assessing the seriousness of the offence, the court should then consider any mitigating factors relating to the offender (eg. age, health, co-operation with the police, voluntary compensation, guilty plea or remorse).

Sentencing framework

The fine is the penalty most frequently imposed by magistrates' court. However it must be recognised that many factors hinder consistency, in particular the duty to give priority to compensation may lead to an apparently lenient fine for a defendant on a low income.

The progression, based on seriousness, is as follows:—

— Consider discharge
— Consider compensation order alone or with other penalties
— Consider compensation and/or fine
— If serious enough consider a community penalty (ie. an attendance centre order (12-36 hours), a community service order (40-240 hours unpaid work), a probation order (6 months- 3 years, with or without requirements), or a combination order (1-3 years probation plus 40-100 hours community service))
— If too serious for a community penalty, consider custody
— if custody is justified, decide on length of sentence
— If significantly greater punishment than 6 months is appropriate, commit for sentence

Note: Whichever sentence is selected, custody and community penalties must be commensurate with the seriousness of the offence and fines must reflect seriousness. The one exception is where 'protection of the public from serious harm' is involved for violent or sexual offences only, which will usually be a reason for committing to the Crown Court for sentence. If in any doubt seek advice from the clerk.

Compensation should always be considered, even where custody is used. It should be awarded only in clear, simple, uncomplicated cases, otherwise consult the clerk. Further guidance is given at page 7.

Custody and community penalties

The law requires the court to take certain information into account before deciding on sentence. There must be a pre-sentence report in relation to custody and most forms of community penalty. Custody can only be used when the offence is so serious that no other sentence is justified. Community penalties can only be used where the offence is serious enough. When considering particular community penalties rehabilitation is a proper consideration in relation to probation orders and the probation part of a combination order.

Compensation Orders

The restrictions on liberty imposed by the sentence chosen must be commensurate with seriousness and the sentence must be the most suitable for the offender.

The justices' clerk/court clerk

Sentencing is a complex field and the justices' clerk or court clerk must advise the bench on the maximum penalties and powers available and assist as to the nature of the options and statutory restrictions, especially those relating to custodial sentences.

A Practice Direction states that

'If it appears to him necessary to do so, or he is requested by the justices, the justices' clerk has the responsibility to.... advise the justices generally on the range of penalties which the law allows them to impose and on any guidance relevant to the decisions of the superior courts and other authorities.'

Priorities

Compensation is an order in its own right, and should be treated as such — particularly where the offender has insufficient means to pay a fine as well.

Damages

Where compensation is to be awarded for damage to, for example, a window, the cost must be proved or agreed.

Payment by instalments

An order for compensation should normally be payable within 12 months, but this can be exceeded up to a three year limit where the circumstances justify it.

Giving reasons

Section 35, Powers of the Criminal Courts Act 1973 states that

'A court shall give reasons on passing sentence if it does not make (a compensation) order in a case where this section empowers it to do so'.

Powers and limitations

Magistrates have power to award compensation for personal injury loss or damage up to a total of £5,000 for each offence. The compensation may relate to offences taken into consideration. There are exceptions including injury, loss or damage due to a road accident unless the damage results from an offence under the Theft Act 1968 or the offender is uninsured and the Motor Insurers Bureau will not cover the loss – if in any doubt, seek advice from the clerk.

An order for compensation should be considered whether or not there is an application by or on behalf of the victim. An award in the magistrates' court will not preclude a civil claim. 'Personal injury' need not be a physical injury. An award can be made, eg. for terror or distress caused by the offence.

Criminal Injuries Compensation Board

The Criminal Injuries Compensation Scheme is intended to compensate victims of violent crime and particularly those who are seriously injured. The minimum award is currently £1,000. Courts are encouraged to order offenders to compensate the victim whether or not the injury comes within the scope of the Criminal Injuries Compensation Scheme, in order to bring home to offenders the personal consequences of their actions. To prevent double compensation for the same injury the Scheme provides for an award to be reduced by the amount of any compensation previously ordered by a criminal court.

Suggested compensation

Damages are assessed under two main headings — *general damages*, which is compensation for the pain and suffering of the injury itself and for any loss of facility, and *special damages*, which is compensation for financial loss sustained as a result of the injury — eg. loss of earnings, dental expenses etc. The suggestions given in the table below are for general damages.

The following guidelines are taken from the Home Office Draft Circular issued in August 1993.

The figures below are only a very general guide and may be increased or decreased according to the medical evidence, the victim's sex, age and any other factors which appear to the court to be relevant in the particular case. If the court does not have enough information to make a decision, then the matter should be adjourned to obtain more facts.

	TYPE OF INJURY	SUGGESTED AWARD
Graze	depending on size	up to £50
Bruise	depending on size	up to £75
Black eye		£100
Cut: no permanent scarring	depending on size and whether stitched	£75-£500
Sprain	depending on loss of mobility	£100-£1,000
Loss of a non-front tooth	depending on cosmetic effect and age of victim	£250-£500
Other minor injury	causing reasonable absence from work (2-3) weeks	£550-£850
Loss of a front tooth		£1,000
Facial scar	however small - resulting in permanent disfigurement	£750+
Jaw	fractured (wired)	£2,750
Nasal	undisplaced fracture of the nasal bone	£750
Nasal	displaced fracture of bone requiring manipulation	£1,000
Nasal	not causing fracture but displaced septum requiring sub-mucous resection	£1,750
Wrist	simple fracture with complete recovery in few weeks	£1,750-£2,500
Wrist	displaced fracture - limb in plaster for some 6 weeks, full recovery 6-12 months	£2,500+
Finger	fractured little finger, assuming full recovery after a few weeks	£750
Leg or arm	simple fracture of tibia, fibula, ulna or radius with full recovery in three weeks	£2,500
Laparotomy	stomach scar 6-8 inches long (resulting from exploratory operation)	£3,500

Public Order Act 1986 s 3
Triable either way - see Mode of Trial Guidelines
Penalty: Level 5 and/or 6 months

Affray

ENTRY POINT — COMMUNITY PENALTY

(–) CONSIDER THE SERIOUSNESS OF THE OFFENCE

eg. Single offender

(+)
eg.
Offence committed on bail
Busy public place
Group action
People put in fear
Vulnerable victim(s)
Previous convictions and failures to respond to previous sentences, if relevant

IS IT SERIOUS ENOUGH FOR A COMMUNITY PENALTY?
IS COMPENSATION, DISCHARGE OR FINE APPROPRIATE, OR
IS IT SO SERIOUS THAT ONLY CUSTODY IS APPROPRIATE?

CONSIDER OFFENDER MITIGATION
eg.
Guilty plea: *for a timely guilty plea allow a discount of about a third*
Age, health (physical or mental)
Co-operation with the police
Voluntary compensation
Remorse

DECIDE YOUR SENTENCE
Compare your decision with the entry point - COMMUNITY PENALTY - and check your reasons if you have reached a different sentence

NB. COMPENSATION - Give reasons if not awarding compensation
NB. FINES - If imposing a fine, remember to increase or decrease the amount according to the financial circumstances of the offender

---

Theft Act 1968 s 13
Triable either way - see Mode of Trial Guidelines
Penalty: Level 5 and/or 6 months

Abstracting electricity

ENTRY POINT — FINE

(–) CONSIDER THE SERIOUSNESS OF THE OFFENCE

eg. Short period

(+)
eg.
Offence committed on bail
High usage
Prolonged period
Special equipment
Previous convictions and failures to respond to previous sentences, if relevant

IS COMPENSATION, DISCHARGE OR FINE APPROPRIATE?
IS IT SERIOUS ENOUGH FOR A COMMUNITY PENALTY?
IS IT SO SERIOUS THAT ONLY CUSTODY IS APPROPRIATE?

CONSIDER OFFENDER MITIGATION
eg.
Guilty plea: *for a timely guilty plea allow a discount of about a third*
Age, health (physical or mental)
Co-operation with the police
Voluntary compensation
Remorse

DECIDE YOUR SENTENCE
Compare your decision with the entry point - FINE - and check your reasons if you have reached a different sentence

Guideline fine for this offence is £270 which reflects the average seriousness of an offence of this type

NB. COMPENSATION - Give reasons if not awarding compensation
NB. FINES - If imposing a fine, remember to increase or decrease the amount according to the financial circumstances of the offender

Assault — Actual Bodily Harm

Offences Against the Person Act 1861 s.47
Triable either way - see Mode of Trial Guidelines
Penalty: Level 5 and/or 6 months

ENTRY POINT ∧ **COMMUNITY PENALTY**

 CONSIDER THE SERIOUSNESS OF THE OFFENCE

eg.

Offence committed on bail	Impulsive action
Deliberate kicking	Minor injury
Extensive injuries	Provocation
Group action	
Offender in position of authority	
Premeditated	
Victim particularly vulnerable	
Victim serving public	
Weapon	
Previous convictions and failures to respond to previous sentences, if relevant	

IS IT SERIOUS ENOUGH FOR A COMMUNITY PENALTY?
IS COMPENSATION, DISCHARGE OR FINE APPROPRIATE, OR
IS IT SO SERIOUS THAT ONLY CUSTODY IS APPROPRIATE?

CONSIDER OFFENDER MITIGATION

eg.
Guilty plea: *for a timely guilty plea allow a discount of about a third*
Age, health (physical or mental)
Co-operation with the police
Voluntary compensation
Remorse

DECIDE YOUR SENTENCE

Compare your decision with the entry point - COMMUNITY PENALTY - and check your reasons if you have reached a different sentence

NB. COMPENSATION - Give reasons if not awarding compensation
NB. FINES - If imposing a fine, remember to increase or decrease the amount according to the financial circumstances of the offender

---

Aggravated Vehicle-Taking

Theft Act 1968 s. 12A as inserted by
Aggravated Vehicle-Taking Act 1992
Triable either way - but in certain cases summarily only - consult clerk
Penalty: Level 5 and/or 6 months
Must endorse and disqualify at least 12 months:
Must endorse (3-11 points) if not disqualified

ENTRY POINT ∧ **CUSTODY**

 CONSIDER THE SERIOUSNESS OF THE OFFENCE

eg.

Offence committed on bail	Keys left in car
Avoiding detection or apprehension	No alcohol or drugs involved
Competitive driving: racing, showing off	Minor damage
Disregard of warnings eg from passengers or others in vicinity	Single incident
Excessive speed	Speed not excessive
Evidence of alcohol or drugs	
Group action	
Pre-meditated	
Serious injury/damage	
Serious risk	
Previous convictions and failures to respond to previous sentences, if relevant	

IS IT SO SERIOUS THAT ONLY CUSTODY IS APPROPRIATE?
IS IT SERIOUS ENOUGH FOR A COMMUNITY PENALTY?
IS COMPENSATION, DISCHARGE OR FINE APPROPRIATE?

CONSIDER OFFENDER MITIGATION

eg.
Guilty plea: *for a timely guilty plea allow a discount of about a third*
Age, health (physical or mental)
Co-operation with the police
Voluntary compensation
Remorse

DECIDE YOUR SENTENCE

Compare your decision with the entry point - CUSTODY - and check your reasons if you have reached a different sentence

Endorse licence (3-11 points)

Disqualify at least 12 months unless special reasons apply

NB. COMPENSATION - Give reasons if not awarding compensation
NB. FINES - If imposing a fine, remember to increase or decrease the amount according to the financial circumstances of the offender

Assault on a Police Officer

Police Act 1964 s.51
Triable only summarily
Penalty: Level 5 and/or 6 months

ENTRY POINT → **CUSTODY** ❶

CONSIDER THE SERIOUSNESS OF THE OFFENCE ➕

eg.
Offence committed on bail	Impulsive action
Any injuries caused	Unaware that person was a Police Officer
Gross disregard for police authority	
Group action	
Premeditated	
Previous convictions and failures to respond to previous sentences, if relevant	

IS IT SO SERIOUS THAT ONLY CUSTODY IS APPROPRIATE?
IS IT SERIOUS ENOUGH FOR A COMMUNITY PENALTY?
IS COMPENSATION, DISCHARGE OR FINE APPROPRIATE?

CONSIDER OFFENDER MITIGATION

eg.
Guilty plea: *for a timely guilty plea allow a discount of about a third*
Age, health (physical or mental)
Co-operation with the police
Voluntary compensation
Remorse

DECIDE YOUR SENTENCE

Compare your decision with the entry point - CUSTODY - and check your reasons if you have reached a different sentence

NB. COMPENSATION - Give reasons if not awarding compensation
NB. FINES - If imposing a fine, remember to increase or decrease the amount according to the financial circumstances of the offender

---

Burglary (Dwelling)

Theft Act 1968 s.9
Triable either way - see Mode of Trial Guidelines
Penalty: Level 5 and/or 6 months

ENTRY POINT → **CUSTODY** ❶

CONSIDER THE SERIOUSNESS OF THE OFFENCE ➕

eg.
Offence committed on bail	Day time
Deliberately frightening occupants	Low value
Group offence	No damage or disturbance
Night time	No forcible entry
Professional operation	
Soiling, ransacking, damage	
Previous convictions and failures to respond to previous sentences, if relevant	

IS IT SO SERIOUS THAT ONLY CUSTODY IS APPROPRIATE?
IS IT SERIOUS ENOUGH FOR A COMMUNITY PENALTY?
IS COMPENSATION, DISCHARGE OR FINE APPROPRIATE?

CONSIDER OFFENDER MITIGATION

eg.
Guilty plea: *for a timely guilty plea allow a discount of about a third*
Age, health (physical or mental)
Co-operation with the police
Voluntary compensation
Remorse

DECIDE YOUR SENTENCE

Compare your decision with the entry point - CUSTODY - and check your reasons if you have reached a different sentence

NB. COMPENSATION - Give reasons if not awarding compensation
NB. FINES - If imposing a fine, remember to increase or decrease the amount according to the financial circumstances of the offender

Common Assault

As charge sheet
Triable only summarily
Penalty: Level 5 and/or 6 months

ENTRY POINT ⅄   COMMUNITY PENALTY

(–)

CONSIDER THE SERIOUSNESS OF THE OFFENCE

(+)

eg.
- Offence committed on bail
- Group action
- Offender in position of authority
- Premediated
- Victim particularly vulnerable
- Victim public servant
- Previous convictions and failures to respond to previous sentences, if relevant

eg.
- Impulsive action
- Provocation
- Trivial nature of action

IS IT SERIOUS ENOUGH FOR A COMMUNITY PENALTY?
IS COMPENSATION, DISCHARGE OR FINE APPROPRIATE, OR
IS IT SO SERIOUS THAT ONLY CUSTODY IS APPROPRIATE?

CONSIDER OFFENDER MITIGATION

eg.
- Guilty plea: *for a timely guilty plea allow a discount of about a third*
- Age, health (physical or mental)
- Co-operation with the police
- Voluntary compensation
- Remorse

DECIDE YOUR SENTENCE

Compare your decision with the entry point - COMMUNITY PENALTY - and check your reasons if you have reached a different sentence

NB. COMPENSATION - Give reasons if not awarding compensation
NB. FINES - If imposing a fine, remember to increase or decrease the amount according to the financial circumstances of the offender

---

Burglary (Non-dwelling)

Theft Act 1968 s.9
Triable either way - see Mode of Trial Guidelines
Penalty: Level 5 and/or 6 months

ENTRY POINT ⅄   COMMUNITY PENALTY

(–)

CONSIDER THE SERIOUSNESS OF THE OFFENCE

(+)

eg.
- Offence committed on bail
- Deliberately frightening occupants
- Group offence
- Night time
- Professional operation
- Ram raiding
- Soiling, ransacking, damage
- Previous convictions and failures to respond to previous sentences, if relevant

eg.
- Day time
- Low value
- No damage or disturbance
- No forcible entry

IS IT SERIOUS ENOUGH FOR A COMMUNITY PENALTY?
IS COMPENSATION, DISCHARGE OR FINE APPROPRIATE, OR
IS IT SO SERIOUS THAT ONLY CUSTODY IS APPROPRIATE?

CONSIDER OFFENDER MITIGATION

eg.
- Guilty plea: *for a timely guilty plea allow a discount of about a third*
- Age, health (physical or mental)
- Co-operation with the police
- Voluntary compensation
- Remorse

DECIDE YOUR SENTENCE

Compare your decision with the entry point - COMMUNITY PENALTY - and check your reasons if you have reached a different sentence

NB. COMPENSATION - Give reasons if not awarding compensation
NB. FINES - If imposing a fine, remember to increase or decrease the amount according to the financial circumstances of the offender

Criminal Damage

Criminal Damage Act 1971 s 1
Triable either way or summarily only. Consult Clerk
Penalty: Either way - Level 5 and/or 6 months
Summarily - Level 4 and/or 3 months

ENTRY POINT	FINE

+ CONSIDER THE SERIOUSNESS OF THE OFFENCE **–**

eg.
- Offence committed on bail
- Deliberate
- Fire raising
- Group offence
- Serious damage

Previous convictions and failures to respond to previous sentences, if relevant

eg.
- Impulsive action
- Minor damage
- Provocation

IS COMPENSATION, DISCHARGE OR FINE APPROPRIATE?
IS IT SERIOUS ENOUGH FOR A COMMUNITY PENALTY?
IS IT SO SERIOUS THAT ONLY CUSTODY IS APPROPRIATE?

CONSIDER OFFENDER MITIGATION

eg.
- Guilty plea: *for a timely guilty plea allow a discount of about a third*
- Age, health (physical or mental)
- Co-operation with the police
- Voluntary compensation
- Remorse

DECIDE YOUR SENTENCE

Compare your decision with the entry point - FINE - and check your reasons if you have reached a different sentence

Guideline fine for this offence is £270 which reflects the average seriousness of an offence of this type

NB. COMPENSATION - *Give reasons if not awarding compensation*
NB. FINES - *If imposing a fine, remember to increase or decrease the amount according to the financial circumstances of the offender*

Careless Driving

Road Traffic Act ... s...
Triable only summarily
Penalty: Level 4
Must endorse: (3-9 points)
May disqualify

ENTRY POINT	FINE

+ CONSIDER THE SERIOUSNESS OF THE OFFENCE **–**

eg.
- Excessive speed
- High degree of carelessness
- Serious risk
- Offence committed on bail

Previous convictions and failures to respond to previous sentences, if relevant

eg.
- Difficult weather conditions
- Minor risk
- Momentary lapse
- Negligible/parking damage

IS COMPENSATION, DISCHARGE OR FINE APPROPRIATE?
IS IT SERIOUS ENOUGH FOR A COMMUNITY PENALTY?
(PROBATION IS THE ONLY AVAILABLE COMMUNITY PENALTY FOR THIS OFFENCE)

CONSIDER OFFENDER MITIGATION

eg.
- Guilty plea: *for a timely guilty plea allow a discount of about a third*
- Co-operation with the police
- Voluntary compensation
- Remorse

DECIDE YOUR SENTENCE

Remember injury or damage cannot be *equated* with the degree of carelessness but may *indicate* it

Compare your decision with the entry point - FINE - and check your reasons if you have reached a different sentence

Guideline fine for this offence is £180 which reflects the average seriousness of an offence of this type

Endorse licence (3-9 points) and, if more serious, consider other measures (including disqualification until test passed if appropriate)

NB. FINES - *If imposing a fine, remember to increase or decrease the amount according to the financial circumstances of the offender*

Driving — no insurance

Road Traffic Act 1988 s.143
Triable only summarily
Penalty: Level 5
Must endorse: (6-8 points)
May disqualify

ENTRY POINT ⅄   **FINE**

— CONSIDER THE SERIOUSNESS OF THE OFFENCE

eg.	eg.
Deliberate driving without insurance	Accidental oversight
LGV, HGV, PCV, PSV or minicabs	Genuine mistake
No reference to insurance ever having been held	Insurance held but clearly not covering the driver or use
Offence committed on bail	Recently expired insurance
Previous convictions and failures to respond to previous sentences, if relevant	— weeks?
	— months?
	Responsibility for providing insurance resting with another - the parent/owner/lender/hirer
	Smaller vehicle, eg. moped

IS COMPENSATION, DISCHARGE OR FINE APPROPRIATE?
IS IT SERIOUS ENOUGH FOR A COMMUNITY PENALTY?
(PROBATION IS THE ONLY AVAILABLE COMMUNITY PENALTY FOR THIS OFFENCE)

CONSIDER OFFENDER MITIGATION

eg.
Guilty plea: *for a timely guilty plea allow a discount of about a third*
Co-operation with the police
Remorse

DECIDE YOUR SENTENCE

Compare your decision with the entry point - FINE - and check your reasons if you have reached a different sentence

Guideline fine for this offence is £540 (and £660 for LGV/PCV) which reflects the average seriousness of an offence of this type. The court should have regard to the amount of the insurance premium.

Endorse licence (6-8 points)

IF DELIBERATE THE COURT SHOULD DISQUALIFY

NB. FINES - If imposing a fine, remember to increase or decrease the amount according to the financial circumstances of the offender

---

Dangerous Driving

Road Traffic Act 1988 s.2
Triable either way - see Mode of Trial Guidelines
Penalty: Level 5 and/or 6 months
Must endorse and disqualify at least 12 months
Must endorse (3-11 points) if not disqualified

ENTRY POINT ⅄   **COMMUNITY PENALTY**

— CONSIDER THE SERIOUSNESS OF THE OFFENCE

eg.	eg.
Offence committed on bail	Momentary risk not fully appreciated
Avoiding detection or apprehension	No alcohol or drugs involved
Competitive driving, racing, showing off	Single incident
Disregard of warnings eg. from passengers or others in vicinity	Speed not excessive
Evidence of alcohol or drugs	
Excessive speed	
Prolonged, persistent, deliberate bad driving	
Serious risk	
Previous convictions and failures to respond to previous sentences, if relevant	

IS IT SERIOUS ENOUGH FOR A COMMUNITY PENALTY?
IS COMPENSATION, DISCHARGE OR FINE APPROPRIATE, OR IS IT SO SERIOUS THAT ONLY CUSTODY IS APPROPRIATE?

CONSIDER OFFENDER MITIGATION

eg.
Guilty plea: *for a timely guilty plea allow a discount of about a third*
Age, health (physical or mental)
Co-operation with the police
Voluntary compensation
Remorse

DECIDE YOUR SENTENCE

Remember injury or damage cannot be *equated* with the degree of danger but may *indicate* it

Compare your decision with the entry point - COMMUNITY PENALTY - and check your reasons if you have reached a different sentence

Endorse licence (3-11 points) and disqualify at least 12 months unless special reasons apply

Order re-test

NB. FINES - If imposing a fine, remember to increase or decrease the amount according to the financial circumstances of the offender

Misuse of Drugs Act 1971

Class A Drugs —
production, supply, possession
with intent to supply

Triable either way - see Mode of Trial Guidelines

Penalty: Level 5 and/or 6 months

COMMIT FOR TRIAL

These offences are not usually dealt with in Magistrates' Courts and should normally be committed to the Crown Court for trial

---

Road Traffic Act 1988 s.103
Triable only summarily
Penalty: Level 5 and/or 6 months
Must endorse: 6 points: may disqualify

Driving while disqualified by Court Order

ENTRY POINT 〉

CUSTODY

(+) CONSIDER THE SERIOUSNESS OF THE OFFENCE (–)

eg.
Offence committed on bail
Efforts to avoid detection
Long distance drive
Planned, long term evasion
Recent disqualification
Previous convictions and failures to respond
to previous sentences, if relevant

eg.
Emergency established
Short distance driven

IS IT SO SERIOUS THAT ONLY CUSTODY IS APPROPRIATE?
IS IT SERIOUS ENOUGH FOR A COMMUNITY PENALTY?
IS COMPENSATION, DISCHARGE OR FINE APPROPRIATE?

CONSIDER OFFENDER MITIGATION

eg.
Guilty plea: *for a timely guilty plea allow a discount of about a third*
Age, health (physical or mental)
Co-operation with the police
Remorse

DECIDE YOUR SENTENCE

Compare your decision with the entry point - CUSTODY - and check your reasons if you have
reached a different sentence

Endorse licence (6 points) and consider disqualification

NB. FINES - If imposing a fine, remember to increase or decrease the amount according to the
financial circumstances of the offender

Class B Drugs — Supply: Possession with intent to supply

Misuse of Drugs Act 1971
Triable either way - see Mode of Trial Guidelines
Penalty: Level 5 and/or 6 months

| ENTRY POINT ⅄ | COMMIT FOR TRIAL UNLESS SMALL SCALE SUPPLY, OTHERWISE CUSTODY |

CONSIDER THE SERIOUSNESS OF THE OFFENCE

+

eg.
Offence committed on bail
Commercial production
Large amount
Previous convictions and failures to respond to previous sentences, if relevant

eg. Small amount

–

IS IT SO SERIOUS THAT ONLY CUSTODY IS APPROPRIATE?
IS IT SERIOUS ENOUGH FOR A COMMUNITY PENALTY?
IS COMPENSATION, DISCHARGE OR FINE APPROPRIATE?

CONSIDER OFFENDER MITIGATION

eg.
Guilty plea: *for a timely guilty plea allow a discount of about a third*
Age, health (physical or mental)
Co-operation with the police
Remorse

DECIDE YOUR SENTENCE

Compare your decision with the entry point - CUSTODY - and check your reasons if you have reached a different sentence

Consider forfeiture of all drugs and equipment

NB. FINES - If imposing a fine, remember to increase or decrease the amount according to the financial circumstances of the offender

---

Class A Drugs — Possession

Misuse of Drugs Act 1971
Triable either way - see Mode of Trial Guidelines
Penalty: Level 5 and/or 6 months

| ENTRY POINT ⅄ | COMMUNITY PENALTY |

CONSIDER THE SERIOUSNESS OF THE OFFENCE

+

eg.
Offence committed on bail
An amount other than a very small quantity
Previous convictions and failures to respond to previous sentences, if relevant

eg. Very small quantity

–

IS IT SERIOUS ENOUGH FOR A COMMUNITY PENALTY?
IS COMPENSATION, DISCHARGE OR FINE APPROPRIATE, OR
IS IT SO SERIOUS THAT ONLY CUSTODY IS APPROPRIATE?

CONSIDER OFFENDER MITIGATION

eg.
Guilty plea: *for a timely guilty plea allow a discount of about a third*
Age, health (physical or mental)
Co-operation with the police
Remorse

DECIDE YOUR SENTENCE

Compare your decision with the entry point - COMMUNITY PENALTY - and check your reasons if you have reached a different sentence

Consider forfeiture of all drugs and equipment

NB. FINES - If imposing a fine, remember to increase or decrease the amount according to the financial circumstances of the offender

Misuse of Drugs Acts 1971
Triable either way - see Mode of Trial Guidelines
Penalty: £500 and/or 3 months

Class B Drugs — Possession

Misuse of Drugs Act 1971
Triable either way - see Mode of Trial Guidelines
Penalty: Level 5 and/or 6 months

Cultivation of Cannabis

Class B Drugs — Possession

ENTRY POINT — **FINE**

CONSIDER THE SERIOUSNESS OF THE OFFENCE

eg.
Offence committed on bail
Large amount
Previous convictions and failures to respond to previous sentences, if relevant

eg. Small amount

IS COMPENSATION, DISCHARGE OR FINE APPROPRIATE?
IS IT SERIOUS ENOUGH FOR A COMMUNITY PENALTY?
IS IT SO SERIOUS THAT ONLY CUSTODY IS APPROPRIATE?

CONSIDER OFFENDER MITIGATION

eg.
Guilty plea: *for a timely guilty plea allow a discount of about a third*
Age, health (physical or mental)
Co-operation with the police
Remorse

DECIDE YOUR SENTENCE

Compare your decision with the entry point - FINE - and check your reasons if you have reached a different sentence

Guideline fine for this offence is £180 which reflects the average seriousness of an offence of this type

Consider forfeiture of all drugs and equipment

NB. FINES - If imposing a fine, remember to increase or decrease the amount according to the financial circumstances of the offender

---

Cultivation of Cannabis

ENTRY POINT — **FINE**

CONSIDER THE SERIOUSNESS OF THE OFFENCE

eg.
Offence committed on bail
Commercial cultivation
Large quantity
Previous convictions and failures to respond to previous sentences, if relevant

eg. Small scale cultivation for personal use

IS COMPENSATION, DISCHARGE OR FINE APPROPRIATE?
IS IT SERIOUS ENOUGH FOR A COMMUNITY PENALTY?
IS IT SO SERIOUS THAT ONLY CUSTODY IS APPROPRIATE?

CONSIDER OFFENDER MITIGATION

eg.
Guilty plea: *for a timely guilty plea allow a discount of about a third*
Age, health (physical or mental)
Co-operation with the police
Remorse

DECIDE YOUR SENTENCE

Compare your decision with the entry point - FINE - and check your reasons if you have reached a different sentence

Guideline fine for this offence is £180 which reflects the average seriousness of an offence of this type

Consider forfeiture of all drugs and equipment

NB. FINES - If imposing a fine, remember to increase or decrease the amount according to the financial circumstances of the offender

ENTRY POINT ⟩ **FINE**

⊕ CONSIDER THE SERIOUSNESS OF THE OFFENCE

eg.
Offence committed on bail
Busy public place
Offensive language or behaviour
With group
Previous convictions and failures to respond
to previous sentences, if relevant

eg.
Account should be taken of any time
spent in custody

IS COMPENSATION, DISCHARGE OR FINE APPROPRIATE?
IS IT SERIOUS ENOUGH FOR A COMMUNITY PENALTY?
(PROBATION IS THE ONLY AVAILABLE COMMUNITY PENALTY FOR THIS OFFENCE)

CONSIDER OFFENDER MITIGATION

eg.
Guilty plea: for a timely guilty plea allow a discount of about a third
Age, health (physical or mental)
Co-operation with the police
Remorse

DECIDE YOUR SENTENCE

Compare your decision with the entry point - FINE - and check your reasons if you have
reached a different sentence

Guideline fine for this offence is £90 which reflects the average seriousness of an offence of
this type

NB. COMPENSATION - Give reasons if not awarding compensation
NB. FINES - If imposing a fine, remember to increase or decrease the amount according to the
financial circumstances of the offender

Failing to Stop
Failing to Report

Road Traffic Act 1988 s.170 (as amended)
Triable only summarily
Penalty: Level 5 and/or 6 months
Must endorse: 5-10 points: may disqualify

ENTRY POINT ⟩ **FINE**

⊖ CONSIDER THE SERIOUSNESS OF THE OFFENCE

eg.
Offence committed on bail
Evidence of drinking
Serious injury and failure to to stop
or remain at scene
Serious injury and/or serious damage
Previous convictions and failures to respond
to previous sentences, if relevant

eg.
Failed to stop but reported
Negligible damage
No one at scene but failed to report
Stayed at scene but failed to give full
particulars
Stayed at scene but left before giving full
particulars

IS COMPENSATION, DISCHARGE OR FINE APPROPRIATE?
IS IT SERIOUS ENOUGH FOR A COMMUNITY PENALTY?
IS IT SO SERIOUS THAT ONLY CUSTODY IS APPROPRIATE?

CONSIDER OFFENDER MITIGATION

eg.
Guilty plea: for a timely guilty plea allow a discount of about a third
Age, health (physical or mental)
Co-operation with the police
Voluntary compensation
Remorse

DECIDE YOUR SENTENCE

Compare your decision with the entry point - FINE - and check your reasons if you have
reached a different sentence

Guideline fine for this offence is £360 which reflects the average seriousness of an offence of
this type

Endorse licence (5-10 points) and consider disqualification

NB. COMPENSATION - Give reasons if not awarding compensation
NB. FINES - If imposing a fine, remember to increase or decrease the amount according to the
financial circumstances of the offender

Handling Stolen Goods

Theft Act 1968 s.22
Triable either way - see Mode of Trial Guidelines
Penalty: Level 5 and/or 6 months

ENTRY POINT ⋗ | COMMUNITY PENALTY

(−)

(+) CONSIDER THE SERIOUSNESS OF THE OFFENCE

eg.
- Offence committed on bail
- Adult involving children
- High value
- Organiser or distributor
- Stolen to order
- Previous convictions and failures to respond to previous sentences, if relevant

eg.
- Impulsive action
- Low value
- Single item for personal use

> *IS IT SERIOUS ENOUGH FOR A COMMUNITY PENALTY?*
> *IS COMPENSATION, DISCHARGE OR FINE APPROPRIATE, OR*
> *IS IT SO SERIOUS THAT ONLY CUSTODY IS APPROPRIATE?*

CONSIDER OFFENDER MITIGATION

eg.
- Guilty plea: *for a timely guilty plea allow a discount of about a third*
- Age, health (physical or mental)
- Co-operation with the police
- Voluntary compensation
- Remorse

DECIDE YOUR SENTENCE

Compare your decision with the entry point - COMMUNITY PENALTY - anc check your reasons if you have reached a different sentence

NB. COMPENSATION - Give reasons if not awarding compensation
NB. FINES - If imposing a fine, remember to increase or decrease the amount according to the financial circumstances of the offender

---

Fear of provocation of Violence

Public Order Act 1986 s.4
Triable only summarily
Penalty: Level 5 and/or 6 months

ENTRY POINT ⋗ | COMMUNITY PENALTY

(−)

(+) CONSIDER THE SERIOUSNESS OF THE OFFENCE

eg.
- Offence committed on bail
- Busy public place
- Group action
- People put in fear
- Vulnerable victims
- Previous convictions and failures to respond to previous sentences, if relevant

eg.
- Single offender

> *IS IT SERIOUS ENOUGH FOR A COMMUNITY PENALTY?*
> *IS COMPENSATION, DISCHARGE OR FINE APPROPRIATE, OR*
> *IS IT SO SERIOUS THAT ONLY CUSTODY IS APPROPRIATE?*

CONSIDER OFFENDER MITIGATION

eg.
- Guilty plea: *for a timely guilty plea allow a discount of about a third*
- Age, health (physical or mental)
- Co-operation with the police
- Voluntary compensation
- Remorse

DECIDE YOUR SENTENCE

Compare your decision with the entry point - COMMUNITY PENALTY - and check your reasons if you have reached a different sentence

NB. COMPENSATION - Give reasons if not awarding compensation
NB. FINES - If imposing a fine, remember to increase or decrease the amount according to the financial circumstances of the offender

Making Off without Payment

Theft Act 1978 s.3
Triable either way - see Mode of Trial Guidelines
Penalty: Level 5 and/or 6 months

ENTRY POINT / **FINE**

(−)

CONSIDER THE SERIOUSNESS OF THE OFFENCE

eg.   Impulsive action

(+) eg.
Offence committed on bail
Deliberate plan
Large sum
Two or more involved
Victim particularly vulnerable
Previous convictions and failures to respond
to previous sentences, if relevant

IS COMPENSATION, DISCHARGE OR FINE APPROPRIATE?
IS IT SERIOUS ENOUGH FOR A COMMUNITY PENALTY?
IS IT SO SERIOUS THAT ONLY CUSTODY IS APPROPRIATE?

CONSIDER OFFENDER MITIGATION

eg.
Guilty plea: *for a timely guilty plea allow a discount of about a third*
Age, health (physical or mental)
Co-operation with the police
Voluntary compensation
Remorse

DECIDE YOUR SENTENCE

Compare your decision with the entry point - FINE - and check your reasons if you have
reached a different sentence

Guideline fine for this offence is £180 which reflects the average seriousness of an offence of
this type

NB. COMPENSATION - Give reasons if not awarding compensation
NB. FINES - If imposing a fine, remember to increase or decrease the amount according to the
financial circumstances of the offender

Harassment, Alarm or Distress

Public Order Act 1986 s.5
Triable only summarily
Penalty: Level 3

ENTRY POINT / **FINE**

(−)

CONSIDER THE SERIOUSNESS OF THE OFFENCE

eg.   Single offender

(+) eg.
Offence committed on bail
Group action
Vulnerable victim
Previous convictions and failures to respond
to previous sentences, if relevant

IS COMPENSATION, DISCHARGE OR FINE APPROPRIATE?
IS IT SERIOUS ENOUGH FOR A COMMUNITY PENALTY?
(PROBATION IS THE ONLY AVAILABLE COMMUNITY PENALTY FOR THIS OFFENCE)

CONSIDER OFFENDER MITIGATION

eg.
Guilty plea: *for a timely guilty plea allow a discount of about a third*
Age, health (physical or mental)
Co-operation with the police
Voluntary compensation
Remorse

DECIDE YOUR SENTENCE

Compare your decision with the entry point - FINE - and check your reasons if you have
reached a different sentence

Guideline fine for this offence is £180 which reflects the average seriousness of an offence of
this type

NB. COMPENSATION - Give reasons if not awarding compensation
NB. FINES - If imposing a fine, remember to increase or decrease the amount according to the
financial circumstances of the offender

Police Act 1964 s.51
Triable only summarily
Penalty: Level 3 and/or 1 month

Obstructing a Police Officer

ENTRY POINT ∧ **FINE**

CONSIDER THE SERIOUSNESS OF THE OFFENCE

(+)

eg.
Offence committed on bail
Gross disregard for Police authority
Group action
Premeditated
Previous convictions and failures to respond to previous sentences, if relevant

eg.
Genuine misjudgement
Impulsive action
Minor obstruction
Unaware that person was a Police Officer

(−)

IS COMPENSATION, DISCHARGE OR FINE APPROPRIATE?
IS IT SERIOUS ENOUGH FOR A COMMUNITY PENALTY?
IS IT SO SERIOUS THAT ONLY CUSTODY IS APPROPRIATE?

CONSIDER OFFENDER MITIGATION

eg.
Guilty plea: *for a timely guilty plea allow a discount of about a third*
Age, health (physical or mental)
Co-operation with the police
Voluntary compensation
Remorse

DECIDE YOUR SENTENCE

Compare your decision with the entry point - FINE - and check your reasons if you have reached a different sentence

Guideline fine for this offence is **£180** which reflects the average seriousness of an offence of this type

NB. COMPENSATION - Give reasons if not awarding compensation
NB. FINES - If imposing a fine, remember to increase or decrease the amount according to the financial circumstances of the offender

---

Theft Act 1968 s.15
Triable either way - see Mode of Trial Guidelines
Penalty: Level 5 and/or 6 months

Obtaining by Deception

ENTRY POINT ∧ **COMMUNITY PENALTY**

CONSIDER THE SERIOUSNESS OF THE OFFENCE

(+)

eg.
Offence committed on bail
Committed over lengthy period
Large sums or valuable goods
Two or more involved
Victim particularly vulnerable
Previous convictions and failures to respond to previous sentences, if relevant

eg.
Impulsive action
Short period
Small sum

(−)

IS IT SERIOUS ENOUGH FOR A COMMUNITY PENALTY?
IS COMPENSATION, DISCHARGE OR FINE APPROPRIATE, OR
IS IT SO SERIOUS THAT ONLY CUSTODY IS APPROPRIATE?

CONSIDER OFFENDER MITIGATION

eg.
Guilty plea: *for a timely guilty plea allow a discount of about a third*
Age, health (physical or mental)
Co-operation with the police
Compensation
Remorse

DECIDE YOUR SENTENCE

Compare your decision with the entry point - COMMUNITY PENALTY - and check your reasons if you have reached a different sentence

NB. COMPENSATION - Give reasons if not awarding compensation
NB. FINES - If imposing a fine, remember to increase or decrease the amount according to the financial circumstances of the offender

Social Security - false
representation to obtain benefit

Social Security Act 1986 s.55
Triable only summarily
Penalty: Level 5 and/or 3 months

ENTRY POINT 〉〈   COMMUNITY PENALTY

+   CONSIDER THE SERIOUSNESS OF THE OFFENCE   **–**

eg.

Offence committed on bail
Fraudulent claims over a long period
Large amount
Organised group offence
Planned deception
Previous convictions and failures to respond
to previous sentences, if relevant

eg.

Ignorance of regulations
Offence of omission

IS IT SERIOUS ENOUGH FOR A COMMUNITY PENALTY?
IS COMPENSATION, DISCHARGE OR FINE APPROPRIATE, OR
IS IT SO SERIOUS THAT ONLY CUSTODY IS APPROPRIATE?

CONSIDER OFFENDER MITIGATION

eg.

Guilty plea: *for a timely guilty plea allow a discount of about a third*
Age, health (physical or mental)
Co-operation with the prosecuting authority
Voluntary compensation
Remorse

DECIDE YOUR SENTENCE

Compare your decision with the entry point - COMMUNITY PENALTY - and check your
reasons if you have reached a different sentence

NB. COMPENSATION - Give reasons if not awarding compensation
NB. FINES - If imposing a fine, remember to increase or decrease the amount according to the
financial circumstances of the offender

Taking Vehicle
without Consent

Theft Act 1968 s.12
Triable only summarily
Penalty: Level 5 and/or 6 months
May disqualify

ENTRY POINT 〉〈   COMMUNITY PENALTY

+   CONSIDER THE SERIOUSNESS OF THE OFFENCE   **–**

eg.

Offence committed on bail
Group action
Premeditated
Related damage
Vulnerable victim
Previous convictions and failures to respond
to previous sentences, if relevant

eg.

Keys left in car
Misunderstanding with owner

IS IT SERIOUS ENOUGH FOR A COMMUNITY PENALTY?
IS COMPENSATION, DISCHARGE OR FINE APPROPRIATE, OR
IS IT SO SERIOUS THAT ONLY CUSTODY IS APPROPRIATE?

CONSIDER OFFENDER MITIGATION

eg.

Guilty plea: *for a timely guilty plea allow a discount of about a third*
Age, health (physical or mental)
Co-operation with the police
Voluntary compensation
Remorse

DECIDE YOUR SENTENCE

Compare your decision with the entry point - COMMUNITY PENALTY - and check your
reasons if you have reached a different sentence

Consider disqualification

NB. COMPENSATION - Give reasons if not awarding compensation
NB. FINES - If imposing a fine, remember to increase or decrease the amount according to
the financial circumstances of the offender

Theft (General)

Theft Act 1968 s.1
Triable either way - see Mode of Trial Guidelines
Penalty: Level 5 and/or 6 months

ENTRY POINT ⋀ FINE

CONSIDER THE SERIOUSNESS OF THE OFFENCE

(+)
eg.

	eg.
Offence committed on bail	Impulsive action
Large Amount	Small amount
Planned	Voluntary restitution
Sophisticated	
Vulnerable victim	
Previous convictions and failures to respond to previous sentences, if relevant	

(−)

IS COMPENSATION, DISCHARGE OR FINE APPROPRIATE?
IS IT SERIOUS ENOUGH FOR A COMMUNITY PENALTY?
IS IT SO SERIOUS THAT ONLY CUSTODY IS APPROPRIATE?

CONSIDER OFFENDER MITIGATION

eg.
Guilty plea: *for a timely guilty plea allow a discount of about a third*
Age, health (physical or mental)
Co-operation with the police
Voluntary compensation
Remorse

DECIDE YOUR SENTENCE

Compare your decision with the entry point - FINE - and check your reasons if you have reached a different sentence

Guideline fine for this offence is £270 which reflects the average seriousness of an offence of this type

NB. COMPENSATION - Give reasons if not awarding compensation
NB. FINES - If imposing a fine, remember to increase or decrease the amount according to the financial circumstances of the offender

---

Theft from a Shop

Theft Act 1968 s.1
Triable either way - see Mode of Trial Guidelines
Penalty: Level 5 and/or 6 months

ENTRY POINT ⋀ FINE

CONSIDER THE SERIOUSNESS OF THE OFFENCE

(+)

	eg.
Offence committed on bail	Impulsive action
Adult involving children	Low value
High value	
Organised teams	
Planned	
Previous convictions and failures to respond to previous sentences, if relevant	

(−)

IS COMPENSATION, DISCHARGE OR FINE APPROPRIATE?
IS IT SERIOUS ENOUGH FOR A COMMUNITY PENALTY?
IS IT SO SERIOUS THAT ONLY CUSTODY IS APPROPRIATE?

CONSIDER OFFENDER MITIGATION

eg.
Guilty plea: *for a timely guilty plea allow a discount of about a third*
Age, health (physical or mental)
Co-operation with the police
Voluntary compensation
Remorse

DECIDE YOUR SENTENCE

Compare your decision with the entry point - FINE - and check your reasons if you have reached a different sentence

Guideline fine for this offence is £270 which reflects the average seriousness of an offence of this type

NB. COMPENSATION - Give reasons if not awarding compensation
NB. FINES - If imposing a fine, remember to increase or decrease the amount according to the financial circumstances of the offender

Theft from Vehicle

Theft Act 1968 s. 1
Triable either way - see Mode of Trial Guidelines
Penalty: Level 5 and/or 6 months

ENTRY POINT ⟩ COMMUNITY PENALTY

CONSIDER THE SERIOUSNESS OF THE OFFENCE

+

eg.
Offence committed on bail
High value
Organised team
Planned
Related damage
Previous convictions and failures to respond
to previous sentences, if relevant

eg.
Car unlocked
Impulsive action

–

IS IT SERIOUS ENOUGH FOR A COMMUNITY PENALTY?
IS COMPENSATION, DISCHARGE OR FINE APPROPRIATE, OR
IS IT SO SERIOUS THAT ONLY CUSTODY IS APPROPRIATE?

CONSIDER OFFENDER MITIGATION

eg.
Guilty plea: *for a timely guilty plea allow a discount of about a third*
Age, health (physical or mental)
Co-operation with the police
Voluntary compensation
Remorse

DECIDE YOUR SENTENCE

Compare your decision with the entry point - COMMUNITY PENALTY - and check your
reasons if you have reached a different sentence

NB. COMPENSATION - Give reasons if not awarding compensation
NB. FINES - If imposing a fine, remember to increase or decrease the amount according to the
financial circumstances of the offender

Theft in Breach of Trust

Theft Act 1968 s. 1
Triable either way - see Mode of Trial Guidelines
Penalty: Level 5 and/or 6 months

ENTRY POINT ⟩ COMMUNITY PENALTY

CONSIDER THE SERIOUSNESS OF THE OFFENCE

+

eg.
Offence committed on bail
Casting suspicion on others
Committed over a period
Large amount
Planned
Senior employee
Sophisticated
Vulnerable victim
Previous convictions and failures to respond
to previous sentences, if relevant

eg.
Impulsive action
Newly employed junior
Single item
Small amount

–

IS IT SERIOUS ENOUGH FOR A COMMUNITY PENALTY?
IS COMPENSATION, DISCHARGE OR FINE APPROPRIATE, OR
IS IT SO SERIOUS THAT ONLY CUSTODY IS APPROPRIATE?

CONSIDER OFFENDER MITIGATION

eg.
Guilty plea: *for a timely guilty plea allow a discount of about a third*
Age, health (physical or mental)
Co-operation with the police
Voluntary compensation
Remorse

DECIDE YOUR SENTENCE

Compare your decision with the entry point - COMMUNITY PENALTY - and check your
reasons if you have reached a different sentence

NB. COMPENSATION - Give reasons if not awarding compensation
NB. FINES - If imposing a fine, remember to increase or decrease the amount according to the
financial circumstances of the offender

Public Order Act 1986 s.2
Triable either way - see Mode of Trial Guidelines
Penalty: Level 5 and/or 6 months

Violent Disorder

TV Licence Evasion

ENTRY POINT	FINE

CONSIDER THE SERIOUSNESS OF THE OFFENCE ●

eg.

Offence committed on bail	eg. Accidental oversight
Deliberate evasion	Confusion of responsibility
Lengthy unlicensed use	Very short unlicensed use
Previous convictions and failures to respond	
to previous sentences, if relevant	

IS COMPENSATION, DISCHARGE OR FINE APPROPRIATE?
IS IT SERIOUS ENOUGH FOR A COMMUNITY PENALTY?
(PROBATION IS THE ONLY AVAILABLE COMMUNITY PENALTY FOR THIS OFFENCE)

CONSIDER OFFENDER MITIGATION

eg.

Guilty plea: *for a timely guilty plea allow a discount of about a third*
Age, health (physical or mental)
Co-operation with the prosecuting authority
Remorse/prompt renewal of licence
Visitor to the premises

DECIDE YOUR SENTENCE

Compare your decision with the entry point - FINE - and check your reasons if you have reached a different sentence

Guideline fines for this offence are £180 (Colour) £90 (Mono) which reflect the average seriousness of an offence of this type

NB. FINES - If imposing a fine, remember to increase or decrease the amount according to the financial circumstances of the offender

---

Violent Disorder

ENTRY POINT	CUSTODY

CONSIDER THE SERIOUSNESS OF THE OFFENCE ●

eg.

Offence committed on bail
Busy public place
Large group
People put in fear
Vulnerable victims
Previous convictions and failures to respond
to previous sentences, if relevant

IS IT SO SERIOUS THAT ONLY CUSTODY IS APPROPRIATE?
IS IT SERIOUS ENOUGH FOR A COMMUNITY PENALTY?
IS COMPENSATION, DISCHARGE OR FINE APPROPRIATE?

CONSIDER OFFENDER MITIGATION

eg.

Guilty plea: *for a timely guilty plea allow a discount of about a third*
Age, health (physical or mental)
Co-operation with the police
Voluntary compensation
Remorse

DECIDE YOUR SENTENCE

Compare your decision with the entry point - CUSTODY - and check your reasons if you have reached a different sentence

NB. COMPENSATION - Give reasons if not awarding compensation
NB. FINES - If imposing a fine, remember to increase or decrease the amount according to the financial circumstances of the offender

| Offences Against the Person Act 1861 s.20
Triable either way - see Mode of Trial Guidelines
Penalty: Level 5 and/or 6 months | **Wounding — Grievous
Bodily Harm** |

| ENTRY POINT ⟋ | CUSTODY |

⊕ CONSIDER THE SERIOUSNESS OF THE OFFENCE ⊖

eg.
Offence committed on bail
Deliberate kicking
Extensive injuries
Group action
Offender in position of authority
Premeditated
Victim particularly vulnerable
Victim serving public
Weapon
Previous convictions and failures to respond
to previous sentences, if relevant

eg.
Impulsive action
Provocation

> *IS IT SO SERIOUS THAT ONLY CUSTODY IS APPROPRIATE?*
> *IS IT SERIOUS ENOUGH FOR A COMMUNITY PENALTY?*
> *IS COMPENSATION, DISCHARGE OR FINE APPROPRIATE?*

CONSIDER OFFENDER MITIGATION

eg.
Guilty plea: *for a timely guilty plea allow a discount of about a third*
Age, health (physical or mental)
Co-operation with the police
Voluntary compensation
Remorse

DECIDE YOUR SENTENCE

Compare your decision with the entry point - CUSTODY - check your reasons if you have
reached a different sentence

NB. COMPENSATION - Give reasons if not awarding compensation
NB. FINES - If imposing a fine, remember to increase or decrease the amount according to the
financial circumstances of the offender

Allow a discount of about a third for a timely guilty plea

Suggestions for Road Traffic Offence Penalties

HOW TO USE THE 'SUGGESTIONS'

For the general approach, please refer to the main introduction, noting that it cannot be emphasised too strongly that THE LIST IS NOT A TARIFF.

The recommended approach for serious road-traffic offences is to use scales based on seriousness indicators. These suggestions offer a starting point based on an average offence without aggravating factors. However, please note that suggested starting points are now based on a NOT GUILTY plea to allow a DISCOUNT of up to a third to be given for a prompt guilty plea.

The seriousness of offences differs widely, especially in cases of careless driving, and many road traffic offences are more hazardous when speeds are higher. Experience has proved that drinking and driving offences account for very many accidents, injuries and deaths. The Court of Appeal has consistently upheld higher penalties for offenders with higher alcohol figures, and it is suggested that penalties and especially periods of disqualification should reflect this. When fixing the size of a fine where an order of disqualification is also made, it should be remembered that the impact of disqualification varies from offender to offender and disqualification will frequently itself entail a very heavy financial burden.

The level of penalties must not become out of proportion compared to the level of fines for common criminal offences such as thefts from shops and assaults.

Variable Penalty Points

Variable penalty points offences imply greater variations in sentence. The fine will give a result adjusted to the financial circumstances of the offender but the penalty points chosen should correspond to the seriousness of the offence.

The Multiple Offender

Where on one occasion an offender is convicted of a large number of offences it is suggested that the court should also take an overall view and initially decide upon the maximum total amount of the fines which it is appropriate to impose for all the offences, even though this total may prove to be considerably less than the figure which would result from adding together all the suggested penalties involved.

Companies

When fining companies the position will depend on the financial standing of the company.

T R P Rudin
SECRETARY

Twelfth Edition
September 1993

The Magistrates' Association
28 Fitzroy Square, London W1P 6DD

IMPORTANT

These suggestions may be reproduced for the use of benches provided the front page is included.

SUGGESTIONS FOR COURTS' ASSESSMENT OF PENALTIES FOR MAIN TRAFFIC OFFENCES

The maximum standard levels are at present:

Level 1 - £200
Level 2 - £500
Level 3 - £1,000
Level 4 - £2,500
Level 5 - £5,000

D — Must disqualify at least 12 months (unless special reasons) and endorse. (If disqualifying for a lengthy period, or if driving skill suspect, consider disqualifying until test passed)

E — Must endorse (unless special reasons) and may disqualify)

MD — May disqualify - no power to endorse or assign penalty points

The maximum penalties for 'goods vehicles' also apply to 'vehicles adapted to carry more than eight passengers'. (See offences 7, 8, 9, 21 and 41, 42 and 43)

† Fixed penalty offences
◆ Refer to Guidelines

OFFENCE	PENALTY POINTS	MAXIMUM PENALTY	COMMENTS	FINE
ACCIDENT				
1.◆ Failing to stop	5-10	Level 5 E and/or six months prison	Refer to Guidelines: Should disqualify if serious	£360
2.◆ Failing to report to the police	5-10	Level 5 E and/or six months prison	Refer to Guidelines: Should disqualify if serious	£360
ALCOHOL Over 35µg breath: 80mg blood: 107mg urine				
3. Drunken driving or driving with excess alcohol	(3-11)	Level 5 D and/or six months prison	See Excess Alcohol chart on page 51	
4. Refusing evidential specimen (driving)	(3-11)	Level 5 D and/or six months prison	D 18 months	£720
5. In charge drunk or with excess alcohol or refusing evidential specimen	10	Level 4 E and/or 3 months prison		£360
6. Refusing roadside breath test	4	Level 3 E		£180
DEFECTS				
7.† Brakes	3	Level 4 E but for goods vehicles etc Level 5 E	Consider degree of responsibility	Driver £120 / LGV/HGV Owner £300 / LGV/HGV Driver £210
8.† Steering	3	Level 4 E but for goods vehicles etc. Level 5 E	Consider degree of responsibility	Driver £120 / LGV/HGV Owner £300 / LGV/HGV Driver £210
9.† Tyres (NB. Suggested penalty refers to each tyre)	3	Level 4 E but for goods vehicles etc. Level 5 E	Consider degree of responsibility	Driver £120 / LGV/HGV Owner £300 / LGV/HGV Driver £210
DISQUALIFIED				
10.◆ By court order	6	Level 5 E and/or six months prison	Refer to Guidelines: Entry point for this offence is CUSTODY	
DOCUMENTS				
11. Failing to produce	-	Level 3		£60

OFFENCE	PENALTY POINTS	MAXIMUM PENALTY	COMMENTS	FINE
DOUBLE WHITE LINES				
12 † Failing to comply with system	3	Level 3E		£120
DRIVING				
13. ♦ Dangerous	(3-11)	Level 5 D and/or six months prison	Refer to Guidelines. Entry point for this offence is COMMUNITY PENALTY. Disqualify for at least the compulsory twelve months and order retest	
14. ♦ Careless or inconsiderate	3-9	Level 4 E	Refer to Guidelines: Always consider degree of carelessness	£180
HELMET				
15 † No safety helmet	-	Level 2		£60
INSURANCE				
16 ♦ No insurance	6-8	Level 5 E	LGV/PCV or taxi-cabs	£540 / £660

In fixing the fine regard should be had as to whether the offence was deliberate or inadvertent, whether the offender was made (or any other mitigating circumstances and whether the 'user' or 'permitter' was responsible for the offence. IF DELIBERATE THE COURT SHOULD DISQUALIFY. In any event the court must have regard to the amount of the insurance premium.

OFFENCE	PENALTY POINTS	MAXIMUM PENALTY	COMMENTS	FINE
LICENCE OFFENCES AND LEARNER DRIVERS				
17 † Driving not in accordance with a licence	3-6 where endorsable	Level 3 in some cases E		see below
eg				
† no licence where could not be covered	3-6	Level 3 E		£150
† no licence where could be covered	-	Level 3		£30
† under age	3-6	Level 3 E		£120
† unsupervised in car	3-6	Level 3 E	Consider disqualification	£120
† learner motor cyclist with passenger	3-6	Level 3 E	Consider disqualification	£90
† no "L" plates	3-6	Level 3 E		£60
18 † No excise licence	-	Level 3 or 5 times annual duty (whichever greater)	Actual duty loss plus penalty of approximately twice that amount or £120 whichever greater	
19 No operator's licence	-	Level 4		£450
LIGHTS				
20 † Driving without lights	-	Level 3		£90

OFFENCE	PENALTY POINTS	MAXIMUM PENALTY	COMMENTS	FINE
LOADS				
21 † Construction & Use: Condition/Load etc - danger of injury by:				
condition of vehicle or of accessories or equipment	3	Level 4 E but for goods vehicles etc. Level 5 E	Ordinary vehicle-driver/owner — but consider degree of / LGV/HGV Driver / LGV/HGV Owner — responsibility	£180 / £300 / £600
† purpose of use	3	Level 4 E but for goods vehicles etc. Level 5 E	Ordinary vehicle-driver/owner — but consider degree of / LGV/HGV Driver / LGV/HGV Owner — responsibility	£180 / £300 / £600
† number or manner of carriage of passengers	3	Level 4 E but for goods vehicles etc. Level 5 E	Ordinary vehicle-owner — but consider degree of / LGV/HGV Driver / LGV/HGV Owner — responsibility	£180 / £300 / £600
† weight, position or distribution of load	3	Level 4 E but for goods vehicles etc. Level 5 E	Ordinary vehicle-owner — but consider degree of / LGV/HGV Driver / LGV/HGV Owner — responsibility	£180 / £300 / £600
† insecure load	3	Level 4 but for goods vehicles etc. Level 5 E	Non-LGV/HGV Owner/Driver — but consider degree of / Non-LGV/HGV Commercial — responsibility / LGV/HGV Driver / LGV/HGV Owner	£150 / £180 / £360 / £750
† overloading or exceeding maximum axle weight - commercial vehicle	-	Level 5	Non-LGV/HGV Driver — but consider degree of / Non-LGV/HGV Owner — responsibility / LGV/HGV Driver / LGV/HGV Owner	£180 / £360 / £750

Suggestion refers to conviction on each charge. In addition, for overloading add £30 for each 1% of overload (ignoring the first 10%) but always have regard to commercial gain and damage to roads.

OFFENCE	PENALTY POINTS	MAXIMUM PENALTY	COMMENTS	FINE
OWNERSHIP/DRIVER				
22. Not supplying details of driver	3	Level 3 E		£210
Not notifying DVLA etc.	-	Level 3		£150
PARKING				
23 † Dangerous position	3	Level 3 E		£90
24 † On zig-zags by pedestrian crossing	3	Level 3 E		£90
25 † Obstruction	-	Level 3		£60
26 † Stopping on Clearway	-	Level 3		£90
PEDESTRIAN OR SCHOOL CROSSING				
27 † Offences other than parking (†certain offences only)	3	Level 3 E	Consider disqualification	£90

OFFENCE	PENALTY POINTS	MAXIMUM PENALTY	COMMENTS	FINE
SEAT BELTS				
26 † Not wearing	-	Level 2		£60
29 † Driving with a child not wearing				
† (front)	-	Level 2		£60
† (back)	-	Level 1		£30
SPEEDING				
30 † Exceeding speed limit	3 - 6	Level 3E	Consider disqualification if 30mph over limit	SEE TABLE OF BANDS ON PAGE 50
SPEED LIMITERS				
31 † Speed Limiter not fitted	-			Driver £300 / Owner £420
32 † Speed Limiter not being used or not correctly calibrated	-			Driver £150 / Owner £210
TACHOGRAPH				
33. No tachograph or not used as required	-	Level 5		£240
34. Tachograph falsification	-	Level 5		£360
TAKEN VEHICLES				
35. ◆ Aggravated Vehicle Taking	(3-11)	Level 5 must disqualify at least 12 months and /or 6 months prison	Refer to Guidelines: Entry point for this offence is CUSTODY	
36. ◆ Taking vehicle without consent	-	Level 5 may disqualify only and/or 6 months prison	Refer to Guidelines: Entry point for this offence is COMMUNITY PENALTY	
37. Carried in taken vehicle	-	Level 5 may disqualify only and/or 6 months prison	Consider custody/community penalty	£300
TEST CERTIFICATE				
38. No test certificate	-	Level 3 but for goods vehicles and vehicles adapted to carry more than 8 passengers Level 4		Ordinary vehicles £90 / 3.5 tonnes or over GVW LGV and PCV £120 / Trailers (but dependent on size) £180 / £90
TRAFFIC LIGHTS				
39 † Failing to comply with	3	Level 3 E		£90
TRAFFIC OR POLICE SIGNS				
40 † Failing to comply with (except traffic lights or double white lines)	3	Level 3 (power to disqualify, endorse, test in some cases)	Endorse where required	£90
VEHICLE OFFENCES under the Construction and Use Regulations not shown elsewhere				
41 † Loss of wheel	3	Level 4 E but for goods vehicles etc Level 5	in all cases consider degree of responsibility	Driver £420 / Owner £600
42 † Exhaust emission	-	Level 3 but for goods vehicles etc Level 4	In all cases consider degree of responsibility	Driver £90 / Owner £150
42 † Other offences	-	Level 3 but for goods vehicles etc Level 4	In all cases consider degree of responsibility	Driver £60 / Owner £90

MOTORWAY OFFENCES

OFFENCE	PENALTY POINTS	MAXIMUM PENALTY	COMMENTS	FINE
DRIVING				
44 † Driving in reverse	3	Level 4 E	On main motorway / On sliproad	£360 / £120
45 † Driving in wrong direction	3	Level 4 E	Consider disqualification / On main motorway / On sliproad	£600 / £180
46 † Driving off carriageway	3	Level 4 E	Central reservation / Hard shoulder	£180 / £150
47 † Driving on sliproad against 'No entry sign'	3	Level 4 E		£180
48 † Making U-Turn	3	Level 4 E	Consider disqualification	£480
LEARNERS				
49 † Learner driver or excluded vehicle	-	Level 4 E		£180
SPEEDING				
50 † Exceeding speed limit	3 - 6	Level 4 E*	Consider disqualification if 30mph over limit	SEE TABLE OF BANDS BELOW

*Level 3E in respect of goods and other vehicles restricted to a lower limit

OFFENCE	PENALTY POINTS	MAXIMUM PENALTY	COMMENTS	FINE
STOPPING				
51 † Stopping on hard shoulder	-	Level 4	On main motorway / On sliproad	£120 / £60
THIRD LANE				
52 † Vehicle over 7.5 tonnes or drawing trailer in third lane	3	Level 4 E		£300
WALKING				
53 † Walking on motorway	-	Level 4	On main motorway or sliproad / On hard shoulder or verge	£90 / £60

†SPEEDING - TABLE OF BANDS
Penalty Points: 3 - 6

Maximum penalty: see numbers 30 & 50 above

Guideline for speeding, but consider scene of offence and more for heavy vehicles/LGVs/PCVs

MILES OVER LIMIT	SUGGESTED VARIABLE PENALTY POINTS		SUGGESTED FINE
1 - 14	A fixed penalty will often have been offered	3	£90
15 - 19	A fixed penalty will often have been offered	3	£90
20 - 24	A fixed penalty will often have been offered	4	£120
25 - 29	A fixed penalty may have been offered	5	£150
	Equivalent to 100mph on the motorway - Consider disqualification	6	£180
30 - 34		6	Disqualify for 7 days £210
35 - 39		6	Disqualify for 14 days £240

Above this speed - 40 miles or more over the limit (eg 70 mph in a 30 mph area - 110 mph on the motorway - sharp increase in penalty and disqualification (minimum 21 days).

EXCESS ALCOHOL

The legal limits are:

Breath: 35 micrograms per 100 millilitres
Blood: 80 milligrams per 100 millilitres
Urine: 107 milligrams per 100 millilitres

Between 40 and 52 micrograms per 100 millilitres of breath the suggested fine is £480 and disqualification for 12 months. For amounts in excess of 52 micrograms (breath) or 120 milligrams (blood) or 160 milligrams (urine) then refer to the chart below and read off a datum or entry point for your deliberations.

For breath: take the reading on the left hand side of the chart and go to the diagonal line. Where the reading meets the diagonal, drop vertically to the base line and read off the associated fine and disqualification.

For blood: above 210, go to the right of the diagonal, drop vertically and read off fine and disqualification. Below 210, go left and proceed as above.

For urine: take the reading on the right hand side of the chart and go left to the diagonal line. Where the reading meets the diagonal, drop vertically to the base line and read off fine and disqualification.

IMPORTANT: This only provides a starting point. Always apply circumstances to increase or decrease fine or disqualification.

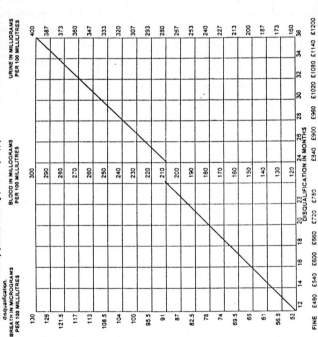

BREATH IN MICROGRAMS PER 100 MILLILITRES — BLOOD IN MILLIGRAMS PER 100 MILLILITRES — URINE IN MILLIGRAMS PER 100 MILLILITRES

BREATH	BLOOD	URINE
130	300	400
126	290	387
121.5	280	373
117	270	360
113	260	347
108.5	250	333
104	240	320
100	230	307
95.5	220	293
91	210	280
87	200	267
82.5	190	253
78	180	240
74	170	227
69.5	160	213
65	150	200
61	140	187
56.5	130	173
52	120	160

DISQUALIFICATION IN MONTHS

12	14	16	18	20	22	24	26	28	30	32	34	36
£480	£540	£600	£660	£720	£730	£780 £340	£900	£960	£1020	£1080	£1140	£1200

CONSIDER CUSTODY ——

REFUSING BREATH BLOOD OR URINE SPECIMENS (DRIVING ETC.) - £720 AND DISQUALIFY 18 MONTHS

Appendix III Home Office Circular 18/1994

The Cautioning of Offenders

The purposes of this Circular are to provide guidance on the cautioning of offenders, and in particular—

—to discourage the use of cautions in inappropriate cases, for example for offences which are triable on indictment only;
—to seek greater consistency between police force areas; and
—to promote the better recording of cautions.

2 This Circular, the terms of which have been discussed with the Association of Chief Police Officers and the Crown Prosecution Service, replaces Circular 59/1990 which is hereby cancelled. Some amendments have been made to the national standards for cautioning established by Circular 59/1990; the revised standards, which should be read in conjunction with this Circular, are attached. The general principles underlying those standards are unchanged: properly used, cautioning continues to be regarded as an effective form of disposal, and one which may in appropriate circumstances be used for offenders of any age.

3 Circular 59/1990 left cautioning decisions to the discretion of the police; there is no intention of reducing this discretion, which in the vast majority of cases is properly used. The decision to caution is in all cases one for the police, and although it is open to them to seek the advice of multi-agency panels, this should not be done as a matter of course. It is important that cautions should be administered quickly, and where such advice is sought it must not lead to unnecessary delay.

4 It is apparent that there is some inconsistency between forces about the circumstances in which they consider it appropriate to administer a caution. It is impossible to lay down hard and fast rules such as that first-time offenders must be cautioned, or that certain minor offences should attract only a caution regardless of the offender's record. Nor does the presumption in favour of diverting juveniles from the courts mean that they should automatically be cautioned, as opposed to prosecuted, simply because they are juveniles. Ultimately the proper use of discretion is a matter of common sense: the questions to be asked in each case are—

—whether the circumstances are such that the caution is likely to be effective, and
—whether the caution is appropriate to the offence.

Serious offences
5 Previous guidance discouraged the use of cautioning for the most serious offences, especially for those triable only on indictment. Statistics indicate, however, that cautions are administered in such cases—there were 1735 in 1992. Cautions have been given for crimes as serious as attempted murder and rape: this undermines the credibility of this disposal. Cautions should never be used for the most serious

283

indictable-only offences such as these, and only in exceptional circumstances (one example might be a child taking another's pocket-money by force, which in law is robbery) for other indictable-only offences, regardless of the age or previous record of the offender.

6 Other offences, less grave in themselves, may nevertheless be too serious for a caution to be appropriate. The factors which will be relevant in making this judgment are too varied for it to be practicable to list them, but they include the nature and extent of the harm or loss resulting from the offences, relative to the victim's age and means; whether the offence was racially motivated; whether it involved a breach of trust; and whether the offence was carried out in a systematic and organised way. Comprehensive lists of such 'gravity factors' have been drawn up by several forces, and these can help in assessing the seriousness of an offence.

7 Efforts should be made to find out the victim's view about the offence, which may have a bearing on how serious the offence is judged to be. It should not, however, be regarded as conclusive. Where a caution has been given and the victim requests the offender's name and address in order to institute civil proceedings, the information should be disclosed, unless there is good reason to believe that it might be used for an improper purpose such as retaliation.

The offender's record
8 Research into a sample of offenders who were cautioned in 1991 indicates that 8 per cent had already received two or more cautions. Multiple cautioning brings this disposal into disrepute; cautions should not be administered to an offender in circumstances where there can be no reasonable expectation that this will curb his offending. It is only in the following circumstances that more than one caution should be considered:

—where the subsequent offence is trivial; or
—where there has been a sufficient lapse of time since the first caution to suggest that it had some effect.

Consistency
9 There are significant variations between forces—and indeed between stations within forces—in the number of offenders who are cautioned as a proportion of those who are either cautioned or convicted. In 1992 this figure for indictable offences varied, as between forces, from 27 per cent to 57 per cent. This discrepancy may result from differing perceptions of the boundary between informal warnings and formal cautions (see below), or of that between formal cautions and prosecutions. Either way, this degree of variation is undesirable. Accordingly, forces which caution a disproportionately high or low number of offenders should ensure that their force guidelines on cautioning are sound and are being interpreted sensibly.

10 Where there is doubt about whether a prosecution should be brought or a caution given in a particular case, it will often be useful to seek the opinion of the Crown Prosecution Service at an early stage in order to avoid disagreement (and in particular the undesirable outcome of an offender escaping without censure of any kind through

being considered to be suitable neither for a caution nor for prosecution). If it is the offender's history, rather than the nature of the offence, which renders the case in the view of the police unsuitable for a caution, the Crown Prosecution Service's attention should be drawn to the fact.

Recording

11 The accurate recording of cautions is essential in order both to avoid multiple cautioning and to achieve greater consistency. This will be made easier when computerised national criminal records are introduced, which will permit a brief description of the offence to be recorded. In the meantime, existing recording systems should be improved, where possible, particularly so as to provide a central force record where this does not already exist. It is essential that records should be checked before a caution is given. When an offender is cautioned on the same occasion for more than one offence, he should be counted as having received one caution only.

12 If a person who is initially suspected of a serious offence is found to have committed a less serious one for which he is then cautioned, it is important that the caution should be recorded as having been given for the lesser offence.

'Informal cautions'

13 There is no intention of inhibiting the practice of taking action short of a formal caution by giving an oral warning, but this should not be recorded as a caution in the criminal statistics nor (unlike a caution) may it be cited in subsequent court proceedings. The expession 'informal caution' used in Circular 59/1990 is confusing and is not recommended.

Supporting cautions

14 Circular 59/1990 made it clear that police officers should not become involved in negotiating reparation or compensation, although these were features which might properly support the use of a caution. In several areas 'caution plus' schemes incorporating voluntary arrangements of this kind have been developed, apparently to the satisfaction of victims. Since caution plus needs further evaluation before a decision can be made on its future, it would be helpful if forces participating in such schemes would monitor the results.

15 In the case of juvenile offenders, it will often be desirable for the police to liaise with local statutory and voluntary agencies about the ways in which assistance might be offered to the juveniles and their families to prevent re-offending. Such support can be especially valuable if a young person is cautioned for a sexual offence.

National Standards for Cautioning (Revised)

Aims

1 The purposes of a formal caution are—

—to deal quickly and simply with less serious offenders;

285

—to divert them from unecessary appearance in the criminal courts; and
—to reduce the chances of their re-offending.

Note 1A A caution is not a form of sentence. It may not be made conditional upon the satisfactory completion of a specific task such as reparation or the payment of compensation to the victim. Only the courts may impose such requirements.

Decision to caution

2 A formal caution is a serious matter. It is recorded by the police; it should influence them in their decision whether or not to institute proceedings if the person should offend again, and it may be cited in any subsequent court proceedings. In order to safeguard the offender's interests, the following conditions must be met before a caution can be administered—

—there must be evidence of the offender's guilt sufficient to give a realistic prospect of conviction;
—the offender must admit the offence;
—the offender (or, in the case of a juvenile, his parents or guardian) must understand the significance of a caution and give informed consent to being cautioned.

Note 2A Where the evidence does not meet the required standard, a caution cannot be administered.

Note 2B A caution will not be appropriate where a person does not make a clear and reliable admission of the offence (for example if intent is denied or there are doubts about his mental health or intellectual capacity).

Note 2C If an offence is committed by a juvenile under the age of 14, it is necessary to establish that he knew that what he did was seriously wrong.

Note 2D In practice consent to the caution should not be sought until it has been decided that cautioning is the correct course. The significance of the caution must be explained: that is, that a record will be kept of the caution, that the fact of a previous caution may influence the decision whether or not to prosecute if the person should offend again, and that it may be cited if the person should subsequently be found guilty of an offence by a court. In the case of a juvenile this explanation must be given to the offender in the presence of his parents or guardian, or other appropriate adult. The special needs of other vulnerable groups should also be catered for, in accordance with the Code of Practice for the Detention, Treatment and Questioning of Persons by Police Officers.

Public interest considerations

3 If the first two of the above requirements are met, consideration should be given to whether a caution is in the public interest. The police should take into account the public interest principles described in the Code for Crown Prosecutors.

Note 3A There should be a presumption in favour of not prosecuting certain categories of offender, such as elderly people or those who suffer from some sort of mental illness or impairment, or a severe physical illness. Membership of these groups does not, however, afford absolute protection against prosecution, which may be justified by the seriousness of the offence.

Note 3B Two factors should be considered in relation to the offender's attitude towards his offence: the wilfulness with which it was committed and his subsequent attitude. A practical demonstration of regret, such as apologising to the victim and/or offering to put matters right as far as he is able, may support the use of a caution.

Note 3C The experience and circumstances of offenders involved in group offences can vary greatly, as can their degree of involvement. Although consistency and equity are important considerations in the decision whether to charge or caution, each offender should be considered separately. Different disposals may be justified.

Views of the victim

4 Before a caution can be administered it is desirable that the victim should normally be contacted to establish—

—his or her view about the offence;
—the nature and extent of any harm or loss, and their significance relative to the victim's circumstances;
—whether the offender has made any form of reparation or paid compensation.

Note 4A If a caution is being, or likely to be, considered its significance should be explained to the victim.

Note 4B In some cases where cautioning might otherwise be appropriate, prosecution may be required in order to protect the victim from further attention from the offender.

Note 4C If the offender has made some form of reparation or paid compensation, and the victim is satisfied, it may no longer be necessary to prosecute in cases where the possibility of the court's awarding compensation would otherwise have been a major determining factor. Under no circumstances should police officers become involved in negotiating or awarding reparation or compensation.

Administration of a caution

5 A formal caution should be administered in person by a police officer, and wherever practicable at a police station. A juvenile must always be cautioned in the presence of a parent, guardian or other appropriate adult. Members of other vulnerable groups must be treated in accordance with Code of Practice C.

Note 5A The officer administering the caution should be in uniform and normally of the rank of inspector or above. In some cases, however, a Community Liaison Officer or Community Constable might be more appropriate, or in the inspector's absence the use of a sergeant might be justified. Chief Officers may therefore wish to consider nominating suitable 'cautioning officers'.

<u>Note 5B</u> Where the person is elderly, infirm or otherwise vulnerable, a caution may be administered less formally, perhaps at the offender's home and in the presence of a friend or relative or other appropriate adult.

Recording cautions

6 All formal cautions should be recorded and records kept as directed by the Secretary of State. The use of cautioning should also be monitored on a force-wide basis.

<u>Note 6A</u> Formal cautions should be cited in court if they are relevant to the offence under consideration. In presenting antecedents, care should be taken to distinguish between cautions and convictions, which should usually be listed on separate sheets of paper.

<u>Note 6B</u> Chief officers may also wish to keep records of cases in which action short of a formal caution has been taken, and the reasons for it. But care should be taken not to record anything about an individual which implies that he is guilty of an offence when the evidence is in any doubt. Offences dealt with by action short of a formal caution may not be cited in court.

Appendix IV National Mode of Trial Guidelines

Mode of Trial Guidelines

The *National Mode of Trial Guidelines* (Lord Chancellor's Department, 1989; *Practice Note* (*Mode of Trial Guidelines*) [1990] 1 WLR 1439, (1991) 92 Cr App R 142)), issued under the auspices of the Lord Chief Justice, state: 'The purpose of these guidelines is to help magistrates to decide whether or not to commit "either way" offences for trial in the Crown Court. Their object is to provide guidance not direction. They are not intended to impinge upon a magistrate's duty to consider each case individually and on its own particular facts. These guidelines apply to all defendants aged 17 and above [of necessity, this must be read as '18 and above' post-CJA 91].

GENERAL MODE OF TRIAL CONSIDERATIONS
Section 19 of the Magistrates' Courts Act 1980 requires magistrates to have regard to the following matters in deciding whether an offence is more suitable for summary trial or trial on indictment: 1 The nature of the case. 2 Whether the circumstances make the offence one of a serious character. 3 Whether punishment which a magistrates' court would have power to inflict for it would be adequate. 4 Any other circumstances which appear to the court to make it more suitable for the offence to be tried in one way rather than the other. 5 Any representations made by the prosecutor or the defence. Certain general observations can be made: (a) The court should never make its decision on the grounds of convenience or expedition. (b) The court should assume for the purpose of deciding mode of trial that the prosecution version of the facts is correct. (c) The defendant's antecedents and personal mitigating circumstances are irrelevant for the purposes of deciding mode of trial. (d) The fact that offences are alleged to be specimens is a relevant consideration; the fact that the defendant will be asking for other offences to be taken into consideration, if convicted, is not. (e) Where cases involve complex questions of law, the court should consider committal for trial. (f) Where two or more defendants are jointly charged with an offence and the court decides that the offence is more suitable for summary trial, if one defendant elects trial on indictment, the court must proceed to deal with all the defendants as examining justices in respect of that offence. A [youth] jointly charged with someone aged [18 or over] should only be committed for trial in the interests of justice. (g) **In general, except where otherwise stated, either way offences should be tried summarily unless the court considers that the particular case has one or more of the features set out [below] and that its sentencing powers are insufficient.**

High value Where reference is made in the guidelines to property or damage of 'high value' it means '... a figure equal to at least twice the amount of the limit imposed by statute on a magistrates' court when making a compensation order'. [Currently £5,000. Note the anomaly whereby the jurisdictional limit for purely 'summary criminal damage' was not increased beyond £2,000 by the CJA 91, which increased maximum compensation in magistrates' courts from £2,000 to £5,000. A proposal to raise the limit to £5,000 is contained in the CJ and PO Bill of 1994].

Presumption of summary trial In relation to every offence dealt with in the guidelines, after the list of relevant considerations, there is a general rider as follows: 'In general, cases should be tried summarily unless the court considers that one or more of the above features is present in the case and that its sentencing powers are insufficient'.

Individual offences

Burglary
1 Dwelling house (1) Entry in the day time when the occupier (or another) is present. (2) Entry at night of a house which is normally occupied, whether or not the occupier (or another) is present. (3) The offence is alleged to be one of a series of similar offences. (4) When soiling, ransacking, damage or vandalism occurs. (5) The offence has professional hallmarks. (6) The unrecovered property is of high value.

In general cases should be tried summarily unless the court considers that one or more of the above features is present in the case *and* that its sentencing powers are insufficient. [Note that under para 28(c) of sched 1 MCA 1980 offences of burglary in a dwelling *cannot* be tried summarily if any person in the dwelling was subjected to violence or the threat of violence.]

2 Non-dwellings (1) Entry of a pharmacy or a doctor's surgery. (2) Fear is caused or violence is done to anyone lawfully on the premises (eg nightwatchman; security guard). (3) The offence has professional hallmarks. (4) Vandalism on a substantial scale. (5) The unrecovered property is of high value.

In general cases should be tried summarily unless the court considers one or more of the above features is present *and* that its sentencing powers are insufficient. [Similarly for the following:]

Theft and fraud 1 Breach of trust by a person in a position of substantial authority, or in whom a high degree of trust is placed. 2 Theft or fraud which has been committed or disguised in a sophisticated manner. 3 Theft or fraud committed by an organised gang. 4 The victim is particularly vulnerable to theft or fraud (eg the elderly or infirm). 5 The unrecovered property is of high value.

Handling 1 Dishonest handling of stolen property by a receiver who has commissioned the theft. 2 The offence has professional hallmarks. 3 The property is of high value.

Social security frauds 1 Organised frauds on a large scale. 2 The frauds are substantial and carried out over a long period of time.

Violence (s20 and s47 Offences Against the Person Act 1861) 1 The use of a weapon of a kind likely to cause serious injury. 2 A weapon is used and serious injury is caused. 3 More than minor injury caused by kicking, head butting or similar forms of assault. 4 Serious violence is caused to those whose work has to be done in contact with the public eg police officers, bus drivers, taxi drivers, publicans and shopkeepers. 5 Violence to vulnerable people (eg the elderly and the infirm). The same considerations apply to domestic violence.

Public Order Act Offences 1) Cases of *violent disorder* should generally be committed for trial. 2) *Affray* 1 Organised violence or use of weapons. 2 Significant injury or substantial damage. 3 The offence has a clear racial motivation. 4 An attack upon police officers, ambulance men, firemen and the like.

Violence to and neglect of children 1 Substantial injury. 2 Repeated violence or serious neglect, even if the harm is slight. 3 Sadistic violence eg deliberate burning or scalding.

Indecent assault 1 Substantial disparity in age between victim and defendant, and the assault is more than trivial. 2 Violence and threats of violence. 3 Relationship of trust or responsibility between defendant and victim. 4 Several similar offences, and the assaults are more than trivial. 5 The victim is particularly vulnerable. 6 The serious nature of the assault.

Unlawful sexual intercourse 1 Wide disparity of age. 2 Breach of a position of trust. 3 The victim is particularly vulnerable. NOTE: Unlawful sexual intercourse with a girl under 13 is triable only on indictment.

Drugs 1) *Class A* a) Supply; possession with intent to supply. These cases should be committed for trial. b) Possession. Should be committed for trial unless the amount is small and consistent only with personal use. 2) *Class B* a) Supply; possession with intent to supply. Should be committed for trial unless there is only small scale supply for no payment. b) Possession. Should be committed for trial when the quantity is substantial.

Reckless driving 1 Alcohol or drugs contributing to recklessness. 2 Grossly excessive speed. 3 Racing. 4 Prolonged course of reckless driving. 5 Other related offences.

Criminal damage 1 Deliberate fire-raising. 2 Committed by a group. 3 Damage of a high value. 4 The offence has a clear racial motivation. *Note*: Offences set out in Schedule 2 to the Magistrates' Courts Act 1980 (which includes offences of criminal damage contrary to section 1 Criminal Damage Act 1971 which do not amount to arson) must be tried summarily if the value of the property damaged or destroyed is £2,000 or less [but see the comments above under the heading 'High value'].

Appendix V: Seriousness, Suitability and Restriction of Liberty

Introduction

This paper has been produced by representatives of the Magistrates' Association, the Association of Chief Officers of Probation and the Justices' Clerks' Society. The paper seeks to give clarity to the specific roles of the sentencer, the clerk and the probation officer in requesting, writing and considering pre-sentence reports. .

The role of the sentencer

After a trial has taken place and the defendant has been convicted OR after hearing the prosecution facts when a defendant pleads guilty—and in both circumstances after hearing any mitigation and seeing a defendant's record (if any), a sentencer must then take a preliminary view of the seriousness of the offence or, if more than one, the offences before the court in order to decide if a pre-sentence report (PSR) is required.

If a PSR is required the bench should give the court duty probation officer some guidance as to why they are asking for a pre-sentence report and these observations must be recorded by the clerk. This is most important as the sentencing will most likely be carried out by a different bench who will not have heard the evidence, if there has been a trial.

The bench at this stage must, however, avoid making a final assessment of seriousness as this would bind a sentencing bench. The following form of words is suggested when announcing an adjournment for a PSR to be prepared:

'The court is adjourning your case until .... so that a pre-sentence report can be prepared. On what we have heard so far, we are considering a community sentence/a custodial sentence.
We must point out to you that the magistrates who deal with your case on ... will not be bound by our view, or by any suggestion in the pre-sentence report about how your case should be dealt with.'

At the final hearing when reports have been prepared and are before the court, the bench should hear all the facts from the prosecution, see the record and read the pre-sentence report, or indicate that this has been done before coming into court. The sentencing bench will then have a clearer view as to seriousness and, where the offence falls into the 'serious enough' category [community sentences, *Chapter 8, post*], will be in a position to establish what type of community disposal it considers to be most suitable for the offender. If it agrees with the proposal in the report the chairman can indicate this so that the defence advocate can decide whether to address the bench. If they do not agree with the proposal in the report the bench should indicate their view in order to give the defence advocate opportunity to address them on all aspects of mitigation.

After hearing all the mitigation the bench will come to a final decision as to seriousness. This means they will decide if the offence before the court should be dealt with by imposing a custodial sentence, a community penalty, a fine or discharge. It is desirable, where appropriate, for the bench to acquaint the probation service with the reasons for not accepting any rejected proposal.

The role of the clerk

The role of the clerk in court was the subject of the *Practice Direction* [1981] 2 All ER 831, as follows (emphasis added):

'1. A justices' clerk is responsible to the justices for the performance of any of the functions set out below by any member of his staff acting as court clerk and may be called in to advise the justices even when he is not personally sitting with the justices as clerk to the court.
2. It shall be the responsibility of the justices' clerk to advise the justices as follows: a) on questions of law or mixed law and fact; and b) as to matters or practice and procedures.
3. If it appears to him necessary to do so, or he is so requested by the justices, the justices' clerk has the responsibility to: a) refresh the justices' memory as to any matter of evidence and to draw attention to any issues involved in the matters before the court; b) advise the justices generally on the range of penalties which the law allows them to impose, and on any **guidance relevant to choice of penalty provided by law, the decisions of the superior courts or other authorities.** [emphasis supplied by the authors of the paper]
If no request has been made of him by the justices, the justices' clerk shall discharge his responsibility in court in the presence of the parties.
4. The way in which the justices' clerk should perform his functions should be stated as follows: a) the justices are entitled to the advice of their clerk when they retire, in order that he may fulfil his responsibility outlined above . . .'

There is no requirement in law that the justice(s) should accept and act upon the advice of their clerk on matters of law. In practice, however, it is accepted that they ought to do so and justices who fail to take the clerk's advice on a point of law may find themselves being ordered to pay the costs of any appeal which may follow (*Jones v Nicks* [1977] RTR 72).

Where any general issues concerning sentencing or PSR preparation arise, these should not be discussed in open court but via the liaison arrangements established jointly between the clerk to the justices and the chief probation officer.

The role of the probation officer

It is very helpful for the report writer to have a preliminary non-binding indication of the level of seriousness identified by the court requesting the PSR. In preparing the report the probation officer should acknowledge how the court interprets the seriousness of the offence initially. Additional guidance is provided in Court of Appeal guidelines, local practices, and the Magistrates' Association sentencing guidelines. [see *Appendix IV* to this work, *post*]

Analysis of current offence(s)

In preparing PSRs probation officers should explore those features of the offence which the court may wish to consider as aggravating and mitigating features when forming its final decision about seriousness. Examples of factors affecting seriousness are detailed in the appendix attached.

Analysing the offence does not mean simply reporting the prosecution version, followed by the defendant's version, without comment. It means presenting the probation officer's analysis, following a consideration of all the versions of the offence. The analysis should reflect an integrated approach, looking at both the

293

offence and the offender's motivation, with the aim of helping the sentencer to understand why the offender committed this particular offence at this time.

The report should not usurp the role of the sentencer by expressing judgments about seriousness, aggravation or mitigation. The preliminary non-binding indication of the court about seriousness should be acknowledged.

Relevant information about the offender

Probation officers should use this part of the pre-sentence report to include personal or social information about the offender which is relevant to the current offence, to past offending, and to the likelihood of re-offending and to any proposed community sentence. This section of the report is usually used to evaluate patterns of offending in the light of the personal and social factors which have contributed to them. This section is also used for information on mitigating factors unrelated to the offence which the court may see as justifying a reduction in sentence, examples of which are also in the appendix.

In the cases of violent or sexual offences any information concerning a risk of serious harm to the public from the offender should be included. This assessment of risk is a most important aspect of the function of the report writer, not only to advise the court, but also ensure the protection of the public.

The conclusion of the pre-sentence report

Where a community sentence is being considered the author should assess the suitability of the offender for the community sentences that might be available, and propose the one most suitable to the circumstances of the offender. In general terms an assessment of suitability for community sentences must take into account:

—seriousness of the offence as indicated by the court;
—the offender's personality, needs and ability;
—the prospect of successful completion (including informed consent or compliance from the offender)
—risk to the public, especially the likely risk of re-offending.

Previous failure to respond to community sentences is likely to be an important factor in assessing suitability, and it may also affect the court's final assessment of seriousness.

The probation service is concerned to ensure that the most suitable offenders are placed on the various community sentences available. It is not desirable for an offender to be placed under a set of obligations which he or she has no motivation to pursue. To perform well on community service, for example, the offender should have the willingness and the social competence which are compatible with the demands that will be made.

Probation programmes can generally meet the needs of those who are more socially inadequate. It is also generally thought better to place those who have a higher risk of reconviction on probation, where the offender can be more closely monitored and where work can take place to address the factors which lead to further offences. The probation service can highlight factors which are associated with successful completion of probation and community service orders. This is of great benefit in assessing the suitability of offenders for different sentences.

In assessing the suitability of an offender for a combination order the probation officer should consider the suitability factors that apply to both probation and community service orders. In general these orders are likely to be indicated in more serious cases where there is both the capacity to complete community service and a higher risk of reconviction.

Finally, the report author has to consider the appropriate level of restriction of liberty of community sentences in the light of the seriousness assessment and the suitability of the offender. Community service orders can be evaluated in terms of the amount of time required to complete the order. A direct comparison for probation orders is not appropriate since liberty is restricted in different ways when an offender is the subject of a probation order. The purpose of probation is to change the behaviour of the offender, and the impact of probation supervision on an individual offender should be greater than that measured by the number of hours the probationer is face to face with the probation officer, or engaged in some probation activity. It is essential that the report writer gives a full account of what is proposed. In the case of probation orders this means detailed information about what will happen whilst the person is under supervision, with specific details of the programmes proposed where day centres or group work programmes are being suggested.

The conclusion of the pre-sentence report must flow logically from the previous material in the offence analysis and the relevant information about the offender. It is the role of the report writer to provide useful information to the court in reaching a final view about seriousness and sentence. Where a proposal is made in a lower band of seriousness than the court indicated in its preliminary view, it should be logically argued and supported by the information the court will need to reach a revised view as to the appropriate sentence.

APPENDIX 1

A. EXAMPLES OF FACTORS AFFECTING SERIOUSNESS

1. **Nature of offence**
Category of offence
Amount of violence used, effect on victim
Whether weapon carried or used
Value of property stolen or damaged, whether recovered, whether housebreaking involved
Class and value of drugs, whether intention to supply

2. **Characteristics of victim**
Whether vulnerable and deliberately selected
Whether abuse of trust

3. **Intention and motive**
Whether aware of likely injury
Whether provoked
Whether racial motivation

4. **Role in offence**
Ring leader or organiser
Whether adult involved children in offence

5. **Location and time**
In public place, onlookers
Whether burglary in hours of darkness, while victim in house, or a pharmacy or

doctor's surgery

6. Gain to offender
Whether offender benefited considerably or little

7. Alcohol/drugs
Role of alcohol or drugs in offence

8. Attitude to offence
Whether guilt, remorse, concern for victim, desire for making reparation

9. Bail
Offence committed whilst on bail is an aggravating factor (s29(2) CJA 1991)

10. Previous relevant convictions and responses
The court, in deciding seriousness, may take into account previous relevant convictions and an offender's failure to respond to previous sentences.

B. EXAMPLES OF FACTORS RELEVANT TO OFFENDER MITIGATION
Youth
Previous good character
Pleas of guilty
Signs of reform and settling down
Completed previous supervision
Co-operated with police
Having treatment for alcohol or drugs problem
Ill health
Effect of custody

NOTE: The Magistrates' Association sentencing guidelines 'entry points' [*Appendix II* to this work, *supra*] are based on a hypothetical first time offender pleading not guilty.

Index

Custody (continued)
  regimes 176
  supervision after 32 192
  suspended sentence 22 56 115 140

D

Dealing with Disadvantage 119
Deception, obtaining by 67
Default periods, fines 227
Deferment of sentence 26
Definite meaning of sentences 93
Definitions 229 239
Dependency on alcohol, treatment for
149
Deportation/deportees 26 196
'Deserts' ('just deserts') 28 30
Detention of young offenders 37 44
  Under PACE Act 1984 45 45 116
Deterrent sentences 34 51 88 92
*Digest of Criminal Justice
Information* 118
Discharges 17 28
Discount for guilty plea 37 46 102 117
Discretionary life sentence 197
Discrimination **118**
*Discrimination and Disparity: The
Influence of Race on Sentencing* 120
Driving offences 64 279
Drugs 66

E

Early release 32 192
  compassionate release 194
  long-term prisoner 193
  sex offenders 196
  short-term prisoner 192
  recall 195
Electronic monitoring, curfew 46 96
Elton, Lord 119
Enforcement 32
*Ethnic Minorities in the Criminal
Justice System* 124
Evidence, of children 36
'Exceptional circumstances' see
Custody
Explanations 113
Extended sentences, abolished 141
Extradited offenders 196

F

Faulkner, David 80 84 174
Financial circumstances 95 157 159
Fines 17 48 95 **156**
  absence of information 158
  default 160 195
  local practices 167
  remission 160
Flexibility towards juveniles 171
Framework for sentencing 28 95 105

G

Gender 126
*Gender and the Criminal Justice
System* 118 126
*General Guide to the Criminal Justice
Act 1991* 28 88 90 96
Grants by probation areas 240
Grave crimes (s53 CYPA 33) 37 44 78
Guardians, liability 160
Guilty by post, young person 173
Guilty plea, discount for 37 46 102
117

H

Harm, serious 134
Hood, Dr Roger 122
Howard, Michael MP 83 84
'How Do You Plead?' 179
Hullin, Roy 124
Hurd, Douglas MP 80

I

Imprisonment, see *Custody*
  prison population 76
Income support, deductions from 162
Information for sentencers 31 136 144
179 *et al*
  s95 CJA 91 118 *et al*

J

Jack, Michael MP 83
'Joy riding' 82
Judicial Studies Board 91 125
Just deserts 28 30

298

Bail

The Law, Best Practice and The Debate
ISBN 1 872870 11 2

Paul Cavadino
Bryan Gibson

'Highly recommended' *Justice of the Peace*

'A sound investment' *The Magistrate*

£14.00 + £1.50 p&p from Waterside Press

Paying Back

Twenty Years of Community Service
ISBN 1 872870 13 9

Edited by Dick Whitfield and David Scott

'Readable and encouraging' *ACOP Bulletin*

'A timely contribution to our criminology' *The Justices' Clerk*

'A book for every bench library' *The Magistrate*

£12 + £1.50 p&p from Waterside Press

With a Foreword by Lord Taylor of Gosforth, Lord Chief Justice

Growing Out of Crime
The New Era ISBN 1 872 870 06 6

Andrew Rutherford

'A brave book' *The Magistrate*

£12.50 + £1.50 p&p from Waterside Press

Drinking and Driving
A Decade of Development

ISBN 1 872870 12 0   Jonathan Black

'A very thorough and competent account' *The Justices' Clerk*

'A useful reference guide' *Probation Journal*

'Strongly recommended' *Justice of the Peace*

£14.00 + £1.50 p&p from Waterside Press

With Contributions on Rehabilitation Courses by

John Cook and John Martin

Criminal Justice *In Transition*

One of a series of books on Criminal Justice from Waterside Press:

Introduction to the Criminal Justice Act 1991

ISBN 1 872870 02 3

The Youth Court

ISBN 1 872870 03 1

Criminal Justice Act 1991 LEGAL POINTS: Commentary & Annotated Guide for Practitioners

ISBN 872870 04 X

Materials on the Criminal Justice Act 1991

ISBN 1 872870 07 4

Bail: The Law, Best Practice and The Debate

ISBN 1 872870 11 2

Paying Back: Twenty Years of Community Service

ISBN 1 872870 13 9

Criminal Justice In Transition

ISBN 1 872870 20 1

The Youth Court One Year Onwards

ISBN 1 872870 14 7

Introduction to the Magistrates' Court

ISBN 1 872 870 01 5

Introduction to the Criminal Justice Process

ISBN 1 872870 09 0